LTD.

Women in Indian Society

The following articles have been printed with the kind permission of the publishers:

Susan Wadley, 'Women and the Hindu Tradition'. First published in *SIGNS Journal of Women in Culture and Society*, Vol. 3, 1, The University of Chicago Press, Chicago, 1977.

Sudhir Kakar, 'Feminine Identity in India'. From Sudhir Kakar, *The Inner World*, Oxford University Press, Delhi, 1978.

Ashis Nandy, 'Woman Versus Womanliness in India: An Essay in Social and Political Psychology'. From Ashis Nandy, *At the Edge of Psychology*, Oxford University Press, New Delhi, 1980. (First published in *The Psychoanalytic Review*, 1976, 63, 2).

Suma Chitnis, 'Feminism: Indian Ethos and Indian Convictions'. Article adapted from 'Feminism in India' which appeared in *Canadian Women Studies*, Vol. 6, 1, Founder's College, York University, Ontario, 1985.

Renuka R. Sethi and **Mary J. Allen**, 'Sex Role Stereotypes in Northern India and the United States'. First published in *Sex Roles: A Journal of Research*, Vol. II, 7/8, Plenum Publishing Corporation, New York, 1984.

V.V. Prakasa Rao and **V. Nandini Rao**, 'Sex Role Attitudes of College Students in India'. First published in *Women in International Development Series*. Working Paper No. 72, Michigan State University, 1984.

Manisha Roy, 'The Concepts of "Femininity" and "Liberation" in the Context of Changing Sex Roles: Women in Modern India and America'. From Dana Raphael ed., *Being Female: Reproduction Power and Change*, Mouton Publishers, The Hague, 1975.

C.S. Lakshmi, 'Feminism and the Cinema of Realism'. First published in *Economic and Political Weekly*, Vol. XXI, 3, Sameeksha Trust Publications, Bombay, 18 January 1986.

Narendra Nath Kalia, 'Women and Sexism: Language of Indian School Textbooks'. First published in *Economic and Political Weekly*, Vol. XXI, 18, Sameeksha Trust Publications, Bombay, 3 May 1986.

Lawrence A. Babb, 'Indigenous Feminism in a Modern Hindu Sect'. First published in *SIGNS Journal of Women in Culture and Society*, Vol. 9, 31, The University of Chicago Press, 1984.

Women in Indian Society

A Reader

Edited by
Rehana Ghadially

 SAGE PUBLICATIONS
New Delhi/Newbury Park/London

First published in 1988 by

Sage Publications India Pvt Ltd
32 M Block Market, Greater Kailash I
New Delhi 110 048

Sage Publications Inc
2111 West Hillcrest Drive
Newbury Park, California 91320

Sage Publications Ltd
28 Banner Street
London EC1Y 8QE

Published by Tejeshwar Singh for Sage Publications India Pvt. Ltd., phototypeset by Mudra Typesetters, Pondicherry and printed at Chaman Offset Printers, Delhi.

Library of Congress Cataloging-in-Publication Data

Women in Indian society: a book of readings/edited by Rehana Ghadially.

   p. cm.
  Bibliography: p.
  Includes index.
   1. Women—India—Social conditions. 2. Sex role—India.
3. Femininity (Psychology) 4. Feminism—India. I. Ghadially, Rehana, 1945–

HQ1742.W666   1988   305.4′2′0954—dc 19   88–11683

ISBN   0–8039–9564–4 (US-hbk)   81–7036–101–X (India-hbk)
        0–8039–9565–2 (US-pbk)   81–7036–102–8 (India-pbk)

Dedicated to my parents
who understood my need
to be free

Contents

Preface

After more than a decade of concern with women's lives, manifested mainly in the form of changes in laws affecting women and concentrated efforts on the part of women's groups to conscientize people, women's studies as a formal discipline is gradually beginning to emerge in this country. A Winter Institute, the second of its kind, for training college and university teachers in the area of women's studies held recently at SNDT University attested to the fact that there is a felt need on the part of the University Grants Commission to start women's courses and women's studies centers in various institutions and universities. This concern with opening women's studies centers is a result of the efforts to improve the status of women made by the government, women's wings of various political parties and grassroots women's organizations. Most importantly, it springs from women's day-to-day experiences and realities.

While a variety of techniques such as organizing conferences, writing research papers, conducting workshops have been adopted by academics to sensitize students, the academic community and the general public, to women's issues, teaching about women in colleges and universities has remained a most neglected area so far. The impetus for preparing a book of this kind came from having taught courses on the psychology of sex differences, the psychology of sex roles and the psychology of women over the past four years in India and abroad. The winds of change around me, the content of one's own experiences and the process of teaching stimulated in me the growth of a new maturity and consciousness. It found me looking at psychological literature in a critical way, a literature that was primarily a product of male thinking. The result was a growing feminist approach to teaching.

I have used my teaching and research experience in this area to select and compile a series of articles that have contributed in a serious way to examining and challenging the roles of women in a rapidly changing society. While the focus of the courses I have taught was on psychology, I felt the need for incorporating other perspectives in understanding women. Women's studies has attracted academics and activists from various other disciplines. The papers in this book include data from anthropology, psychology, sociology, and related social science disciplines.

Such an inter-disciplinary approach is in tune with the values represented by the women's movement, namely, lowering barriers that separate people, nations and disciplines.

This book provides immediate access to some critical areas on the subject of women. The purpose of the book is to raise awareness, stimulate thinking, generate discussion and provide fuel for action in changing relevant aspects of women's lives. Hopefully it will inspire younger scholars to look at their world differently, to attain a new perspective in man-woman relationships and contribute in a serious way to the field of women's studies.

The book is divided into five sections. Each section is preceded by an introduction which briefly describes the papers included in it. Section I presents contextual, analytical, as well as theoretical ideas about women, their role and identity. Section II consists of recent empirical research organized around existing stereotypes about men and women, the socialization of the two sexes and the attitudes people hold towards women. Some forms of violence against women, where these originate from and what can be done to stop them are explored in Section III. Section IV deals with the portrayal of women in diverse kinds of media such as films and television. The papers on growing awareness in Section V speak of the variety of efforts generated in this country regarding sensitizing people to inequalities between the sexes and a search for personhood among women.

I wish to thank my students whose responses in class propelled me into making a commitment to editing this book. My special thanks to Mutalik-Desai for his support and encouragement. I am grateful to S. Krishna-swamy, Pramod Kumar and R.K. Premarajan for giving me their valuable time.

INTRODUCTION

Rehana Ghadially

In the last decade and more, half the human experience, namely, the female half, has received considerable attention from the government, the press and women themselves. The current resurgence of discussion on women's issues is due to the international recognition of the problems of women all over the world, and has resulted in the U.N. declaration of 1975 as Women's Year and the period between 1975–1985 as Women's Decade.

The appointment of the National Committee on the Status of Women in India in 1972 and the publication of its report in 1975 marked the first official attempt in contemporary times to study the status of Indian women and recommend changes to improve their position. The report highlighted that despite constitutional guarantees the roles, rights and participation ot women in all spheres of life were limited. Since the publication of this report, there has been no committee at the national level appointed to systematically and comprehensively reassess the accomplishments of the Women's Decade. However, several reports have been written and none paint an encouraging picture.

There are several ways one can look at the status of women in any society. During the last decade at least three approaches, not necessarily mutually exclusive, were discernible. One was to examine the common demographic indicators that give an overall picture of women's relative standing vis-a-vis men. According to the 1981 census, the sex ratio stood at 933 females per 1000 males. The literacy rate was 46.89 per cent for males and 24.82 per cent for females. The life expectancy at birth for females was 50 years and for males it was 50.9 years. The average age at marriage for females was 18.32 years and for males it was 23.27 years. The female work participation rate was 13.99 per cent and the male work participation rate was 51.62 per cent. Figures regarding economic participation rate for women have very little meaning as the definition of a worker has changed from one census to another. There is agreement however that women's participation in the labor force has declined since the turn of the century. Comparing these figures with the 1971 census data, one notices that the status of women has improved very little and they continue to remain a disadvantaged group. STATS

Many scholars prefer to study the status of women in society in terms of the extent to which women have been assimilated in the nation's developmental programs and the extent of the impact of development policies on women. Development has been defined by the World Conference of the U.N. Decade for Women held at Copenhagen in July 1980 as follows:

> Development is here interpreted to mean total development, including development in the political, economic, social, cultural, and other dimensions of human life as also the physical, moral, intellectual and cultural growth of the human person. Women's development should not only be viewed as an issue in social development but should be seen as an essential component in every dimension of development.

Irrespective of how development has been defined and irrespective of the developing country studied, some common trends have emerged from the literature. The changes taking place in society and especially the input of modern technology for accelerating growth have solved less and created more problems for women. While the new technologies have created employment opportunities for women and increased the household income of women of some classes, they have at the same time displaced women from the labor force, forced women to migrate and has not reduced the drudgery in traditional women's work as much as initially anticipated.

The major reason why development has brought little or no benefits for women is that the pattern of development has been superimposed on a pre-existing system with social structures severely in disfavor of women. The development planning itself being male biased has not been conducive to the creation of a much needed ideological and institutional change. For a developing country the talent and potential of every citizen regardless of sex, religion or caste is important and ignoring any section of society will be tantamount to saying that we do not wish to develop.

The statistical profile and the developmental approach provide us with a wealth of information that leave no doubt about the disadvantaged position of women. Hidden behind the demographers' figures and the jargon of developmental specialists are women themselves who have felt helpless and overwhelmed by the problems they face by virtue of simply being female. This pervasive sense of powerlessness has forced many women to seek succor from welfare agencies, social organizations, government authorities and, more recently and importantly, from women's groups.

What has been the reality for these women? A list of the kinds of problems faced by women as exemplified in the reports sent between 1979 and 1983 by various women's groups to a well-known, city-based feminist magazine resulted in the following breakdown. Rape was a major issue with grassroots autonomous women's groups. This was followed by a concern for conditions of women at work. It included demands for equal wages for equal work, maternity benefits, creche facilities and the need to organize working women. Another major issue was the portrayal of women in media—the depiction of violence against women and stereo-typing of sex roles in theatre and other aspects of media and the need for censorship. A cluster of issues such as dowry deaths, organizing training camps for women activists, leadership training and sexual and mental harassment ranked fourth. The fifth group of problems included abolition of the *devdasi* custom, providing water facilities in rural areas, alcoholism among men and analyzing the roots of women's oppression. The final set of concerns included wife-beating, training women for health care, parti-cipation of men in housework, setting up special courts for women, educa-tion of scheduled caste women and protest against the rise in price of food items.

Demographic factors, marginalizing of women in the developmental process and an oppressive social reality highlight the miserable plight of women and the long struggle ahead of them.

The struggle for the upliftment of women began in India in the nineteenth century. It was an off-shoot of the fight against colonialism and the aspira-tion for national freedom. Enlightened freedom fighters, some of them products of western education, could see parallels between the political impotency of a nation of 'men' and an all encompassing oppressiveness of women. These political leaders, social reformers, missionary workers—virtually an all male hegemony—were interested in improving the status of Indian women. They were supported in their struggle by a few emanci-pated women such as Sarojini Naidu, Saraladevi Chaudhrani, and Saroj Nalini Dutt and together they worked toward the abolition of sati, female infanticide, encouraging women's education albeit of the traditional kind, supporting widow remarriage and a variety of other issues that degraded women. By contrast, in contemporary times, the effort to improve the status of women has been taken by women themselves. According to one estimate, in 1985 there were as many as fifty-five autonomous women's organizations/activist groups all over India. This did not include women's wings of political parties, media groups, religious organizations and unions.

No matter how much we would like to avoid thinking about it, earlier efforts to improve the status of women and the contemporary women's movement is, to a considerable extent, the product of an idea that had its birth in the West. However, our own historical and cultural experiences have provided its own unique momentum and direction. Unlike western women, Indian women's identity is deeply embedded not in the marital twosome, but in the entire family, caste, class and community. To untangle her true self from this morass of intertwining network is no mean task. It is precisely this rootedness, that has made it impossible for even Indian feminists to seriously challenge the family as the single-most oppressive institution. Her role in the family is either given a heavy white-wash or new roles are added to the existing ones. Contrary to western women, Indian women are also committed to the idea of gradual change. Radicalization and innovativeness in lifestyle are not yet part of the Indian women's consciousness.

Paradoxical though this may seem the lot of women as a result of these efforts has changed for the better and yet things have remained the same. The reason for this is that women have lived in two types of reality—the legal and the social. For the last 150 years, liberal thinkers have tried to amend archaic and sexist laws derogatory to women. With one or two exceptions, such as Muslim Women Protection of Rights on Divorce Act, 1986 and the New Rape Bill, 1983 which failed to take into account power-rape, the legal reality, in general, has been moving in a progressive and optimistic direction. The optimism is best manifested in the Dowry Prohibition (Amendment) Bill, 1986. However, the psychological and social realities in which women live have remained virtually unchanged. The hierarchy and power relations of traditional institutions produce people who are mutilated. The myths, customs and values that shape people's perception of and attitude toward women are too fossilized for any significant dent to be made to transform their lives for the better. Yatras, protest marches, street plays, poster exhibitions, training camps, formal teaching, consciousness-raising groups, Women's Day celebrations have been organized to raise the consciousness of the people. The impact of this is yet to be systematically studied and analysed. Without a change in the consciousness no social transformation will be able to set women free.

Laws have been challenged and changed through lobbying by enlightened groups, by publicizing a particular case and finally with a stroke of a pen. However, few have been able to redefine themselves, focusing not on large abstractions but on the immediate transformation in their daily lives, making that crucial inner journey. This bifurcation in approaches—one legal and the other creating psychosocial awareness and bringing about change—that is seen in improving the status of women is also apparent in terms of what areas of women's lives have deserved priority by way of effort and attention.

At the international level, the U.N. organized women's conferences have been concerned with the participation of women in the development process. This has included equal representation of women in education, politics and labor. Traditionally, their lack of participation in these spheres has been explained away as due either to the demands on their 'natural' role as a mother which is seen as being antithetical to their public role, or intellectual and personality differences springing from biological variables that made it difficult or even impossible for women to participate in traditional male endeavors. The second approach is best exemplified among feminist groups working at the grassroots level. They have been primarily concerned with atrocities committed against women. It must be noted that both the area and the approach adopted to understand and solve women's problems, apply equally to all sections of women, regardless of their social background.

It will be obvious to the reader that this selection tilts toward urban, middle class women. Given the complexity of Indian social reality and the tremendous diversity of its people, it would be an empty claim that this anthology does justice to all women, especially women belonging to the lower classes, the minority communities and rural women. These groups deserve to be studied in their own right. Studies on lower class and rural women had to be omitted as there is insufficient research on them and contrary to the major focus of this anthology it takes a pre-dominantly developmental and economic focus. Minority women are almost invisible in social science literature, and where studies have been made on them they are seen as embedded in the practice of traditional and archaic customs like purdah, rather than seen as seriously questioning and challenging these customs. To the extent that these women are not included for study, the reality that social science presents to us will remain limited and distorted. All said and done, the themes represented in this anthology have a certain universal appeal and to that extent it helps us in understanding the essential condition of all women.

The psychosocial realm of women is the main focus of the anthology. It reflects a concern over the hold of traditional, religious and mythical ways of thinking about women and its impact on controlling women's daily life. It highlights the gradual questioning and growing challenge of holding on to this traditional ideal. The myths and ideals are operationalized in the differential socialization of the two sexes. Through the use of a variety of techniques of socialization such as imitation, role-modelling, and selective reinforcement, children's behavior is channelized to take a particular shape and form. This differential treatment is meted out by a variety of social agents such as parents, teachers, peers and symbolic agents such as television and books. The end product is a package of personality traits attributed to women and men: what psychologists label as femininity and masculinity. A compartmentalized, straitjacket, either-or concept of sex roles is implied by the feminity masculinity conception. Liberal minded agents of socialization are minimizing the push toward stereotyping and thereby facilitating the emergence of an androgynous person who is flexible, adaptive and displays both masculine and feminine characteristics.

This volume also focuses on the concern over objectification of women. This area deserves our complete attention and energy. To objectify is to depersonalize, to make substandard, to make women not quite human. To objectify is to define a woman in terms of her anatomical and physical attributes. In the minds of men this view of women arouses a strong undercurrent of sexuality. The explosive mixture of object and sexuality make women an easy target for male violence. Our bodies are the material representation of ourselves, both to others and to ourselves. The relationship between our physical selves and our psycho-social selves is not only close, but subtle and profound. In a patriarchal set-up, rape, incest, wife-beating, tinkering with women's reproductive system, etc., are the most compelling forms of control exercised over women's bodies. Men's power over the circumstances and exigencies of women's physical selves, have reduced them to a state of child-like dependence and obedience. Until conditions change, women remain deprived of the possibility of being independent and autonomous persons.

Awareness of inequality and oppressiveness is a precondition to any kind of social change. While consciousness-raising groups have often been described as the hallmark of new feminism in the West, sustained activity in a variety of fields by autonomous women's groups has been the prime generator of greater social awareness about women's problems in India. At some points in their lives, many women are forced to re-examine their relationships with others, especially men. This reassessment, usually with the help of some social support, has led to a new awareness and a commitment to know more about women and womanhood.

The crucial role (though often detrimental) played by mass media has been recognized. However, alternative forms of raising public consciousness regarding women's problems need to be worked on urgently. A growing scholarship and the need to develop courses and programs in women's studies in educational institutions will go a long way in educating teachers, students and lay persons in recognizing women's sense of worth, her rights and her presence in the world.

Increasing importance is being given to science in our country as a tool for reaching knowledge and truth. Social sciences focus specifically on human behavior. The impact of social sciences on the conduct of our lives has already been significant. Feminists, however, are less than happy about the view of social reality that sexist social scientists have given us. They question and challenge both its content and methodology. Sociologists and psychologists have criticised their respective disciplines for being preoccupied with the activities, interests and experiences of men and for blatantly generalizing their findings to women. Feminist criticism of social sciences has resulted in research which focuses on women, done for and by women. Although these tenets are not rigidly adhered to, a growing body of information has accumulated that has been aptly labelled as women's studies or feminist literature. The methodologies by which knowledge is gathered has also not escaped their critical attention. Prestigious research methods have required the researchers to manipulate and control reality, to remain aloof and distant from it. This objectivity has resulted in hard or quantitative data. According to Jessie Bernard, the entire research process has a built-in machismo element. The recognition of what Stanley and Wise call 'the personal', 'the direct experience' and the near impossibility of doing away with emotional involvement has resulted in soft or qualitative data. The preference among feminists for soft data has provided a healthy corrective to choice of research methods.

The division of methodologies into bipolar dichotomies such as hard or soft, quantitative or qualitative is both arbitrary and unfortunate as most research approach presents a happy mix of both kinds of emphasis. While it would be a futile experience to put methodologies on a continuum of sexism, according to Stanley and Wise, it would definitely be worth the while for all scholars to keep in mind how social reality is constructed, what factors and assumptions play a role in its construction and whether it takes cognizance of women's experience of reality. The validity of the new and emerging reality is no longer at stake. What is at stake is what we wish to do with this evidence, how we translate it into action and policy decisions that create social conditions for the nourishment and fulfillment of all.

I

CONTEXT

The roles women play in society and the images we have of them have developed not simply from the exigencies of biology and social situations but are rather deeply rooted in the myths and legends and the religion of the culture. This is especially true of Indian culture. In the West, the Virgin Mary is hardly presented as a model that ought to be emulated whereas in India, Sita is considered just that. This has made the task of social change particularly difficult. Philosophers, sages and theologians have at one time or another given attention to what a woman is. In a society where men have controlled knowledge and have interpreted the classical texts, it is not surprising, as S. Ruth says, women have lost the power of naming, of explaining and defining for themselves the realities of their own experience.

In a patriarchal culture, what we get is a masculinist definition of ideals and images of women. These ideals and visions are not women's creations. They are not born out of their own experiences. The perspective developed by social sciences is influenced by the culture's ideology. The sociological perspective identified in the functional framework reserves instrumental functions for men and expressive functions for women. The psychological perspective views her as passive, masochistic and dependent. Marriage and motherhood are considered mandatory for fulfillment and identity formation. Women are absent from history, and political science has simply by-passed her. These views have been seriously challenged and are in the process of being revised.

In her paper 'Women and the Hindu Tradition' Susan Wadley speaks of the duality of women in Hindu ideology. Identified with nature, she is a giver of birth and protector of her children. On the other hand she is evil and destructive. How her sexuality is controlled determines her essentially benevolent or malevolent nature. Everyday behavior and roles she is expected to play are dictated by this mythical view of femaleness. Sudhir Kakar in his paper 'Feminine Identity in India' looks at a woman's development and transition through the various stages of her life-cycle from a psycho-analytic perspective. A variety of social agents prepare her for motherhood, a role in which her identity finds completion. The inspiration of ideal womanhood comes from the mythical figure of Sita. The assimilation of this ideal serves as a defense against the recognition and acceptance of one's sexuality. In 'Woman versus Womanliness' Ashis Nandy directs our attention to the dynamics that keep women in their constricted place in society. The centrality of motherhood in a culture inevitably produces certain kinds of sons and men. A challenge to this all-consuming role contains the seeds of liberation. Suma Chitnis warns us of the pitfalls of adopting a Western model of liberation in her treatise 'Feminism, the Indian Ethos and Indian Convictions'. According to her, greater sensitivity to the historical as well as the contemporary social context, coupled with Indian women's particular brand of psychological strength would be worth examining to provide alternative paths to equality.

WOMEN AND THE HINDU TRADITION

Susan Wadley

Introduction

Most of the world views Hindu women as degraded, downtrodden slaves. Yet the percentage of Indian women in the professions compares favorably with those of the West: Indian women comprise 7.1 per cent of the doctors, 1.2 per cent of the lawyers and 10.9 per cent of the scientists, in spite of incredibly low literacy rates for the overall female population (18.4 per cent of Indian women are literate). Clearly, Indian women present a paradoxical situation for the interpreter of South Asian society. The view of the Hindu women as downtrodden represents one behavioral reality; her participation in the highest political and social arenas is another undeniable reality.

This situation cannot be fully explored in one short paper and this paper is concerned only with Hindu ideology and practice relating to women and their roles: the aim is to suggest factors of Hindu belief and practice which may affect changes in women's secular roles in South Asia. I am concerned first with Hindu definitions of femaleness. For this discussion the primary source materials are both ancient and modern scriptures and mythology.

Although the village practitioner of Hinduism may not be consciously aware of the sophisticated textual statements sometimes referred to, he/she has command of myths and folk beliefs which restate many classical statements. Part I continues with a discussion of Hindu norms and expectations for women's behavior. Again, the sources are primarily literary traditions. In Part II, I turn to a consideration of women's actual place in Hindu practice. Here I draw primarily on anthropological descriptions. Lastly, in Part III, I suggest some factors of Hindu orthopraxy which affect or may affect changes in women's secular roles in South Asia.

PART I
Hindu Ideology and Women

In discussing women in Hinduism, one must first consider how the nature

of femaleness is portrayed in Hindu ideology.[1] Beliefs about what a female
is underlie both the role models religious figures present and advocate for
women and the place of women in Hindu religious practice. These beliefs
about the nature of femaleness also affect the potential for change in the
roles of women in Hindu South Asia.

Femaleness: The Hindu Perspective

The concept of the female in Hinduism presents an important duality: on
the one hand, the woman is fertile, benevolent—the bestower; on the
other, she is aggressive, malevolent—the destroyer. A popular statement
characterizes the goddess in all her manifestations thus: 'in times of prosperity she indeed is Lakshmi, who bestows prosperity in the homes of
men; and in times of misfortune, she herself becomes the goddess of
misfortune and brings about ruin' (Jagdisvarananda, 1953, quoted in
Babb, 1970). In a similar vein, Brenda Bech discusses the name of the
South Indian goddess, Mariyamman, noted for her dual character. Using
Sanskrit and Tamil etymologies, *mari* means death or rain while the folk
etymology has *mari* meaning 'to change', while *amman* means 'lady' or
'mother', (Beck, 1971) so that the goddess is in fact recognized as the
'changing lady'—a clear acknowledgement of her dual character. Both
goddesses and women—for there is no differentiation of super-human and
human in Hindu belief (Wadley, 1975)—reflect these characteristics of the
female as both benevolent, fertile bestower and malevolent, aggressive
destroyer[2] (Hart, 1973).

[1] Hinduism is a classical religion, with ancient and established textual and authoritative
traditions. But it differs from Christianity, Judaism and Islam in that it lacks a single
authoritative text: rather, it has thousands, produced over a 3,000 year period. In general,
the *Vedas*, written over a period of a thousand years, are the ultimate source to which Hindus
refer. However, most Hindus are themselves unfamiliar with the contents of the Vedas, and
Hinduism as it is practised today is more non-Vedic than Vedic. In addition, within the
geographic space of South Asia, Hinduism assumes varied forms and often appears more
diversified than unified. Thus any particular practice or belief found among a group of
Hindus may, in fact, be contradicted elsewhere or denied by Hindus of other groups or
regions. Clearly, not even the textually-based but varied 'great traditions' of Hinduism could
be fully explored in a brief paper; further, the 'little traditions' or local practices that are not
based on written texts, provide endless complications of interpretation and acknowledgement
of belief and practice. As a further complication, Hinduism is a way of life, most actions,
whether cooking or ploughing, have religious elements. In this paper, I attempt to be faithful
to the Hindu tradition in its multiple forms. If I have not succeeded, I apologize.

As a guide to the reader, I use 'textual', 'authoritative' or 'great tradition(al)' to refer to
written texts or material from written texts, usually in Sanskrit. 'Non-authoritative' implies
practices without written scriptural sanction, although they may be equally authentic in the
minds of their practitioners.

[2] Without detailing the historical development of Hindu beliefs about women, some
crucial factors of this duality must be noted. Early Vedic literature (pre-600 BC) brought by

Two facets of femaleness relate to this duality, and perhaps provide a cultural logic for it. The female is first of all *sakti* (energy/power), the energizing principle of the universe. The female is also *prakriti* (Nature)— the undifferentiated Matter of the Universe. I shall examine each of these in turn, elaborating their role in illuminating the dual character of the Hindu female.[3]

In Hindu cosmology, the universal substratum from which all being arises is known as *brahman*: 'Invisible, inactive, beyond grasp, without qualifications, inconceivable, indescribable . . . ever aloof from manifestation' (*Mandukya Upanishad* quoted by Danielou, 1964). From this unmanifest substance, beings are made manifest through the tension created by the opposition of cohesion (Visnu) and disintegration (Siva).[4] This tension defines *sakti*—the manifesting power, the creative principle. The Hindu notion of divinity rests upon that of *sakti* (power) (Wadley, 1975; Danielou, 1964): greater power is what distinguishes gods from men. So, *sakti* underlies both creation and divinity; and *sakti* is female. Therefore, all creation and all power in the Hindu world is based on femaleness—there would be no being without energy/power.

Although without the female there would be no energy in the universe, in fact all beings contain their share of *sakti*, their share of power and energy, with which they are endowed by birth along with their defining qualities (*guna*) and actions (*karma*) (Marriott and Inden, 1972). Furthermore, the *sakti* that is part of an individual at birth can be increased or decreased through later actions. For example, a woman by being a true and devoted wife (*pativrat*, literally 'one who fasts for her husband'), increases her *sakti*. Various austerities, particularly sexual abstinence, also increase a person's *sakti*. But even though both men and women have *sakti*

---

the Aryan migrators from the North emphasizes the prosperity and benevolence of female figures. Later developments in Hindu literature introduce the dangerous image of females. Women are the source of sacred power—frequently bad or dangerous sacred power. This developing emphasis on female power, including potential danger, probably reflects an incorporation of Dravidian beliefs (already existing in India prior to 600 BC) into the Aryan religious complex. The earliest available Dravidian literature (specially, Tamil literature) refers frequently to dangerous female power, a theme not found until later in the Sanskrit literature of the Aryans.

The modern Hindu, however, does not know about historical developments but only their result: the dual image of femaleness as simultaneously bad and dangerous, good and fertile.

[3] The following discussion is abbreviated and generalized, due to the necessities of space. Hopefully, no injustice is done to the Hindu tradition. I wish to thank Barbara D. Miller and Bruce W. Derr for their many readings and helpful suggestions. In addition, H. Daniel Smith aided in clarifying points from the great traditions.

[4] The beings of the universe are necessarily manifest or they could not be known; they are not necessarily a total representation of *brahman*; for each god, goddess and being represents a part of the Unknowable that is *brahman* itself.

as a personal attribute, the woman embodies *sakti*, the original energy of the universe.

A common metaphor is that woman is the field or earth into which man puts his seed. 'By the sacred tradition the woman is declared to be the soil, the man is declared to be the seed; the production of all corporeal beings (takes place) through the union of the soil with the seed'[5] (Buhler, 1964). The image of field or earth also symbolizes a second facet of femaleness: woman is *prakriti* (Nature). Nature is the active female counterpart of the Cosmic Person, *purusa*, the inactive or male aspect. Moreover, Nature is Matter; the Cosmic Person is Spirit. But whereas *prakriti* represents the undifferentiated matter of Nature, *purusa* provides the Spirit, which is a structured code. Thus, *purusa* (Cosmic Person) is code (differentiated Spirit), as opposed to *prakriti*, which is Nature (undifferentiated Matter). The union of Spirit and Matter, code and noncode, inactive and active, leads to the creation of the world with all of its differentiated life forms. No life exists without both Matter and Spirit; *prakriti* and *purusa* are in all beings. This relationship can be represented diagrammatically (Figure 1).

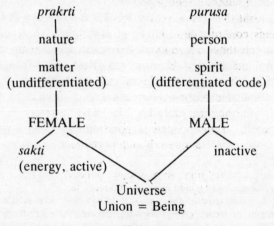

Figure 1

The unity of *purusa-prakriti* underlies the beliefs regarding biological conception. Here we find that the male contributes the hard substances: the bones, nerves and structuring elements of a child. The woman contributes the soft substances: the flesh, skin, blood, and unstructured parts of a child (Inden and Nicholas, 1970). Whichever partner dominated at the time of conception, determines the sex of the child. The *Laws of Manu* speak on this point: 'On comparing the seed and the receptacle, the seed is

[5] G. Buhler (1964). The Laws of Manu were supposedly written by the first man, Manu. While most Hindus are not personally familiar with the laws of Manu, the laws do express a corpus of beliefs about women which are still prevalent in India.

declared to be more important: for, the offspring of all created beings is marked by the characteristics of the seed' (Buhler, 1964). The hard substance (seed) is structure (culture?) as opposed to the soft substance which is nonstructure (Nature?). Women, then, are automatically more Nature than men. The Nature and nonstructure in them dominates over coded Spirit and structure.

Uniting these two facets of femaleness, women are both energy/power and Nature (Ortner, 1974); and Nature is uncultured. In fact, the Aryan vernacular languages of ancient India are called Prakrit ('Uncultured' or 'Natural'), as opposed to the priestly religious language Sanskrit (literally, 'Cultured'). Uncultured Power is dangerous. The equation, Woman = Power + Nature = Danger, represents the essence of femaleness as it underlies Hindu religious belief and action about women. The equation summarizes a conception of the world order that explains the woman/goddess as the malevolent, aggressive destroyer.

As we saw above, however, the Hindu view of woman is not only one of danger—woman is also the benevolent, fertile bestower. Fertility is easily comprehended, for woman is the necessary receptor of man's seed: she, like the closely conjoined images of cow and earth, represents growth, prosperity and fertility. Benevolence and goodness, however, are more complex. One possible explanation of female benevolence is that woman is capricious, therefore she sometimes uses her Uncultured Power for human benefit. Recent studies have provided a sharper insight (Babb, 1970; Beck, 1971): 'good females—goddess or human—are controlled by males; that is, Culture controls Nature'.

A popular myth presents the male controlling dangerous female Power, thus rendering that Power positive and benevolent. Kali, the Black One, one of the many wives of Siva, was sent by the gods to oppose a demon and his army when the gods could not control him themselves. Kali defeated the demons. Delighted with her victory she performed a savage killing dance so furiously that the earth trembled beneath her weight and its destruction appeared imminent. The gods, frightened and unable to stop her, sent Siva to induce her to desist. Entranced in her bloody rampage and not noticing him, Kali continued killing and dancing. So Siva lay down at her feet. When eventually Kali was about to step on him, she realized that it was her husband upon whom she was placing her feet—an inexcusable act for the Hindu wife. She stopped her rampage and the earth was saved—because her husband had regained control over her.[6]

---

[6] It should be noted that there are also destructive and malevolent male deities in Hinduism. The goddesses alone do not cause all the trouble of the world. However, there seems to be a basic difference between male and female destructiveness. Male deities and demons appear to be logical in the trouble they cause. Unlike Kali, they do not get carried away with the idea

The benevolent goddesses in the Hindu pantheon are those who are properly married and who have transferred control of their sexuality (Power/Nature) to their husbands. Symbolically, a woman is 'a part' of her husband, his 'half-body'. Rules for proper conduct mandate that she transfer her powers, as they accumulate, to her husband for his use. Mythology is replete with stories of the properly chaste wife who aids her husband in winning his battle by virtue of her proper behavior and ensuing transfer of power (it is probable that females, in the last analysis, win all battles). In the following two myths the gods' triumph depends on the control of female power.

There was once a continuous twelve-year war between the gods and the demons. The gods were losing badly and Indra felt that there was no way except for losing his life. At this time, Indrani said to her husband: 'Don't be afraid. I am a faithful wife. I will tell you one way by which you can win and protect yourself.' After saying this much, Indrani bound the *rakhi* (a bracelet, literally 'protection') on the wrist of her husband. After she bound the *rakhi*, Indra again went to war and defeated all the demons (Wadley, 1975).

There was a demon named Jalandhar. He had a very beautiful and faithful wife named Branda. Because of the power accruing to him from the faithfulness of his wife, the demon conquered the whole world. The gods were in trouble and arrived at this solution: changing a dead body into the shape of Jalandhar, Visnu threw it into the courtyard of Branda's family. Then Visnu gave life to the body and, in this way, Branda embraced another man and marred her faithfulness. Owing to her loss of faithfulness, Jalandhar's power was weakened and Visnu killed him in a big war (Wadley, 1975).

According to Hindu cosmology, if a female controls her own sexuality, she is changeable; she represents both death and fertility; she is both malevolent and benevolent. If, however, she loses control of her sexuality (Power/Nature) by transferring it to a man, she is portrayed as consistently benevolent. There are two images, then, of the woman in Hinduism, linked by the basic conceptions of the nature of femaleness: the fact that the female is both *sakti* (Power/Energy), and *prakriti* (Nature).

As Power and Nature, and controlling her own sexuality, the female is potentially destructive and malevolent:

---

of mere killing. In discussing this matter with Guy Welbon, we came up with the distinction of plotted versus plotless action. Male destruction has an end goal; female destruction often does not. The logic (and Culture?) of the male dominates his action; the non-logic (and Nature) of the female dominates her actions.

Kali (the Black One): Bearing the strange skull topped staff, decorated with a garland of skulls, clad in a tiger's skin, very appalling owing to her emaciated flesh, with gaping mouth, fearful with her tongue lolling out, having deep-sunk reddish eyes and filling the regions of the sky with her roars . . . . (Jagadisvarananda, 1953, quoted in Babb, 1970).

With the control of her sexuality transferred to men, the female is fertile and benevolent:

Lakshmi (the Goddess of Fortune): 'She who springs forth from the body of all the gods has a thousand indeed countless, arms, although her images are shown with but eighteen. Her face is white, made from the light streaming from the lord of sleep (Siva). Her arms made of the substance of Visnu are deep blue: her round breasts made of *soma*, the sacrificial ambrosia, are white . . . . She wears a gaily coloured lower garment, brilliant garlands, and a veil . . . . He who worships the Transcendent Divinity of Fortune becomes the lord of all the worlds' (Karapatri, 'Sri Bhagavati Tattva', quoted in Danielou, 1964).

The Ideal Hindu Woman

Understanding the dual character of the Hindu female's essential nature (her *sakti* and *prakriti*), provides a backdrop for understanding the rules and role models for women in Hindu South Asia. A central theme of the norms and guidelines for proper female behavior, especially in the male-dominated classical literature, is that men must control women and their power. But whether in classical texts or folk traditions, the dual character of the Hindu female emerges definitely, and is seen most clearly in the roles of wife (good, benevolent, dutiful, controlled) and mother (fertile, but dangerous, uncontrolled).

I draw on a variety of materials to explicate these roles. Rules for proper conduct are explicitly laid down in Hindu lawbooks, collectively known as the *Dharmasastras* (the Rules of Right Conduct). Mythology, written and oral, in Sanskrit and in the vernaculars, provides many examples of female behavior and its consequences, thus setting up explicit role models for the Hindu woman. Folklore yields yet other beliefs about female behavior. Finally, social organization and structure mesh with, allow for, and reinforce these beliefs about the proper conduct of women (Wadley, 1976).

The dominant norms for the Hindu woman concern her role as wife. Classical Hindu laws focus almost exclusively on this aspect of the woman. Role models and norms for mothers, daughters, sisters, etc., are less prominent and are more apt to appear in folklore and vernacular traditions. In addition, in most written traditions, the emphasis is on women's behavior in relationship to men: wife/husband; mother/son; daughter/ father; sister/brother. Role models for female behavior concerning other females (mother/daughter; sister/sister) are almost nonexistent in any of the literature. In contrast, two female/female relationships—mother-in-law/daughter-in-law and husband's sister/wife—are common themes in folklore and oral traditions but not in the more authoritative religious literature. These two relationships are vital to the well-being of women, but of little concern to men.[7] That they do not occur as important themes in the male-oriented and written literature of the Sanskrit tradition is not surprising. Rather, they surface in the popular oral traditions of women themselves. The male orientation in classical literature is also apparent in differing depictions of the husband/wife and brother/sister relationships. With these factors in mind, let us examine norms for female behavior in Hindu South Asia.

The basic rules for women's behavior are expressed in the following passages from the *Laws of Manu*, written early in the Christian era. These passages stress the need to control women because of the evils of the female character. The first set is excerpted from a section dealing with the duties of women:

By a young girl, by a young woman, or even by an aged one, nothing must be done independently, even in her own house.

In childhood a female must be subject to her father, in youth to her husband, when her lord is dead, to her sons; a woman must never be independent . . . .

Though destitute of virtue, or seeking pleasure (elsewhere), or devoid of good qualities, (yet) a husband must be constantly worshipped as a god by a faithful wife . . . .

By violating her duty towards her husband, a wife is disgraced in this world; (after death) she enters the womb of a jackal, and is tormented by diseases (the punishment) of her sin.

She who controlling her thoughts, words, and deeds, never slights her lord, resides (after death) with her husband (in heaven), and is called a virtuous (wife) (Buhler, 1964).

The following set is excerpted from the section regarding the duties of wife and husband:

Day and night, women must be kept in dependency by the males (of)

<hr>

[7] In what is essentially a sex-segregated society, women's primary day-to-day interactions are with other women, often in a joint family setting.

their (families), and if they attach themselves to sensual enjoyment, they must be kept under one's control . . . .

Considering that the highest duty to all castes, even weak husbands (must) strive to guard their wives . . . .

Women do not care for beauty, nor is their attention fixed on age: (thinking) '(it is enough that) he is a man', they give themselves to the handsome and the ugly.

Through their passion for men, through their mutable temper, through their natural heartlessness, they become disloyal towards their husbands, however carefully they are guarded in this (world).

Knowing their disposition, which the Lord of creatures laid in them at the creation, to be such, (every) man should most strenuously exert himself to guard them (Buhler, 1964).

Thus, women, because of their evil inclinations and birth, are to be kept under the control of men at all stages of their lives. The ideal women are those who do not strive to break these bonds of control. Moreover, the salvation and happiness of women revolve around their virtue and chastity as daughters, wives and widows.

These themes are not relegated merely to laws in ancient Sanskrit texts. They continually reappear in later Sanskrit and vernacular writings as well as in oral traditions. One of the most popular religious texts in India is the *Ramayana*, found in Sanskrit and in most vernaculars. This text tells the story of Rama, an incarnation of Visnu, sent to earth to destroy the menacing demon Ravana as he was on the verge of upsetting the right moral order of the earth. In the *Ramayana*, Rama's wife Sita exemplifies the behavior of the proper Hindu wife, devotedly following her husband into forest exile for fourteen years, and eventually, after being kidnapped for a time by the evil Ravana whom Rama finally destroys, proving her wifely virtue by placing herself on a lighted pyre. When she remains unscathed by the flames, the gods above pour flowers down upon her. In a happy ending her husband accepts her back into his household.

The story of Rama and Sita is well known to most Hindus and is enacted yearly, with greater or lesser splendour, in villages and cities all over India. Pictures of Sita following her husband to the forest, of Sita being kidnapped by Ravana, of Sita on the pyre, are found in a great many homes, on the walls of shops and even in government offices. Famous cinema stars portray Rama and Sita in gargantuan film epics. The message of the *Ramayana* is clear, and remarkably similar to that of the more esoteric and inaccessible lawbook written years before.

Sita is to most Hindu women the epitome of the proper wife. She represents the ideal towards which all should strive. Other wives in the Hindu tradition also provide popular role models. Women who have committed *sati* (burning themselves on their husbands' funeral pyres), are acclaimed as goddesses and are honored with shrines and rituals. The theme of the devoted wife also recurs in connection with calendrical rites. Throughout North India, women yearly worship the goddess Savitri. Her renown emanates from her extreme devotion to her husband, through which she saves him from the god of death. The story of Savitri is held up as a prime example of the lengths to which a wife should go in aiding her husband. The good wife saves her husband from death, follows him anywhere, proves her virtue, remains under his control and gives him her power.

These aspects of wifely behavior and norms are also found in oral traditions, with one crucial addition: the wife's desire for her husband and her dismay at his absence. The theme of love between husband and wife is minor in the classical written literature, whether Sanskrit or vernacular; rather, devotion and dutifulness dominate.[8]

However, the traditions of women, those created and perpetuated by women alone, continuously reiterate the longing for a husband's return and their mutual love as these examples illustrate:

One seer of wheat I will eat for one year,
    eat for one year,
(But) I will not allow my husband to go.
I will keep him before my eyes, (and) I
    will not allow my husband to go.
I will not allow you to go for the whole night,
O beautiful wife, I will not allow you to go
    for the whole night (Srivastava, 1974).

The above discussion emphasizes, as does the literature, the wife's regard for and duties to her husband, not his towards her, though this theme does emerge partially in the oral traditions. The textual traditions contain few injunctions for husbandly behavior beyond stating that a man must marry to procure sons who are needed for his salvation. One passage from Manu is critical, however, stipulating that men should treat their women well or women will destroy them:

[8] This is not to say that the written traditions provide no examples of wifely love. However, the emphasis switches as we move from written (men's) to oral (women's) traditions. Moreover, there is one notable example of male/female love in the written traditions in the pairing of Radha and Krishna. In many parts of India, this pair is not believed to be married. And Radha is seldom recognized as an ideal. She does provide a possible role model, but not one which is advocated.

Women must be honoured and adorned by their fathers, brothers, husbands, and brothers-in-law who desire (their own welfare) . . . . The houses on which female relations, not being duly honoured, pronounce a curse, perish completely, as if destroyed by magic. Hence, men who seek (their own) welfare, should always honour women on holidays and festivals with (gifts of) ornaments, clothes and (dainty) food (Buhler, 1964).

Thus, women ideally have some recourse when ill-treated—using their power, they can destroy. But, as we saw above, the best of wives (Sita) will worship their husbands even when abused.

The wifely role is pre-eminent in Hinduism. There are other roles but they are not generally considered normative patterns. Rather, they provide expectations for possible behavior. The woman as mother is the most critical of the other female roles.

The norms for mothers are less explicit than those for wives. Whereas mythology and lawbooks provide endless examples of the good wife, there are no prime examples of the good mother. However, it is the goddesses as mothers rather than as wives who are village guardians, who are worshipped regularly for their protection and aid, and who are feared. A common name for many goddesses is 'Mother'; a goddess is never called 'Wife'.[9] The wifely role is one of subordination, of devotion in any circumstances, of dutifulness. It is the mother who gives, who must be obeyed, who loves, and who sometimes rejects (Wadley, n.d.). Although there are no popular and well-known role models of the mother treating her children well, the mother as a giving, loving individual, although sometimes cruel and rejecting, is present at a sub-conscious but critical level in Hindu thought.[10]

It is the mother, transformed into the mother goddess whose devotees are her 'children', who is both the bestower and destroyer. Mothers and mother goddesses represent clearly the dual character of Hindu females. They can give and take away, whether from children or devotees. As such, the mother role is not acclaimed as proper or ideal behavior; rather, her danger is accepted because she is necessary. The mother, also, more than the wife, represents the polluting aspects of the Hindu female as well as representing the purifying milk. In her very biology—a biology necessary for motherhood but not for wifehood—the mother is a contradiction.[11]

[9] As one of the complications of this facet of motherhood, the goddesses who are said to have children are seldom called mother; rather, it is the goddesses who do not have children *per se* (Durga, Kali, Santoshi, Sitala) who are known as 'Mother'.

[10] The imagery and psychology of the 'Mother' in Indian thought presents complications in interpretation and meaning far beyond the potential and scope of this paper.

[11] The woman is especially impure and inauspicious just before and during childbirth. Yet their milk is a most pure substance. Her monthly menses are polluting, but not equalled by

Last, mothers and the mother goddesses are in control of their sexuality; wives are not. Again, we find the opposition of Lakshmi, the wife and Kali, the mother.

Hinduism also includes women who are totally malevolent, who never change from an evil maliciousness. These figures, primarily ghosts of women who died in childbirth or in other inauspicious ways, but also witches, are the antithesis of the wife. Beck has suggested that they themselves have lost control of their sexuality and cannot channel their actions towards any positive end (Beck, 1971). If this interpretation is correct, we obtain the following model of women's roles in Hinduism:

Wife	Mother	Ghost
Culture via male control	Nature but in self control	Nature but out of control
Good	Good/Bad	Bad
Subordinated	Worshipped	Appeased

Expectations for other female behavior can be summarized briefly. The daughter obeys her father and the sister is under the protection of her brother (and fervently desires his protection as he is her primary link with her natal home, especially in North India). The husband's mother is threatening and the husband's sister is an unreliable ally in the husband's home. The expectations for these latter three come mostly from women's oral traditions and reflect women's concern for their day-to-day welfare.

Norms for women in Hinduism derive from two separate, though related, sources. First, the male-dominated literature prescribes control and subordination of the woman. Second, folk and oral traditions, often created and propagated by women, yield norms that are concerned with women's welfare and emphasize the behavior of crucial male kin (the husband as lover, the brother as protector, the son as security) as well as female kin (the mother-in-law, the husband's sister). In both these realms we find the mother—not merely as the bearer of children, but also as the mother of

---

the pollution of childbirth. To what extent Hindu perceptions of the female are based on biological functions, it is hard to say. I have not attempted to deal with the relationship between female biology (pollution/purity) and perceptions of the female in Hinduism. Others have suggested that they are closely intertwined, with which I would agree. However, purity/pollution and femaleness presents another set of problems which must be dealt with elsewhere. I should note, however, that Hindu mythology does explicitly relate the low ritual status of women to:

a her monthly periods
b her ability to bear children.

the devotee—given extreme importance. The wife is the woman under male control; the mother is the woman in control of herself and her 'children'. These two figures dominate Hindu thought about women.

PART II

Women in Hindu Religious Practice

Women are active religious practitioners, but they have little religious authority—legitimate, textually sanctioned religious power—which is limited to a small group of men. Paradoxically, however, at the popular level, women are prominent religious participants, both as specialists and non-specialists.

To comprehend the place of women in Hindu religious practice, a brief summary of Hindu social organization is necessary. As is well known, India is a society based on hierarchies, including not only that of caste but also that of kinship and others. The many thousands of castes in India are grouped into five broader social classes: the four varna that originated in ancient times (Brahman, priest; Ksatriya, warrior; Vaisya, tradesman; Sudra, worker) and the untouchable. One's membership (via a specific caste) in a particular varna is of little importance most of the time.[12] However, religious activity is sometimes based on varna membership. Specifically only male members of the first three varna have access to the sacred texts of the *Vedas*, the earliest and most authoritative of the Hindu scriptures. Women, Sudras and Untouchables are not allowed to know, or sometimes even to hear, the *Vedas*. Further restrictions dictate that only Brahman men are to use the *Vedas* in approaching the gods, i.e., in rituals. Thus, men of the top three varnas are 'twice born' (i.e., can wear the sacred thread after a ritual second birth and can know the scriptures). And only Brahman men can perform Vedic rituals. Women, therefore, are no worse off than a great many men in terms of access to the principal authoritative sources of religious power.[13]

Women's access to the *Vedas* and other authoritative texts apparently underwent revision sometime around 600 BC. Previously, women had been able to undertake fasts for themselves, to hear and learn the *Vedas*, etc. By the time of Manu, women were no longer allowed to hear the *Vedas* or

---

[12] Many people cannot name their varna, though Brahmans generally know theirs. Aside from religion, it appears to have been of minor importance until recently when varna is regaining popularity both as an urban classification and for political purposes.

[13] Untouchables, both men and women, are generally the most maligned members of Hindu society. Higher caste men and women can enter temples, but until recently untouchables could not enter many temples. (Untouchability is outlawed in the Indian constitution, but is still practised in many parts of India).

to be major participants in rituals. During this time, perceptions of women as dangerous were developing among the Aryan population. Most probably, these redefinitions of the nature of femaleness affected women's positions in ritual activities (Pinkham, 1941).

Fortunately, Hindu religious activity is not based solely on Vedic rituals. The dominant form of ritual activity today is that of *bhakti*, or devotion to a deity. Stemming from the *Bhagavad Gita* and gaining strength from an anti-Brahman, anti-Vedic movement which started in about AD 700, *bhakti* (devotion) and associated ritual forms do not require the services of a priest to approach one's chosen deity.[14] One result is that women have direct access to the gods, and thus to salvation. Today, *puja* (devotional ritual) is the principal form of ritual activity in India. Vedic rituals are reserved for life-cycle rites and other male-dominated occasions, such as the opening of a new temple.

Although women may approach the deities directly through *bhakti* rituals, men continue to be recognized as legitimate religious specialists.[15] Males are temple priests; males conduct life-cycle rites; males are the leaders of most public rituals. To understand the female as religious specialist, we must first understand the varying roles of male specialists. Table 1 summarizes the discussion of Hindu religious specialists and their social characteristics.

The best-known Indian religious specialists are the priests—the caretakers of temples and the family priests who conduct life-cycle rites. Priests are called by various terms: in North India, two (*pandit, purohit*) refer only to Brahmans; the third (*pujari*) often refers to a lower-caste priest/caretaker of a temple. Normally, *pandits* are temple priests. *Purohits*—family priests—serve their patrons whenever called, sometimes daily, sometimes only for major life-cycle rites. Both must be Brahman males. *Pujaris* are often lower-caste males who function as priests at the temples of local deities who lack scriptural sanction. In addition, the wives of Brahman priests often act as specialists for life-cycle rites or on other ritual occasions. Generally, they are experts in oral tradition, knowing the songs or stories associated with a particular rite or the unwritten rules for women's correct ritual behavior. Their husband's role has scriptural sanction; theirs does not.

---

[14] Priests are still found in most temples; however, temple worship is not necessary for the followers of *bhakti* (and the early *bhakti* movement was anti-temple as well as anti-Brahman).

[15] By the term religious specialist, I mean:

    a someone who is paid for religious/ritual services,

    b someone who conveys religious instruction, or is a guide in ritual practice, or performs rituals for others.

People who provide essential ritual services (such as the flower grower or the washerman) but not religious instruction or guidelines, are not considered religious specialists.

Table 1
RELIGIOUS SPECIALIZATION IN HINDUISM

Specialist	Male	Female	Textually Sanctioned
Priest:			
Pandit	x(B)	(wife)	x(not wife)
Purohit	x(B)	—	x
Pujari	x	—	—
Actor as God	x(B)	—	?
Shaman	x	x	—
Exorcist	x	—	—
Client in jajmani system	x	(wife)	—
Yogi/Sadhu	x	seldom	x
Personality cult-leader	x	x	—
Devadasi	—	x	x(South India only)

Explanation: x(B) means, must be Brahman.
(wife) indicates 'plays role by virtue of wifehood'.

A related specialist, often also called *pandit*,[16] is the astrologer. He is the expert who provides essential information and advice at the time of marriages and births and fixes auspicious dates for journeys and other undertakings. The astrologer is also a Brahman male.[17]

Brahman men dominate still other forms of public ritual. For example, various forms of religious folk operas and plays are found throughout India: in these, the actors portraying a deity are all male—whether the deity be male or female. In fact, the actor as the deity, is worshipped as a manifestation of the deity, and because worship of the actor as deity is required, the actor must usually be a Brahman.

Less legitimate participants in public rituals, are more likely to be non-Brahman males. Possession rituals which are not textually sanctioned, appear to be male-dominated; many exorcists and shamans are non-Brahman.[18] Occasionally, a shaman will be female. Shamans and exorcists

[16] Pandit is also an honorific used for any Brahman male, including those who do not perform priestly functions.

[17] Modern astrologers are sometimes female—you find their ads in English language newspapers or big hotels. To what extent traditional astrologers might have been female is unknown. I have not seen any reference to them in the literature.

[18] Exorcists and shamans come from any caste and from either sex, although female shamans are rarely mentioned in the literature and female exorcists may be non-existent. Some authors have claimed that the shamans/exorcists (the two are often confused) are the non-Brahman counterparts of priests. I believe that the situation is vastly more complicated than that as Brahman shamans are common, for one thing. I should mention that there are also possessions related to illness where a religious specialist is not possessed; rather, a victim is (especially young women facing the tribulations of her husband's home).

are religious power figures who lack textual sanction; their power comes from oral traditions and societal recognition. As such, they provide access to religious power for those normally forbidden such access: non-Brahman males and all females.

Other ritual specialists must also be considered, particularly those who are specialists by virtue of their position in the *jajmani* system, a system of inherited patron-client ties found throughout most of South Asia. Several of the clients (workers who provide services in return for payment) have primarily ritual connections with their patrons. One such client is the barber and his wife, who are necessary figures in most life-cycle rites. In addition to providing services (hair cutting, bathing the new infant, bathing the groom, etc.), they instruct and guide their patrons through the proper ritual forms. The midwife is another such ritual guide. None of these have textual sanction for their roles as religious specialists *per se*, and the instruction they provide is usually based on local traditions.[19]

Other specialists are the sadhus and yogis. Many play no vital role in Hindu religious practice beyond that of a 'presence', while others are important lecturers and teachers. Occasionally, a woman will be a yogini. Both male and female yogis are sanctioned by various textual traditions. However, the yogi is considered to be outside the caste system and removed from family ties; he/she is outside society and its structures. All members of society can thus opt for being non-members. These non-members lacking caste *and* sexual distinctions, are sanctioned by the classical texts.

Popular, nonclassical religious specialists in Hinduism can be either male or female—the 'personality cult' leader such as Guru Maharajji or The Mother. Women are less often the figureheads of such movements than men; nevertheless, female leaders do recur regularly and are sanctioned by society if not by textual tradition.

Traditionally, only one religious specialist so far as I know was always female—the *devadasi* (votary of God). Found in South India, the *devadasis* were nominally married to the god of the temple but allowed mates. Their offspring were legitimate: the girls were often, in turn, dedicated to the temple; the boys might become professional musicians. The *devadasi* was always felt to be distinct from the 'dancer'; her role was definitely religious. Outlawed by the British, the institution of the *devadasi* fell into disrepute,

---

[19] Other clients in the *jajmani* system have connections which are the provision of ritual services often based on conceptions of purity/pollution. Here we find the washerman, sweeper and leather-worker. However, like the flower grower mentioned in note 16, they are not considered religious specialists as they provide no religious instruction and play no role in rituals *per se* (On the other hand, all activity by a Hindu can be considered religious, in which case everyone is a specialist).

although its traditions of dance still exist with some descendants and as 'dance' are having a revival in both East and West. Traditionally, the *devadasi* was a religious specialist who had textual sanction only in South India (Devi, 1972).

These facets of religious specialization are summarized in Table 1. Textually recognized specialists are, with one exception, Brahman men. Women and non-Brahman men are religious specialists, but are only rarely sanctioned by authoritative traditions. Thus, women, like low caste men, have religious power in Hinduism, but nonlegitimate, nonauthoritative power.

Clearly, then, Hindu women have considerable religious involvement. Women as nonspecialists are 'invisible' religious practitioners, since most of their observances are performed non-publicly (in the home or 'domestic' sphere) and their role is not textually sanctioned; indeed, the *Laws of Manu* forbid a woman to fast or participate in rituals without her husband. Yet, if we look at folk religious practices rather than the Hinduism of the texts, women, along with low caste men, are the primary actors.

Women alone perform a large number of the yearly calendrical rituals in both rural and urban India and are essential to most others.[20] In Karimpur, a village in North India, women are the instigators and prime participants in twenty-one of the thirty-three annual rites (Wadley, 1976). Women also dominate nine of the twenty-one annual rites in the village Mohana near Lucknow[21] (Majumdar, 1958) and are apparently the sole participants in nine of the twenty two festivals in the annual cycle of Rampur, a village north of Delhi[22] (Lewis, 1965). The exact 'great tradition' status of the rites of women—which are all based on *puja* (devotional ritual) rather than on Vedic fire sacrifices—has yet to be determined. However, most festivals which can be easily identified as having no 'great tradition' ties are women's festivals. I suspect that if the rituals of women do have textual sanction, their performance varies widely and reflects manifold local differences.

Women's participation in life-cycle rites is definitely part of the 'little tradition'. Women surround these rituals, in which they are mere accessories, with local folk practices. During actual ceremonial time, women's

[20] The evidence in the following discussion comes from rural North India. Comparable evidence is lacking for most of the rest of India. Urban data comes from my personal experiences in Delhi and Agra.

[21] Majumdar, *op. cit.*, lists more than twenty-one early rites, but provides no descriptions of the others. Identification of the participants by sex could only be made for these twenty-one.

[22] Available evidence of these festivals in the three villages suggests that there is some variation in which festivals are organized and run by females versus males, with only a few always being male or female. The variation in local practice needs further investigation. Also, most authors list caste variation in participants; sexual variation must be culled from descriptions.

practices clearly dominate: taking a marriage or a birth ceremony as a whole, men's rites take very little time, although the men's rites are a crucial subsidiary (to women).[23]

Much of India is a society with strict sexual segregation. Purdah is generally associated with sexual division of labor and existence in separate worlds (Papanek, 1971). As a corollary, women's concerns are very different from those of men. This separation is found also in religion: the many folk practices of women focus on the prosperity and well-being of the family. Women's rites seek the protection and well-being of crucial kinsmen (especially husband, brother and son), the general prosperity and health of family members, and 'good' husbands. This emphasis is found in both calendrical and life-cycle rites. Men's rites do not seek 'good' wives or ones who will have a long life; rather, they are concerned with a good wheat crop, ridding the village of disease, etc. (Wadley, 1976).[24] It is not surprising to find this religious division of labor in the sexually-segregated purdah society of traditional India.

Women's religious practices are influenced in part by conceptions of the female: her danger provides a justification for her not being an active participant in the most authoritative rites; yet within the domestic sphere women are vital religious practitioners who have developed a subsidiary religious realm of largely folk, or local, non-textual traditions. The sexual segregation of Hindu society also articulates with the role that religion plays in drawing women together: female solidarity is continuously reinforced through religious practices. Moreover, many women's rites relate to their dual roles as wives and mothers. But females, such as the mother goddesses, who protect most villages in India are, nevertheless, frequent objects of worship by both men and women.

PART III

The Potential for Change

There can be no doubt that Hindu perceptions of femaleness are powerful and pervasive: women are threatening; their sexuality is destructive to men, whose energy they sap, yet their fertility is needed for bearing their sons. One result is a deep-seated fear of women aligned with a recognition of their power. Women are thus banned from the dominant sources of religious power and authority, but in fact, they obtain power and prosperity through their own religious practices. Moreover, social practices and

---

[23] In some religions, men make fun of and laugh at the women's rites and generally put up with them in a condescending fashion.

[24] For some of this material, I would also like to thank William Houska for his insights into male-female orientations in North Indian rituals.

religious ideology seem to be mutually reinforcing: for example, a woman worships her brother, who is indeed her protector, and she is secluded (and kept in need of protection) because it is believed that she can be dangerous.

Yet India, a country where Hindus constitute 83 per cent of the population, was ruled by a woman. This fact initially appears disconcerting and contrary to most outsiders' impressions of South Asian and Hindu women. Indeed, it is in contradiction with the image of the properly behaved wife given above. But Mrs. Gandhi's role apparently was not a contradiction to the residents of India. A brief look at some Indian impressions of Mrs. Gandhi illustrates an important aspect of the potential for change for Hindu women.

During the height of Mrs. Gandhi's power, a famous Indian artist had completed a portrait of her as Durga riding on a tiger (Lukas, 1976). Durga is one of the goddesses considered to be a wife of Siva. However, she, like Kali, has a vast potential for aggression and destruction. She does not remain under her husband's control and controls her own sexuality. Yet Durga is generally beneficent (especially in contrast to Kali)[25] and is worshipped as a mother goddess throughout India. We are being told by the artist, I suspect, that Mrs. Gandhi was the mother as epitomized by the goddess—a mother who is generally kind, but one who repulses her children (devotees, citizens) at times.

Similarly, the Hindu villager was apt to describe the Prime Minister as *devi*, the goddess. And in a poem dedicated to Indira Gandhi published in a popular English language magazine just after the Bangladesh war, we find these phrases: 'Presiding deity of our country's fate' and 'Of noble grace and looks and yet defiant, thunder in her eyes . . . .' (Dhamija, 1972). Mrs. Gandhi is the goddess, not Sita of the *Ramayana*, the devoted wife who obeys her husband's every wish,[26] but the Mother, the goddess who epitomizes the dual character of the Hindu female. As such, she is easily comprehended in Hindu terms. The Hindu female can be aggressive: her essential nature makes her exactly that. Thus, Hindu conceptions of the female place the Hindu woman in a position opposite to that of the American woman who is generally believed to be passive by nature. Hindu women need only take advantage of their defining characteristics whereas American women must overcome theirs. As a result, when the Hindu woman does act as Durga (or as Mrs. Gandhi), there is a ready explanation for her behavior and acceptance of the woman in a dominating role

[25] If Mrs. Gandhi has been portrayed as Kali, the implications probably would be vastly different.

[26] It should be mentioned that Mrs. Gandhi did play on the image as the 'proper Hindu woman', looking meek, with covered head and mild manners on many public occasions.

(after all, Durga does save the world). Thus, Hindu beliefs about the nature of the female and corresponding religious role models (but not the ideal type—the wife), contains an ideology that can and seemingly does provide a meaningful code for women actively involved in non-wifely roles.

Until recently, Hindu ideology has been Brahman (high caste) male dominated. Even today, almost 80 per cent of India's population is rural, and literacy rates remain low. But this situation is rapidly changing. Women, through schooling and mandatory learning of Sanskrit in many states, can now study the scriptures, forbidden to them for the past two thousand years, although a female *pandit* (as novel as a female Catholic priest would be) is yet to be seen. With the relaxation of purdah restrictions in both urban and rural areas, women are not as sexually segregated as previously; their freedom of movement allows them more opportunities for forming alliances with other women, and women's participation in public rituals is enhanced.

Since the early nineteenth century, many Indians have agitated for reform of traditional religious-based rules for women. Practices such as *sati*, bans on widow remarriage, and prepuberty marriage have already been outlawed, and divorce and abortion are legal, although social practice lags behind the laws. Other social practices based on Hindu orthopraxy continue to impede women's secular status. Purdah is still rigidly followed in some rural areas and aids in denying women economic equality. Daughters are not desired because of economic liabilities with regard to hypergamous marriages and dowries, both aspects of Brahmanical orthopraxy, especially in the North. The sex ratio continues to decrease—from 972 females per thousand males in 1962 to 930 females per thousand males in 1971—suggesting that female mortality is high. A recent study suggests that Brahmanical practices are one aspect of discrimination against females and they contribute to the benign neglect of female children, resulting in juvenile female deaths (Miller, 1976). The Hindu-based desire for sons forces women into unwanted pregnancies and denies them control of their sexuality.

Many questions remain. Manuals for the proper conduct of women are now popular. These include material ranging from how to guarantee the birth of a son, to the necessary yearly rituals, to decorating the house. The content of these needs to be examined. The recent popularity of a 'new' goddess: 'The Mother of Peace' (*santoshi mata*), in both rural and urban North India needs investigation, including the phenomenon of a sellout film featuring this goddess and her all-abiding concern with family, but particularly with the husband/wife tie. Are these phenomena signs of change or a reaffirmation of traditional, male-dominated values?

There is potential for further change. Hinduism provides a conception of the world in which women are necessary but powerful and dangerous. Traditionally, this power and danger has been controlled through religious laws prescribing women's proper behavior as being under the control of men. Yet women (and the mother especially) do control others; the mother in Hindu thought becomes the Hindu woman in control of herself. As such, she provides an alternative role to that of the dutiful wife. Women's religious practices, meanwhile, are not authorized by the religious authorities but do provide for female solidarity and for alternative sources of religious power. Women's ritual practices, however, emphasize kinship and family relationships, reinforcing the view of woman as wife. Thus, despite the ideology of the powerful aggressive woman, most Hindu women probably will continue to be motivated by the Hindu conception of the women as dutiful wife, and will perform their yearly rituals for their husbands' long life, the presence of many sons, and so forth. But, as women take more powerful positions in India's changing society, they will find validation for their new roles in long-standing Hindu textual traditions.

The fearful goddess (Candika), devoted to her devotees reduces to ashes those who do not worship her and destroys their merits (Devi Mahatmya, quoted in Danielou, 1964).
Yet,
For those who seek pleasure or those who seek liberation, the worship of the all-powerful Goddess is essential. She is the knowledge-of-the-Immensity; she is the mother of the universe, pervading the whole world (Karapatri, *Sri Bhagavati Tattva*, quoted in Danielou, 1964).

FEMININE IDENTITY IN INDIA

Sudhir Kakar

Whether her family is poor or wealthy, whatever her caste, class or region, whether she is a fresh young bride or exhausted by many pregnancies and infancies already, an Indian woman knows that motherhood confers upon her a purpose and identity that nothing else in her culture can. Each infant borne and nurtured by her safely into childhood, especially if the child is a son, is both a certification and a redemption.

At the same time, each individual woman approaches motherhood at her particular crossroads of *desa, kala, srama* and *gunas* (Kakar, 1978), and with her unique constellation of values, expectations, fears and beliefs about the role and the experience of mothering. She meets her new born infant with the emotional resources and limitations of her particular personality; these are the 'matrix' of her child's infancy.[1] Her identity as a Hindu woman has evolved out of the *particulars* of her life cycle and childhood, out of the dailiness of her relationships as daughter in her parents' family and as wife and daughter-in-law in her husband's family, and out of the universals of the traditional ideals of womanhood absorbed by her from childhood onwards. Whether a particular mother is reserved or responsive to a particular infant, and in what circumstances, depends on a wide range of variables, not the least of which is her ordinal position in her original family (whether she was a firstborn female or the fourth daughter in a row, or the first little girl after a string of sons . . .) as well as the sex and ordinal position of the infant who now needs and claims her love and care. It is not the purpose of this study to explore the range of individual maternal receptivity. Rather, we will focus on the vivid ideals of womanhood and motherhood in India, the common themes which in a traditional society such as India pervade and circumscribe the identities of individual women.

First of all, where and when tradition governs, an Indian woman does not stand alone; her identity is wholly defined by her relationships to

---

[1] For a psychoanalytic consideration of some of these issues, see, for example, Grete L. Bibring et al., 'A Study of the Psychological Processes in Pregnancy and of the Earliest Mother-Child Relationship', *The Psychoanalytic Study of the Child*, Vol. 16, New York: International Universities Press, 1961, pp. 9–72, and H.A. Moss, 'Sex, Age and State as Determinants of Mother-Infant Interaction', *Merrill-Palmer Quarterly*, 13, 1967, pp. 19–36.

others. For although in most societies, a woman (more than a man) defines herself in relation and connection to other people, this is singularly true of Indian women. The dominant psycho-social realities of her life can be condensed into three stages:

First, she is a daughter to her parents.
Second, she is a wife to her husband (and daughter-in-law to his parents).
Third, she is a mother to her sons (and daughters).

How, then, do daughters fare in 'mother India'? The frank answer is that it is difficult to know, at least as exhaustively and 'in depth' as I would like to. The reason for this lies in the fact that data, of all kinds, are uneven or unavailable. Anthropological accounts refer, implicitly or explicitly, to the development of boys, and skim the subject of female childhood or skip it altogether. Myths, too, are sparing of their bounty towards daughters, for in a patriarchal culture myths are inevitably man-made and man-oriented. Addressing as they do the unconscious wishes and fears of men, it is the parent-son rather than the parent-daughter relationship which becomes charged with symbolic significance[2] (Karve, 1968).

These limitations are real enough, but they need not be forbidding. On the contrary, they challenge the psycho-analytic researcher to mine the existing material thoroughly and to construct an interpretive bridge for future work. There are, for example, in anthropological accounts, both a consistent indication of the marked preference for sons all over India, and at the same time, somewhat paradoxically, abundant allusion to the warmth, intimacy and relaxed affection of the mother-daughter bond.[3] Statistical

---

[2] Although the patrilineal and patrilocal family type is dominant all over India, there are some castes and communities, especially in southern India which are matrilineal and in which women enjoy relatively greater freedom. For the similarities and contrasts in kinship organization of different regions in India, see Irawati Karve, *Kinship Organization in India*, 3rd edn., Bombay: Asia Publishing House, 1968.
My remarks are intended to apply only to the dominant patriarchal culture where by unconscious necessity it is the mother who is of primary symbolic significance, or, as the Jungians would put it, the mother is the primary constituent of a man's anima. The problem of feminine figures in the myths of a patriarchal society is compounded by the fact that these animas are not solely male projections but also represent some aspects of feminine psychology in these cultures. The reason for this intertwining of anima images and feminine psychology is that very early in childhood, girls learn to accurately perceive and conform to the patriarchal images of femininity entertained by the men around them in the household. In this connection see Marie-Louise von Franz, *The Feminine in Fairy Tales*, Zurich: Spring Publications, 1972.
[3] The anthropological accounts which have a bearing on this section are T.N. Madan, *Family and Kinship: A Study of the Pandits of Rural Kashmir*, Bombay: Asia Publishing House, 1965; Leigh Minturn and John T. Hitchcock, 'The Rajputs of Khalapur, India' in *Six*

documentation reminds us of the higher rate of female infant mortality, and calls attention to the fact that whatever health care and schooling are available in India, daughters are the last to receive it.[4] In the realm of literature, although the mainstream mythology and classical texts of Hinduism have been the preserves of men, there are parts of the oral tradition—ballads, folk-songs and couplets sung by women in different parts of the country, a few folk-tales—which give us clues to the psychological constellation of daughterhood in India. Leavened with clinical impressions, these various sources can be judiciously drawn together to sketch a portrait of Indian girlhood.

The preference for a son when a child is born is as old as Indian society itself. Vedic verses pray that sons will be followed by still more male offspring, never by females. A prayer in the *Atharvaveda* adds a touch of malice: 'The birth of a girl, grant it elsewhere, here grant a son' (*Atharvaveda* quoted in Das, 1962). As MacDonell observes:

> Indeed daughters are conspicuous in the *Rigveda* by their absence. We meet in hymns with prayers for sons and grandsons, male offspring, male descendants and male issue and occasionally for wives but never daughters. Even forgiveness is asked for ourselves and grandsons, but no blessing is ever prayed for a daughter. When *Agni* is born it is as if it were a male infant. They clap their hands and make sounds of rejoicing like the parents of a new-born son. There is no such rejoicing over the birth of a daughter (MacDonell quoted in Das, 1962).

Cultures: Studies of Child-rearing, ed. B.B. Whiting, New York: John Wiley and Sons, 1963, pp. 301–61; L. Minturn and W.W. Lambert, *Mothers of Six Cultures*, New York: John Wiley, 1964; Oscar Lewis, *Village Life in Northern India*, New York: Vintage Books, 1958; S.C. Dube, *Indian Village*, New York: Harper and Row, 1967; M.N. Srinivas, *Marriage and Family in Mysore*, Bombay: New Book Co., 1942; Edward B. Harper, 'Spirit Possession and Social Structure', in *Anthropology on the March*, ed. B. Ratnam, Madras: The Book Centre, pp. 165–97; and Aileen D. Ross, *The Hindu Family in its Urban Setting*, Toronto: University of Toronto Press, 1961. Two other useful studies, essentially descriptive, based on intensive interviewing with women who represent the progressive, well-educated parts of Indian society are: Margaret Cormack, *The Hindu Woman*, Bombay: Asia Publishing House, 1961, and Promilla Kapur, *Love, Marriage and Sex*, Delhi: Vikas Publishing House, 1973. For older, impressionistic yet sensitive studies of Indian women, see Mary F. Billington, *Woman in India* (18–?), New Delhi: Amarko Book Agency, 1973, and Frieda M. Das, *Purdah, the Status of Indian Women*, New York: The Vanguard Press, 1932.

[4] The infant mortality rate in 1969 for females was 148.1 as compared to 132.3 for males; the life expectancy between 1961–71 was 45.6 for females, 47.1 for males, while the number of girls enrolled in the educational system in 1970–1 was 18.4 per cent as compared to 39.3 per cent for boys. See the relevant statistical tables in Indian Council of Social Science Research, *Status of Women in India: A Synopsis of the Report of the National Committee on the Status of Women* (1971–4), New Delhi: Allied Publishers, 1975, pp. 140–75.

The ancient *Pumsavana* rite, still performed over pregnant women in traditional Hindu households, is designed to elicit the birth of a male infant and to magically change the sex of the unborn child if it be a female.

Contemporary anthropological studies from different parts of India and the available clinical evidence assure us that the traditional preference for sons is very much intact.[5] At the birth of a son drums are beaten in some parts of the country, conch-shells blown in others and the midwife paid lavishly, while no such spontaneous rejoicing accompanies the birth of a daughter. Women's folk-songs reveal the painful awareness of inferiority— of this discrepancy, at birth, between the celebration of sons and the mere tolerance of daughters. Thus, in a north Indian song the women complain:

> Vidya said, 'Listen, O Sukhma, what a tradition has started!
> Drums are played upon the birth of a boy,
> But at my birth only a brass plate was beaten.' (Lewis, 1958).

And in Maharashtra the girl, comparing herself to a white sweet-scented jasmine (*jai*) and the boy to a big, strong-smelling thorny leaf (*kevada*), plaintively asks: Did anyone notice the sweet fragrance of a *jai*? The hefty *kevada* however has filled the whole street with its strong scent' (Karve, 1968).

Of course there are 'valid' ritual and economic reasons—we will come to the psychological ones later—for 'sexism' in Indian society. The presence of a son is absolutely necessary for the proper performance of many sacraments, especially those carried out upon the death of parents and imperative to the well-being of their souls. In addition to her negligible ritual significance, a daughter normally is an unmitigated expense, someone who will never contribute to the family income and who, upon marriage, will take away a considerable part of her family's fortune as her dowry. In the case of a poor family, the parents may even have to go deep in debt in order to provide for a daughter's marriage. The *Aitareya Brahmana* (like other older texts) probably refers as much as anything else to the economic facts of life when it states flatly that a daughter is a source of misery while a son is the saviour of the family[6] (Das, 1962).

[5] See, for example, Minturn and Hitchcock, *op. cit.*, pp. 307–08; Madan, *op. cit.*, p. 77; Dube, *op. cit.*, pp. 148–49; Cormack, *op. cit.*, p. 11. See also, William J. Goode, *World Revolution and Family Patterns*, New York: The Free Press, 1963, pp. 235–36; and D.G. Mandelbaum, *Society in India*, Vol. 1, Berkeley: University of California Press, 1970, p. 120. Cases of post-partum depression, for example, are much more commonly reported among mothers who give birth to a daughter than among those who have a son. See M.R. Gaitonde, Cross-Cultural Study of the Psychiatric Syndromes in Out-Patient Clinics in Bombay, India, and Topeka, Kansas', *International Journal of Social Psychiatry*, 4, 1958, p. 103.

[6] A contemporary Bengali proverb expresses this thought more bluntly, 'Even the piss of a son brings money; let the daughter go to hell.'

As in other patriarchal societies, one would expect the preference for sons over daughters, the cultural devaluation of girls, to be somehow reflected in the psychology of Indian women. Theoretically, one possible consequence of this kind of inequity would be a heightened female hostility and envy towards males, together with a generally pronounced antagonism between the sexes. I do not have sufficient evidence to be categorical; yet my impression is that these phenomena do not, in general, characterize the inner world of Indian women. The dominant myths, for example—unlike, say, *A Thousand and One Nights*—show little evidence of strain in relationships between the sexes. And, as I have shown elsewhere, aggression occurring between members of the same sex is significantly greater than between members of opposite sexes in India (Kakar, 1974).

It can be argued that male dominance and strong taboos against feminine aggression may inhibit the expression of female resentment against men and serve to redirect this hostility against male children. For if a woman perceives that the sole and fundamental premise of the absolute status hierarchy between the sexes is merely gender, and if she is prevented from expressing her age and resentment at this state of affairs, either because of cultural taboos, social inferiority or her dependence upon men, then her unconscious destructive impulses towards male children are liable to be particularly strong, this being her only possible revenge against a pervasive oppressive masculinity. Again, excepting certain communities, this does not appear to be characteristic of Indian women, given the evidence of songs, tales and other kinds of folklore (Kakar, 1974).

The third possibility is that girls and women in a dramatically patriarchal society will turn the aggression against themselves and transform the cultural devaluation into feelings of worthlessness and inferiority. There is scattered evidence that such a propensity indeed exists among many communities of Indian women, that hostility towards men and potential aggression against male infants are often turned inward, subsumed in a diffuse hostility against oneself, in a conversion of outrage into self-deprecation. At least among the upper middle class women who today seek psychotherapy, the buried feeling, 'I am a girl and thus worthless and "bad" ', is often encountered below the surface of an active, emancipated femininity. One patient, for example, staunchly maintained that her parents' separation took place because of her father's disappointment that she was born a girl and not a boy, although in fact, as she herself was aware, the parents had separated shortly before her birth. Some of the traits connected with low self-esteem—depressive moodiness, extreme touchiness and morbid sensitivity in interpersonal relations—come through in the testimony of modern, educated Indian girls in the non-clinical interviews reported by Margaret Cormack in *The Hindu Woman*. And their less educated, rural sisters give vent to similar feelings through the medium of folk-songs: 'God Rama, I fall at your feet and fold my hands and pray to you, never again give me the birth of a woman' (Karve, 1968).

I have deliberately used the words 'possibility' and 'propensity' in the above discussion rather than ascribe to Indian women a widespread depressive pattern. In the first place, for the cultural devaluation of women to be translated into a pervasive psychological sense of worthlessness in individual women, parents' and other adults' behavior and attitudes towards the infant girls in their midst—the actualities of family life—must be fully consistent with this female depreciation. Secondly, the internalization of low self-esteem also presupposes that girls and women have no sphere of their own, no independent livelihood and activity, no area of family and community responsibility and dominance, no living space apart from that of the men, within which to create and manifest those aspects of feminine identity that derive from intimacy and collaboration with other women. And, in fact, these two circumstances exist in India, to mitigate the discriminations and inequities of patriarchal institutions.

From anthropological accounts and other sources, we know of the special kind of lenient affection and often compassionate attention bestowed by mothers on their infant daughters throughout their lives.[7] 'I turn the stone flour mill with the swiftness of a running deer; that is because my arms are strong with the mother's milk I drank', (Karve, 1968). This, and other couplets like it, sung by women all over India, bear witness to the daughter's memory of her mother's affection for her and to the self-esteem and strength of will this has generated in turn. Thus, in infancy, the most radical period of emotional development, Indian girls are assured of their worth by whom it really matters: by their mothers.

The special maternal affection reserved for daughters, contrary to expectations derived from social and cultural prescriptions, is partly to be explained by the fact that a mother's unconscious identification with her daughter is normally stronger than with her son.[8] In her daughter, the mother can re-experience herself as a cared-for girl. And, in Indian society, as we shall see later, a daughter is considered a 'guest' in her natal family, treated with the solicitous concern often accorded to a welcome

[7] See Ross, *op. cit.*, pp. 150–1; Dube, *op. cit.*, pp. 148–9; Srinivas, *op. cit.*, p. 173; Whiting, *op. cit.*, p. 303; Harper, *op. cit.*, pp. 171–72; Madan, *op. cit.*, p. 77; and Cormack, *op. cit.*, p. 9. Folk songs from all over India also bear witness to this close mother-daughter tie. See, for example, songs no. 4, 5, 6, 7, 8, and 9 in Karve, *op. cit.*, p. 205.

[8] As Helene Deutsch expresses it: 'In her relation to her own child, a woman repeats her own mother-child history.' See *The Psychology of Women*, Vol. 1, *op. cit.*, p. 205. See also Nancy Chodorow, 'Family Structure and Feminine Personality', in *Woman, Culture and Society*, ed. M. Rosaldo and L. Lamphere, Stanford: Stanford University Press, 1975, pp. 52–53.

outsider, who, all too soon, will marry and leave her mother for good. Mindful of her daughter's developmental fate, the mother re-experiences the emotional conflicts her own separation had once aroused, and this in turn tends to increase her indulgence and solicitude towards her daughter.

In addition to her mother's empathic connection with her, as an Indian girl grows up her relationships with others within the extended family further tend to dilute any resentment she may harbour for her brothers. Among the many adults who comprise a Hindu family there is almost always someone in particular who gives a little girl the kind of admiration and sense of being singled out as special that a male child more often receives from many. In such a family system, every child, irrespective of sex, stands a good chance of being some adult's favourite, a circumstance which softens the curse of rivalry, envy and possessiveness which often afflicts 'modern' nuclear families. And, of course, when a girl is the only daughter, such chances are increased immeasurably. Thus in folk-tales, however many sons a couple may have, there is often one daughter in their midst who is the parents' favourite.

Finally, in traditional India, every female is born into a well-defined community of women within her particular family. Although by no means does it always resound with solidarity and goodwill, the existence of this discrete sphere of femininity and domesticity gives women a tangible opportunity to be productive and lively, to experience autonomy and to exercise power. It also allows a special kind of inviolate feminine privacy and familiar intimacy. Getting along with other women in this sphere, learning the mandatory skills of householding, cooking and childcare, establishing her place in this primary world: these relationships and these tasks constitute the dailiness of girlhood in India. Moreover, this 'developmental apprenticeship' and the activities that transpire in this feminine sphere are independent of the patriarchal values of the outside world. And when necessary, other women in the family—her mother, grandmother, aunts, sisters and sisters-in-law—are not only an Indian girl's teachers and models but her allies against the discriminations and inequities of that world and its values. Often enough, in the 'underground' of female culture, as reflected in ballads, wedding songs and jokes, women do indeed react against the discriminations of their culture by portraying men as vain, faithless and infantile.[9] All these factors help to mitigate (if not to prevent) the damage to a girl's self-esteem when she discovers that in the eyes of the culture she is considered inferior to a boy, a discovery which usually coincides with the awareness of gender identity in late childhood.

[9] Thus in many ballads whereas the women are depicted as tolerant, self-sacrificing and faithful, the men are weak, timid and faithless. See Sankar Sen Gupta, *A Study of Women of Bengal*, Calcutta: Indian Publications, 1970, p. 107.

Late childhood marks the beginning of an Indian girl's deliberate training in how to be a *good woman*, and hence the conscious inculcation of culturally designated feminine roles. She learns that the 'virtues' of womanhood which will take her through life are submission and docility as well as skill and grace in the various household tasks. M.N. Srinivas, for example, reports on the training of young girls in Mysore:

> It is the mother's duty to train her daughter up to be an absolute docile daughter-in-law. The *summum bonum* of a girl's life is to please her parents-in-law and her husband. If she does not 'get on' with her mother-in-law, she will be a disgrace to her family, and cast a blot on the fair name of her mother. The Kannada mother dins into her daughter's ears certain ideals which make for harmony (at the expense of her sacrificing her will) in her later life (Srinivas, 1942).

In the *bratas*, the periodical days of fasting and prayer which unmarried girls keep all over India, the girl's wishes for herself are almost always in relation to others; she asks the boons of being a good daughter, good wife, good daughter-in-law, good mother, and so forth.[10] Thus, in addition to the 'virtues' of self-effacement and self-sacrifice, the feminine role in India also crystallizes a woman's connections to others, her embeddedness in a multitude of familial relationships.

If the self-esteem of Indian girls falters radically during the years of early puberty, this is intimately related to the fact that at precisely this developmental moment, a time of instinctual turbulence and emotional volatility, her training in service and self-denial in preparation for her imminent roles of daughter-in-law and wife is stepped up. In order to maintain her family's love and approval, the 'narcissistic supplies' necessary for firm self-esteem, the girl tends to conform, and even overconform, to the prescriptions and expectations of those around her.

The adult personality of Indian women is not only moulded through this (unconscious) manipulation of her precarious feelings of worthiness as an adolescent, it is also distinctly influenced by the culturally sanctioned maternal indulgence of daughters. As we have noted above, daughterhood in India is not without its rewards, precisely because the conditions of

---

[10] For example, in the *Dasa Puttal Brata* of Bengali girls it is wished that 'I shall have a husband like Rama, I shall be *sati* like Sita, I shall have a *devara* (younger brother-in-law) like Lakshman, I shall have a father-in-law like Dasharatha; I shall have a mother-in-law like Kausalya; I shall have sons as Kunti had, I shall be a cook like Draupadi, I shall acquire power like Durga; I shall bear the burden like earth; I shall be like Sasthi whose offspring know no death.' See Akshay Kumar Kayal, 'Women in Folk-Sayings of West Bengal', in Sen Gupta, *op. cit.*, p. xxii.

womanhood are normally so forbidding. In contrast to the son's, a daughter's training at her mother's hands is normally leavened with a good deal of compassion, for which, as ever, there are traditional as well as psychological explanations. Manu expressly enjoins that kindness be shown to the daughter as she is 'physically more tender and her emotions are more delicate', and other ancient commentators forbid any harshness towards her, even in words (Das, 1962). The learned Medhatithi puts the whole matter into its 'proper', that is, its ritual, perspective:

> By reason of the marriage having taken the place of *Upanayana*[11] it follows that just as in the case of men all the ordinances of the *Srutis*, *Smritis* and custom become binding upon them after the *Upanayana*, before which they are free to do what they like and are unfit for any religious duties, so for women also there is freedom of action before marriage, after which they also become subject to the ordinances of the *Srutis* and *Smritis* (Das, 1962).

Little wonder that for an Indian girl rebellion against the fearsome constraints of impinging womanhood, with its singular circumscription of identity, becomes impossible. She internalizes the specific ideals of womanhood and monitors her behavior carefully in order to guarantee her mother's love and approval, upon which she is more than ever dependent as she makes ready to leave home. For all the reasons described above, the irony of an Indian girl's coming-of-age is that to be a good woman and a felicitous bride she must be more than ever the perfect daughter.

Sita: The Ego Ideal

For both men and women in Hindu society, the ideal woman is personified by Sita, the quintessence of wifely devotion, the heroine of the epic *Ramayana*. Her unique standing in the minds of most Hindus, regardless of region, caste, social class, age, sex, education or modernization, testifies to the power and pervasiveness of the traditional ideal of womanhood: Sita, of course, is not just another legendary figure, and the *Ramayana* is not just another epic poem. It is through the recitation, reading, listening to, or attending a dramatic performance of this revered text (above all others) that a Hindu reasserts his or her cultural identity as a Hindu, and obtains religious merit. The popular epic contains ideal models of familial bonds and social relations to which even a modernized Hindu pays lip service, however much he may privately question or reject them as irrelevant to the task of modern life.

[11] The sacrament for boys, usually occuring between the ages of five and eight, which initiates them as full-fledged members of the society.

Sita, like the other principal figures in the epic—Rama, Lakshman, Hanuman—is an incomparably more intimate and familiar heroine in the Hindu imagination than similar figures from Greek or Christian mythology are in the fantasies and deliberations of an average westerner. This intimate familiarity is not meant to suggest historical knowledge, but rather a sense of the mythical figure as a benevolent presence, located in the individual's highly personal and always actual space-time. From earliest childhood, a Hindu has heard Sita's legend recounted on any number of sacral and secular occasions; seen the central episodes enacted in folk plays like the *Ram Lila*; heard her qualities extolled in devotional songs; and absorbed the ideal feminine identity she incorporates through the many everyday metaphors and similes that are associated with her name. Thus, 'She is as pure as Sita' denotes chastity in a woman, and 'She is a second Sita', the appreciation of a woman's uncomplaining self-sacrifice. If, as Jerome Bruner remarks, 'In the mythologically instructed community there is a corpus of images and models that provide the pattern to which the individual may aspire, a range of metaphoric identity',[12] then this range, in the case of a Hindu woman, is condensed in one model. And she is Sita.

For western readers unacquainted with the myth, the legend of Sita, in bare outline, goes like this: One day as King Janaka was ploughing, an infant sprang up from the ground whom he named Sita.[13] The child grows up to be a beautiful girl whom the king promises to give in marriage to any man who can bend the wonderful bow in his possession. Many suitors—gods, princes, kings, demons—vie for Sita's hand but none is even able to lift the bow, until Rama, the reincarnation of Vishnu and the hero of the epic, comes to Janaka's country and gracefully snaps the bow in two. After their wedding, Sita and Rama return to Ayodhya, which is ruled by Rama's father, Dasharatha.

After some time Dasharatha wants to abdicate in favour of Rama who is his eldest son. But because of a promise given to the mother of one of his younger sons, he is forced to banish Rama to the forest for fourteen years. Rama tries to persuade Sita to let him proceed in his exile alone, pointing out the dangers, discomforts and deprivations of a homeless life in the forest. In a long, moving passage Sita emphasizes her determination to

[12] Jerome S. Bruner, 'Myths and Identity', *Daedalus*, Spring 1959, p. 357. In a study carried out in the north Indian province of Uttar Pradesh 500 boys and 360 girls between the ages of 9 and 22 years were asked to select the ideal woman from a list of 24 names of gods, goddesses and heroes and heroines of history. Sita was seen as the ideal woman by an overwhelming number of respondents: there were no age or sex differences. See P. Pratap, 'The Development of Ego Ideal in Indian Children', unpublished Ph.D. Thesis, Banaras Hindu University, 1960.
[13] The name Sita means a furrow, a universal symbol for the feminine genitalia.

share her husband's fate, averring that death would be preferable to separation. Her speech is an eloquent statement of the *dharma* of a Hindu wife:

> For a woman, it is not her father, her son, nor her mother, friends nor her own self, but the husband, who in this world and the next is ever her sole means of salvation. If thou dost enter the impenetrable forest today, O Descendant of Raghu, I shall precede thee on foot, treading down the spiky *Kusha* grass. In truth, whether it be in palaces, in chariots or in heaven, wherever the shadow of the feet of her consort falls, it must be followed (Shastri, 1962).

Both Rama and Sita, mourned by the citizens of Ayodhya who adore their prince and future king, proceed to the forest in the company of Rama's brother Lakshman. The *Ramayana* then recounts their adventures in the forest, most prominent and terrible among them being Sita's kidnapping by the powerful king of the demons, Ravana, and her abduction to Lanka. In Lanka, Ravana's kingdom, Sita is kept imprisoned in one of the demon-king's palaces where he tries to win her love. Neither his seductive kindnesses nor his grisly threats are of any avail as Sita remains steadfast in her love and devotion to Rama.

Meanwhile, Rama raises an army from the *Vanar* (monkey) tribes in order to attack Lanka and bring back Sita. After a long and furious battle, he is victorious and Ravana is killed. Doubting Sita's fidelity through the long term of her captivity, Rama refuses, however, to accept her again as his wife until she proves her innocence and purity by the fire ordeal in which the fire-god Agni himself appears to testify to her virtue. The couple then return to Ayodhya where amidst the citizens' happy celebrations Rama is crowned king.

But Sita's ordeal is not yet over. Hearing of rumours in the city which cast suspicion on the purity of his queen, Rama banishes her to the forest where she gives birth to twins, Lava and Kusha. She and her children live an ascetic life in a rustic hermitage, but Sita's love for Rama unfaltering. When the twins grow up, she sends them back to their father. On seeing his sons, Rama repents and Sita is brought back to Ayodhya to be reinstated as queen. On her arrival, however Rama again commands her to assert her purity before the assembled court. His abiding mistrust, this further demand, prove too much for the gentle queen who calls on her mother, the earth, to open up and receive her back. The earth obliges and Sita disappears where she was born.

How are we to interpret the legend of Sita? Philip Slater has pointed out that a myth is an elaborately condensed product, that there is no one 'correct' version or interpretation, for no matter how many layers one peels off, there will still remain much to be explained (Slater, 1968). In the interpretation that follows, I will set aside such elements as social history, religious ritual and artistic embellishment, although I am only too well aware of their importance to mythmaking. Rather, my aim is to attend to the themes in the Sita legend from a psycho-analytic and psychosocial perspective. In this kind of interpretation we must ask questions such as: How does the myth influence the crystallization of a Hindu woman's identity and character? What role does it play in helping to ward off or assuage feelings of guilt and anxiety? How does it influence her attitude towards and images of men? How does it contribute to the individual woman's task of 'adapting to reality' and to the society's task of maintaining community solidarity? And finally do the different mythological versions of a single underlying theme correspond to different 'defensive editions' of unconscious fantasy at different life stages of those to whom the myths speak (Arlow, 1961).

The ideal of womanhood incorporated by Sita is one of chastity, purity, gentle tenderness and a singular faithfulness which cannot be destroyed or even disturbed by her husband's rejections, slights or thoughtlessness. We should note in passing that the Sita legend also gives us a glimpse into the Hindu imagery of manliness. Rama may have all the triats of a godlike hero, yet he is also fragile, mistrustful and jealous, and very much of a conformist, both to his parents' wishes and to social opinion. These expectations, too, an Indian girl incorporates gradually into her inner world.

The legend of Nala and Damayanti provides a variation on the ideal of the good wife; Damayanti cheerfully accompanies Nala, her husband, into the forest after he has gambled away everything they own, including his clothes. And when he leaves her sleeping in the forest at night, taking away half of the only garment she possesses to clothe his own nakedness, Damayanti does not utter a single word of reproach as she wanders through the forest, looking for her husband. The 'moral' is the familiar one: Whether treated well or ill a wife should never indulge in ire.

In another popular myth: Savitri, in spite of the knowledge that her chosen husband is fated to die within a year, insists on marrying him and renouncing the luxuries of her palace to join him in his poverty. When at the end of the year, Yama, the god of death, takes away her husband, Savitri follows them. Yama assures her that as she has loved her husband faithfully, she need not sacrifice her own life. Savitri replies that wherever her husband goes she must follow for that is the eternal custom: 'Deprived of my husband, I am as one dead!' (Roy, n.d.).

In the Savitri myth, the ideal of devoted fidelity to one man takes on an added dimension and categorical refinement: Exclusive devotion to one's husband becomes the prerequisite for the all-important motherhood of sons. Thus, as Savitri follows Yama to his country, the land in which all wishes come true, she refuses to accept his assurance that with her husband's death all her wifely obligations have expired. Only through her demonstration of wifely devotion, even after her husband's death, can she finally persuade Yama to revive him and grant her the boon of offspring: 'Of Satyavan's loins and mine, begotten by both of us, let there be a century of sons possessed of strength and prowess and capable of perpetuating our race'.[14] (Roy, n.d.).

To be a good wife, is by definition, to be a good woman. Thus Markandeya discourses to Yudhishthira of 'wives restraining all their senses and keeping their hearts under complete control. They regard their husbands as veritable gods. For women, neither sacrifice, nor *sraddhas* (penances), nor fasts are of any efficiency. By serving their husbands only can they win heaven' (Roy, n.d.). This is the ideal, purveyed over and over again, in numberless myths and legends, through which the Hindu community has tried to mould the character and personality of its female members. Moreover, a woman is enjoined that her devotion to her husband should extend also to his family members, especially to his parents. A married woman's duties have been nowhere more fully described than in Draupadi's advice to Satyabhama, Lord Krishna's wife:

Keeping aside vanity, and controlling desire and wrath, I always serve with devotion the sons of Pandu with their wives. Restraining jealousy, with deep devotion of heart, without a sense of degradation at the services I perform, I wait upon my husbands . . . Celestial, or man, or Gandharva, young or decked with ornaments, wealthy or comely of person, none else my heart liketh. I never bathe or eat or sleep till he that is my husband hath bathed or eaten or slept . . . When my husband leaveth home for the sake of any relative, then renouncing flowers and fragrant paste of every kind, I begin to undergo penances. Whatever husband enjoyeth not, I even renounce . . . Those duties that my mother-in-law had told me in respect of relatives, as also the duties of alms-giving, of offering worship to the gods . . . and service to those that deserve our regards, and all else that is known to me, I always discharge day and night, without idleness of any kind (Roy, n.d.).

[14] The Savitri myth is also a striking demonstration of Ernest Jones's thesis that the conscious fantasy of dying together possesses the unconscious significance of the wish to have children. See E. Jones, 'On "Dying Together" with Special Reference to Heinrich von Kleist's Suicide' and 'An Unusual Case of Dying Together', *Essays on Applied Psychoanalysis*, London: Hogarth Press, 1951, pp. 9–21.

I have quoted from the ancient texts in detail in order to emphasize the formidable consensus on the ideal of womanhood which, in spite of many changes in individual circumstances in the course of modernization, urbanization and education, still governs the inner imagery of individual men and women as well as the social relations between them in both the traditional and modern sectors of the Indian community.

Together with this function as a more or less conscious ideal which leaves indelible traces in the identity formation of every Hindu woman, the Sita myth also plays an unconscious role as a defence against the anxiety aroused by a young girl's sexual impulses, whose expression would almost seem to be invited by the nature of family life in traditional India. Freud has clarified for us the universal themes of infantile psycho-sexual development in terms of the vicissitudes of the libido. He left it primarily to others to differentiate among the social influences and cultural variations. Thus, sexual development in Hindu daughters is *socially* influenced by the communal living pattern, the close quarters of the extended family and the indulgent adult attitudes towards infant sexuality. In this intimate daily setting where constant close contact with many members of the family of both sexes and several generations is part of a little girl's early bodily experience; where the infant girl is frequently caressed and fondled by the many adults around her; and where playful exploratory activities of an explicitly sexual nature among the many cousins living in the same house or nearby in the neighbourhood are a common early developmental experience, often indulgently tolerated by the more or less 'permissive' adults—a promiscuous sexual excitation, as well as the fear of being overwhelmed by it, looms large in the unconscious fantasies of an Indian girl. Later, as she leaves childhood behind, the identification with Sita helps in the necessary renunciation of these promiscuous sexual fantasies of childhood, in the concentration of erotic feeling exclusively on one man, and in the avoidance of all occasions for sexual temptation and transgression. Sita sets the compelling example: Although Rama's emissary, the monkey-god Hanuman, offers to rescue Sita from her ordeal of imprisonment in Lanka by carrying her on his shoulders and transporting her through the air to her waiting husband, she must refuse the offer since it means touching Hanuman's body, and of her own free will she may, on no account, permit herself to touch any man except her husband. This enigmatic tension between the memory of intense and pleasurable childhood sexuality and the later womanly ideal which demands restraint and renunciation, between an earlier indiscriminate 'availability' and the later unapproachability, may account for that special erotic presence in Indian women which has fascinated the imagination of many writers and artists.

Perhaps the most striking mythological elaboration of the connection between the young girl's sexuality, in particular, her fantasied erotic wishes towards her father, and her later repudiation of these wishes by transforming them into their opposite, aloofness and chastity, is the myth of Arundhati, who, next to Sita, is the most famous chaste wife in Hindu mythology. I have reproduced the myth in detail not only to illustrate this aspect of feminine identity in India but also because of its special relevance for psycho-analytic theory, for it explicitly acknowledges the existence of infantile sexuality:

Brahma (the Creator) had displayed desire for his daughter, Sandhya (Twilight), as soon as she was born, and she had desired him. As a result of this, Brahma cursed Kama (Eros), who had caused the trouble, to be burnt by Siva. When everyone had departed, Sandhya resolved to purify herself and to establish for all time a moral law: that new-born creatures would be free of desire. To do this, she prepared to offer herself as an oblation in the fire. Knowing of her intention, Brahma sent the sage Vasistha to instruct her in the proper manner of performing *tapas*. Vasistha disguised himself as a *brahmacharin* with matted locks and taught her how to meditate upon Siva. Siva then appeared to her and offered her a boon, She said, 'Let all new-born creatures be free of desire, and let me be reborn as the wife of a man to whom I can just be a close friend. And if anyone but my husband gazes upon me with desire, let his virility be destroyed and let him become an impotent eunuch.' Siva said, 'Your sin has been burnt to ashes, purified by your tapas. I grant what you ask; henceforth, creatures will only become subject to desire when they reach youth, and any man but your husband who looks upon you with desire will become impotent.' Then Sandhya, meditating upon the chaste Brahmin for her husband, entered the sacrificial fire. Her body became the oblation, and she arose from the fire as an infant girl, named Arundhati. She grew up in a sage's hermitage and married Vasistha.[15] (Das, 1962).

[15] *Siva Purana*, 2. 2. 5. pp. 1–68, 6. pp. 1–62. The translation is from W. O'Flaherty, *Asceticism and Eroticism in the Mythology of Siva*, London: Oxford University Press, 1973, pp. 64–65. A perusal of Hindu law texts reveals that our ancient law-givers—Manu, Kautilya, Kullika, Medhatithi—were obsessed with the chastity of young unmarried girls. The punishments for all conceivable kinds of chastity-violation, depending on the castes of the actors, their sex (whether the violator is a man or a woman), the degree of consent and so on, are elaborately detailed. Thus, for example, if a man forcibly 'pollutes' a maiden with his fingers, the fingers shall be amputated and he shall pay a fine of 500 panas. If the man is of equal caste, the fine is reduced. If the fingers have been inserted with the consent of the maiden, the fingers are not amputated and the fine is reduced to 200 panas. If the initiative is taken by the girl, the punishment is lighter or non-existent; instead her guardians are to be punished in so much as they presumably did not keep a proper watch on her. There are similar fines in the case of an older woman seducing a young girl, depending on their castes and the 'violation'.

Another version of the myth offers a diametrically opposite resolution of the conflict. Here the 'plot' works to lift the repression of childhood memories and to remove defences against erotic impulses and guilt feelings, and, according to the principle of the identity of opposites, the daughter of Brahma is reborn not as the most chaste of women, but as Rati, the incarnation of sexuality and the goddess of sexual pleasure. The unconscious fantasy elaborated in this version belongs, of course, to adolescence rather than to the oedipal years of childhood.

On still another level, the identification with Sita contributes to the Hindu woman's adaptation to married life in her husband's extended family and to the maintenance of this family as a functioning unit. Such a family, composed as it is of other men besides her husband, affords the Hindu wife temptations and opportunities for sexual transgression, the indulgence of which would destroy the necessary interdependence and cooperation of the Indian family. At some level of consciousness, every Hindu couple is aware, for instance, of Sita's exemplary behavior towards Rama's brother Lakshman during the fourteen years of their exile together. There exist, of course, elaborate codes and rituals of social behavior and discretion between the male and female members of an extended family, such as the injunction that the elder brother never directly address his younger brother's wife (nor enter her room when she is alone). Like most taboos, these are broken in fantasy. In a Bengali folk-song, for example, a woman expresses her desire for amorous relations with the elder brother of her husband, regretting that he is not the younger brother so that her desire might be gratified.[16] These taboos are designed to preclude intolerable jealous passions and disruptive rivalries; the reigning presence of Sita in the Indian inner world, in all her serene forbearance, is an important psychological reinforcement of these special codes.

The short description of daughterhood and the elaboration of the Sita ideal of womanhood cannot fully account for an Indian woman's emotional preparation for motherhood. Her chronological and developmental stage of life at marriage, her experiences and relationships within her husband's family, and the meaning of childbirth in her particular personal and social setting: these factors too are paramount; taken together, they are the 'psycho-social matrix of infancy' in India.

Life Stage at Marriage

An Indian girl is usually married during early adolescence, between the

[16] *Rangila bhasur go tumi keno deyor haila na.*
   Tumi jodi haita re deyor khaita batar pan
   (Aar) ranga rasa kaitam katha juraito paran.
   Sen Gupta, *op. cit.*, p. 94.

ages of twelve and eighteen; the average age of a Hindu bride is fifteen to sixteen.[17] In urban areas, or among higher castes, where daughters are more likely to receive some kind of formal education, the age may be somewhat higher. The traditional ideal holds that a girl should be married soon after her first menstrual period, for it is feared that 'if she remains long a maiden, she gives herself to whom she will'. The custom of early marriage, it seems, recognizes and is designed to guard against the promiscuous resurgence in adolescence of a girl's playful childhood sexuality and the threat this would pose to Hindu social organization. To marry one's daughters off propitiously is considered one of the primary religious duties of Hindu parents. Indeed: 'Reprehensible is the father who gives not his daughter at the proper time'. If married at eleven or twelve, the girl may remain in her parents' home for another three to four years before moving away to live with her husband. In any case, when she joins her husband's family, she is still a young adolescent and vulnerable to the universal psychological problems of this age.

First of all, before her departure for her husband's family and household, a very special relationship tends to develop between an Indian girl and her mother (Ross, 1961), who becomes at this time, naturally enough, her daughter's confidante and counsellor in the bewildering turmoil of adolescence and the newness of the prospect of marriage. Although the relationship between daughter and mother is surely characterized by the tension between the conflicting modalities of 'getting away' and 'coming nearer', the daughter none the less seeks to recreate the emotional closeness to the protective mother of her childhood. She has also formed intimate attachments to girl friends of her age in the village or neighbourhood among whom the secret fears and delights concerning the physical changes of puberty are shared, and fantasies about men and marriage are collectively evoked as each girl tries to envision and secure a clear sense of herself as a woman. These processes—the renunciation of dependency on the 'preoedipal' mother, the integration of what she was as a girl with the woman she is now suddenly becoming, and the acceptance of her inevitable marriage to a stranger—all these require time, her mother's support and love, the reassuring exchange of confidences with peers, and the 'trying out' of new, as yet unexperienced identities in fantasy. This whole process of feminine adolescent development is normally incomplete at the time an Indian girl gets married and is transplanted from her home into the unfamiliar, initially forbidding environment, of her in-laws.

The alien, often threatening, and sometimes humiliating nature of the

---

[17] The mean age according to the 1961 census was 15.8 years. For a discussion of the subject, see K.P. Singh, 'Women's Age at Marriage', *Sociological Bulletin* 23 (2), 1974, pp 236–44. See also William J. Goode, *op. cit.*, pp. 232–36.

setting in which an Indian girl's struggle for identity and adult status takes place cannot be stressed enough. In much of northern India, for example, the exogamous rule, that the bride comes from a village which does not border on the groom's village, strictly applies. In some other parts of the country, marriage customs are governed by a further rule which stipulates that a man who lives in a *gotra* village, that is, a village which is predominantly composed of a related caste group, is unacceptable as a potential bridegroom for any daughter of the village. In his study of social life in a village in Delhi, Oscar Lewis found that the 266 married women of the village came from 200 different villages, a pattern repeated by those who married outside this, their native village.[18] Consequently, this small village of 150 households was linked with over 400 other villages in its region; at the same time, no woman in the village could call for company, or in a moment of crisis or loneliness, on a friend or neighbour or relative known to her from childhood.

Whatever the contribution of these marriage rules to the integration of Indian society, and it is considerable, this integration is ultimately based on the insistence that women not only renounce their erotic impulses and primary loyalties to their parents—a universal developmental requirement—but also sever their attachments, in fact and in fantasy, to all the other boys and men they have known during their early lives who inevitably belong to one of the forbidden extended kinship or village groups. Instead, upon marriage, an Indian woman must direct her erotic tenderness exclusively towards a man who is a complete stranger to her until their wedding night, and she must resolve the critical issues of feminine identity in unfamiliar surroundings without the love and support of precisely those persons whom she needs most. Little wonder that the themes of the young girl pining for her parental home, her grief at separation from her mother, constantly recur in popular folk-songs and ballads.[19] The staunch presence of ideal feminine figures like Sita and Savitri is crucial to overcoming the traumatic transition which an Indian girl undergoes at precisely the most sensitive and vulnerable period of her development.

---

[18] Lewis, *op. cit.*, p. 161; see also Karve, *op. cit.*, p. 137 for evidence on the widespread existence of this custom.

[19] Here is an example from Bengal (freely translated):

O, Kaffu a bird, you are from my mother's side.
Speak, O speak in the courtyard of my parents.
My mother will hear you:
She will send my brother to fetch me.
O what sorrowful days have come!
I wish to get out of this,
I wish to reach my father's house.

(Sen Gupta, *op. cit.*, p. 149).

Status within Her Husband's Family: Not Wife but Daughter-in-law

An Indian girl's entry into the married state and the new world of social relations within her husband's family thus does not take place under auspicious psychological conditions. In spite of her inner ideals and conscious resolutions to be a good wife and an exemplary daughter-in-law, a bride comes into her husband's family with a tremendous burden of anxiety and nostalgia, with a sense of antagonism towards her mother-in-law who has, after all, usurped the place of her own sorely missed and needed mother, with a mixture of shy anticipation and resentment towards her husband's sisters and other young female relatives who have presumed to replace the sisters and cousins and friends at home, and with ambivalent feelings of tenderness and hostility towards the unknown person who is now her husband and claims her intimacy.[20] And if her husband turns out to be unworthy, she knows that there is no going back for her. Manu enjoins: 'Though destitute of virtue or seeking pleasure elsewhere, or devoid of good qualities, yet a husband must be constantly worshipped as a god by a faithful wife' (Buhler, 1964). And: 'By violating her duty towards her husband, a wife is disgraced in this world, after death she enters the womb of a jackal and is tormented by the punishment of her sin' (Buhler, 1964). These precepts, in spirit, if not in these precise words, have been instilled into Hindu girls from the age of earliest understanding. For, as mentioned above, although treated with indulgence and demonstrative affection in the years immediately before her marriage, an Indian girl is so indulged partly because of her status as a guest in her own house. Her 'real' family is her husband's family. Whatever her future fortunes,

---

[20] Folk-lore especially singles out the *sas* (mother-in-law) and the *nanad* (sister-in-law) as the natural enemies of the young bride. See Karve, *op. cit.*, p. 130. Here are lines from some of the songs in Bengal depicting the bride's plight (and her anger) in these two relationships. 'My husband's sister is nothing but a poisonous thorn, her poisonous stings give me much pain'; 'My mother-in-law expired in the morning, if I find time in the afternoon after eating lunch, I will weep for her.' In north India the bride sings:

O my friend! My in-laws' house is a wretched place.
My mother-in-law is a very hard woman
She always struts about full of anger,

and so forth. There are also many songs which complain of the husband's indifference. For example, see songs no. 39, 40, 41 in Karve, *op. cit.*, pp. 209–10. The presence of hidden hostility towards the new husband can also be inferred from the results of a Thematic Apperception Test administered to forty school girls in the South who were shown a picture of a death scene, with a covered unidentifiable body in the centre of the room and a doctor nearby consoling a young woman. In the stories written by the girls, by far the largest number (45 per cent) 'saw' the covered figure as the body of a dead husband. See D. Narain, 'Growing up in India', *Family Process*, 3, 1964, pp. 132–33.

when she marries an Indian girl knows that, in a psychological sense, she can never go home again.[21]

In the social hierarchy of her new family, the bride usually occupies one of the lowest rungs. Obedience and compliance with the wishes of the elder women of the family, especially those of her mother-in-law, are expected as a matter of course. Communication with the older men is minimal (if it exists at all) since they, as mentioned earlier, are traditionally expected to maintain a posture of formal restraint in the presence of the newcomer. Unflinchingly and without complaint, the new daughter-in-law is required to perform some of the heaviest household chores, which may mean getting up well before dawn and working till late at night. Any mistakes or omissions on her part are liable to incur sarcastic references to her abilities, her looks or her upbringing in her mother's home. For it must be noted, once again, that the new bride constitutes a very real threat to the unity of the extended family. She represents a potentially pernicious influence which, given family priorities, calls for drastic measures of exorcism. The nature of the 'danger' she personifies can perhaps best be suggested by such questions as: Will the young wife cause her husband to neglect his duties as a son? As a brother? A nephew? An uncle? Will social tradition and family pressure be sufficient to keep the husband-wife bond from developing to a point where it threatens the interests of other family members? Will 'sexual passion' inspire such a close relationship in the bridal couple that the new girl becomes primarily a wife rather than a daughter-in-law and her husband transfers his loyalty and affection to her rather than remaining truly a son of the house?

These are, of course, not either/or choices; however, custom, tradition and the interests of the extended family demand that in the realignment of roles and relationships initiated by marriage, the roles of the husband and wife, at least in the beginning, be relegated to relative inconsequence and utter inconspicuousness. Any signs of a developing attachment and tenderness within the couple are actively discouraged by the elder family members by either belittling or forbidding the open expression of these feelings. Every effort is made to hinder the development of an intimacy within the couple which might exclude other members of the family, especially the parents. Oblique hints about 'youthful infatuations', or outright shaming, virtually guarantee that the young husband and wife do not publicly express any interest in (let alone affection for) each other; and they are effectively alone together only for very brief periods during the night. If women's folk-songs are any indication, even these brief meetings

---

[21] Literally, of course, she may return to visit her family and village of origin; this is particularly likely in the case of a new, young wife at the time of confinement and childbirth.

are furtive affairs. There is hardly a song which does not complain of the ever wakeful *sas* (mother-in-law) and *nanad* (sister-in-law) preventing the bride from going to her husband at night. Madhav Gore's study of a sample of Indian men of the Agarwal community further confirms that these constraints, masterminded by the older women, usually succeed in their aims: 56 per cent of the men described themselves as being closer to their mothers than to their wives, while only 20 per cent felt they were closer to their wives (Gore, 1961).

I do not intend to imply that marriage in India lacks intimacy—that mutual enhancement of experience within culturally determined patterns of love and care which is the commonly held criterion of a 'good marriage' in the West. Rather, in India, this intimacy develops later in married life, as both partners slowly mature into adult 'householders'. Ideally, parenthood and the shared responsibility for offspring provide the basis for intimacy, rather than the other way around as in the West. This postponement of intimacy is encouraged by the family, for in the years of middle age the husband-wife bond no longer seems to threaten the exclusion of other family members, but incorporates or rather evolves out of the responsibility to take care of the next generation. Thus it is not antithetical to communal and family solidarity but, in its proper time, a guarantor of it.

Has the newly-married girl's situation in her husband's family no redeeming, or even relieving, features? I have neglected to point out that an Indian girl prepares for the harsh transition of marriage for some time before her actual departure for her husband's household. Stories, proverbs, songs, information gleaned from conversations with newly-married friends who come back home on visits, all more or less 'prepare' her for her role as an obedient daughter-in-law. Moreover, as in many other parts of the world, puberty rites such as seclusion during her menstrual period, or fasting on certain days, are designed to separate the young girl, both physically and symbolically, from her parents and to enable her to tolerate 'oral deprivation', for in her husband's household, at any meal, she will be the last one to eat.

These and other procedures bring the Indian girl to the end of childhood and introduce her, in a measured, ritual way, to the realities of womanhood. If married *very* young, the bride's initiation into her new life and family is gradual, interspersed with long visits to her parents' home where much of the accumulated loneliness and resentment can be relieved by the indulgent love showered on her by everyone, and particularly by her own mother's constant presence as a sympathetic listener and a gentle mentor. The young wife's isolation in her husband's home, moreover, is not necessarily as extreme as I have implied. She often develops relationships of informal familiarity and friendly consolation with certain younger members of her husband's family; and it usually happens that one or another of the many children in the family forms a strong attachment to her. But above all, it should be emphasized that the suspicion and hostility towards her rarely degenerate into deliberate oppression. This reflects a cultural tradition of restraint and prudence, which manifests itself in the Hindu conscience. Respect for and protection of the female members of society are a prime moral duty, the neglect of which arouses anxiety and a sense of being judged and punished. Manu, the law-giver, a misogynist by modern standards, leaves no doubt about the virtuous treatment of the female members of the family: 'Where women are honoured, there gods are pleased; but where they are not honoured, no sacred rite yields rewards . . . Where the female relations live in grief, the family soon wholly perishes; but that family where they are not unhappy ever prospers . . . The houses on which female relations, not being duly honoured, pronounce a curse, perish completely, as if destroyed by magic' (Buhler, 1886). Thus, the head of the family, or other elder males who feel themselves entrusted with the family's welfare, gently but firmly seek to mitigate the excesses of the mother-in-law and the elder women. On balance, however, the conclusion is unavoidable that the identity struggle of the adolescent Indian girl is confounded by the coincidence of marriage, the abrupt and total severance of the attachments of childhood, and her removal from all that is familiar to a state of lonely dependency upon a household of strangers.

Pregnancy and the Anticipation of Motherhood

The young Indian wife's situation, in terms of family acceptance and ience, emotional well-being, changes dramatically once she becomes pregnant. The prospect of motherhood holds out a composite solution for many of her difficulties. The psychological implications of her low social status as a bride and a newcomer; the tense, often humiliating relationships with others in her husband's family; her homesickness and sense of isolation; her identity confusion; the awkwardness of marital intimacy, and thus, often, the unfulfilled yearnings of her sexual self—these are tangled up in a developmental knot, as it were. With the anticipation of motherhood, this knot begins, almost miraculously, to be unravelled.

The improvement in an Indian wife's *social* status once she is pregnant has been universally noted by cultural anthropologists (Lewis, 1965). Elder family members, particularly the women, become solicitous of her welfare, seeing to it that she eats well and rests often. Many irksome tasks, erstwhile obligations and restrictions are removed, and gestures of pride and affection towards her as a daughter-in-law of the house increase markedly.

The growing feeling of personal well-being throughout the course of pregnancy is also reinforced by social customs. Thus, in many parts of India, the expectant mother goes back to stay at her own mother's house a few months before the delivery. This stay helps her to strengthen her identification with her mother, a prerequisite for her own capacity for motherhood. The anticipation of the birth itself, in spite of the primitive medical facilities available, does not seem to provoke strong anxiety or fears of dying since she knows her own parents, the all-powerful protectors, will be constantly at her side during labor. Once having given birth, the new mother can bask in her delight in her child and also in her satisfaction with herself, all of this taking place in a circle of greatly pleased and highly approving close kin.

This unambiguous reversal in an Indian woman's status is not lost on her; moreover, the belief that pregnancy is a woman's ultimate good fortune, a belief that amounts to a cultural reverence for the pregnant woman, is abundantly broadcast in the favourite folk-tales and familiar myths of Hindu tradition. Thus, this passage from a Bengali tale: 'Suddenly it seemed that God had taken notice of the prayer. The youngest queen, Sulata, was expecting. The king was overjoyed at the happy news. His affection for Sulata grew even more. He was always looking after her comforts and attending to her wishes' (Majumdar, 1911).

The roots of this solicitous respect for the pregnant women lie deep in a religious and historical tradition which equates 'woman' with 'mother' and views the birth of a male child as an essential step in the parents' and the family's salvation. 'To be mothers women were created, and to be fathers men', Manu states categorically (Buhler, 1964). Further on in the Laws, appraising the status of motherhood, he adds, 'The teacher is ten times more venerable than the sub-teacher, the mother a hundred times more than the father' (Buhler, 1964). 'She is a true wife who hath borne a son' Shakuntala tells Dushyanta as she reminds him of his forgotten marriage vows, for wives who produce children are 'the root of religion and of salvation. They are fathers on occasions of religious acts, mothers in sickness and woe' (Roy, n.d.). And the goddess Parvati, with divine disdain for convention, remarks: 'Among all the pleasures of women, the greatest pleasure is to unite with a good man in private, and the misery that arises from its interruption is not equalled by any other. The second greatest misery is the falling of the seed in vain, and the third is in childlessness, the greatest sorrow of all' (O'Flaherty, 1973).

Numerous passages in legends and epics vividly describe the suffering of the souls of departed ancestors if a couple remain childless and thus unable to guarantee the performance of the rituals prescribed for salvation. 'Because a son delivers his father from the hell called put', Manu says, 'he was therefore called put-tra a deliverer from put by the self existent himself"[22] (Buhler, 1964). Hindu society is of course not unique in revering motherhood as a moral, religious, or even artistic ideal,[23] but the absolute and all-encompassing social importance of motherhood, the ubiquitous variety of motherhood myths, and the function of offspring in ritual and religious (not to mention economic) life all give to motherhood in Indian culture a particularly incontrovertible legitimacy.

Subjectively, in the world of feminine psychological experience, pregnancy is a deliverance from the insecurity, doubt and shame of infertility: 'Better be mud than a barren woman', goes one proverb. Moreover, until very recently, in Hindu society, as among the Jews, Muslims and certain West African tribes, a childless wife could be repudiated (even if not divorced) by her husband who was permitted then to take another wife. On the positive side, pregnancy marks the beginning of the psychological process which firmly establishes a Hindu woman's adult identity. The predominant element in this identity, the ideal core around which it is organized, is what Helene Deutsch has called 'motherliness'. Its central emotional expressions are those of tenderness, nurturing and protectiveness, directed towards the unborn child. Many of the other psychic tendencies generally associated with the young woman's life-stage now become subordinate. The need for emotional closeness with her 'preoedipal' mother and the wish to be loved can be transformed into the wish to love; hostility, especially towards her new surroundings, can be directed towards the protection of her child from the environment; the longing of her reawakened sensuality can be temporarily sublimated, given over to physical ministrations to her child.

To be sure, the development of motherliness as the dominant mode in a Hindu woman's identity and its harmony with other personality traits vary among individual women. Nonetheless, a Hindu woman's 'motherliness' (including manifestations of maternal excess) is a relatively more inclusive element of her identity formation than it is among western women. Given her early training and the ideals of femininity held up to her, motherhood does not have connotations of cultural imposition or of confinement in an isolating role.

For an Indian woman, imminent motherhood is not only the personal fulfilment of an old wish and the biological consummation of a lifelong promise, but an event in which the culture confirms her status as a renewer

---

[22] Although it is primarily the son who is responsible for the performance of these rites, in case a couple has no son the rites may be performed by the daughter's son.

[23] The Hindu attitude is similar to Malinowski's characterization of the Melanesians: 'The woman shows invariably a passionate craving for her child and the surrounding society seconds her feelings, fosters her inclinations, and idealizes them by custom and usage.' See B. Malinowski, *Sex and Repression in Savage Society*, New York: Harcourt, 1927, p. 21.

of the race, and extends to her a respect and consideration which were not accorded to her as a mere wife. It is not surprising that this dramatic improvement in her social relations and status within the family, the resolution of her emotional conflicts and the discovery of a way of organizing her future life around the core of motherliness tend to be experienced unconsciously as a gift from the child growing within her. The unborn child is perceived as her savior, instrumental in winning for its mother the love and acceptance of those around her, a theme which recurs in many legends and tales. Thus Rama repents and is ready to take Sita back for her exile in the forest after he sees his sons for the first time; Dushyanta remembers and accepts Shakuntala as his legitimate wife after he comes face to face with his infant son; while in the two Bengali folk-tales of Sulata and Kiranmala, it is through their children's instrumentality that the injustice done to the mothers is redressed and they assume their rightful places as queens. In the case of a Hindu woman, at least in the imagery of the culture, maternal feelings of tenderness and nurturance occur in combination with a profound gratitude and the readiness for a poignantly high emotional investment in the child.

WOMAN VERSUS WOMANLINESS IN INDIA: AN ESSAY IN SOCIAL AND POLITICAL PSYCHOLOGY[1]

Ashis Nandy

I

At the level of values, human progress can be seen as an expanding awareness of the subtler and more institutionalized forms of inequity and the suffering born of it. Person-to-person aggression and personal sadism have been punished since almost the dawn of civilization. For its survival, every society had to do that. But, as Bertrand Russell was fond of pointing out, social ethics always lags behind private ethics, so slavery, racism, colonial exploitation, and genocide were not only permitted but often encouraged. Of course, some controls were maintained. The sacred texts everywhere defined social rights and social wrongs and prescribed limits to group violence, but the observance of such limits was not informed with an understanding of the less obvious forms of ill-treatment of man by man and of the social institutions and psychological defenses which supported them. Civilization grew for many centuries before men such as Owen, Marx, and Kropotkin formulated ambitious explanations of intra-species aggression in terms of social groupings till then seen as 'naturally' different.[2] Today the idea of a continuum between the exploiters and the exploited, between the aggressors and their victims, is commonplace. It was not so only a century ago.

There were still other, and subtler, forms of inequity. It was Sigmund Freud who pointed out the inequities associated with biological strata like age and sex. Though Friedrich Engels had noted earlier the vulnerability of women in general, and western women in particular, in some ways he had merely extended the formal model of class analysis to the condition of

[1] I am grateful to M.P. Sinha, R.L. Owens, and D.L. Sheth for their comments on an earlier draft of this paper. The essay was first delivered as a lecture at the Nehru Memorial Museum and Library, New Delhi, India.
[2] Erik Erikson (1968) has called attention to the manner in which men legitimized these differences with reference to the latent construct of 'pseudo-species'.

woman (Engels, 1942). Freud, being more cynical, had less faith in human nature and even less willingness to grant that economic institutions were the only means of oppression human intelligence and nature could devise. He traced the root of inequity to a more fundamental stratificatory system 'designed' to derive its strength from man's evolutionary experience, namely, psychobiological growth. As a pioneer he understandably directed attention to the biological stratum which was most vulnerable at the time, namely, children. For the first time in human history he systematically analyzed how over the centuries man has exploited children, using them to express sadistic and narcissistic impulses. He also showed how man has built enormous defenses to deny to himself his cruelty and exploitation. There were times when infanticide and the torture of children were wide-spread in the world. Yet some of the most sensitive and humane thinkers of the age never protested. In fact, torturers of children included men such as Milton and Beethoven. Child labor was acceptable till about fifty years ago in, reputedly, the most civilized parts of the world. Sexual abuse of children was common. Some of the greatest Greek philosophers en-thusiastically supported the homosexual use of children. One even gave elaborate instructions on how to perform well in this sphere, though he was kind enough to advise that one should not stimulate the genitals of a child when indulging in buggery because that might lead to premature sexual growth in the child and might be bad for his morals (De Mause 1974). It would be rash to conclude that the man was a vicious hypocrite. He was no more a hypocrite than the defenders of the democracy of Greek city states which rested on the slavery of the masses. They just did not have a large enough span of moral awareness. Human morality had not acquired that much depth at that time.

Gregory Zilboorg's deservedly famous paper suggests something very similar for the man-woman relationship (Bettelheim, 1962; Zilboorg, 1944). Here, too, oppression results from attempts to deny one's deepest anxieties which are projected to an exploitative relationship institutionalized over centuries. The most socially valued attributes of the male, Zilboorg argues, are a result of natural selection imposed upon him by the female original power to instinctively sense which mate was biologically fitter. This primal dominance arouses in man insecurity, jealousy, and hostility toward woman. He has a phylogenetic awareness that his primordial role is 'highly specialized as no more than a temporary and ephemeral appendage of life', as a 'parasitic' fertilizer[3] (Salzman, 1971). Till now he has had no civilizational awareness that he has been trying to work through this basic hostility by limiting the full possibilities of woman by sheer oppression

[3] Ontogenetically, too, it is the female sex which is primal, not the male.

It is an indicator of how far man has succeeded in these efforts that in many societies the evolutionary and biological primacy of woman has given way to an institutionally entrenched jealousy of man on her part. It is this complex psychosocial phenomenon which Freud so appropriately called penis envy[4] (Erikson, 1964). I do not think, as many defenders of woman do, that Freud was wrong in his analysis. There is enough data from some of the major western societies to support him. He merely missed the historical tragedy that was involved in this reversal of roles.

All this is by way of a long digression. The point is this: the present awareness of the constricted role of woman in Indian society and in public affairs is part of an ongoing process of civilizational change and must be so analyzed. This demands that we identify the structure of defenses, individual as well as cultural, which has given meaning to the role of woman in Indian society and which has been challenged in recent times by new waves of social consciousness. Only then can we hope to isolate and control the long-term processes of social and psychological changes in this sphere.

I shall give an example. Everybody knows that the survival rate of boys in India is much higher than that of girls. But only scattered individuals and groups feel passionately about it, in spite of the fact that the number of vulnerable young girls in India is larger than that of the landless laborers. Even fewer persons are sensitive to the fact that this indirect female infanticide—or, to use Johan Galtung's term, structural violence toward woman—is mainly a function of maternal neglect, a weird expression of woman's hostility toward womanhood and also, symbolically, toward her own self. This classic instance of the psychological defense of turning against self by identifying with the aggressive male draws attention to the way in which some social institutions have made woman herself a participant in her self-repudiation and intra-aggression. The oppressive reality for woman, one might suggest, is now only partially outside her. A part of that reality has been introjected through a long historical process of social learning. And the learning has been thorough. It has been said that man's cruelty toward man is exceeded only by man's cruelty toward woman. But even man's cruelty toward woman is no match for the cruelty of woman toward woman.[5]

[4] A sensitive interpretation of Freud's view of womanhood and its humanist implications can be found in Erikson (1964).

[5] For an early psychological analysis of woman's identification with the aggressive male and her hostility toward womanhood see Menninger (1942). It may seem a little too obvious to be important, but in a society like ours, a major obstacle to the equal treatment of woman by man in job situations is the pressure exerted by the insecure female relatives of both male and female job-holders.

To ignore this aspect of womanhood in India is merely to strike a moralistic posture congruent with the strident tones of the female liberators of women in the West; it abridges Indian awareness of some of the latent justifications of oppression in this society. Such a statement itself challenges vested interests and arouses the anxiety of many, so I shall begin at the very beginning, with a consideration of the linkage between the Indian's traditional world image and his means of livelihood.

II

An agricultural society has its own distinctive symbiotic relationship with nature. Since the time of neolithic agriculture, this distinctiveness has lain in the central role of woman in society and culture. It was she who was primarily involved in 'gentling and nurturing and breeding'; it was her 'capacity for tenderness and love' which gave the earliest agricultural settlements of man their touch of 'security, receptivity, enclosure, nurture'; and it was she who made fully possible the growth of civilization (Mumford, 1961).

A number of studies have found that such a society tends to emphasize the feminine principle in nature, to see nature as a mother who is irascible and unpredictable, propitiable only through a wide variety of rites and rituals.[6] Particularly in societies where nature continues to be the dominant partner in the man-nature dyad, important themes in folklore and religious texts are often the fecundity and bounty of nature as well as her frequent denial of sustenance to men who have poor means of controlling the fickle mother and are totally dependent upon her for survival. This is indeed true of India. Though the Brahmanic tradition attempted to limit the dominance of woman in society, the pre-Aryan dominance of woman was retained in many areas of life, particularly in the symbolic system.[7] This undeniably is a matrifocal culture in which femininity is *inextricably* linked with *prakriti*, or nature, and *prakriti* with *leela* or activity.

The concept of *adya shakti*, primal or original power, is entirely feminine in India. It is the male principle in the godhead, *purusha*, that is reliable but relatively passive, weak, distant, and secondary. That is why the deities that preside over those critical sectors of life which one cannot

[6] Barbara Smoker (1975), making the point that the Judeo-Christian god was 'the original male chauvinistic pig', has tried to show how the position of woman in the original peasant culture of the West changed in response to a 'divine sex change'. Gradually the fertility goddesses gave way to a patriarchal god who was perceived as the creator of man after his own image.

[7] The Aryan attempt to contain the importance of woman was more successful in the Brahmanic and Brahmanized sectors than in the rest of society, where women retained much of their traditional freedom and prerogatives (Zimmer, 1956).

control—such as the success of crops and the occurrence of famines (food), protection against cholera and smallpox (personal survival), and childbirth and child health (perpetuation of race)—are all motherly figures.

All the more cruel rituals, which are mentioned as indicators of Indian medievalism, have centered on the goddesses: *sati*, or the enforced ritual suicide of women after the death of their husbands; child sacrifices at Sagar Sangam; infanticide to ensure the longevity of dams, bunds, and buildings; and human sacrifices of various forms. The *thugs*, or men who robbed after quasi-ritual murder of unwary travellers, considered themselves devotees of Kali. For that matter, most of the marginal groups, such as thieves and dacoits, have sought meaning as social beings by being devotees of one black goddess or another, that is, at another level, by identifying—and identifying with—an aggressive, treacherous, annihilating mother. In other words, the ultimate authority in the Indian mind has always been feminine. It is this authority that the traditional Indian male propitiates or makes peace with through symbolic or real aggression against his own self and by identifying with what he sees as the passive, weak, masculine principle in the cosmos.

III

There is a congruence between this structure of authority and the traditional family and socialization systems. Studies of child rearing done in the more orthodox sectors of Indian society have repeatedly shown that in the critical years of life the mother is the only true and close authority to which the child is exposed. In his relationships with others, the Indian child has a wide spectrum of predefined roles and role-specific behavior. There is distance and fragmentation of self in these interpersonal relationships. It is only with respect to his mother that he is his whole self and recognizable as an individual (Gore, 1968; Narayan, 1964).

Associated with this, in the son, is a deep feeling of ambivalence toward a controlling yet discontinuous mother. He often sees her as a treacherous betrayer, mainly because of her intermittent presence and nurture which are in turn due to the exigencies of her familial role, social obligations, mores, and taboos.[8] The Indian's fantasy life is to a great extent organized

[8] An important element in her familial and social roles is the fact that she is expected to be the main socializing agent for her children, responsible for meting out both rewards and punishments. This fosters the child's ambivalence toward her. In many societies, the responsibility for administering punishment is mainly the father's. Here he is, on the whole, an outsider to the reward-punishment system for the children. There is also the possibility that the Indian wife resents the husband's social superiority and dominance and, unable to express it, displaces her unconscious destructive impulses toward him to her son (Kakar, 1974; Slater, 1968).

around this image of an angry, incorporative, fickle mother, against whom his anger is directed and from whom, through a process of projection, counter-aggression is feared (Carstairs, 1957; Spratt, 1966; Whiting, 1966). His model of male identification, too, is the father who is more a mother's son than a woman's husband, and therefore is swayed by the same fantasies and fears.

For the Indian mother, on the other hand, the son is the major medium of self-expression. It is her motherhood that the traditional family values and respects; her wifehood and daughterhood are devalued and debased. The woman's self-respect in the traditional system is protected not through her father or husband, but through her son. It is also through the son—and for that matter on the son—that she traditionally exercises her authority.[9]

Here, thus, is a case of psycho-ecological balance. What the nature and economy emphasize, the family and the cultural system underscore. No wonder all major social reforms and attempts at social change after the beginning of British rule have centered on woman and femininity. It is by protesting against or defying the traditional concepts of woman and womanhood that all Indian modernizers have made their point. On the other hand, all forms of conservatism and protests against modern western encroachments on the Indian society have taken shelter in and exploited the symbol of motherhood.

IV

The mother-son relationship is, thus, the basic nexus and the ultimate paradigm of human social relationships in India. To an extent this is true of all cultures, but only in a few cultures have the loneliness and self-abnegation of woman as a social being found such elaborate justification in her symbolic status as a mother. Since motherhood is a compensatory mechanism, society can manipulate and control a woman by forcing her to take on her motherly identity whenever cornered and a man by forcing him to take on the son's role whenever in crisis. The culture tends to shape critical public relations to fit or exploit that symbolic paradigm.

Yet simultaneously, Indian society inculcates in women a certain self-doubt and in men a certain ambivalence toward womanhood. This ambivalence is very different from the ambivalence which the western man feels towards woman or the universal fear which Zilboorg, Bettelheim, and Salzman diagnose. In this society, except for small sectors in which

[9] As is well known, the Indian family underemphasizes the wife's role and overemphasizes the mother's to blur the outlines of the nuclear family and de-emphasize it as the basic unit of family life. Though a huge majority of Indians stay in nuclear households, the values associated with the extended family system are a major influence on intra-family relationships.

martial values predominate, the man's fear is not that he will lapse into womanliness and thus lose his masculinity or potency. In fact, potency here is not generally something men strive for, protect, or protest in the external world. The masculine fear here is that a man may run afoul of the cosmic feminine principle, that woman will betray, aggress, pollute, or at least fail to protect.

There are two major corollaries of such an uncertainty about the cosmic feminine principle. The first of these can be stated in the form of a dialectic but is perhaps a matter of the various planes at which the Indian man lives his psychological life. At one plane, he is continually afraid that he may become too independent of the maternal principle of authority, too defiant as a son of the power of cosmic motherhood, and too close to open anger towards his mother. On the other, he is constantly anxious that he will be incorporated by an all-encompassing, powerful mother, lose his autonomy and individuality altogether, and be reduced to the 'safe' but ineffective role of the father.

Secondly, bisexuality in India has always been considered an indicator of saintliness and yogic accomplishments. Perhaps it is considered an indicator of having successfully coped with or transcended one's deepest conflicts about femininity and masculinity. Perhaps it has something to do with the traditional concept of *ardhanarishwara*, or bisexual god, associated with the deity that combines godly grandeur with yogic asceticism, namely Siva. However it be, one who is closer to godliness is expected to show a little less concern with the worldly division between the sexes and a little more ability to transcend the barriers imposed by one's own sexual identity. He is expected to subscribe to values which are unbound by the society's prevalent sexual identities[10] (Nandy, 1976).

In India, unlike in many western societies, the softer forms of creativity and the more intuitive and introspective styles of intellectual and social functioning are not strongly identified with femininity. Nor is masculinity that closely linked to forceful, potency-driven, 'hard', and hardheaded modes of intrusive behavior. Sex-role-specific qualities here are differently distributed. In fact, the concept of potency in Indian high culture has always had a private, introversive quality about it. The Brahman's concept of ritual and intellectual potency has nothing in common with the manifest extroversive concept of potency in the modern West. Brahmanic potency is 'derivable', as it was in medieval Europe's monastic orders, from displaced sexual potency through abstinence and denial of one's sexual self.

---

[10] One would expect this idealization of bisexuality to lead to understanding and tolerance of the other sex (Kestenberg, 1956). One wonders why this has not happened in India's high culture. Perhaps what the culture values is not so much bisexuality as transexuality. It is in India's low cultures that bisexuality as a value has had its fullest impact.

This has another aspect. In the twilight zones in which creative minds dwell, there is always a certain emphasis on the ability to turn inward and live in one's own inner world; the ability to accept intuition, tenderness, and *caritas* as values; a certain sensitivity to one's natural environment and to the 'latent' communications among men; and the capacity to use media of self-expression which mobilizes feelings, imagery, and fantasies. In the West this has invariably meant becoming more feminine. That is why psychological studies of creative men in the West frequently show that one of the best predictors of creativity in men is the extent of their psychological femininity. In the western context, Berdyaev has argued that the figure of Christ is androgynous and that 'all creators must be so if they are to conceive and bear greatly and whole' (Mackinnon, 1970; Barron, 1969; Berdyaev, 1954). Understandably too, there are elements of pathos and loneliness associated with such a search for bisexuality in societies where, even at the level of symbols, males dominate.[11]

My own studies of creative men in India roughly corroborate this finding but with one important caveat. The Indian, apparently, is not more creative only when he is more feminine or, to put it less obtusely, when he can better accept his feminine self. His creativity also consists in his being able to identify the cosmic feminine principle with his own internal concept of authority and then in defying this authority and simultaneously making large-scale symbolic reparations for this defiance. This is a major ingredient of the relationship between womanliness and creativity in India. The isomorphism between one's inner controls and society's concept of authority sharpens one's sensitivity to the basic symbolic system of the culture and makes one more rooted in the culture's style of self-expression. On the other hand, this defiance of one's final and most intimate authority gives an edge to one's defiance of the shared concept of authority outside. And you do not have to be a psychologist to recognize that this defiance is one of the cornerstones of creative effort.

There is another aspect of this linkage between creativity and womanliness in India. Public defiance rationalizes one's more guilt-provoking private defiance. If this public defiance of authority is linked to the cause of woman, either as an exercise in reform geared to her good or as a purely intellectual exercise in understanding her problems, the structure of rationalization becomes stronger and more usable. It binds the moral anxiety triggered by defiance of one's internal authority and, at another level, atones for that defiance. This atonement—through working for the cause of woman or in its intellectualized version, through understanding

---

[11] On the tragedy which accompanies the search for bisexuality in the West, see the fascinating study of Kubie (1974).

woman and femininity—has been perhaps the single most important theme in the history of social creativity in India.

Many years ago someone pointed out to me how formidable and powerful the women are in the *Mahabharata*, the epic which perhaps summarizes the Indian ethos better than any work of social science, and how the story revolves round them. It struck me then as an original viewpoint, and over the years I have been convinced that it is correct in more senses than one. When one looks at the styles of creative self-expression during the last two hundred years, a period characterized by a fast tempo of social change and the breakdown of many aspects of the older life style, one cannot but marvel at the crucial role that woman as a symbol and womanliness as an aspect of Indian identity have played. This dynamic is clearer in some parts of the country than in others, because some communities, such as Bengal, have a greater capacity than others to superbly dramatize the psychological problems of the society at large.[12] Perhaps Bengal's tribal base, unsure Brahmanization, deep symbiotic links between means of livelihood and cultural products, and strong feudal traditions have something to do with this (Nandy, 1975).[13] At least from Rammohun Roy through Ishwar Chandra Vidyasagar in the area of social reform, from Bankim Chandra Chatterji through Sarat Chandra Chatterji to Satyajit Ray in literature and arts, from Vivekananda to Aurobindo in religion, womanhood as a symbol and womanliness as a subject of study have been the center pieces of creative consciousness in different sectors of Bengali life.

Whether in Bengal or the country as a whole, certain closely related modes of symbolic adaptation have dominated India's distinctive style of entry into the modern world. What came as if in a flux in the British period was an entire authority system which involved the invalidation at many levels of the traditional equation between femininity and power, the old concept of propitiation through rituals and magic, and the primal mythical personification of nature as an inviolate cosmic mother. Some like Rammohun Roy and Ishwar Chandra Vidyasagar, tried to redraw the traditional definition of womanly identity, trying to introduce into it new elements drawn from reinterpreted traditions and to endogenize certain western themes. Their own deeper ambivalence toward woman found in these efforts a personal adaptive device. I have shown elsewhere how much this was true of Roy, and some of the new biographies of Vidyasagar

---

[12] How far this helps the society to work through these problems by providing tentative solutions—and nonsolutions—is, however, a different issue.

[13] Kakar provides interesting comparative data on seven Indian subcultures which show Bengal to be exceptional in its concern with the destructive and threatening aspects of the mother and its unconcern with the Oedipal conflicts between the father and the son.

do not leave us in much doubt on this score either (Mitra, 1969; Ghosh, 1958). Some with mass appeal like Sarat Chandra Chatterji and Govar-dhanram Tripathi among writers, and Vidyasagar and Gandhi among reformers, tried to legitimize woman's wifely role in particular and public role in general by stressing in them aspects of her motherliness.[14] Some others like Ramkrishna Paramhansa and Aurobindo found in motherhood the supreme concept of a new godhead, rooted in tradition on the one hand and capable of balancing the overemphasis on masculinity in the Semitic religions on the other. In fact, their appeal to many westerners was this concept of a godhead that could be counterpoised against the patri-archal orientations dominating the western view of man and nature. Still others like Bankim Chandra Chatterji and Vivekananda linked this tradi-tional image of sacred motherhood to the modern concept of motherland, hoping thereby to give a new sanctity to the concept of nation in an essentially apolitical society. Even Gandhi tried to give a new dignity to women by making a new equation between womanliness and political potency, denying in the process the western association between maleness and control over public affairs and statecraft, rejecting the martial tradition in India, which, like martial traditions in most other societies, debased womanhood, and abrogating the colonial identity which equated feminity with passivity, weakness, dependence, subjugation, and absence of mascu-linity (Erikson, 1969; Rudolph and Rudolph, 1966). Man's conservatism as well as his modernity, his success as well as his failure, rested on this equation.

V

In sum, the redefinition of womanhood in present-day India has required a redefinition of the concept of man and of public functioning. In this ongoing process, the emancipation of woman and her equality with man have been important but not the main issues. They may today lead to vicious debates in small groups of already privileged modern women, but the majority in the hinterlands have never considered these themes rele-vant for social analysis and intervention. Naturally, to make the issues of emancipation of woman and equality of sexes primary, one needs a culture in which conjugality is central to male-female relationships. One seeks

[14] In fact, this redefinition through the new norms of sex-role-specific behavior was tried also by Rammohun Roy in Brahmoism, the new religious ideology he evolved, and by Ishwar Chandra Vidyasagar in his style of reform and the rationalizations he offered for them. Nirupama Pota's ongoing study of the four most creative writers of twentieth-century Hindi literature (Jay Shankar Prasad, Suryakant Tripathi Nirala, Sumitra Nandan Pant, and Maha-devi Verma) suggest something roughly similar.

emancipation from and equality with one's husband and peers, not with one's son. If the conjugal relationship itself remains relatively peripheral, the issues of emancipation and equality must remain so too.[15]

Thus in conclusion I must confront the basic yet commonplace paradox of every social interpretation of the Indian woman: why do some women in India reach the pinnacles of public power and recognition while women in general have kept out of large areas of public life?[16] According to some, the ascendancy of certain women is proof that Indian culture does not intrinsically discriminate against women. According to others, these women are exceptions that prove nothing. To psychologists, who, as you know, are used to thinking in strange ways, there is always a continuity between the commonplace and the exceptional. I have already said that, in India, competition, aggression, power, activism, and intrusiveness are not so clearly associated with masculinity. In fact, in mythology and folklore, from which norms often come for traditionally undefined social situations, many of these qualities are as frequently associated with women. The fantasy of a castrating, phallic woman is also always round the corner in the Indian's inner world.

That is why in some areas of life, disjunctive with the traditional life style and not having clearly defined or well-developed norms, women do not start with as much handicap as they do in many other societies. Obvious examples of such areas are politics and public affairs and some scientific and religious activities.[17] Here public success does not seem to detract from private womanliness. In other words, in such instances the Indian woman can more easily integrate within her feminine identity the participation in what by western standards are manly activities but in India are either not defined in terms of sex roles or are tinged with transexual or bisexual connotations. In these areas, Indian women do not have to fight the same battle that their western sisters have to fight, though some of them do pretend to give battle to existing norms here too.[18]

[15] The theme of equality between sexes has been less dead, because it also relates to equality between the son and the daughter. From Rammohun Roy to Jawaharlal Nehru, a number of reformers have made it an important plank in their ideologies of social change.

[16] In the forthcoming *Women in India*, Veena Das seems to argue that men in India are also kept out of large areas of life. If women do not have access to men's life, men also do not have access to women's life.

[17] I must remind those who may be surprised by my inclusion of some aspects of religious activity in this list that traditional Hinduism is not an organized religion. Some highly organized Hindu sects which have sprung up during the last 150 years are thus clearly discontinuous with the older life style. In such sects women often play important roles.

[18] I must reluctantly draw attention to the fact that in India the truly creative women in these areas have rarely been feminists, ardent or otherwise. There the battle has been fought by men who have presumed that the plight of women in other areas of life extend to these too.

That, of course, is shadow boxing. I am not concerned here with those for whom the search for freedom and dignity as women has become a search for a new neurotic stability which they hope will defend them as successfully against self-awareness as the now crumbling defenses once did. For the more sensitive woman, the challenge is nothing less than redefinition of herself. The first task that faces her is to devise means of de-emphasizing some aspects of her role in her family and society and emphasizing others, so that she may widen her identity without breaking totally from its cultural definition or becoming disjunctive with its psycho-biological distinctiveness. In the West that may mean defying the limits of conjugality and giving a new dignity to the maternal role of woman; in India it may involve transcending the partial identity imposed by mother-hood and winning a new respect for conjugality. Partial identities always extract a price from those who live with them, either as victims or as beneficiaries. Indian women have paid terribly for Indian insensitivity, but they have also extracted a heavy toll from a society which has not yet learned to live with all aspects of womanhood. In that respect theirs is not what Rollo May would call a case of 'authentic innocence' but that of 'pseudoinnocence'. This innocence leads one to participate in a structur-ally violent system because of the unawareness of one's power to intervene in the real world and because of the indirect psychological benefits of being a victim.

But then, ultimately this is no different from ancient wisdom. Victims and beneficiaries of a system, even common sense admits, are rarely ever exclusive groups. Modern psychology only strengthens one's belief that no marauder can hope to be a marauder without being a prey and no prey can be a prey without being a marauder.

FEMINISM: INDIAN ETHOS AND INDIAN CONVICTIONS

Suma Chitnis

A Personal Response

One of the most distinctive features of women's studies as an academic discipline is that many of the scholars in the discipline have been attracted to it by deeply personal questions regarding the status of women. Most often these questions are born out of their own painful encounter with life, as battered wives, unwanted daughters or toiling mothers, as women discriminated against, oppressed or exploited within and outside their homes. However, frequently, they also occur as a less tortured but equally committed response to the powerful statements of feminism.

The Promptings of an Indian Consciousness

My own involvement in women's studies belongs to the second category. It was stimulated by a session on Gender Roles that I attended at the World Congress of Sociology at Toronto in 1974. As I listened to the angry tirade against their patriarchal social order, launched by the American and European feminists at that meeting, I was deeply conscious of the fact that the situation of Indian women, in many ways worse than that of the situation of American and European women did not arouse me similarly. Puzzled by my own placidity, and called upon to respond to these colleagues from the vantage point of my own experience, I made an effort to examine some of their issues with reference to the Indian context. As I did so I discovered that although the deprivations, exploitations and oppressions suffered by women are almost identical in the two societies there are basic differences in the value systems and historical circumstances in which they are pitched. These differences seemed to account significantly for the difference between my attitude to the issue of the status of women and that of my North American colleagues.

As feminism arrived in India soon afterwards in the mid-seventies, I noticed many Indians respond to the feminist statement much as I had done in Canada. Well formulated though it was the western statement of feminism seemed to jar upon their sensitivities. In fact it turned several Indian women away from the cause. By now the women's cause has gained substantial strength in the country. A growing number of women are willing to speak out and to act. Nevertheless a large section of the population recoils from the feminist rhetoric. It is possible that they do so because they are too entrenched in tradition to recognize their oppression. But one must also consider the possibility that they respond as they do for the simple reason that it does not take adequate note of the historical circumstances and values that render the women's issue different in India from the issue in the West.

Since the situation of women in India is in fact quite miserable and a great deal needs to be done on their behalf, it is a pity that the Indian statement of their problems is often couched in statements that sound alien and which, therefore, fail to hit the mark. In order that the women's cause in the country gain the massive support that it needs it is important that Indian feminists understand the Indian context thoroughly and that they phrase their criticisms, their arguments and their demands on behalf of women with sensitivity to the Indian society.

Distinctiveness of Context

Quite apart from this pragmatic consideration, the articulation of the distinctiveness of the Indian context is important, in as much as a recognition of differences of context of each country or culture, and a careful consideration of the implications of these differences, is necessary from the point of view of bringing greater depth to an understanding of the problems concerning gender discrimination. Although networks linking social science research across the world are growing rapidly there is a general tendency to observe and to describe realities in terms of concepts and theories shaped in the context of western experience, and to pass over the distinctive feature of non-western cultures. In the process, the contours of multicultural reality are flattened, sometimes beyond recognition (Hans, 1984).

There are at least three specific points on which the perceptions and the sentiments of a noticeably large number of Indian women seem to diverge from those of the western-influenced feminists. By far the most conspicuous of these is the average Indian woman's disapproval of feminist anger. The second is their somewhat mixed and confused reaction to the feminist emphasis on patriarchy, and particularly on men as the principal oppressors. The third is their relative inability to tune in to the demands for equality and personal freedom. Understanding the roots of each of these three reactions is important from the point of view of gearing both activist feminism, and women's studies in India to the Indian ethos and Indian convictions.

An Exasperated Response

It is possible to understand and to sympathize with the anger in western feminism when one recognizes the gap between what is professed and what is practised by way of the commitment to equality in western society. Regardless of whether they are based on capitalist or on socialist political ideologies, all the countries of Europe and North America claim equality as one of the core principles of their political philosophies. Beginning with the liberal ideals of Locke and Rousseau, that triggered the French Revolution on to the Declaration of Independence that led to the birth of the American constitution and the consolidation of the U.S.A. as a democratic federation, European and American societies have since the last three or four decades of the eighteenth century loudly asserted equality. Yet, they have refused to accept women as equals. Long and painful suffragette movements, bitter struggles for the acceptance of the idea of equal pay for equal work, continuing battles on behalf of women's right to abortion and to the practice of birth control, are some of the visible marks of the gender inequality that has persisted and that women have had to fight for in spite of the commitments that were made. Under the circumstances, feminist anger in the West may be seen as women's cry against the hypocrisy of a culture that accords centrality to the values of equality and individual freedom but nevertheless denies equality to women.

A Hierarchical Society

The situation in India is altogether different. Indian society has always been highly hierarchical. The several hierarchies within the family (of age, sex, ordinal position, affinal and consanguinal kinship relationships) or within the community (particularly caste, but also lineage, learning, wealth, occupation and relationship with the ruling power) have been maintained and integrated by means of a complex combination of custom, functionality and religious belief. The harshness and oppressiveness of all these hierarchies is somewhat relieved by a strong sense of deference to superiors, a sense of mutuality, a series of behavioral codes which bend superiors to fulfil their obligations to their inferiors and, above all, by a philosophy of self-denial, and the cultural emphasis on sublimating the ego.

The concept of equality, as a correlate of the concept of individual freedom, is alien to Indian society. It was first introduced into Indian culture through western education and through the exposure of western-educated Indians to liberalism, at the beginning of the nineteenth century.

But it did not become an operational principle of Indian life until the country achieved independence and adopted a democratic system of government forty years ago. At that point the constitution granted women political status fully equal to that of men. Thus Indian women did not have to bear the kind of injustices that women in the West had to suffer because of the continuing gap between political ideals and realities. Nor did they have to suffer the indignities European and American women have had to experience in the course of their efforts to bridge this gap.

Liberalism, Social Reform, Nationalism and the Women's Cause

In fact, Indian history reveals an almost opposite experience. As western educated Indians came to be acquainted with European liberalism, they were inspired to reflect upon their own value system and to examine the inequalities, injustices and oppressions of their own culture. This introspection stimulated a strong movement for social reform. Significantly, the removal of practices and customs that led to suffering for women figured prominently in the agenda for social reform.

Raja Ram Mohan Roy's tenacious struggle for the abolition of sati, marks the beginning of the movement for reform on behalf of women. Launched during the third decade of the nineteenth century, this movement constitutes an important landmark in the Indian effort towards the emancipation of women. Several aspects of this movement deserve consideration as features that illustrate the uniqueness of the Indian context and mark the issue of feminism in India as distinctly different from the issue in the West.

The most distinctive feature of this movement is that it was initiated by men. It was only towards the end of the century that women joined the fray. The list of names of the men who championed the cause of women is long . . . Raja Ram Mohan Roy, Ishwar Chandra Vidyasagar, Keshav Chandra Sen, Malabari, Phule, Agarkar, Ranade, Karve . . . to mention but a very few. The record of the reforms they undertook to achieve is impressive. It reveals that their efforts spanned action to abolish the practice of sati, the custom of child marriage, the custom of disfiguring widows, the ban on the remarriage of upper caste Hindu widows and a host of other evil practices that affected women. It further reveals that while they concentrated on removing evil practices these men were also actively engaged in advancing the status of women by promoting their education, by obtaining for them legal rights to property, and by requiring the law to take cognizance of their status by providing them with some basic rights in matters such as adoption.

Conflict of Purpose

An equally significant feature is that these nineteenth and early twentieth century benefactors of women pushed reform on behalf of women in the face of total unwillingness on the part of the British government to interfere with Indian customs. The British, it may be noted, were unwilling to interfere with Indian custom for the simple reason that they feared that tampering with tradition would make them unpopular and destabilize their rule. Thus, as rulers, concerned about the stability of their empire in India, they were willing to put aside their liberal values and moral convictions, and to allow their subjects to continue with inhuman practices against women. It was only because of the dogged persistence of their western-educated Indian subjects that they were compelled to move. The quality of this doggedness is evident in the fact that when, towards the end of the century, the interests of the reform movement clashed with that of the nationalist movement for freedom, several of the reformers, who happened also to be committed nationalists, chose to accord priority to reform. Since this conflict between the obligation to reform and the commitment to the struggle for self-rule, that occurred towards the end of the nineteenth century, was highly significant in shaping the status of women in the twentieth century, it may be pertinent to look at it in some detail.

The Birth of Nationalism

The opportunity to acquire western education and through it to be exposed to European morals and philosophy that some of the Indian elite obtained at the beginning of the nineteenth century had critical implications for Indian thought, morals and culture. The first impact of European liberalism on Indians was, as pointed out earlier, to stimulate them to reflect upon their own culture, question some of the customs and practices that they had earlier accepted with equanimity and to move in the direction of reform. It was this impulse that generated the social reform movement and guided its course through the first three quarters of the nineteenth century. Throughout this period western-educated Indians looked up to their British rulers. They admired what they considered to be their superior morals and philosophy and believed that as responsible liberals their rulers would bring about the reforms and changes required to advance Indian society towards the liberal value system.

However, towards the last three decades of the nineteenth century the Indian outlook regarding the British began to change. Having experienced British timidity about reform, even those who had earlier admired the British were growing to be disillusioned with British rule and sceptical of British intentions. This scepticism combined with the growing impact of liberal political ideology to generate a desire for political freedom and self-rule, to give birth to a nationalist movement for political freedom and self-rule. The spirit of this movement is best summed up in Lokmanya Tilak's famous statement, 'Swaraj (self-rule) is my birth-right and I shall have it'.

Division Over the Issue of Reform

The nationalist movement for freedom was born out of the same ideology and sentiments that had generated the movement for reform, and most of the social reformers of the nineteenth century were also committed nationalists. However, towards the end of the nineteenth century there was a serious split in the Indian leadership which came to be divided into two factions, viz., those who wished to accord the struggle for freedom priority over reform and those who preferred to combine the struggle for freedom with the struggle for reform. The former group consisting of nationalists totally disillusioned by the British, was powerfully led by Tilak. The latter consisting of those who continued to hold some hopes about the British as benevolent rulers was led by several political moderates. Tilak's impatience for reform came from his antagonism against the British, which was so firm that he rejected everything European, including European reform. Reforms involving women, in particular, appeared to him as unnecessary concession to western ways. Inevitably this antagonism sharpened the rift between the two groups to the point at which some nationalists looked upon reformers as traitors to the cause of freedom.

The story of how the two factions came to merge makes interesting political history. It is not possible to go into the details here. What matters is that the British attitude to reform continued to be so lukewarm that the moderates were, eventually, also disillusioned and disappointed enough to give up their separate stand and join the nationalists. As they did so, their aspirations for the advancement of the status of women in India came to be enmeshed in the concept of the new society that the nationalists began to dream of establishing in independent India.

Stree Shakti and New Direction for Nationalism

Meanwhile, at about the time of this merger which occurred towards the dawn of the twentieth century, politics in the country was beginning to take a new shape. Initially, under the leadership of Tilak, the struggle for freedom had been a militant movement. But as the implications of militancy began to unfold there was a strong feeling that a poor country like India must use some other strategies against the superior military powers of the British. The answer came in the form of Gandhi's brave new philosophy of *Ahimsa* or nonviolence. One of the basic tenets of this philosophy is that, in order to fight a nonviolent revolution, it is necessary to build moral power. As Gandhi emerged as the country's political leader, he called for the people to arm themselves morally and declared that the eradication of untouchability, the acceptance of equality for women, liberation from crippling superstition and fear, and the cultivation of humanism were critical to this armament. Thus Gandhi directly declared that equality for women would be one of the central objectives of his political program.

In addition he did much more while explaining the concept of *Ahimsa*, he likened the moral power in a nonviolent struggle to the pure and gentle, but firm and tenacious strength which, he emphasized, women continuously display in life. Finally, at the organizational level, he emphasized that nothing less than the total involvement of the entire population in the nonviolent struggle for freedom would be adequate, and in this context he pointed out that it was imperative to involve women in the mass movement. With all the persuasiveness and charisma at his command, he urged women to step cut of their homes and join him.

Support and Religion

If Gandhi could communicate the concept of *stree shakti* (the moral power of womanhood) to the Indian masses so convincingly, it was because the Hindu religion carried a highly positive concept of the feminine principle. Unlike Christianity, Judaism or Islam, the image of God in Hinduism is not exclusively male. The female principle complements and complete the male. The polytheistic Hindu pantheon consists of divine couples such as Shiva and Shakti, Purusha and Prakriti, Rama and Sita. Together the male and the female represent the specific power for which they are venerated. In addition, the Hindu pantheon consists of a number of goddesses or *devis*. It is significant that the deities of knowledge (Saraswati) and wealth (Laxmi) are female. Correspondingly, there is a distinctive place for women in the practice of the Hindu religion. Women, particularly those who are virgins or virtuous wives, are believed to have special spiritual powers. Their prayers, penances or supplications to God are believed to earn grace more readily than the prayers of men. Several of the most important religious sacrifices, ceremonies and rituals can only be performed by a married couple. They cannot be performed by single men, single women, widows or widowers.

The Establishment of Equality

Inspired by reformers and encouraged by what Gandhi put before them from the Hindu religion, women had come out in large numbers to participate in the struggle for freedom. By the time the country obtained independence in 1947, they had already established themselves as equals in political life. Both as a tribute to the equality of their participation, and as a reaffirmation of Gandhi's commitment to equality of the sexes, the Indian constitution explicitly and categorically granted sex equality. Indian women have political rights fully equal to those of men. What is more, the constitution declares that women, together with the former untouchable castes and tribals living in remote areas, are to be recognized as 'weaker sections' of the population, and to be specially assisted to function as equals.

Living Up to a Promise

The Indian government has tried to live up to this promise. Since 1947 each of the seven Five Year Plans has carefully provided for the health, education, employment and welfare of women. More importantly, planners have been alert and dynamic in defining plan obligations to fit in with changing times. Up to the Fifth Plan the emphasis was on providing women with 'welfare' and 'protection'. Almost as though it was a response to feminism, the Sixth Plan made a striking departure with a new emphasis on involving women as 'partners in development'.

In addition to the constitutional safeguards and Plan provisions, there are a host of provisions in the legal and the political structure of the country that affirm and reaffirm the equality of the sexes: for example, property rights, the provisions for divorce, employment and health. If a cross-cultural or multinational analysis of legal provisions for women is made, India is likely to emerge as one of the most progressive countries. For instance, the Directive Principles of the Constitution safeguard the principle of equal pay for equal work, and labor legislation ensures generous maternity leave provisions. Not only does the Indian government officially support and sponsor the use of contraceptives for birth control, but it has also legalized the medical termination of pregnancy. Several committees and commissions have been appointed to look into the problems of women. When International Women's Year commenced in 1974, India was ready with a sensitive and comprehensive report on the status of women, prepared by a parliamentary committee appointed a few years earlier (*Towards Equality*, 1974).

In the face of the western feminist this cry that women have been neglected by society in general, and by the government in particular, does not quite appeal to Indian women. They see that the legal safeguards and equal opportunity facilities that are being fought for in many of the countries which claim long traditions of equality and individual freedom are already available to them in principle. Thus they react with the feeling that feminism is alien.

The Indian Problem

None of this means that the situation of women in India is satisfactory or acceptable. Regardless of all the factors cited, the fact remains that the country measures poorly in terms of any of the indicators that are normally issued to measure the status of women. The ratio of women to men, in the population of the country is low (933 F to 1000 M), accounted for by poor care of female infants and of women in their child-bearing years. The disadvantaged status of women is also evidenced in the low level of their literacy (24.8% as compared to 46.9% for men) their poor representation in the workforce (45 million females) and the fact that their dropout rate from primary and middle school is at least 10 per cent higher than it is for men.

Even more painful evidence of their inferior status is that female infanticide, sati and child marriage which nineteenth century reformers had fought hard to abolish by law, linger, particularly in rural India. Practices such as the denial of remarriage to upper caste Hindu widows, polygamy, and dowry, similarly made illegal, continue. Worse yet, some of these practices have gained strength in new forms. For instance, the use of amniocentesis to determine the sex of the foetus, and the use of the right to medical termination of pregnancy to abort the female foetus is, in a sense, a return to female infanticide. Or again, the widespread incidence of bride burning and dowry deaths reflect the traditional practice of dowry in a new and ghastly form. Thus, in spite of constitutional and legal provisions aimed at facilitating their status as equals, women continue to suffer.

The Indian problem really lies in the fact that women do not make proper use of the existing legal and political rights and facilities. There are several reasons for this. The mass of Indian men and women are not yet fully aware of their new rights and opportunities. The bureaucracy they must deal with in order to exercise these rights, or to obtain redress for grievances, is too complex, too slow, too distant, and even too expensive for them to use. It has none of the immediacy, the approachability and the visible efficacy of the caste or tribal council or the village *panchayat* which they, as an essentially rural people were accustomed to use.

More specifically, women's poor utilization of voting rights is primarily due to their low level of political awareness and sense of political efficacy. They do not yet appreciate their potential power and political leverage as citizens of a democracy. They are ignorant about issues, and are not being encouraged to become interested. Even educated women are apathetic. On the other hand, political parties consider women candidates a poor risk and are unwilling to invest in them. Women themselves find that an active political career is difficult to combine with homemaking. Thus the women who are active in politics are either the wives or daughters of politicians, or women who have entered politics as social workers or as students.

Women's failure to exercise their employment rights is due to quite another set of reasons. Poverty compels both men and women in the country to take up any available work. Because unemployment is high they are obliged to accept the terms of the employers, who often evade or slip through the requirements of law. Women are particularly vulnerable to such exploitation because they are too timid to argue. They suffer from the additional limitation of having to accept work that fits in with their obligations as wives, mothers and home-makers. Trade unions are relatively insensitive to women's needs and in any case the sectors in which women work are poorly unionized.

By far the most serious tragedies that occur—dowry deaths, suicide, impoverishment of widows—arise out of women's failure to use the legal safeguards and redress provisions with reference to marriage, divorce, dowry and property. Their general inability to use the law is further aggravated in situations in which they have to fight a husband or a father. In the role allocation within Indian culture, these are the persons upon whom women normally depend to handle court matters. Better legal aid facilities are needed to enable women to use the legal system against these persons.

The Value System

While the factors listed above are visibly responsible for the poor status of women in India the greatest obstacle to change in the directions of equality is the value system by which women abide. Women are conditioned to revere the father, and to serve the husband as a devotee serves God. Devotion to the husband is cultivated among girls of all religions, but it is particularly idealized and firmly institutionalized in the Hindu concept of *pativrata*. The term *pativrata* (literally translated as 'one who is vowed to her husband') connotes a wife who has accepted service and devotion to the husband, and his family, as her ultimate religion and duty. The ideal of the *pativrata* is romanticized through legend, folklore and folksong, and reaffirmed through ceremonies of different kinds. It may be pertinent to illustrate with one of the legends, the legend of Savitri and Satyavan.

According to this legend, on the death of Satyavan, Savitri, his virtuous wife or *pativrata* followed Yama, the God of Death, imploring that he should not take her husband. Yama tried to reason with her and to convince her that this was not possible, as all humans must die. However, when she refused to turn back, he said that he had to respect her as a *pativrata* and offered her a boon if she would comply. Promptly Savitri asked for sons. As Yama agreed to grant her wish, she pointed out that as a true wife she would have to bear them by her husband and none else. Yama could not go back on his word. He was forced to yield and Satyavan was saved. To this day Hindu women commemorate Savitri with a celebration and ritual performed annually, on a fixed day. Even educated, urban women follow the practice devotedly.

Similarly, Sita, the wife of Prince Rama, the legendary hero of the *Ramayana*, is worshipped as the virtuous wife who not only followed her noble husband into fourteen years of exile, but suffered indignity and the suffering that he as a 'just' king was forced to inflict upon her in deference to the wishes of his subjects. Both Savitri and Sita, exhibit sharp wit, intelligence, resourcefulness, tenacity and affection. These qualities have never been held up for emulation. Tradition has only emphasized women's self-immolation.

Taking Cognizance of the Indian Reality

The women's cause in India could gain enormously if it takes cognizance of these realities. In most countries the feminist struggle needs to be directed towards obtaining legal and political rights for women. In India, legal and constitutional rights are already extensively available to women. The problem is that they are not adequately used.

The foregoing paragraphs briefly speculate upon the reasons for this non-utilization. Women's studies in India must explore into these reasons thoroughly. Similarly, feminist statements must highlight the poor utilization of existing rights and provisions and underline the point that legal and constitutional provisions are futile unless they are backed by appropriate attitudes and public commitment. The feminist struggle, in turn, must focus on cultivating the attitudes required for building the necessary public commitment. While doing so it is important to recognize that it is useful to build upon what has been achieved in the past. Indian feminism is particularly fortunate in that the reforms that nineteenth and early twentieth century reformers were able to achieve on behalf of women, constitute a firm base.

Similarly, although Indian tradition has for the major part encouraged the subservience of women, applauded their self-effacement, and thus promoted their subjection, it contains several elements that can be developed towards establishing equality for women and towards a new assertion of the full dignity of their personhood. It is important that Indian feminism grasps firmly at these elements as features to build upon. For instance, feminists could work towards building new attitudes among women by highlighting the spiritedness, the intelligence and the resourcefulness of figures like Sita and Savitri. There are several other points at which they can usefully draw from tradition. But, in order to do so they must give conscious and careful thought to how folklore, folksongs, epics and age-old models of virtuous womanhood can be bent to speak for the new value system. Feminists tend to turn away from traditional images, and in the process snap vital links of communication with the masses (Berger and Luckmann, 1984).

The Larger Context

The feminist message in India also misses its mark when it names men as oppressors. The feminists almost exclusively blame men for the unhappy situation of women.

Firstly, the mass of Indian women are unlikely to be able to make the fine distinction between sorrow and oppression. Sorrow is real, it is the substance of their life, and they know it intimately. But they know it as hunger, poverty, ill-health, disease, the death of their infant children, the free use of their bodies by powerful landlords to whom they are bonded in labor, bound as laborers, or tenants, or by contractors or employers for whom they work. They know it as the impotence of their husbands, fathers, brothers or sons to help them when this happens. They know it as the ruthlessness of custom, the burden of tradition, the unrelenting demands of ritual. They know it as the beatings of a drunken husband or father, or as anger unleashed without reason as the brute force of men. Feminists must make a special effort to indicate how sorrow, as the mass of women experience it, is compounded by oppression.

Secondly, although there can be no dispute about the fact that Indian society is oppressively patriarchal, it must be remembered that in India patriarchy is only one from among the several hierarchies that oppress women. Some of the most oppressive of these are the hierarchies of age, of ordinal status, of relationship by marriage. Conceptually and analytically some of these may be seen to be mere extensions of patriarchal oppression, but it is important to recognize that they are not experienced as oppression by the male. Most women in India experience family violence as the cruelty of the mother-in-law or the husband's sisters. In most families, the principal oppressor is the husband's mother, or his unmarried or widowed sisters, not the husband. In many incidents of bride-burning, or suicide attempted by women unable to bear ill-treatment within the family, the person who has driven the woman to death is almost invariably one of her female relatives. Even in cases in which the husband has been held guilty of a crime against his wife, the victims have generally named his mother or sisters as abettors.

On the other hand, men in Indian history have often stood out as 'benefactors' facilitating the advance of women. Biographies and autobiographies of nineteenth as well as twentieth century women clearly indicate that those who stepped out of the beaten track to pursue education, to take up social work or politics, or to enter occupations or professions that were considered to be the exclusive preserve of men, have almost invariably been encouraged, supported, and actively helped by a husband, a father or a brother—most frequently by a husband. The reformers who initiated action in support of equality and freedom for women were all men. So were most of those who pioneered the education of women.

Similarly, there is an Indian tradition by which men and women unrelated to each by blood or marriage, but belonging to the same neighbourhood, village, caste or circle of acquaintance, address each other by the kinship term that would be appropriate. A special feature of this tradition is one by which interaction between contemporaries of the opposite sex is channelized into the brother-sister relationship. This is probably a mechanism, through which the culture which rigidly segregates the sexes renders such interaction 'safe' by equating the two to siblings and thus imposing upon them the sex taboos normal to a brother-sister relationship. But it is important that, in the process, it provides for a mechanism by which members of the opposite sex may offer each other warmth, protection and emotional support without the tension or aggressiveness of sexual possession or dispossession.

Yet another unique relationship between men and women exists within the joint family. This is the relationship between a woman and her husband's younger brother—she is expected to maintain distance from all his elder brothers, but is allowed to interact almost as freely with his younger brothers as she would with her own. In fact often in a joint family the husband's younger brother is a woman's sole friend. He may stand up on her behalf against his own mother in situations in which his elder brother, her husband, may not. Not infrequently both may silently or even secretly protect or support each other against the tyranny of elders—even of her own husband.

Confrontation vs. Compromise

Under the circumstances, it is possible to appreciate that the firm tone of western feminism, relentlessly critical of males, can strike a discordant note in the ethos of Indian life. In fact, the roots of the discord go much deeper into the Indian philosophy of life. This may be illustrated with reference to the difference in the manner in which contradictions and conflicts are handled in the two cultures. In the West there is a compulsion to a logical resolution of conflict to confrontation and categorical choice. In contrast, the Indian culture places a greater value of compromise on the capacity to live with contradictions and to balance conflicting alternatives.

The author had occasion to observe this difference at a workshop on the identity of women, to which both Indian and American women who had stepped out of their traditional tracks to pursue careers as writers, researchers, academics, etc., were invited to discuss their experiences in life. At one point in the discussion one of the Indian participants used the word 'compromise' to describe her accommodation of the conflicting demands upon her in life. All the American participants took a negative view of her situation. To them the term connoted a denial of autonomy and freedom, an unhappy compulsion to accommodate into her plans and aspirations something that she would have been more comfortable without. In contrast, the overwhelming majority of the Indian women seemed to consider compromise positively to view it as the most acceptable accommodation of conflicting obligations, of pressures satisfactorily resolved. It was interesting to observe that both sets of participants were about equally placed in the ladder of professional achievement.

The history of men's involvement in the movement for the liberation of women, their education and the advancement of their status, the position that men in the Indian culture have traditionally held as caring brothers and affectionate fathers, and the weight that the Indian value system accords to the capacity to compromise could and should be carefully employed to co-opt men in the movement for the advancement of the status of women in India. If this is skilfully done the women's movement could be lifted from its current status as a feminist issue to the status of a much larger issue of human rights, which is what in essence it is.

Towards a Cultural Redefinition of Selfhood in India

Illustrations could be multiplied. But the gist of this issue is that it is important to take careful note of the differences in the ethical and cultural contexts of feminism in western and in Indian societies. In the West, feminism—together with some of the ethnic movements such as that conducted by American blacks—has taken on the responsibility of bridging a longstanding cultural gap between an ideology of individual freedom and equality and a reality in which women (and some of the ethnic minorities) are discriminated against severely.

India is, as yet, new to the ideology of personal freedom. Both Indian men and Indian women have hitherto functioned under rigid hierarchies; learned to curb their freedom; condition themselves to suppress their needs, silence their senses, and sublimate their selves in a philosophy of self-denial, self-effacement and service. Political freedom from British rule and the adoption of democracy and its accompanying value system have opened up for them totally new opportunities for personal freedom, self-hood and autonomy. The challenge to feminism in India is to help Indian women realize this self-hood in full measure.

The temptation to follow the paths blazed by western feminists, in research as well as in action, may be irresistible. However, one hopes for a revival of sensitivity to the uniqueness of the Indian situation and of the capacity to respond to this uniqueness by forging new ways.

II

STEREOTYPE

Indian social scientists, especially psychologists, have yet to give serious attention to the scientific study of sex roles. Sporadic and indirect attention has thrown some light on this important aspect of behavior.

In the popular mind there exists stereotypical expectations and beliefs regarding gender differences in behavior and personality characteristics. These personality differences presumably also make the two sexes better able to perform given roles in society. There also exist beliefs regarding the causes of these gender differences. When scientific evidence on the behavior and personality of the two sexes is examined the stereotypical beliefs turn out to be only partially true.

Overwhelmingly, the data shows no real gender difference and points to the decisive role cultural and social conditioning play in shaping human behavior. The selves that we become—masculine, feminine or androgynous—are the result of our attempts to meet social expectations. Since cultural conditioning propels us to behave in certain restricted ways, it leaves a good part of our potential underdeveloped. The kinds of attitudes we hold toward sex-roles color the nature of social transactions between the sexes. They also act as psychological barriers to social change. There is pan-cultural evidence to indicate that women hold more progressive attitude toward sex roles than men.

In their paper 'Sex Role Stereotypes in Northern India and the United States' Renuka R. Sethi and Mary J. Allen compare sex trait stereotypes in two very distinct cultures. It highlights the presence of some crosscultural similarities and differences. While there is distinct cluster of personality traits associated with females, the overall stereotypical differences between the two sexes in India are fewer than in U.S.A. V.V. Prakasa Rao and V. Nandini Rao in their article 'Sex Role Attitudes of College Students in India' examine what demographic variables could shape students' sex role attitudes. It points to the importance of some familial factors in shaping young people's attitudes toward sex roles.

In their paper 'Parental Sex Role Orientation and Sex Stereotypes of Children' Sukanya Das and Rehana Ghadially combine the study of personality characteristics and sex role attitudes. They contrast the self-description of children of both sexes with parents having liberal attitudes toward woman's role in society with those of children of parents holding traditional attitudes. Children from liberal families are more likely to see themselves in an androgynous way and are also less likely to stereotype occupations by sex than children from traditional homes. The understanding of women's changing role requires a truly inter-disciplinary effort. Manisha Roy meets this challenge and takes a macro level view in her paper, 'The Concepts of "Femininity" and "Liberation" in the Context of Changing Sex Roles: Women in Modern India and America'. Women's personality characteristics are not fixed by her anatomy but are contingent upon the particular social role that she is playing at different stages in her life-cycle.

SEX ROLE STEREOTYPES IN NORTHERN INDIA AND THE UNITED STATES

Renuka R. Sethi and Mary J. Allen

Until recently psychological research was limited primarily to the western world. A quest for basic knowledge about the behavior and development of people in other parts of the world, concern for social action and greater family mobility have led to an increased interest in crosscultural research. The sex roles of children and adults comprise one area of research that is currently of great interest and significance all over the world and has far-reaching implications for our academic, professional, economic, and social lives.

Reviews of crosscultural research lead to the following universal conclusions: all cultures distinguish between behaviors considered appropriate for males and females, differences between males and females appear early in life and continue to be reinforced and maintained through differential socialization of males and females (Hoyenga and Hoyenga, 1979; Hyde and Rosenberg, 1980). Recent research with Brazilian children (Tarrier and Gomes, 1981) provides evidence that sex role stereotypes increase with age and are related to social class. Generally speaking, in most cultures, males are expected to be more aggressive, assertive, and achievement-oriented, while females are expected to be more nurturant, sensitive, and responsible (Whiting and Edwards, 1973). There seems to be a fairly high degree of similarity between cultures in traits and roles that are ascribed to males and females (Williams, Giles, Edwards, Best, and Daws, 1977; Williams, Daws, Best, Tilquin, Wesley, and Bjerke, 1979; Williams, Best, Tilquin, Keller, Voss, Bjerke, and Baarda, 1981; Rowland, 1977). For example, a study comparing West German students with United States students, employing the Extended Personal Attributes Questionnaire, revealed substantial crosscultural similarity on all scales and significant sex differences; both groups showed higher masculinity (instrumental) scores for males and higher femininity (expressive) scores for females (Runge, Frey, Gollwitzer, Helmreich, and Spence, 1981). Sex role distinctions are also evident in terms of occupations, with males more likely to be involved in pursuits requiring strength and technical skills, while women are more frequently engaged in tasks requiring skills in child rearing, homemaking, and interpersonal relations (Hoyenga and Hoyenga, 1979). Children's games and toys, adult hobbies and leisure time pursuits, language, and dress also reflect variability between the sexes (Maccoby and Jacklin, 1974).

Several of the studies demonstrating crosscultural similarity have been based on findings from western countries (Williams et al., 1977, 1979, 1981; Runge et al., 1981). It is likely that a comparison of countries with greater cultural diversity might reveal differential sex-role ascriptions. Some anthropological evidence supports the fact that besides certain apparently universal sex differences, societies vary in behaviors considered differentially-appropriate for males and females. Mead's (1935) classic study of three New Guinea tribes, the Arapesh, the Mundugumor, and the Tchambuli, reveals strong support for crosscultural variations. Certain societies allow a wide range of behaviors in each sex role category. In some societies, both sexes share particular roles equally (e.g., the Arapesh and the Mundugumor); in others, though infrequent, a reversal of roles is evident (e.g., the Tchambuli). While in some societies, political and military authority and particular occupational roles (e.g., medicine) are reversed for males, these roles are also shared by females in other societies such as India, Israel, and Russia (Hyde and Rosenberg, 1980).

The diverse response patterns among individuals of varying cultural and ethnic backgrounds demonstrate the influence of cultural values and socialization in sex role behavior. Each culture has a set of institutional structures and practices to teach sex roles. Individuals learn to be male or female by learning effective means of communications and social behaviors which are required for their gender. Such culturally related sex role behaviors are particularly apparent in such Asian countries as India where religion, culture and tradition have deep roots and have significant influence on the individual's personality and behavior. Parents, siblings, and other members of the extended family, along with cultural mores, have a significant role in the timing, techniques, and emphasis on sex role development and training (Nyrop, Benderly, Cover, Cutter, and Parker, 1975).

Studies of children and adults in Indian society have demonstrated sex differences in training and behavior. Minturn and Hitchcock (1973) report that the play behavior of Rajput children in India is based on observational learning: 'Both sexes have their own type of fantasy play which is modelled on adult work. The little girls play at cooking and the boys at farming' (p. 334). In a study of reaction to frustration among Indian college students, Devi (1967) found that males respond with more overtly aggressive reactions; females report more withdrawal and regressive reactions. Currently in India, personal observations suggest that industrialization and migration have brought about some obvious changes in stereotyped concepts of masculinity and femininity affecting such factors as household composition, residence patterns, sleeping arrangements, specific kinship relationships, and male and female attitudes and behavior (Nyrop et al., 1975; Zinkin, 1958). A recent study of sex role attitudes, marriage and career among Indian college men and women (Ghadially and Kazi, 1980) has provided evidence to suggest that the role played by males and females in Indian society is gradually changing. Findings indicate a significant difference between 'traditional' and 'non-traditional' males and females on the above issues.

The purpose of this study is to investigate current sex role ascriptions in India. The Bem Sex Role Inventory (BSRI) currently is used as a research tool for investigating sex roles in the United States. The items on the BSRI were empirically derived based upon the theory that sex role is not a bipolar dimension (with masculinity and femininity at opposite extremes), but is two-dimensional (Bem, 1974). People may be high in both masculine and feminine characteristics (androgynous), high on just one set of characteristics (masculine or feminine), or low in both (undifferentiated).

Item selection for the BSRI was based upon presenting a list of personality characteristics to two groups of judges. One group was told to rate each characteristic on the desirability of each trait for American males; the other group was given the same instructions, but told to rate the desirability of each trait for American females (e.g., 'In American society how desirable is it for a man/woman to be truthful?'). Items for the masculinity or femininity scales were selected if the two sets of desirability ratings were significantly different (p < .05) for both male and female judges. The Social Desirability scale is made up of items not related to gender. Twenty items were selected in this way for each scale (Bem, 1974). Research has demonstrated that the BSRI is useful (Bem, 1975) and valid (Bem, 1977; Bem, Martyna, and Watson, 1976) for exploring sex role based upon an individual's self-description in terms of society's definitions of differentially desirable traits in American males and females.

At the present time, the BSRI has not been employed widely in crosscultural studies of sex role stereotyping. However, the studies that have presented crosscultural data using the BSRI have demonstrated that the measure, if adequately translated, can serve as a valid discrimination between the sexes. In a study of sex role orientation comparing American and Israeli students, Maloney, Wilkof, and Dambrot (1981) found no differences between the two nations in the mean masculine and feminine BSRI scores. But compared to American males, fewer Israeli males were classified as androgynous and the latter's total masculinity scores were lower. A significant cultural difference was also noted by the authors in comparing total masculinity and femininity scores for the gender within each group. The difference in the American group was greater than the difference in the Israeli group. This is to be expected, since the items on the BSRI were selected to discriminate between American sex role stereotypes. A test based on Israeli norms should show the opposite effect.

The present study partially replicates Bem's (1974) item selection study using subjects in India. In addition to the 60 items on the BSRI, 44 items were added by the authors to explore sex differences in areas not included in the BSRI, but deemed to be significant personality traits in the culture being studied. It has been suggested (LeVine, 1970; Werner, 1979) that in any crosscultural study, ethnographic information about the culture being studied is essential and helpful, both in anticipating distinctive dispositions and in the interpretation of results. One of the authors is originally from India and is familiar with the culture. The 44 items were compiled by her based upon discussions with 10 Indian adult males and females in the Los Angeles area. These additional items tap power (e.g., powerful, submissive), family relationships (e.g., has strong family loyalty, feels obligation to family), and various personality traits (e.g., docile, religious, polite, protective).

Method

Subjects

Subjects were volunteer students at two major universities in northern India with a mean age of 20.57 (SD = 2.97). Nine subjects were eliminated because of errors in filling out the questionnaire, leaving 225 subjects, 112 men and 113 women. All subjects were from the middle socioeconomic class and were tested in groups in their classrooms.

Procedure

Subjects were informed that this is a study designed to investigate what traits are desirable for males and females in Indian society. Approximately one-half of the male subjects and one-half of the female subjects were asked to rate each of the personality characteristics on its desirability for men in Indian society. The remaining subjects were asked to rate each personality characteristic on its desirability for women in Indian society. For each characteristic, subjects were to ask 'Is it desirable for Indian men (women) to _____?' and give a rating from 1 to 7, where a rating of 1 meant the characteristic was not at all desirable and a rating of 7 meant the characteristic was extremely desirable. Rating between 1 and 7 indicated intermediate levels of desirability; if subjects believed that a characteristic was moderately desirable in Indian men (women), they were asked to assign the number 3, 4, or 5. When a subject did not understand a word or was unfamiliar with it, a clarification was provided by the investigator using dictionary definitions. All forms and instructions were done in English.

Results

Each of the 104 items on the questionnaire was analyzed using a two-way factorial ANOVA with sex of subject and sex of cue as independent variables. Effects were considered significant if $p < .05$. Based upon the main effect for sex of cue, each item was classified as 'male', 'female', or 'neutral', depending upon which sex, if either, was rated higher on the item. Relationship between American categories (Bem, 1974) and Indian categories for specific items are shown in Table 1. A chi-square test for independence relating Bem's categories to the Indian categories for Bem's 60 items was highly significant, $X^2 (4) = 45.06$, $p < .001$.

Fifteen of the tests for interaction were significant at the $< .05$ level. Each interaction was classified as ordinal if the rating trends among both 'competitive' higher for male than for female cues, but male subjects rated the male cue higher than did female subscripts. Disordinal interactions occurred if the sexes' rating trends rank-ordered the cued sexes differently and were of two types—each sex group rating itself higher, and each sex group rating the other higher. Parenthetical material in Table 1 labels variables with these interaction patterns.

Table 1 also provides the grand mean for each item (averaging across sex of cue and rater) as a measure of overall trait desirability in the Indian culture. Grand means ranged from 1.76 (uncooperative) to 6.38 (faithful) on a scale that could, theoretically, range from 1.0 to 7.0. The mean desirability rating for Indian male traits ($M = 4.66$, $SD = 1.08$) was not significantly different from the mean desirability rating for Indian female traits ($M = 4.53$, $SD = 1.17$), $t(39) = .40$, ns. Traits were classified as highly desirable ($M > 5.5$), desirable ($3.5 < M < 5.49$) or less desirable ($M < 3.5$). A chi-square test for independence of item desirability and classification category (male, female, or neutral) was not significant, $X^2(4) = 1.96$, *ns*.

Discussion

Of the 104 traits, 41 (39%) had a main effect from sex of cue, and 63 (61%) did not. In addition, 41 of the 60 BSRI traits (68%) were in the same category in the American and Indian samples. Thus, for this set of traits, gender and cross-cultural similarity were the more common results.

Table 1
RELATIONSHIP BETWEEN AMERICAN AND INDIAN CATEGORIES AND MEAN DESIRABILITY RATINGS*

Indian category	American category			None
	Male	Female	Neutral	
Male	4.23 Acts as leader (D_S)			5.25 Adventurous
	3.32 Aggressive			3.13 Authoritarian
	5.58 Ambitious			2.87 Boisterous
	4.53 Athletic			6.31 Hard working
	5.77 Competitive (O)			5.14 Powerful
	4.01 Dominant			5.62 Protective (O)
	4.12 Forceful (D_S)			2.91 Rigid
	5.13 Has Leadership abilities (O)			
	5.29 Independent			
	4.00 Masculine			
	6.02 Strong personality			
	5.32 Willing to take risks			
Female		6.09 Affectionate (O)	5.66 Reliable	4.52 Charismatic
		3.08 Childlike (O)	3.86 Secretive	4.03 Delicate (O)
		5.49 Eager to soothe hurt feelings		3.24 Docile
		3.82 Feminine		4.68 Domestic
		2.77 Flatterable		5.92 Generous
		2.81 Gullible		3.94 Innocent
		6.00 Sensitive to the needs of others		6.03 Polite
		3.20 Shy		4.77 Religious
		5.68 Soft-spoken		3.29 Submissive
		5.05 Tender (O)		
		5.66 Warm		
Neutral	4.95 Analytical	6.30 Cheerful	5.28 Adaptable	4.62 Altruistic
	4.41 Assertive	5.34 Compassionate	2.58 Conceited	2.81 Chauvinistic (D_S)
	3.97 Defends own beliefs (D_S)	5.05 Does not use harsh language	3.58 Conventional (D_S)	5.68 Considerate
	4.16 Individualistic		6.20 Friendly	2.38 Cunning
	5.83 Makes decisions easily	6.32 Gentle	6.37 Happy	5.39 Disciplinarian
	5.48 Self-reliant	6.16 Loves children (D_O)	6.18 Helpful	2.71 Dogmatic
	5.38 Self-sufficient	6.11 Loyal	1.90 Inefficient	2.89 Egotistic
	5.82 Willing to take a stand	6.06 Sympathetic	2.04 Jealous	4.95 Enterprising
		6.05 Understanding	5.91 Likable	6.38 Faithful
		4.33 Yielding	2.77 Moody	2.62 Family oriented
			6.32 Sincere	5.46 Feels obligation to elderly
			4.53 Solemn	5.63 Feels obligation to family
			5.60 Tactful	3.77 Frugal
			3.06 Theatrical	5.43 Fun loving
			6.03 Truthful	2.72 Gossipy
			2.85 Unpredictable	5.76 Has strong family
			2.15 Unsystematic (D_S)	

Indian category	American category			None
	Male	*Female*	*Neutral*	
				loyalty
				6.35 Intelligent
				2.23 Intolerant
				5.43 Modest
				4.21 Quiet
				3.88 Reserved
				4.27 Structured
				3.35 Subservient
				3.43 Talkative
				2.78 Timid
				1.76 Uncooperative
				6.26 Wise

* Parenthetical notes refer to significant interactions: O denotes an ordinal interaction, D_S denotes a disordinal interaction with the sexes rating themselves higher, D_O denotes a disordinal interaction with the sexes rating each other higher.

Differences between American and Indian sex roles may be attributed to differences in technology, economic base, religion, and cultural heritage. The many similarities in spite of these factors may be attributed to a common British influence, the parallel development of division of labor in prehistory, and an increasing western influence in India.

There is considerable overlap between traits considered related to gender in the American and Indian samples. Differences between the countries never reversed stereotypes, but did move items from the gender-related to the neutral category. Nearly half of the BSRI's masculine and feminine items did not reveal significant gender difference in India. The largest agreement across countries was with respect to Bem's neutral items; all but two were also not gender related in India.

In both countries a number of traits are considered more desirable for the same gender. If we use Parsons' (Parsons and Bales, 1955) instrumental-expressive dichotomy, a number of traits related to instrumentality appear more desirable in males, and a number of traits related to expressiveness appear more desirable in females. It is considered more desirable for men to act as leaders, to have leadership abilities, and to be aggressive, ambitious, competitive, dominant and forceful. It is considered more desirable for women to be sensitive to the needs of others, tender, warm, eager to soothe hurt feelings and affectionate. In addition, it is more desirable for women to be childlike, flatterable, and gullible, a trio of traits with a mean desirability rating of only 2.89.

Several interactions between sex of subject and sex of cue occurred. Since Bem (1974) analyzed her data using t tests instead of ANOVAs, it is not clear if interactions would have been found in her data too. Bem classified a trait as gender related if the t test was significant for both male and female subjects, paralleling no interactions or ordinal interactions in the present study. Using this criterion, two of the male-related Indian items (acts as a leader and forceful) would be omitted, so that cross-national agreement would hold true for 10 of Bem's 20 male items.

Bem (1974) classified an item as neutral if t tests comparing male to female cues were not significant among male or female raters and if a t test comparing male to female judges' ratings was not significant. This would compare to the present study's classification criterion using no interaction or ordinal interactions, plus the requirements that the main effect for sex of rater was not significant. Using these added criteria, the following items could no longer be considered neutral in the Indian sample: adaptable (female judges' ratings were higher), secretive (male judges' ratings were higher), and the four items with disordinal interactions. For purposes of describing sex role stereotypes, the classification of items based upon main effects seems more appropriate. Since Bem's goal was to create a measure of sex role from a large pool of potential items, her t test strategy seems appropriate for her goals. She was more interested in large consistent differences than in using the most powerful analytical tool available.

Examining the items that are gender related in the United States but not in India, it appears equally desirable for Indians of both genders to have traits related to assertiveness (assertive, defends own beliefs, individualistic, self-reliant, self-sufficient and willing to take a stand). These assertive traits were all more desirable in males in the American sample. In the author's opinion, most western observers would conclude that Indian women are not assertive. But Indians and some western observers familiar with the culture (e.g., Zinkin, 1958) have long recognized the subtle strength of Indian women in their interaction with men. The data support the conclusion that this assertiveness is as desirable in women as it is in men and that both Indian men and women share this common attitude valuing assertiveness in all people.

Some of Bem's female traits related to expressiveness (compassionate, gentle, loves children, sympathetic and understanding) were not gender related in India. In all, 44 traits that were not on the BSRI were analyzed. Among these items were several related to family ties and responsibilities. Of these, none showed a gender difference. It appears to be equally desirable for Indian males and females to be family oriented, to feel obligations to the elderly and to the family, and to have strong family loyalty. This is not surprising in a culture where children are highly valued, where family has greater importance than the individual, where the elderly have high social status within their families and in society, where family relationship and obligations are highly valued (Nyrop et al., 1975), and where there are no government-sponsored social security benefits or nursing homes.

It is significantly more desirable for Indian males to have traits such as adventurous, hard-working, authoritarian and powerful. When these are connected with the other Indian male traits, a constellation that seems to be related to entrepreneurial tendencies occurs: acts as a leader, aggressive, ambitious, competitive, dominant, forceful, had leadership abilities, independent, and willing to take risks.

It is more desirable for Indian women to be docile, domestic, generous, innocent, polite, religious and submissive. This is in strong contrast to the entrepreneurial traits considered more desirable in Indian males. These stereotypes probably have a strong influence on career choice and domestic arrangements in Indian society. Nyrop et al. (1975) report that

> in 1970/71 women science graduates numbered 48,000 of whom 60 per cent were school teachers, compared with 25 per cent of the male graduates. Only 100 of the 2,090 officers in the elite Indian Administrative Services (IAS) were women, although many more were employed in the lower ranks of government service. Of the 6,500 women enrolled in commerce colleges, most will seek jobs as accountants, clerks, book keepers or saleswomen (p. 249).

Thus, Indian women—even those with higher education and technical training—gravitate toward service professions, while their male counterparts are more likely to develop careers involving technical or political leadership.

In the present study, both genders had a range of traits including low and high desirability ratings, and the tests comparing them were not significant. Although the genders had different roles, there is no evidence that one role is superior or more desirable than the other. Of course, it is possible that the desirability ratings obtained in the present study are not adequate indicators of social status. In addition, the distinction between attitude and behavior must be made. Perhaps Indian culture highly values a number of traits in both genders, but attributes higher status to a male displaying these traits. Mandelbaum (cited by Nyrop et al., 1975), summarizing attitudes toward family roles in Indian society, concludes that 'their political ideology on this matter has commonly outpaced their family behavior' (p. 203), with traditional arranged marriages and marital relationships still common among educated Indians.

Items with high desirability ratings describe traits that Indian culture values, regardless of gender. Items with mean ratings of at least 5.5 appear to form six clusters of traits: ability (intelligent, wise, and makes decisions easily, M = 6.15); interpersonal warmth (happy, cheerful, friendly, sincere gentle, affectionate, sympathetic, understanding, sensitive to the needs o others, polite, warm, generous, considerate, soft spoken, tactful, and likable, M = 6.01); trustworthiness (faithful, helpful, truthful, loyal, reliable, and protective, M = 6.50); interpersonal strength (strong personality and willing to take a stand, M = 5.92), motivation (hard-working competitive, and ambitious, M = 5.88); and family orientation (has strong family loyalty, feels obligation to family, family oriented, and loves children M = 5.79). Most of these highly desirable traits are gender neutral in India, but of the gender-related items, those related to Interpersonal Warmth tend to be more desirable in women and those related to motivation tend to be more desirable in men. Items related to Ability and Family Orientation are all gender neutral.

Gender and crosscultural similarity are supported by the data. In contrast to American results, traits related to assertiveness and some traits related to expressiveness are not related to gender in India. In addition, in Indian males and females a number of traits related to ability and family orientation are equally highly desirable.

Data for this study were collected in northern India. Generalizing results to all of India may be questionable, especially in view of the tremendous diversity in India of language, religion and customs. Historically, northern India has been more often invaded and influenced by other cultures especially by Muslim societies.

There is need for further research of this type in other parts of India and in other cultures to clarify sex roles as they exist today. In addition, studies comparing immigrants in the United States to their native populations or their conceptions of sex roles would provide interesting information on the acculturation of immigrants toward American norms.

SEX ROLE ATTITUDES OF COLLEGE STUDENTS IN INDIA

V.V. Prakasa Rao and V. Nandini Rao

Introduction

In traditional Indian families the roles of wife and mother are clearly defined and separated from that of the father. The domestic roles of men and women do not overlap and are not interchangeable. Men have always attended to the tasks outside the household. The woman has a complex constellation of roles: manager of the household; caretaker of the children; and distributor of love and affection. She routinely performs such tasks as cleaning, sweeping, and decorating the house; washing vessels; cooking and serving food; looking after children; and welcoming and entertaining guests (Mukherjee, 1958; Sen Gupta, 1960; Rao and Rao, 1982; Ross, 1961; Jacobson, 1977a; Wadley, 1977; Mandelbaum, 1970; Dube, 1978; Dube, 1963; Altekar, 1962; Prabhu, 1962). Despite the rigid differentiation of roles, unqualified generalizations about sex roles would be misleading because of differences in caste, sect, region, language, and religion. For example, lower caste and untouchable women not only do household work but also engage in agricultural and nonagricultural work outside the household.

A brief survey of the status of women reveals that women are considered inferior and less desirable while men are viewed as superior and desirable. Male children are more highly valued than female children, and they are socialized in different ways. Female children are still considered an economic liability to the family, not only until they are married but, to some extent, throughout their lives. The socialization process emphasizes modesty and adaptation for females, while it teaches male children to be aggressive, assertive, superior and independent (Baig, 1976; Nanda, 1976; Jain, 1975; de Souza, 1975). The different qualities of males and females are reinforced from childhood by all the major institutions. 'Guided by traditional concepts of proper feminine behavior and aware that their actions are inextricably linked to family honor, prestige, and ultimately material rewards, women typically carry out their roles as chaste daughters and dutiful wives' (Jacobson, 1977a: 8).

Although the status of women in India can be studied through various stages in life, emphasis will be given to the roles of wife and mother in the present study of sex roles. Once a woman is married, her role as a wife is clearly defined. Traditionally she lives with her husband, in a patrilineal joint family household where she is likely to play a submissive role and adapt to fit into her husband's family. Rules of proper conduct for the Hindu wife and husband are clearly laid down in such books as the *Mahabharata*, the *Ramayana*, and other *Dharma Shastras*. These works have a great influence in shaping the behavior of wives. Sita, Savitri Gandhara and other characters in these stories exemplify the proper and ideal behavior of wives. Religious teachings prepare girls to play subordinate roles in their husband's families. Ross described the young wife's function in the new family as 'mainly a servicing one, and the husband-wife relationship structurally quite different from that of the North American family, in which it is the pivot around which the family revolves' (1961 152–154).

The status of a wife improves upon the birth of children. As a mother she is given higher esteem in the family, a greater degree of independence, and the right to have her voice heard in the women's quarters (Mandelbaum, 1949: 103). Because of the importance accorded to a son who is believed to save the father from going to hell, the position of a mother with sons improves even more. Mother-son relations are described as strong, close, affectionate, dependable and tender.

The mother's influence gradually increases in domestic as well as outside matters. The mother is obeyed, makes important decisions and enjoys certain rights. Dubois observed during his visit to India in the nineteenth century that the Hindu mother was the pivot of life in the family. The mothers showed 'a shrewdness, a savingness and intelligence which would do honor to the best housewives in Europe' (1928: 192). They also enjoy the confidence of their husbands and are the guardians of family property, money and jewels. They make important decisions with regard to the arrangement of family, the marriages of their children and the distribution of alms and charities.

Although, ideally, a woman plays a submissive and subordinate role in the family, in reality, the woman in India exercises considerable power in family matters in addition to being the sole authority in the household. The traditional dominant role of a woman in the domestic aspects of the family has not received as much attention as the subordinate role of women. Ross recognizes the woman's influence and states that,

her position as a consultant meant in reality that in most families she shared the responsibility of making the major family decisions with the father . . . The mother is well qualified to act as advisor to the head of the house, for as she is the pivot around which the family revolves she is in a strategic position in relation to the whole gamut of household intrigue. Through her relationships with the women of the household and larger kin groups she knows all the intimate details of the lives of family members and is thus in a position to advise her husband and later her sons, and so control their decisions . . . In this way, 'mothers' may have great power although the traditional picture of the Hindu women shows her in a state of submission to husband and elders (1961: 102).

Both indigenous and foreign writers have observed the influence of the women on their husbands' decisions not only as consultants but also as mediators. Children are much closer to their mothers than to their fathers. There is a distance between the father and the children, especially sons. Children are reluctant to approach the father because of the status differences. Usually, it is the mother who acts as a mediator between the children and their father and sees that the children's desires are conveyed. With respect to the importance of the wife's advisory role, Srinivas observed that 'no important decision was taken, however, without the wife's consent if not permission, and frequently, the push to take a decision came from the wife' (1977: 231). Jacobson noted that women,

> help make important decisions in other family matters, especially in the selection of mates for their children. Men do some of the scouting, but, through their network of ties with women in other towns and villages, women frequently have access to information vital for evaluating prospects (1977b: 62–63).

Since the turn of the century, the status of women has been changing because of industrialization and urbanization, the independence movement, spatial mobility, the principle of democracy, social legislation, and contacts with the outside world. Many parents want their daughters to have higher education and equal occupational opportunities. With the expansion of the occupational structure, women are entering the world of paid employment in unprecedented numbers. Women have also gained considerable political power as a result of their participation in the independence movement. Women are in political positions at every level from village councils to the national government. The impact of these socio-cultural changes on the sex role attitudes of the student population has not yet been examined. Since these changes have produced liberal attitudes toward sex roles in many developed countries, it is appropriate to examine the relationship between social changes and sex role attitudes in a developing country like India.

The large number of women working outside the home does not necess arily mean that women's household responsibilities and duties have declined New roles may be added to the traditional roles increasing women's burden. Husbands and other relatives may not oppose women seeking employment but unequivocal support that includes sharing the household responsibilities appears to be lacking. Kapur captures the ambivalent atti tudes of men when she states that husbands 'like their wives to take up jobs but dislike them to change at all as their attitude towards their roles and status at home is concerned, and dislike their traditional responsibi lities being neglected which results from their preoccupation with out-of home vocation' (1970: 407). In the process of fulfilling responsibilities at home and at work, some employed women may face role conflict while in other cases roles of men and women are being redrawn to cope with the changing conditions in the family.

This study examines the attitudes of the college students toward the mother, wife, husband and father roles. It was expected that the sex of the respondents would have significant influence on their attitudes toward the three sex roles. More specifically, it was hypothesized that females would be more likely to express liberal attitudes toward all three roles than males. The analysis identifies the factors related to the sex role attitudes of the male and female respondents and also determines the factors that explain the greatest variance in sex role attitudes. This enables us to identify the factors that vary between the sexes in explaining the variance in sex role attitudes.

Methods

Data for the study were collected from 210 graduate students who enrolled in three major universities in Andhra Pradesh. Questionnaires were administered by teachers of these universities and the students completed the instruments in the classroom in the fall of 1982. The sample was 56 per cent male and 44 per cent female. The mean age for the group was 22.8 years (ranging from 19 to 29). About 87 per cent of the students were Hindus; the remaining 13 per cent are of various other religious groups. The average education for fathers was 13.0 years and for mothers 10.4 years. Nearly 54 per cent of the students came from families whose fathers were in high-ranking positions such as executives, managers, teachers, professionals, businessmen and in the IAS (Indian Administrative Service). The average income for the father was Rs. 1568 per month (US $1 = Rs. 11). The respondents had an average of 2.3 brothers and 2.4 sisters. A majority of the sample came from rural communities. Half of the sample lived in nuclear families while the other half lived in joint families.

The wife role, the mother role, and the father role, which are considered the dependent variables in the study, were operationalized by using a slightly revised scale dealing with 'Traditional Wife Role', 'Traditional Mother Role', and 'Traditional Father Role', developed by Scanzoni (1975). The wife role is considered traditional if the interests of husband and children are emphasized and placed ahead of those of the wife. It is considered modern if the wife role emphasizes reduced commitment to the notion of subordination of the wife's interest. A thirteen item scale was used to measure attitudes toward the *wife role*. The mother role is treated as traditional if the interests of children are placed ahead of the mother's or if mother-centered considerations superordinate the individual-centered considerations. Five items were used to measure attitudes toward the *mother role*. The husband's role is considered traditional if the emphasis is given to the husband as head and as unique provider of the family. Modernism is indicated by weaker congruence with the traditional patriarchal ideology. Two items measuring attitudes toward the *husband role* constituted the scale. Respondents were asked to indicate their choice for each of the items in the three scales to one of the five responses: strongly disagree; disagree; sometimes agree and sometimes disagree; agree; and strongly agree. The responses were summed for each of the three dependent variables. The highest possible score for wife role is 65, for mother role is 25, and for husband role is 10 while the lowest possible scores are 13, 5 and 2 respectively. For each of the three scales, a lower score indicates a 'traditional' emphasis while a high score indicates a 'modern' emphasis. Mean values for the positions of wife role, mother role and husband roles were 37.5, 14.7 and 4.2 respectively. In order to determine the reliability of the three subscales, Cronbach's *alpha* was computed. Coefficients of internal consistency are .74 for wife role, .68 for mother role and .62 for father role.

Findings and Conclusions

Table 1 includes the *mean* values of the male and female Indian students' attitudes toward the wife, mother and father roles. Both male and female students expressed traditional sex role attitudes on 12 statements on this scale and liberal attitudes on six items. On the remaining two items, females expressed liberal attitudes while males embraced traditional views.

In considering the *wife role*, both males and females in this study think that a woman's most important task is caring for children and husband, that she obtains more satisfaction through children, that she is suited for certain kinds of jobs, that she should give up her new job if it inconveniences the family members, and that she should work only when there is

Table 1
SEX ROLE ATTITUDES SCALE ITEMS AND THE MEAN VALUES FOR
MALES AND FEMALES

	Males	Females	
Items	$\bar{X}$	$\bar{X}$	T-Test
Wife Role			
1. A wife's most important task in life should be taking care of her husband and children	1.79	2.09	*
2. A woman's greatest satisfaction in life comes through her children	2.16	2.17	–
3. If she works, she should not try to compete (get ahead)	3.20	3.63	**
4. A wife should not have equal authority with her husband in making decisions	3.59	4.14	**
5. If she has the same job as a man who has to support his family, she should not expect the same salary	3.59	3.87	–
6. A woman is suited for only certain kinds of jobs because of emotional and mental nature	2.58	2.98	*
7. A wife should give up her job whenever it inconveniences her husband and children	2.40	2.67	*
8. If a mother of young children works, it should be only while the family needs the money	2.56	2.74	–
9. A woman's place should be in the home†	3.59	3.82	–
10. A woman should be protected first by her father, then by her husband, and finally by her son	2.24	2.77	**
11. Woman should not mix freely with males in her social relations†	3.26	3.36	–
12. A woman should give more importance to the needs of her family than her personal ambitions and needs†	2.35	2.73	*
13. Although a woman is highly educated, she should be encouraged to assume domestic role†	2.62	2.58	–
Mother Role			
14. A working mother cannot be just as warm and affectionate with her children as a mother who does not work	3.03	3.39	*
15. The parents get more satisfaction when a son does well (get ahead) in his occupation			

	Males	Females	
Items	$\bar{X}$	$\bar{X}$	*T-Test*
than when a daughter gets ahead in hers	2.71	3.35	**
16. A marriage is incomplete without children	2.96	2.75	–
17. A young girl should not be permitted as much independence and freedom as boys	2.62	3.25	**
18. School-going children are likely to suffer if mother works	2.77	2.84	–
Father Role			
19. A married man's chief responsibility should be to support his wife and family	1.77	1.84	–
20. The husband should be the head of the family	2.12	2.51	*
Traditional Wife Role Attitudes	30.42	33.41	**
Traditional Mother Role Attitudes	14.09	15.58	**
Traditional Father Role Attitudes	3.89	4.35	–
Sex Role Attitudes	48.40	53.34	**

* Significant at .05 level or higher
** Significant at .01 level or higher
† These items are developed by the authors

financial need. The woman should be protected throughout her life; she should give importance to the family needs over her own; and she should assume the domestic role even if she is educated. At the same time the students disagree with the statements that a woman should compete with men in her job, that she should not have equal authority in the family, that she should not expect the same salary for a similar job, that her place should be in the home, and that she should not mix freely with men.

With regard to the *mother role*, both sexes report that a marriage is not complete without children and that school-age children suffer if mother works. By contrast, they disagree with the statement that a mother cannot be warm and affectionate with her children if she works. It is interesting to find that males and females differ with regard to children's success and their freedom. Males feel that parents get more satisfaction from a son's success than a daughter's and that girls should not be granted as much freedom and independence as boys. Female students express more liberal attitudes toward these issues.

In considering the *father role*, both sexes agree that a man should have the major responsibility of supporting the family members and that he should be the head of the family.

116/V.V. PRAKASA RAO AND V. NANDINI RAO

T-test was used to detect significant differences between males and females on attitudes toward the three sex roles. In general the students embraced traditional attitudes toward the wife role and the father role, but females expressed significantly less traditional attitudes toward the wife role than males. The sexes did not differ in their attitudes toward the father role. Females expressed more liberal attitudes than males toward the *mother role*.

An examination of the attitudes of the sexes by item of the subscale points out some apparent inconsistencies in their attitudes toward the three roles. For example, the respondents think that a husband should be the head of the family and should support the family, but at the same time, they do not think that the woman's place should be in the home and they do think that a wife should have equal authority with her husband in making decisions. This apparent inconsistency can be explained by the fact that although women seem to play dependent, docile, subordinate and secondary roles in the family, they exercise great influence. The finding is consistent with the observation made by Carstairs (1975: 235) that the 'women could be quite strong-minded beneath their submissive demeanor, and that they were very good in getting their own way.' Srinivas (1977: 231) also observes that the relationship between husband and wife changes as they mature in marital bond, and that 'the balance was tilted in favor of the wife, but this was concealed more or less effectively by symbols of wifely deference, and expressions of devotion to the lord and master.' These observations lead to the conclusion that the husband has the responsibility of supporting the family but, at the same time, the wife does exercise considerable power in making important decisions in the family.

Neither males nor females in this study agree with the statement that 'women should not mix freely with males in their social relations.' This is a surprising finding in a society where segregation of the sexes is common. It may be that the respondents have defined 'mixing freely' in a very restricted sense. For instance, in India merely talking to a person of an opposite sex and going to restaurants with him/her without ever being physically touched can be defined as 'mixing freely'. Even this kind of mixing is generally confined to the educational setting, especially outside the classroom situation. Male and female students are still segregated in social, educational, political and religious settings. At weddings, feasts, social parties, temples or shrines and other informal gatherings, there is a tendency for males and females to sit separately. Even among educated urbanites, sexual segregation is observed outside the home. Hence, it may be concluded that the expression of liberal attitudes here is based on a restricted sense of 'mixing freely'.

It is interesting to note that both sexes agree that a woman's most important task is to take care of her husband and children, that her greatest satisfaction comes from children, and that she should assume domestic roles even if she is highly educated. Although the enrolment of women in educational institutions has been steadily increasing and the political and economic status of women is continually rising, for most educated women family needs are more important than their personal ambitions. An expression of these traditional attitudes finds rationale in the argument that a key to improvement in a woman's position at home does not lie in her adding to the family income. It is even argued that the working woman's status is much worse than that of those other similarly placed women who do not work. Because of these common notions, 'working women in India often leave their jobs in mid-career to devote themselves wholly to domestic responsibilities' (Madan, 1975: 71); careerism has not yet relegated the family to the background in the lives of working women. Even if women work, Karve cautioned that 'in the final analysis everywhere women have to move towards establishing harmony in the domestic as well as outdoor roles in the interest of the family, nation, and society at large' (1975: 129).

Neither male nor female respondents believe that 'a working mother cannot be as warm and affectionate with her children compared to a non-working mother.' This finding can be explained in two ways. First, there is a common notion that motherhood is more important than womanhood. It is the sole responsibility of a mother to provide expressive function for the children. Second, in many cases working mothers do not have to spend much time attending the domestic chores after work because of the availability of help (relatives or servants). This allows her to spend more time with her children. This argument finds support in the observation made by Srinivas that 'educated Indian women are able to hold demanding jobs and be housewives and mothers at the same time thanks to the availability of servants, and to their ability to draw upon their wide kin-networks for help in crises' (1977: 236). Consequently, many female students feel that they can successfully blend traditional household responsibilities and modern occupational obligations into their social lives.

In this study the males consistently expressed more traditional attitudes than the females. This finding is similar to the conclusions observed in American studies (Scanzoni, 1976, 1978; Duncan and Duncan, 1978; Sexton, 1979; Rao and Rao, 1983; Tomeh, 1978). The same pattern is reported by Tomeh (1981) in her study of sex role attitudes among Korean students.

Table 2 presents the correlation coefficients between the background variables and the three sex role attitudes. Females were more likely to have liberal attitudes toward the wife, mother, and father roles than males. Higher caste respondents expressed liberal attitudes toward the wife role and the father role while lower caste respondents embraced

Table 2

ZERO-ORDER CORRELATIONS BETWEEN THE BACKGROUND
CHARACTERISTICS AND SEX ROLE ATTITUDES OF THE
INDIAN STUDENTS (N = 210)

Characteristics	Sex Role Attitudes[1]			
	SRA	TWR	TMR	TFR
Sex	.242**	.232**	.197**	.119*
Age	−.008	−.016	−.011	.039
Religion	−.023	−.016	.000	−.077
Caste	−.219**	−.271**	−.038	−.120*
Father's Education	.276**	.304**	.144**	.131*
Mother's Education	.145*	.178**	.070	−.002
Father's Occupation	.137*	.155**	.091	.009
Mother's Employment Status	.001	.016	−.012	−.039
Father's Income	.055	.077	−.020	.057
Mother's Income	−.069	−.053	−.092	−.011
Number of Brothers	−.020	.039	−.017	.077
Number of Sisters	−.042	.022	−.134*	.003
Community Size	.202*	.221**	.117*	.008
Family Type	−.003	.024	−.078	.039

[1] SRA = Sex Role Attitude
   TWR = Traditional Wife Role Attitude
   TMR = Traditional Mother Role Attitude
   TFR = Traditional Father Role Attitude
   *Significant at .05 level
   **Significant at .01 level or higher

traditional attitudes toward these roles. The mother role attitudes were
not significantly related to the respondent's caste. Father's education is
significantly and positively related to the attitudes toward the three sex
roles. The higher the father's education, the more liberal the students'
attitudes toward all three roles. The mother's education was strongly
related to the wife role attitudes but not to the mother and father role
attitudes. A positive significant relationship is found between the father's
occupation and the wife role attitudes; the children of fathers with high
occupational status expressed liberal attitudes toward the wife role.
Number of sisters is negatively associated with the mother role attitudes.
The students with large numbers of sisters expressed traditional mother
role attitudes. Community size is positively related to the wife and mother
role attitudes.

In order to determine the relative contribution of each independent
variable in explaining the variance in the dependent variables while the
other independent variables are statistically controlled, a stepwise

multiple-regression analysis was computed for the total sample and for the sub-samples of males and females with the wife role, the mother role, and the father role as criterion variables. The thirteen demographic and socio-economic variables formed the item pool from which the optimal models were constructed for each group of respondents.

Table 3 presents the effects of the strongest independent variables on the three sex roles for the total sample. The three-variable model for the wife role attitudes indicates that female students who had fathers with higher levels of education, living in large communities tended to express less traditional attitudes. Based on the standardized regression coefficients (*beta* weights) and the increments in R^2, it is obvious that the explained variance in the wife role attitudes is relatively small. Of the three predictor variables in the model, father's education, the most powerful explanatory variable, explained 9.4 per cent of the total variance while sex and community size explained 1.7 per cent and 1.9 per cent respectively in the wife role attitudes. Sex and number of sisters emerged as the most salient predictors of the student's attitudes toward the mother role. Females and the students who reported fewer sisters expressed more liberal attitudes toward the mother role. Sex is the most powerful predictor explaining 3.9 per cent of the variance in the criterion variable while number of sisters explained 1.9 per cent of the variance in the same variable. Not a single predictor entered into the regression equation in explaining the variance in the father role attitudes of the students when the effect of independent variables was removed.

For male students, stepwise regression equations were computed for the three sex role attitudes. The number of brothers is the only predictor explaining the variance in the wife role attitudes. Males with larger number of brothers tend to express more traditional attitudes toward the wife role. Number of brothers explained 5.6 per cent of the variance in the criterion variable. Number of sisters is the only predictor explaining the variance in the mother role attitudes of males. The more sisters a male had, the more traditional were his attitudes toward the mother role. Number of sisters explained 9.2 per cent of the variance in the criterion variable. It is equally surprising to find that not a single variable emerged as a predictor in explaining the variance in the father role attitudes of males.

For the three sex role attitudes, father's education emerged as the only significant predictor, explaining 18.2 per cent of the variance in the wife role attitudes of female students. If the father's education was high, females were likely to hold less traditional attitudes toward the wife role. Father's education also emerged as the only powerful predictor explaining 7.8 per cent of the variance in the mother role attitudes of female students. The

Table 3

STEPWISE MULTIPLE REGRESSION ANALYSIS OF THE STRONGEST
PREDICTORS OF SEX ROLE ATTITUDES OF THE
INDIAN STUDENTS (N = 210)

Predictors	B (unstandardized)	Standard Error of B	Beta (standardized)	R²	T-Test
Wife Role					
Father's Education	.360	.078	.306	.094	4.64
Sex	2.163	1.071	.141	.111	2.11
Community Size	.571	.273	.142	.130	2.09
Mother Role					
Sex	1.445	.500	.197	.039	2.89
Number of Sisters	−.323	.157	−.139	.058	−2.06
Father Role					
No variables entered in the Model					

higher the father's education, the more liberal the attitudes of females toward mother role. Finally, caste was the only significant predictor explaining 7.4 per cent of the variance in father role attitudes. Higher caste females expressed less traditional attitudes toward the father role than lower caste females.

In the regression analysis:

1. only a few predictors explained the variance in the wife, mother and father roles;
2. the explained variance in the three sex role attitudes was small.

In general, the background variables did not produce significant differences in the students' attitudes toward the three sex roles. For example, changes in the units of independent variables did not result in similar changes in the father role attitudes, thus implying a consensus on the part of the students about the importance of the father role.

For the total sample, sex was the only significant predictor explaining the variance in attitudes toward the wife and the mother roles. Males expressed more traditional attitudes while females embraced less traditional attitudes. Consideration of the changes occurring in Indian culture such as urbanization, technological development, employment of women, increase in female enrolment in educational institutions, and western influence on social attitudes toward the acceptance of women's employment should be taken into account in examining the differences in sex role attitudes between males and females. The less traditional attitudes of females toward the sex roles can be explained in terms of the perceived changes in status, power, and prestige of employed women. Outside employment is seen as a sign of independence and equality between the sexes. It is considered a means to escape the traditional 'status trap'. Additionally, the central government has been advocating equality of women as a basic condition for the social, economic, and political development of the nation, and has given high priority to the development of mechanisms to release women from their dependent and unequal status (Indian Council of Social Science Research 1975: 1–5).

In addition to sex, father's education and community size are both powerful predictors of attitudes toward the mother. These demographic characteristics generally have similar correlations with American students' sex role attitudes. Fathers with higher education have daughters with more liberal attitudes toward the wife and mother roles. It should be noted that, although some of the demographic variables explained the variance in the sex role attitudes of the Indian students, their attitudes are still fairly traditional. Hence, caution should be used when the findings are compared with those from other cultures. The observations made by Jones are worth mentioning here:

> perhaps nowhere in the world is traditionalism stronger than in the India of today. A modernizing country, India, nevertheless embraces techniques and norms which have been extant for millenia. Truly a land of contrasts, this country is probably the most paradoxical in that modern values and methods are initiated and perpetually challenge traditional values and methods, while seemingly affecting little change (1980: 1).

Implications: These findings may be interpreted in terms of methodological as well as theoretical implications. Although students who are male, come from high income families, are unmarried, come from rural communities, and major in liberal studies seem to be over-represented in the sample, the sample can be considered typical of a university student population in India with only a few exceptions. The sample is sufficiently diversified that sex role attitudes do vary with sample characteristics. The findings of the study may be generalized to the student population attending the universities in India, but, because of regional, economic, language, caste and other socio-cultural differences, these findings cannot be generalized to the Indian total population.

Since few studies have been conducted about sex role attitudes of Indian students and factors affecting these attitudes, we cannot compare our findings with those of other studies. Conclusions drawn from this study should be considered tentative until further testing is done to validate the findings not only by using a cross-section of student population but also by using large samples of all ages and all social groups from the larger population.

Like many developing societies, India is undergoing tremendous structural changes that are affecting various dimensions of the family. In recent times, the status of women is changing socially, politically, and economically. By attending colleges and universities, entering the occupational world, and moving into the political arena, women are contributing to the development of Indian society. The question that remains is to what extent these structural and situational changes affect the sex role attitudes of women in India. This study reveals that, although both males and females expressed traditional attitudes toward sex roles, female attitudes are less traditional than male attitudes. Both sexes expressed traditional attitudes toward the father role; females expressed less traditional attitudes toward the wife role than did males; and females held more liberal attitudes toward the mother role than males. Despite their less traditional sex role attitudes, the actual role performance of females in the family has not changed much. Employed women are responsible for both the domestic chores and outside work. Husbands rarely participate in household tasks. Women are expected to blend the domestic roles and the employee roles in the interest of the family. The availability of servants and relatives who do most of the household tasks has relieved employed women from most domestic chores although they are still expected to supervize them. Thus, one finds little change in the traditional expectations of male and female roles in the family although women's status in the occupational world is changing.

The findings of the study may have implications for marriage in the future since women expressed less traditional sex role attitudes. It may be argued that males and females should reconcile their sex role attitudes before they are married. Since most marriages are arranged by the parents, however, it is unlikely that the differences in sex role attitudes between potential mates will enter into the process of mate selection. Although tremendous changes are taking place in India, they have left the institution of family largely untouched. People are still traditional and have not accepted egalitarian relations in the family.

PARENTAL SEX ROLE ORIENTATION AND SEX STEREOTYPES OF CHILDREN

Sukanya Das and Rehana Ghadially

In society the two sexes have been stereotyped in terms of different tasks, previleges and role patterns that are traditionally assigned to them. Sex stereotypes refer to the constellation of different traits, activities, values and behavioral characteristics attributed to and used to describe and differentiate two sex groups in a socio-psychological set up. Ashmore and Delboca (1979) reviewed the definition of sex stereotypes used by researchers and identified four generally accepted characteristics. A sex stereotype is usually considered to be cognitive, it is a set of beliefs, it deals with what men and women are like, and it is shared by the members of a particular group.

The aspects of sex stereotypes such as sex trait stereotypes and sex role attitudes are closely linked. Sex trait stereotypes are the psychological characteristics and behavior traits (masculine and feminine) which are believed to characterize men and women. Sex role is defined in terms of activities of social significance in which the two sexes participate with differential frequency. Sex stereotypes are the product of biological and social conditioning. Socialization for the development of appropriate sex traits and roles starts from childhood and passes through the phases of adolescence and adulthood. Adolescence is a period of transition which involves changes in physiological and psychological dimensions. With growth of cognitive skill, interaction with the environment and socialization experience, the sex role behavior of adolescent children gets more strengthened. Differential socialization of the two sexes within the family, school and in wider socio-cultural set-up is perhaps the single most important contributor to sex stereotyping in children.

Boys are encouraged and reinforced to develop masculine characteristics (aggression, dominance, independence, sense of adventure and achievement-oriented) whereas girls are encouraged to acquire feminine characteristics (submissive, nurturance, dependence, less achievement-oriented). The existence of sex stereotypes have been sufficiently documented from studies on children (Williams and Best, 1982) and college students (Bem, 1974; Spence and Helmreich, 1978). Studies (Williams and Best, 1982;

Ward and Sethi, 1983; Rao and Rao, 1984) have indicated the presence of sex stereotypes among children and adults across cultures. Further, there has been evidence to show higher sex trait stereotyping among boys compared to girls (Sutton-Smith et al, 1963).

Besides sex trait stereotypes, occupations have also been sex stereotyped. Studies (Gettys and Cann, 1981; Panek, Rush and Greenwalt, 1977; Archer, 1984) have indicated sex typed preference for various occupations and activities among pre-adolescent and adolescent groups. Even among young children, boys engage themselves in gardening and outdoor play whereas girls engage in household work (Kuhn, Nash and Brucken, 1978). Children are able to classify and label different occupations for men (policeman, scientist, sports superstar) and women (teacher, nurse, housewife) appropriately (Siegel, 1973; Franken, 1983).

The sex stereotypes both traits and occupations that children and adults hold are related to a variety of biological, psychological and other environmental variables. The sex of the child (Maccoby and Jacklin, 1974) and age level (Gordon, 1975) determine its patterning. Different family variables like education of parents, socio-economic status and family size influence the development of sex role behavior. Various parental antecedents like sex of the parent (Bronson, 1959) and their characteristics like parental dominance (Hetherington, 1967), parental masculinity and femininity (Spence and Helmreich, 1978) and parental sex role attitude (Minuchin, 1965; Verma, 1981) are found to influence sex stereotypes among children. Child rearing practice (Block, 1983; Barry, Bacon and Child, 1957) and parent-child relationship (Bandura and Walters, 1963; Block, Block and Morrison, 1981) also determine children's sex role development.

From the review of literature it is clear that parents are primary socializing agents, that sex of the child is an important determiner of the kind of child-rearing practice and the particular developmental stage of the child are important in shaping the personality of young people. On the basis of the above, the following hypotheses were formulated:

1. The children—both boys and girls—of traditional families will exhibit higher sex trait stereotypes followed by children of incongruent and non-traditional families.
2. Boys and girls will exhibit greater masculinity and femininity respectively.
3. Sex trait stereotypes will increase with age. The masculinity scores of late adolescent boys will be higher than their early counterparts. Similarly, femininity scores of late adolescent girls will be higher than their early counterparts.
4. The children of traditional families will indicate higher occupational

stereotypes followed by children of incongruent and non-traditional families.

5. The occupational stereotypes of boys will be higher than girls.
6. The occupational stereotypes will increase with age. Late adolescent boys and girls will indicate higher stereotypes than their early counterparts.

Method and Procedure

Sample

A total sample of 240 families was selected from three different cities in Orissa. Each family included father, mother and their one child. All the families were matched in terms of parents' education level, income, number of adolescent children and family size. The families were divided into three types depending on parent's attitude towards women's role in society—traditional, incongruent and non-traditional. Each group consisted of 80 parents.

The sample also included children of both sexes studying in high school and junior college level. There were 40 boys and 40 girls in each family group. They were divided into early adolescents (12–14 years) and late adolescents (15–17 years) age groups. These children attended schools with similar medium of instruction, strength of students, co-education facility, and similar management structure. The purpose of selecting children from these schools was to minimize the differential impact of social agents other than the family on children's sex stereotypes.

Design

A $3 \times 2 \times 2$ factorial design with three types of families (traditional, incongruent and non-traditional parental sex role orientations), two sex groups of children (boys and girls), and two age groups (early and late adolescents) was used. The number of respondents in each cell was equal. The main purpose was to see the impact of parental sex role orientation on the sex trait stereotypes and occupational stereotypes of children.

Measuring Instruments

Parental Sex Role Orientation: An Indian adaptation (Verma, 19?1) of Hawley's Sex Role Modernity Scale was used. It consists of 35 items dealing with attitude towards women's role in society in five areas. The score varies from 35 to 175. A high score on the scale indicates traditional sex role orientation.

Sex Trait Stereotypes: The sex trait stereotypes of children were measured by Ward and Sethi's (1983) Indian adaptation of Bem's Sex Role Inventory (Bem, 1974). This is a self descriptive measure consisting of twenty masculine, twenty feminine and eighteen neutral items. The highest possible score for both masculine and feminine items could be 100 and the lowest 20. A high score on the scale for the masculine and feminine items indicates greater amount of masculine or feminine traits in the subject.

Occupational Stereotypes: The occupational stereotypes of children were measured by a list of 34 items consisting of various occupations and activities. Items were selected from occupational stereotypes scales used in different studies (Shepard and Hess, 1975; Franken, 1983). The sex stereotyping of occupational items were cross-checked with Indian data (Census of India, 1971). Twelve masculine, twelve feminine and ten neutral items were chosen for the scale. The subjects were classified as sex typed (masculine/feminine) or non-sex typed. The highest possible score was 24 and the lowest was 1. High scores indicate high occupational stereotyping.

Procedure

The data were collected from three cities, viz., Bhubaneswar, Berhampur and Rourkela which constitute central, south-east and north-west zones of Orissa respectively. A total of 12 schools and four colleges were covered. As a first step, Family Information Sheet and Sex Role Modernity Scales were attached together and distributed among the students. They were requested to give them to both their parents and return within four days. The families were divided into three types according to sex role orientation scores of parents. The scores ranged from 42 to 171, with a mean of 96.73 and SD of 10.64. The respondents (both parents) were divided into bipolar categories. Eighty couples whose scores fell between 42 to 80 were labelled as non-traditional and another 80 couples whose scores fell between 120 to 171 were labelled as traditional. Finally, the incongruent group was formed consisting of parents whose scores fell differently in either of these bipolar categories. Out of 618 families surveyed, 240 were selected for the present study. All the non-Oriya parents were dropped to make it a unicultural sample.

The sex trait stereotypes and occupational stereotypes scales were distributed at school to children of these three family groups. The two scales were attached together and given to all children with proper verbal instructions. They were asked to return them within 5 days.

Results

Data were analyzed using a three factor analysis of variance (ANOVA). The sex trait stereotypes results indicated a significant family type effect

(F = 4.30, P <.05), sex of the child effect (F = 123.34, P <.01) and a significant family type into sex of the child interaction effect on masculinity test scores (Table 1). A significant family type effect (F = 4.58, P <.05), sex of the child effect (F = 149.34, P <.01) and a significant family type and sex of the child interaction effect (F = 12.52, P <.01) on femininity test scores was also found (Table 2). Results presented in Table 3 show that the children of traditional families showed greater discrepancy while describing themselves in masculine and feminine terms whereas children of non-traditional families were closer to each other in their self descriptions. The scores of children of incongruent families fell in between. The mean masculinity scores was highest for children of non-traditional families. This was due to the high masculinity scores of girls of non-traditional and incongruent families. Similarly, the mean femininity scores was highest for children of non-traditional families followed by incongruent and traditional families because of increased femininity scores of boys of non-traditional and incongruent families.

Table 1
A SUMMARY OF ANOVA ON MASCULINITY TEST SCORES

Source of variance	DF	F
A (Type of Families)	2	4.30*
B (Sex of the child)	1	123.34**
C (Age of the child)	1	0.39
AB	2	19.17*
AC	2	0.28
BC	1	1.43
ABC	2	0.22
within cell (error)	228	0.29
*P <.05	**P <.01	

Table 2
A SUMMARY OF ANOVA ON FEMININITY TEST SCORES

Source of variance	DF	F
A (Type of families)	2	4.58*
B (Sex of the child)	1	149.34**
C (Age of the child)	1	0.04
AB	2	12.52**
AC	2	0.26
BC	1	1.42
ABC	2	0.14
within cell (error)	228	0.23
*P <.05	**P <.01	

Boys' mean masculinity scores was highest in traditional families followed by incongruent and non-traditional families. Similar pattern was noticed for girls' mean femininity scores of the three families. The mean masculinity scores of boys were found to be higher than girls across the three families. Similarly, mean femininity scores of girls were found to be higher than boys across these families (Table 3).

Table 3
MEANS OF MASCULINITY AND FEMININITY SCORES
OF TWO SEX GROUPS OF CHILDREN
FROM THREE DIFFERENT FAMILIES

Sex	Traditional	Incongruent	Non-traditional	Total
Mas. Boys	86.8	79.07	75.27	80.38
Girls	33.52	47.92	65.07	48.83
Total masculinity scores	**60.16**	**63.49**	**70.17**	**64.60**
Fem. Boys	30.15	43.82	60.07	44.68
Girls	86.47	80.4	78.92	81.93
Total femininity scores	**58.31**	**62.11**	**69.49**	**63.30**

Table 4
MEANS OF MASCULINITY AND FEMININITY SCORES
OF TWO SEX AND AGE GROUPS OF CHILDREN
FROM THREE DIFFERENT FAMILIES

	Boys		Girls	
	Masculinity	Femininity	Masculinity	Femininity
Early adolescents	77.8	46.21	48.2	79.95
Late adolescents	82.91	43.15	46.15	84.08
Total	80.35	44.68	48.83	81.93

The effect of the age of children was not significant. Nevertheless there was a trend of masculinity and femininity scores of late adolescent boys and girls respectively to be slightly higher than their early counterparts. Whereas the mean masculinity and femininity scores of late adolescent girls and boys respectively was slightly lower than their early counterparts.

For occupational stereotypes, results indicated a significant family type effect ($F = 57.74$, $P < .01$), sex of the child effect ($F = 27.94$, $P < .01$) and a significant family type and sex of the child interaction effect ($F = 5.06$, $P < .01$) (Table 5). The children of traditional families exhibited greater occupational stereotypes followed by children in incongruent and non-traditional families. Boys' mean occupational stereotype scores were found to be higher than girls' across the three families. The mean occupational stereotype scores of boys was highest in traditional families followed by incongruent and non-traditional families. Similar trend was found for girl's mean scores (Table 6). While there was a trend for late adolescent boys and girls to show higher occupational stereotyping than their early counterparts, the increase was not significant (Table 7).

Table 5
A SUMMARY OF ANOVA ON OCCUPATIONAL STEREOTYPES

Source of variance	DF	F
A (Type of families)	2	57.74**
B (Sex of the child)	1	27.94**
C (Age of the child)	1	3.10
AB	2	5.06*
AC	2	0.0
BC	1	0.08
ABC	2	0.0
within cell (error)	228	0.36
*p <.05	**P <.01	

Table 6
MEANS OF OCCUPATIONAL STEREOTYPE SCORES
OF TWO SEX GROUPS OF CHILDREN
FROM THREE DIFFERENT FAMILIES

	Traditional	Incongruent	Non-Traditional	Total
Boys	23.30	20.89	17.50	20.56
Girls	22.80	16.13	13.65	17.54
Total	23.07	18.51	15.57	19.05

Table 7
MEANS OF OCCUPATIONAL STEREOTYPE SCORES
OF TWO SEX AND AGE GROUPS OF CHILDREN

	Boys	Girls	Total
Early adolescents	20.44	16.94	18.69
Late adolescents	21.01	18.11	19.56
Total	20.72	17.52	19.12

Discussion

The results are discussed under the following two headings:
1. Sex trait stereotypes (Masculinity/Femininity)
2. Occupational stereotypes.

Sex Trait Stereotypes

The results will be discussed in the context of framed hypotheses. The hypothesis that children of traditional families will exhibit higher sex trait stereotypes, i.e., boys and girls of traditional families will exhibit higher masculinity and femininity scores respectively, followed by incongruent and non-traditional families was confirmed (Table 3). A liberal attitude towards women's role in society on the part of non-traditional parents gets transmitted to the children. This transmission can occur in a variety of ways.

There is evidence to show a close relationship between given sex role orientation and certain personality characteristics. Modern or egalitarian sex role orientation is found to be positively related to greater autonomy, achievement, whereas negatively to succorance, social recognition and dominance (King and King, 1985; Greenberg and Zeldow, 1977). Traditional sex role attitude is found to be significantly related to perceiving larger personality differences between the two sexes (Spence and Helmreich, 1978). Thus parents with a given sex role orientation are expected to display these personality characteristics. They become role models for the children who emulate similar personality characteristics from childhood through observation learning, imitation and mechanisms of identification (Bandura and Walters, 1963).

In a study of overall modernity syndrome in six developing countries including India, Inkles and Smith (1974) have identified several dimensions of an overall modern person. These dimensions are, for example, openness to new experience, readiness for social change, interest in acquisition of relevant information, proper time orientation, sense of efficacy and finally a liberal sex role orientation. They even found a high and consistent correlation among these dimensions. Krishnamurthy (1987) used the Indian adaptation of overall modernity scale on college students and found a close association between modernity and persuability. Persuability reflects one's tendency to entertain and accept new ideas and thereby oppose the traditional value orientation. Hence it can be argued that non-traditional families are displaying other characteristics of overall modernity. Given this kind of outlook, non-traditional parents in the sample have encouraged their children to incorporate both masculine and feminine qualities. It supports earlier findings (Ketty and Worell, 1976) where parental emphasis on non-stereotypic aspects of personality (intellectual interests for daughters and warmth for sons) were important determinants of children's androgyny. These androgynous children will be more flexible in their sex roles as adult which will help them to adapt to a rapidly changing society. Bem (1975) also has noticed greater adaptability of androgynous students.

Studies (Germaine, 1975; Donaldson and Nichols, 1978) have shown other correlates of sex role modernity like reduced fertility, late marriage and overall family size. Moreover, the emphasis on cognitive consistency (Newcomb, 1956) do provide further support for the given sex role ideology and its related attitudes and behavior. Traditional and non-traditional sex role orientation of parents thus account for children's stereotypic or flexible personality traits respectively.

The socialization practice is also found to be related to given parental sex role attitude (Verma, 1981; Das, 1986). As expected mothers with modern sex role attitude treat their sons and daughters less differentially through encouraging them for independence and achievement compared to their traditional counterparts (Verma, 1981). Similarly non-traditional parents are found to emphasize both masculine (independence) and feminine (nurturance) qualities among their children compared to their incongruent and traditional counterparts (Das, 1986). This suggests that less sex differentiated socialization practice of non-traditional parents fosters less sex trait stereotypes among their children. In contrast, the distinct sex differentiated socialization practice of traditional parents facilitate children's greater sex trait stereotypes.

The hypothesis that boys and girls will exhibit greater masculinity and femininity respectively was confirmed (Table 3). Studies (Bem, 1974; Williams and Best, 1982) on children and adults indicate more masculine traits (instrumental, independent, aggressive, dominant, adventurous) among boys and feminine traits (expressive, submissive, dependent, emotional, affectionate) among girls.

It can be argued that acquisition of sex appropriate personality characteristics among children reflects their conformity to societal norms and conventions as deviation from these norms leads to negative consequences (Deaux, 1976).

According to social learning theorists (Bandura and Walters, 1963) children acquire the stereotypes relating to masculine and feminine personality as a result of their identification with same sex parental model. This identification is facilitated as a result of selective reinforcement.

Sex differential child-rearing practice of parents (Barry, Bacon and Child, 1957; Das 1986) and similar socialization pressure from other agents like teachers (Serbin et. al., 1973), peers (Hartup, 1983) and media (Kalia, 1979) further strengthen the acquisition of sex appropriate behavior.

Cognitive developmental theory has emphasized children's cognitive skill like awareness of gender identity, stability permanence and consistent self-categorization which guides the perception of gender stereotypes and consequent development of gender attributes (Kohlberg, 1966). According to Bem's (1981) gender schema theory sex typing occurs because of the growth and readiness of cognitive structure. It helps both sexes to encode and organize information regarding culturally prescribed sex roles and thereby assimilate them into their self-concept.

The present study also indicates the significant interaction effect of family type and sex of child on sex trait stereotypes. The wide difference between the masculinity and femininity scores of children from traditional families shows their greater discrepancy or stereotyping which gradually narrows down in incongruent and non-traditional families. The narrowing of this difference may be due to their emphasis on balancing both masculine and feminine characteristics. Higher masculinity scores of girls in non-traditional families compared to femininity of boys indicate the higher value and status associated with masculine qualities. In addition sex reversed qualities among girls are tolerated to some extent whereas boys reject opposite sex behavior (Bussey and Perry, 1982).

Occupational Stereotypes

The hypothesis that children of traditional families will exhibit higher occupational stereotypes followed by incongruent and non-traditional families was supported (Table 6). Parental sex role attitudes not only influence children's sex trait stereotypes but also determine their perception of different occupations and activities.

Sex role orientation is closely related to the perception of sex appropriateness of various activities and occupations. Traditional sex role attitude adheres to rigid differentiation of labor on the basis of sex. For example, in traditional families the father is the breadwinner and the mother performs a purely domestic role. However, studies (Burlew, 1982; Tangri, 1972) have identified a close association between a liberal sex role orientation on the one hand and pursuit of higher education, career salience, choice of male dominated disciplines and occupations along with acceptance of traditional role responsibilities among women. Sex role liberal men have been found to be more willing to permit their wives to work than traditional men (Ghadially and Kazi, 1980). Men with working wives are more likely to participate in child care and household tasks (Pleck, 1981). As a result of this, children in traditional homes are conveyed the idea that certain activities or tasks are done by members of one sex and a different set of tasks or chores are executed by members of the other sex. Children in non-traditional homes on the other hand are witness to juggling of activities and tasks between parents and no particular task thereby gets identified with any one sex. This perception of sex linked task or lack of it evidently gets extended to a wider variety of jobs and occupations in society and hence the greater stereotypy of children of traditional families compared to non-traditional ones.

Studies (Young, 1984; O'Neil, 1981) have indicated a close association between personality traits (masculinity/femininity) and choice of jobs or occupations. The feminine jobs usually call for qualities like nurturance, helping others, interpersonal skill whereas occupations labelled as masculine require autonomy, competition, leadership etc. Children in traditional families as noted earlier, describe themselves in sex stereotyped terms whereas children of non-traditional families have incorporated both masculine and feminine characteristics. As a result, children from traditional families see some occupations as suited for females and others suited for males whereas children from non-traditional families see both the sexes suited for any job. Closely related to this idea is the finding (Lemaku, 1983) that females in non-traditional professions display higher masculine traits whereas women in traditionally female dominated occupations show more feminine traits. Hence girls of non-traditional families will perceive any occupation as suited to them whereas girls of traditional families will perceive jobs as sex-linked.

The relationship between sex role attitude and personality traits of individuals have been established. Men and women with traditional sex role attitude are more likely to be masculine and feminine respectively. Whereas those with non-traditional attitudes are likely to be androgynous in nature (Spence and Helmreich, 1978). Repetti (1984) has noted that mother's femininity and father's masculinity are strongly associated with their children's sex stereotyping of occupations and toys. Thus it can be argued that greater stereotypes will be reflected in the perception of occupational roles among children of traditional families compared to their counterparts from incongruent and non-traditional families.

The hypothesis that the occupational stereotypes of boys will be higher than girls was also confirmed (Table 7). While both the sexes have been found to show occupational stereotypes (Siegel, 1973), greater occupational stereotypes have been noticed among boys compared to girls (Franken, 1983). It can be explained by referring to the greater status and value attached to male roles as well as greater socialization pressure on boys to reject opposite sex behavior (Feinman, 1981; Macoby and Jacklin, 1974). Parents tolerate 'tomboyish' behavior among girls whereas reject 'sissy' behavior among boys. As a result of which girls adopt more flexible perception regarding variety of occupations they can engage in.

Family type and sex of child also show their significant interaction effect on children's occupational stereotypes. It supports the earlier explanation regarding socialization style of traditional and non-traditional families. Boys and girls of traditional families are strictly disciplined for their distinct sex appropriate tasks whereas non-traditional parents reinforce them to adopt occupations irrespective of its sex appropriateness rather to display the required potentialities. Therefore occupational stereotypes are more prevalent in traditional group which has gradually decreased in incongruent and non-traditional families.

The hypothesis that sex-trait stereotypes and occupation stereotypes will increase with age i.e., late adolescent boys and girls will indicate higher stereotypes than their early counterparts was not confirmed (Tables 1, 2, 5). However, the trend was in the expected direction (Tables 4, 7). The emergence of only a trend and lack of a significant finding may be due to several factors. The two adolescent phases in the sample were too close in time to permit the emergence of significant development in a short time. The examination of more discrete and temporally apart age groups would show the change more distinctly. Besides, sex role learning is comparable to the phases of virtually any kind of learning where initial growth rate, i.e., gains in development is greater in earlier stages and the learning curve stabilizes at later ages.

While parents still regulate and monitor children's behavior in sex-appropriate direction, the intensity of it is considerably reduced compared to the earlier periods. During adolescence, the impact of school, peers and the mass media is also important in shaping behaviors. However, it appears that the role of these socializing agents is to fortify further what has already been learnt at home.

Overall results indicate that parental beliefs and attitudes regarding women's role in society appear to be crucial in shaping the personality structure of children. Modern parental outlook and egalitarian sex role attitude is conducive to the development of androgynous adults, and in contrast, conservative attitude results in stereotyping. The findings from incongruent families show that even modernity of one of the parents, irrespective of gender, contributes in the decrease of sex stereotyping of the children. It is interesting to mark the acculturation of flexibility among incongruent and non-traditional parents in their socialization pattern. In conclusion, the greater preference for masculine traits and occupations among both boys and girls suggests the need to reconsider the importance of feminine traits and values of our culture, so that boys can be encouraged to assimilate those traits in their personality configuration and become androgynous persons.

THE CONCEPTS OF 'FEMININITY' AND 'LIBERATION' IN THE CONTEXT OF CHANGING SEX ROLES: WOMEN IN MODERN INDIA AND AMERICA

Manisha Roy

The theoretical assumption underlying this comparative analysis is that women in every society are socialized and enculturated toward a set of roles. However, the roles are not always amenable to change over time. Some institutions which function as socializing agents change at different paces. Some lag behind, clashing with the values of other faster moving institutions. Many women in both modern India[1] and America find themselves caught in this unbalanced situation. When this occurs they must make compromises between the economic, social and familial demands on them and their personal aspirations. Some cultures offer less scope for such compromise than others and the source of this difference can be found in the sociocultural history of a society and in the pattern of female socialization for adulthood. Change in roles within the milieu of each culture, changes within that culture and the many factors influencing any given individual have been rendered somewhat controllable by focusing on only two crucial concepts in the role change of modern woman in two countries, India and America.

The two concepts—'femininity' and 'liberation' (or freedom)—were used as a heuristic device to contrast differences and effects in the social-ization process of women in these two cultures, and to show the deep-seated and far-reaching implications in various sociological, economic and psychological aspects of women's roles. It is suggested that the values and ideologies expressed in language and its connotative usage have a reci-procal and enduring impact on human behavior and thought on both cognitive and affective levels. Thus, cultural notions such as 'femininity' or 'masculinity' or 'individualism' contribute toward the formation of an

---

[1] Although the Indian data used in this paper came from one particular state, Bengal, the premises and conclusions made in this study overlap greatly with those of other parts of India. I wish to thank Gunhild Bisztray of University of Chicago for a very encouraging discussion and help on the library research leading to formulating my ideas in this paper.

individual's self-image. This is especially true in the case of the self-conscious, literate, middle classes of the cultures described here.

As we will see below, the use of these value concepts helps clarify a number of puzzles encountered by both Western and Indian observers. My intimate contact for a decade with American culture as an anthropologist and an Indian woman and my lifelong contact with my own culture has led me to believe that these concepts are valuable indicators, operators and predictors in the realm of women's roles in both private and public arenas.

Methods and Data

The observations, analysis and conclusions reached in this study are based on field work in urban West Bengal and urban Southern California between 1965 and 1970. The socioeconomic group spanned the broad category of the middle class with a Hindu literate cultural background in Bengal and a white Judeo-Christian literate background (at least four years of college education) in California. In addition to the anthropological method of participant observation plus both unstructured and structured interviews, I used a number of published materials in sociology, psychology and literature. In the case of both cultures so-called soft data offered by literature, and mass media of various kinds formed a larger part of the background material. Though often fictionalized and exaggerated, the radio, television and the popular journals have been extremely valuable supplementary sources of information in this research. The age of the women studied ranged from 5 to 70, with the majority around 30. I also interviewed men although my primary concern was with women.

Concepts

Let us delimit the cultural meaning and connotation of the concepts of 'femininity',[2] liberation and freedom first for the Indian culture and then for America. In Bengali the term 'femininity' has none of the implied connotations that the Sanskrit word *naritva* has, such as the ideal feminine virtues of docility, obedience, self-sacrifice, etc. The qualities are desirable

---

[2] The term in classical Sanskrit that comes closest to the lexical meaning of the English term 'femininity' is *naritva* a compound of *nari* (woman) + *tva* (a suffix meaning 'the content of', 'related to'). The word has an ideal connotation and is often used in formal writing or speeches to refer to Indian womanhood. The etymological meaning (related to women) mentioned above is nearly lost in common usage. In modern Bengali, this term is hardly used to refer to woman. The Bengali word (common usage) 'femininity' is *meyeli*, a compound of *meye* (girl, daughter or woman) + *li* (a case ending for adjectives meaning 'related to', 'in connection with'). In real usage the word is used either to mean 'effeminate' (pejorative when referred to a male) or feminine in a very neutral sense such as *meyeli* clothes, *meyeli* jewelry, *meyeli* talk and so on.

in a women but not oppositional, that is, feminine versus masculine. This lack of opposition between masculine and feminine attributes contrasts strongly with the American meaning of 'femininity' with the implicit 'non-masculine' emphasis.

Further, in Bengal, a woman is not more desirable or admirable because she is more especially feminine. She is not more or less feminine. She is feminine simply by virtue of being a woman. Once a woman, she may be more or less gentle or demure even as she may be more or less pretty, taller or shorter. Some of these qualities are as desirable and becoming in men as they are in women depending on a man's role or the context of his behavior. Therefore, the concept *meyeli* (feminine) does not embody a set of attributes which constitutes a clearcut identity connected only with a female and desirable in the eyes of men and the society at large as occurs in America.

In India a woman's femininity does not depend on her ability to attract the opposite sex with sexual and personality factors determined by male standards (Roy, 1975a). In other words, the physical attributes designed to attract the male do not constitute a major part in the cultural definition of femininity. What is stressed are indicators/signs (*lakshan*)—both physical and mental, which indicate that she will successfully play out her future female roles. Hence a prospective bride is evaluated on indicators which promise the successful fulfillment of the daughter-in-law, wife and mother roles. What makes a woman feminine and attractive depends on what point she is in her life-cycle and how well she is playing her roles. A little girl is attractive because she plays her role of daughter and of sibling ably. A young woman is attractive because she is an able wife and daughter-in-law (sister, sister-in-law, etc.), a good neighbour and friend of both sexes.

The implications of such cultural notions are clear. The behavioral adjuncts change with changing roles and age. So loss of specific physical attributes that occur as one ages is not threatening to women. Parenthetically it might be valuable to mention that the concept of femininity just outlined is somewhat changing in urban India where the model of a woman is beginning to be a mixture of movie star, novel heroine and westernized city woman. However, the majority of Bengali population (even men) has not yet integrated these modern western notions sufficiently to support the emergence of such ideas (Roy, 1973). A modern woman tries to strike a compromise by compartmentalizing[3] her 'modern role'

---

[3] Milton B. Singer (1972) first used this term in the context of Indian cultural change to demonstrate how compartmentalization is used as an adaptive strategy to cope with the incongruity that may be generated by simultaneous 'traditional' and 'modern' practices. An actor achieves a compartmentalization of two spheres of conduct and belief that would otherwise collide. The shift between the two may be symbolized by shift in clothes, language and even behavior which two or more settings may demand.

from her 'traditional roles'. For example, a female physician may behave very much like a masculine woman (in the American sense) in her clinic and swing back to a 'feminine wife' or a 'daughter-in-law' at home as she changes from her work clothes to her domestic sari.

A further behavior, aggressiveness (as expressive of independent thinking and behavior) is used in America today as a negative attribute when applied to women. It seems as if the American concept of femininity in both the traditional and modern senses excludes such attributes as 'aggressiveness', because it is a masculine trait. Aggressiveness is quite acceptable in a Bengali woman, provided her particular role calls for it. For example, a woman over forty who is a matron-mother may rule over her children, her husband and even her neighbors and still not be called aggressive or a 'bossy female'. She is allowed this seemingly 'unfeminine' behavior because she has reached a status in her life-cycle where this is acceptable. A young woman can act aggressively provided she is socially clever and capable of using the right symbols and expressions to assert her authority in the right context. *What really matters in Indian society is how well a woman acts out her role(s) vis-a-vis other roles in a given context.* And she is socialized by her family to acquire cues for relevant behaviors and the culture supports and reinforces such behaviors. Socialization and ideology seem to be in harmony.

The roles a woman is socialized into are mostly ascribed roles determined by birth or marriage. Thus her self-concept is framed in the context of her roles. She is not a person if she is stripped of her roles. Her personal gratification or frustrations are also connected with her role as daughter, wife, mother or grandmother, rather than as woman. If she is unhappy, she tries to find explanations in her actions and behavior, in her roles or in things over which she has little control. She is not encouraged to delve into her own psyche or to have self-doubts. This is possible because the Indian culture offers less confusion between role-expectations and the real contexts of behavior. Even in a somewhat changing socio-economic scene a woman can count on cues from her traditional roles to help her combine behavioral and affective contents. For instance, she can extend the role patterns of behavior rather than create new ones, as when a woman treats her male office colleagues as she would her male cousins. In Bengali society, cousins cover a range of various emotional components and, since the nature of modern roles themselves is fluid, such extensions are feasible and often necessary.[4]

The discontinuities in cultural conditioning that Ruth Benedict talked about seem to appear more often in America that in India. For example,

---

[4] I discuss this aspect of role-overlap and compositeness within a Bengali family in another paper (Roy 1973).

in modern America a married woman is ascribed a number of roles, each role implying certain privileges and obligations. Conflict may arise if a woman claims the privileges of more than one role without accepting the corresponding obligations, which her early socialization may not have included.

An example from my field notes indicates how a Bengali woman may visualize herself in her roles. A woman of forty relates the following:

At the age of forty, looking back, I often try to think how my life has been. I was born in a happy family with my father and uncles always spoiling me. When I did well in my school work, my grandmother always warned me not to do too well, because the books would not tell me how to be a good daughter-in-law and a mother. She meant I would be a lot better off if I paid heed to her and watched other women do their duties. I felt like rebelling at that time. But when my family began to negotiate for my marriage at the age of 19, even before I finished my B.A., I did not rebel and in fact I even welcomed the idea of getting married.

For the first five years of marriage I used to feel very home-sick for my father's house. I felt frustrated with my husband. Gradually I became close to my husband's family and began to sympathize even with my husband. In a big household he could not possibly pay much attention to me. Then I discovered compensations in marriage. I was so delighted for example, to have my first son. He took me away from everything including my husband for about 5–6 years. He filled my life. Only then I began to understand what my grandmother used to mean . . . Yes, I missed my friends and my cousins and those carefree days of my school and college; but this is life and I would not like to go back to those days anymore.

Of course, life does not go on the same way always. I was very unhappy when my son had to go to England for his higher studies; I felt my whole life was empty. But I adjusted to the situation. At least I had a son. What could I have done without one? I know gradually he will go even further away. He will marry and, who knows, perhaps his wife would not like the idea of staying with us. Suppose he marries an English girl! I think of all this. But then I am getting old and it is good for me to think of Him, the God, and get involved in puja and meditation. Ten years ago I used to laugh at this suggestion, now I see why my widowed aunt spends seven or eight hours in her puja room . . . No, I do not have regrets. God gave me a husband who is alive and a son who is good and respectable. What else should a woman need?

Or, to quote from the life history of a 50 year old articulate and sensitive informant:

> I am beginning to think at the age of 50 that something is wrong with life itself. We plan to be happy and do all sorts of things that our mothers and grandmothers and fathers taught us. I tried my best to be a good wife, a daughter-in-law and a good mother. I enjoyed doing it most of the time but often I felt tired and did not see much point in anything. I found out, for example, that my son no matter how much he loved me would go away someday and would love his wife. This is the way life is. But this knowledge could not make me accept it totally. I am often convinced that we women are born to suffer.

These two views are not that much in contrast with the attitude of a 30 year old modern woman, a college professor who is also married and has three young children:

> Well, there are moments when I wonder about what I really wanted and what happened to me. But then, who can plan about life? In a sense, I ought to feel quite happy and smug compared to my classmates. At least I have a good job in a respectable college with a principal as a boss who is not impossible to get along with. At home, I must admit, my mother-in-law is quite understanding about the time I spend outside home. Because she knows that unless I add to the family income, things are going to be difficult. Also, I have a feeling she prefers that I am not around all the time. She can feel important in her son's household and do things she likes such as bossing the maids around. Besides, the children love her. That solves the babysitting problem. As for my husband, frankly, I don't have time to worry about him. During the first years of our marriage I used to grumble about his frequent business trips and his apparent neglect of me and the family. Now I think it's even good not to have him around that much. We meet everyday but hardly have time to be close or intimate. He is a kind and distant person. And I feel proud that I have a husband who allows me to work and does not demand much. Considering all, I have to say that life could be worse.

All these women seem to express the common theme that none of them is confused as to their roles nor would they consider stepping out of their present role(s)—which in India means stepping out of life. They all accept the pain and the plan of life as given and as resulting from a combination of uncontrollable factors. By the same token they also have experienced occasional happiness and satisfaction, again resulting from a combination of factors not necessarily under their control.

A series of published sociological studies explore the current sex role stereotypes and self-concepts of college students in America. Findings from the first research (Broverman et al., 1968) show that 74 male and 80 female college students indicated more frequent high valuation of stereotypically masculine than feminine characteristics. Among some bipolar items the positively valued masculine traits formed a cluster of related behaviors which entail competence, rationality, assertion, independence. The feminine traits formed a cluster of related behavior entailing submissiveness, warmth, expressiveness, dependence, impulsiveness, minimum logic, etc. The results from another research conducted by the same team in 1972 showed similar notions still persist. For example, responses to the sex role questionnaire from 599 men and 383 women showed that stereotyped masculine characteristics are still valued more than the stereotyped feminine characteristics.

Since feminine traits are negatively valued it would follow that women tend to have more negative self-concepts than do men. A woman is faced with a contradiction. Since having masculine traits is more desirable in this culture, if she wishes to be feminine she risks being an inferior human being. On the other hand, if she adopts the desirable masculine traits in order to become more acceptable, she gives up being the socially sanctioned 'nice feminine woman' which may damage her self-image. This double-bond partially results from a notion of 'femininity' based on traits and attributes which reflect the demands of an industrial economy which values competition rather than the emotional needs of an individual. Further, this concept of 'femininity' fosters ambivalence and an increasing polarization between the two concepts masculinity and femininity, yielding a hostile sex-struggle in personal as well as public spheres of male-female interaction.[5] Bengali culture has not as yet developed indigenous symbols to express a changed attitude about the concept of 'femininity' among the youth, as appears to be the case in contemporary middle class America.

Data collected in 1942 and 1943 (Komarovsky, 1946) of 153 undergraduate students showed that while there were a number of permissive variants of the feminine attributes for women of college age (such as being

[5] Findings from Broverman, et al. (1970) do not show any indications to support the current belief that such polarization is being reduced, at least among the youth of the university campuses. The rhetoric on the campuses stressing a neutral attitude toward homosexual/lesbian movements may not reflect the attitudes of the wider culture as much as the wishful thinking of small groups of individuals. The effect of the clothes and hairstyle of today's youth tends to blur the male-female distinction.

good sport, glamour girl) they always were expressed with reference to the male sex-role. As a school girl, a woman may have been encouraged to compete with boys intellectually, but from adolescence on she was expected to underplay her intellectual ability—a decisively masculine trait—and prepare herself to be more feminine and consequently attractive to men. This conflict between two types of sex-roles that women were encouraged to internalize may clash with educational roles as well as family roles. Whereas in early childhood a girl is encouraged to prepare herself for a desexualized modern role, in college she is definitely discouraged from doing so. The goals set by each role are mutually exclusive and the fundamental personality traits each evokes are diametrically opposed.

One significant side effect of such contradictory socialization is expressed very aptly by Jessie Bernard in her study *American Family Behavior* (1942). She points out that women after marriage often discover the fallacy of the sex stereotypes. They also discover that their husband, the sturdy American male, often cuts an inferior figure in intimate, inter-personal relations and familial crisis situations. These discoveries are doubly traumatic, for as a wife, a woman cannot express these feelings to others. As a consequence she either learns to delude herself perpetually into an acceptable inferior status of wife or falls into another pattern of behavior of babying the husband—an inversion of the cultural stereotype. A third alternative is to face her situation and run the risk of breaking a marriage (which is also culturally not acceptable).

I was studying both men and women in southern California during the summer of 1970, at various stages of the dissolution of their marriages. Some of the autobiographical data illustrates the problem of socialization mentioned above. Many informants perceived their childhood and adolescence socialization as directly connected with their marital maladjustments. One woman, aged 32, with a B.A. degree from a well-known midwestern university, born of white Protestant parents related the following:

When I was five or six my mother told me many times that I had to play with certain kinds of toys and behave like a little lady. I was given toys which looked like miniature kitchen and bedroom stuff. I often played with the girls next door and we imitated our mothers in our games, mostly doing housework. By the time I went to school my first IQ test indicated that I was far above average in intelligence and my parents made a big thing out of it. I was encouraged to read a lot and do well in Maths and Science. When I was 14 or 15, unlike many of my friends' mothers, my mother did not seem to bother too much over my dating situation. I grew up without much emphasis on clothes, cosmetics, etc. I went out with my dad a lot watching baseball games . . . . I went to a college away from my home town and that's where for the first time I faced difficulty with my self-image as a girl. I was doing well at school winning scholarships from the very beginning, but suddenly the whole atmosphere made me aware that doing well at school was not enough. My dorm friends constantly talked about boys and sex and future marriage. A few of my friends from high school still corresponded with me and we all agreed that we would like to go for graduate school and never get married. None of us except one, whose mother was a community college professor, got direct encouragement from home. With my parents, it was odd; because they never said anything one way or the other, except for my mother, who began to write letters to me in my junior year, the main theme of which was consistently the same advice regarding making myself more attractive to boys. I hardly ever dated till my junior year. I met my future husband one Saturday evening in the library; he told me he was impressed by my seriousness. My husband was in his second year of graduate school in physics when we got married and despite my desire to go to graduate school I decided to take up a job so that we could settle down and have a little extra. We both agreed that I would go back to school after he finished his Ph.D. After two years I became pregnant with our first child—not an unplanned one. I wanted to be a mother at that time. We had two other sons within the next four years. My rationale was that once I had them all, I could go back to school when they grew up fast. When my third son was a year old we moved to California with a better job for my husband. Meanwhile I stopped working. I noticed my husband did not mind my being a fulltime housewife and mother at all. We began to drift apart. In his new job he hardly had time to do anything with me or the family. I began to feel very weary and hemmed in. I loved my kids, yet I felt as if I had to get out. I was not quite sure what bothered me most. I felt cheated. The worst thing was that my husband did not understand it at all. He accused me of being too much of an intellectual. We began to argue a lot, and then fight and gradually life together became unbearable . . . Suddenly I realized I should not have been married. I felt I was married to a stranger and I appeared a stranger to myself. I craved to go back to my third year of college and do it all over again. I wish I were free to do what I wished—anything, something else, I do not quite know what.

This woman's statement shows the results of a process of conflicting socialization and indicates an awareness of a very crucial notion of self consciousness and a sense of lack of freedom. When real life experience cannot feed into the positive self-image of a woman she begins to feel hemmed in. The need for 'liberation' or 'freedom' is also very intricately and subtly connected with a woman's identity as a female and the cultural image of femininity.

In the rapidly changing technological world of America, change in life style also precipitates change in values and ideas. However, achievement in technology and science does not necessarily mean freedom of choice in personal life, although it does mean a greater choice in the availability of certain roles. But, although the western industrial revolution, by increasing the productive capacity has brought material comfort within the reach of the majority, the process through which this has been achieved has generated tensions and frictions.

Human beings in a technological civilization often live in a state of isolation. Many values take on meanings predominantly in economic terms. The individual's consciousness of freedom appears to be confined at a level of economic consumption and there is a lack of cognizance of the individual's innate potential. The very promise of individual freedom that one expects from technological progress becomes subverted by its own vicious circle of progress and material gain at the cost of individual psychic sacrifice. This predicament is visible in many aspects of the rising consciousness among women.

For over a century, since the beginning of the industrial revolution, women's routine work at home formed the infrastructure of the modern industrial economy. They have also become the most flexible and vulnerable group of consumers induced by advertisement to react not only to goods but also to education and even such intangibles as a new brand of 'love' (Henry, 1963). Values emanating from such a life-style often clash with the new inner aspirations and psychic needs of women. When she talks of liberation an American woman is perhaps craving for a liberation which may be available to her Indian counterpart despite and perhaps because of an underdeveloped economy where there is less freedom of choice but also less conflict. Roiphe (1973) in her review of the television series *An American Family*, a candid production of an American family over seven months, poignantly says:

I feel badly that I can do so few things for myself with my own hands, that I am a consumer and my children, like me, buy before they build. I have no household goods, or any other kind, to keep me civilized, and . . . I feel often as if I have been set too free. Culture, if it means anything, must mean the binding of the individual into the social fabric. My threads are all undone . . .

I wish we could return to an earlier America when society surrounded its members with a tight sense of belonging, of being needed. Maybe it's better to be . . . tribal and ethnocentric than urbane and adrift.

However, one must remember that even the concept of liberation varies according to the socioeconomic, educational and cultural backgrounds. When an upper-middle class housewife is hemmed in by her home and successful husband, her lower class counterpart in the slum aspires for the same comfort which will liberate her from her hand-to-mouth existence. At the same time, the middle class, university educated self-conscious woman is fighting for her liberation against discrimination in a job market on the one hand, and against her own internal conflict regarding her self-image, on the other.

Conclusion

The crux of the problem presented above, then, is to show a need for a compromise between individual needs (both psychic and intellectual) and social needs. It seems, in Bengali society, that such a compromise is offered by minimizing the possibility of the development of a self-conscious personality among women. This is done by making the self-image of a woman coincide with socially prescribed and culturally supported roles. In America, on the other hand, the conflict between socially prescribed roles and individual self-image is becoming sharper as more women and men are trying to release themselves from previously defined social roles.

By drawing data and observation from two very different cultures, I am not suggesting one is better than the other. Comparison, a bias of a social analyst, is desirable only because it highlights the problems. While I try to remain an 'objective' analyst, in understanding some problems with which modern women struggle, I close this paper with a very subjective notion. I strongly believe that there is nothing teleological or inevitable about the predicament that modern women face today. Despite all the historical and economic antecedents, individuals are free to change the course of history. Thus, I am convinced women will achieve the goal of liberation that their inner beings are craving for, if they understand the situation in proper perspective, and act.

Rejoinder

Since the writing of this article in 1975 women's lives in terms of role choices have changed considerably in America and to some extent in middle and upper-class India. The struggle for economic and social equality through the Women's Liberation Movement began to bear fruit in the eighties when employment of women, including some high positions, exceeded that of half of the population for the first time. Has this economic success, along with wider role choices contributed to a better self-image for women? What seemed the primary goal in the seventies was achieved at a high emotional price. So-called masculine traits such as competitive skills and the commitment to success may not help the professionally successful women to become emotionally satisfied. Commitment and emotional security from caring and loving relationships seem to clash with the commitment to professional success. Increasing overlap of man's and woman's roles both outside and in the home began to create a new confusion regarding the definition of masculinity and femininity. Acquiring so-called masculine traits of aggressiveness and competitiveness is not guaranteeing improved self-image in the long run. Feeling good about being a woman has become very complex during this decade (Marshall, 1984).

The changes in Indian urban middle class may be comparable to the American situation of the seventies. Indian women in this class are questioning their traditional roles of dependence on men and unsatisfactory social and cultural ideals. Compartmentalization is less successful due to certain structural changes in the family and the increased economic struggle. The rate of divorce in Indian cities during the last decade indicates, among other things, women's need to be free of the dependence on marriage. Obviously some of the traditional roles are failing to offer a satisfactory self-image for some women. The concept of femininity, as it has been defined in this paper, may not be fully applicable to the westernized conscious women of the urban middle class. However, ideas and values do not change in India as rapidly as they may appear to change in America, where the swings of the pendulum seem to always bring back the past values even if for a short time.

III

VIOLENCE

The one issue that has inflamed feminists more than any other is that of violence against women. According to one estimate, as many as thirty specific forms of violence against women have been identified. These range from sterilization abuse, through pornography to outright murder. Violence against women is often seen as an assault against her body but more importantly it is a negation of her integrity and personhood. The fear of sexual violence has been a powerful factor in restricting women's behavior and sense of freedom.

On 8 March 1984, autonomous women's groups across the country celebrated International Women's Day. Their activities centered around the theme of violence against women. An examination of their reports sent to a feminist magazine showed a growing concern over dowry deaths, abuse of amniocentesis test, rape, prostitution, sexual harassment and wife-beating. Power rape, i.e., rape of helpless women by men in positions of authority, is particularly an indigenous phenomena. This list revealed the depth of hatred men feel toward women. Of all the laws, rape and more specifically dowry laws have been most often amended in the last ten years. This attests further to the importance of these issues in women's lives. The emotional destruction resulting from these acts of aggression have yet to be seriously examined in this country.

The struggle against violence is the struggle against the unequal distribution of power—both physical and economic—between the sexes. The challenge lies not only in re-defining hierarchical relationships between the sexes but hierarchical interactions in all aspects of interpersonal relationships. People in positions of power—upper caste men, police, labor contractors, military personnel—dismiss violence done to lower caste and class women as insignificant. Women accept the male view of what is important and in violent encounters, end up blaming themselves, the victims, rather than castigate the perpetrators. As Heilbrun states, 'until women adopt a model of action that sustains the primacy of their own claim they will not achieve full equality.'

This section includes some frequently talked about and others not so frequently mentioned yet powerful forms of violence against women. The cruelty that exists in our most intimate and valued relationship is the essence of Flavia's paper 'Violence in the Family: Wife-Beating'. It explodes the myths and falsehood existing about wife-abuse. She suggests structural changes in the family and society to minimize this problem. These changes being slow in coming, she recommends some immediate courses of action to ease the situation.

Closely related to this essay on the problem of wife-beating is the one on 'Bride-Burning: The Psycho-Social Dynamics of Dowry Deaths' by Rehana Ghadially and Pramod Kumar. The paper discusses the psychological dynamics involved in criminal victimization and how this victimization is only now being minimized by vital social support from women's groups and enlightened changes in the law.

Female infanticide practised in the nineteenth century and its more modern counterpart female foeticide are common ways of getting rid of a daughter and thereby minimizing the family's burden of bringing her up and saving up a dowry for her marriage. In the article 'Sex-Determination and Sex Pre-Selection Tests: Abuse of Advanced Technologies', Vibhuti Patel summarizes the literature on the misuse of this technique. She challenges those in favor of its use and provides her own arguments as to how, this technique is another way of oppressing women. Action taken to ban the use of this test is also touched upon in this paper.

S. Krishnaswamy's article 'Female Infanticide in Contemporary India: A Case Study of Kallars of Tamil Nadu' warns us that this practice is not dead as many people would like to believe. Groups on the margin of Indian society, economically disadvantaged, with no access to modern sex-determination and abortion techniques resort to the gruesome murder of female infants. The paper mentions the prevalence, origin and nature of this custom among the Kallar community.

Sohaila Abdulali explores a virtually unexplored field in her article 'Rape in India: An Empirical Picture', and provides us with the extent and variety of situations in which rape occurs. Rape is used as a means to maintain all forms of hierarchical structures and institutionalized forms of inequality.

VIOLENCE IN THE FAMILY: WIFE BEATING

Flavia

The recent murder of a housewife by her husband and mother-in-law has focused public attention on the gravity of wife beating. Gomati Shah, a Gujarati Jain girl was married at the age of sixteen. She lived with her husband in Bombay in a lower middle class industrial area for only six months and then went back to her parents' house in Gujarat, unable to bear the cruelty of her husband and in-laws. She returned to Bombay because her husband and in-laws wanted her back. She was reluctant to return and told her mother, 'If I go back they will kill me'. Yet she was sent back by her parents and the village panchayat. A mutual friend living in Gujarat stood guarantee that she would not be beaten after her return. But the in-laws laid down a condition that her six uncles living in Bombay should not interfere. So the uncles stayed away. Every night, Gomati would be beaten brutally, at times burnt with a hot iron.

Unable to bear the disturbance each night, the neighbors complained to the police at Kalachowki. But the police did not take any action as they felt it was a domestic matter. The neighbors then informed the uncles in Walkeshwar. The uncles came over on 28 September. Gomati Shah and her husband were called to the police station at the request of the uncles. Gomati was interrogated in the presence of her husband. By then she was already in bad shape. Her body was swollen, and some of her wounds were infected. When Gomati was asked whether she was facing any problems at home, she replied that she was not. The uncles went back home and so did Gomati and her husband. The uncles then sent for the mother. But before the mother could arrive, Gomati died on 2 October 1980.

The women's liberation movement in India has rallied around the issue of rape. Many women's groups from different cities came together and agitated for changes in the outdated rape laws and for reopening the Mathura case. Another aspect of violence against women—that of wife beating—seems to get camouflaged under the term 'dowry deaths'. The deaths which occur within the home is the ultimate manifestation of the violence suffered by most Indian women in varying degrees. The term 'dowry deaths' is an over simplification of a far more complex social phenomenon of power relationships within the family. We prefer to call them plain 'wife-murders'. And most of these women are harassed for a long time before they are murdered or driven to suicide and for every woman who dies in her home, there must be a million more who are beaten and harassed, economically deprived and mentally humiliated.

Wife beating is perhaps the most prevalent form of violence against women. In U.S.A. many researchers in this field agree with Judge Stewart Oneglia's estimate that '50 per cent of all marriages involve some degree of physical abuse of the woman' (Langley and Levy 1977, p. 20). Such statistics are not available in India, but there is little doubt that they would far exceed the American statistics.

There seems to be a reluctance on the part of most groups working towards social change to take up the issue of domestic violence, and power relationships within the family. The problem is viewed as a general problem of domestic discord. The counselling which takes place sees the couple as a unit for counselling, although the way the problem affects the partners within the marriage is very different. It is socially acceptable that within the family the man is the master and the woman is the inferior and subordinate partner. Social pressures force women to maintain this status quo. A woman who does not accept the traditional role of submissiveness and subordination needs to be 'advised' or 'tamed' into accepting this position, and any means including violence is justified in achieving this goal. Counsellors and social workers also contribute implicitly towards this ideology when they question a woman who gets beaten: 'What did you do to provoke him?'.

There have been very few attempts to deal with and understand the problem of violence against women in the family. Usually, violence is seen as a natural occurrence and social workers seek to save the marriage by making the women more understanding and more adaptable. It is essential to understand the complexity of this phenomenon before we begin to struggle against it and provide support structures for those who seek to break out of these oppressive marriages.

Very little is actually known about the problems, the situation, and what needs to be done regarding wife beating. Thus we often rely on myths and cliches. To study the nature and the extent of wife beating in Indian society, we decided to undertake a survey in order that we might be able to provide insights into the dynamics of marital violence and why the victims are often deprived of a reasonable solution to opt out, in trying to solve the problems of violence in their marriage. It was with the hope that bringing these problems into the open would perhaps assist in starting an active struggle against this form of oppression—which touches every woman in India either in physical or mental form and bringing it into the forefront of the women's movement.

This is a study of a very small number of battered women—25 from middle class and 25 from working class backgrounds. The most startling factor that emerged at the onset of the survey was that we did not have to establish contact with battered women through marriage counsellors or at homes for battered women. Many of the women we personally knew gave us contacts of friends or relatives who were being constantly beaten. This survey has been possible only because these women assisted us and talked openly about themselves. Whether these women are crushed, whether these women die or commit suicide, whether they can fulfil their desire to live out an independent life away from male dominance depends partly on us: on whether we can respond to their needs and create the conditions whereby they don't have to live with this emotional and physical torture.

At the end of the first month we published some case studies in newspapers and women's magazines and received a tremendous response from all over the country. For the purpose of discussion we present some of our findings and analysis below.

Survey Results

1 The age of women who reported being beaten ranged from 16 to 65.
2 The educational background of the women ranged from illiterates to post graduates.
3 60 per cent of these women lived in nuclear families and the rest in joint families. The family structure did not have much effect on marital violence.
4 50 per cent of the women were beaten within the first 6 months of marriage.
5 60 per cent of the women had children, disproving the fact that the presence of children leads to a decrease in violence.
6 The monthly income of the family ranged from Rs. 150 to Rs. 5,000.
7 60 per cent of the men from middle class did not touch alcohol while in the working class a large percentage were habitual drinkers. Not all of them beat their wives when they were drunk.
8 The women from the middle class backgrounds had husbands who were lawyers, journalists, public prosecutors, executives and successful businessmen.
9 The immediate causes of violence as reported by the women were:
    a) Arguments over money
    b) Jealousy and suspicion of the woman's character
    c) Instigation by in-laws

   d) Housework

   e) Alcohol

   f) Woman's desire to work outside the home, or woman's high self-esteem (she thinks too much of herself)

   g) Disputes over children

   h) Extra marital affairs on the part of the husband

10 The forms of violence encountered included:

   a) Beating with hand and fist

   b) Beating with sticks or iron rod

   c) Kicking the abdomen/sitting on the stomach while the women were pregnant

   d) Beating with utensils or knives and ladles

   e) Throwing women against objects or bashing their heads against the wall

   f) Burning the breasts, vagina, etc.

   g) Excessive sexual demands and sexual perversions

11) The injuries suffered were:

   a) Deep cuts requiring stitches

   b) Broken bones

   c) Miscarriages

   d) Nervous breakdowns

12 Most women had tried to find some assistance at some time. These included:

   a) Going to the parental family

   b) Staying with friends

   c) Staying alone

   d) Seeking advice of counsellors

   e) Seeking advice of religious heads

   f) Complaining to the police

   g) Going to rescue homes

13 About 50 per cent of the women had jobs.

In our study the dowry factor did not emerge as the major factor contributing to wife beating. At best it served as an excuse among others.

Myths and Reality

Before we go on to analyze the findings of our survey and shatter the prevailing myths regarding wife beating we would like to go into the social and cultural causes of wife beating.

After marriage the woman becomes the property of the husband. The definition of the rape law says 'forced intercourse with a woman other than his wife'. This statement implies that a husband can rape his own wife or have intercourse without her consent. Even though society does not actually say that a man has the right to beat his wife, no one denies that he has the right to tame the woman he marries, or make her bow to his will. So when a man cannot tame his wife in any other way he uses force.

Aggression and violence are considered to be positive male qualities. The man who is not assertive in his marriage becomes an object of ridicule. He is called 'henpecked'. Women themselves accept the subordinate role within marriage unquestioningly. Time and again we see in movies how a modern liberated girl is transformed into a traditional woman (who covers her head and touches the feet of her husband and mother-in-law) by her husband by putting her through an Agni Pariksha. Is it then a wonder that the common, average man applies the same principle to his marriage and tries to tame his wife by beating her? Society either pretends that wife beating does not exist or treats it as a very light matter. During our survey when we went to police stations to collect information they laughed outright!

1 The first myth is that *middle class women do not get beaten*. The women came from all sections of the society, belonged to different religions, all educational levels and from all socio-economic classes. About 20 per cent of the women from the middle classes were working. If we hear more about wife beating in slums or in chawls, it is because these women have less privacy. The middle and upper class women are beaten behind closed doors. They live in total isolation and are oppressed further because they have to keep up the pretence of a successful marriage. Working class women talked quite openly about the violence that they experienced in their homes, and generally it seemed to affect them less psychologically. This could also be because working class women accept the violence, and thus do not see it as being something related to them as individuals. Middle class women begin to question and doubt themselves.

2 Another myth is that *the victim of violence is a small fragile, helpless woman belonging to the working class*. But in fact, women holding responsible jobs as doctors, lecturers, journalists and models get beaten by their husbands. Many of the women interviewed were quite capable of managing their lives. So there is no stereotype portrait of a battered woman.

3 When we talk about the man who beats his wife we think about *a man from the lower strata of society, a man who is frustrated in his job, an alcoholic, or a paranoid person, aggressive in his relationship with the*

world at large and his wife is just one of the victims. We found professionals like lawyers and doctors beating their wives. Sixty per cent of the middle class women who were interviewed said that their husbands did not touch alcohol. Among the rest only 20 per cent of the men beat their wives after the consumption of alcohol. Among the working class although 80 per cent of the men consumed alcohol, in most cases they beat their wives while they were sober and wanted money to buy their drink. There were some cases both in the middle classes and the working classes when the husband was very angry with the wife, went out to get drunk and came back to give her a good thrashing. In the wives' description of their husbands it was evident that these men are not over-aggressive in their day-to-day transactions with people—men or women. If three quarters of all Indian women get beaten by their husbands, are we to assume that 75 per cent of our male population is paranoid and needs to be in mental asylums?

4 Another myth is that of *provocation*. This myth victimizes the woman further. The burden of guilt falls on the woman and increases her shame and degradation. This myth also conveys the message that women who get beaten are masochistic and they want to get beaten.

5 Another oft exploited myth is that *long standing battering relationships can change for the better*. We found in our survey that, at best, with the passage of time the violent assaults are reduced in severity and frequency. But the women continue to live in a state of fear and uncertainty because they can never predict when, where and under what circumstances the violence may suddenly erupt. And many times the violent situation escalates to homicide and suicide.

6 The myth that the *loving husband does not indulge in wife beating* is also false. We found that the husband can be extremely kind and loving specially after a violent assault.

7 Another myth is that *since the women don't leave their husbands they do not mind the beatings or that they actually like it*. It is often asked: 'Why do women continue to live in a situation where they are eventually murdered or are driven to suicide? Why don't they seek a way out?' The theory of learned helplessness gives an insight into the mental state of passive resignation experienced by these women.

The Theory of Learned Helplessness

Most women interviewed, attempted to break away from their husbands during the first year of their marriage. They often went to stay with their mothers. But in most cases the women were told to try harder, that it would not happen again; that she should have a child. But a woman we interviewed said:

There was nowhere that I could go, nothing that I could do. I had tried to escape—it had no effect. So the only way left was to learn how to survive within the house. Getting out of this house and breaking the marriage was out—so I learnt to grin, laugh, bear with it. I laughed a lot. Why? If I cried or talked about my problems few people believed I am beaten, and that also severely, because I don't look sad, tearful and unhappy all the time. Funny, isn't it?

In an experiment conducted by psychologist Martin Seligman (1972) dogs were trapped in a cage and were given electric shocks. Initially the dogs reacted violently and tried to break free. But when they realized that there was no way out, no matter what their response, they ceased voluntary movement. They became submissive, listless and passive. Even when the shocks became more intense there was no reaction. Eventually, when the cage door was opened the dogs refused to leave and did not avoid the shocks. They had to be repeatedly dragged to the exit to teach them again the process of voluntary response. The dogs had learnt to be helpless and passive.

When the middle class women were beaten for the first time they were numb with shock. Every woman interviewed said 'I did not know that educated men beat their wives'. They had not seen wife beating in their parents' home (except in one case). Their initial reaction was to deny it even to themselves. They said the shame and humiliation of the first beating had left a permanent scar on their psyche. They became silent and withdrawn. They did not tell anyone. This reluctance to confide ranged from a few weeks to five years. After the initial shock they began to question their worth. They began to wonder whether there was something wrong with their behavior, their upbringing or their education. They tried to change their behavior, their actions and their mode of dressing in order to please the husband and in-laws. But soon they began to realize the fact that they got beaten, no matter what their response. The repeated assaults threatened their physical safety and survival became a major issue.

It is at this stage that women seek help. But wherever they go they are sent back. We report the case histories of two women, one from the middle class and one from the working class. Sudha, the wife of a motor mechanic says:

I was desperate, but I could not return to my mother's house because I had two younger sisters and my mother felt that if I came back it would be difficult to get them married. So I stayed on. Once I was so desperate I poured kerosene over myself, but my husband entered the room and stopped me before I could light the match. I was expecting my first child. When I went to my mother's house for delivery I stayed for three years. But finally my mother grew frantic because my younger sisters were not getting proposals. So she took me, my daughter, 10 tolas of gold and Rs. 2000 and left me in my husband's home. Today I have three children and I live as a prisoner in my own home.

Prema, a working woman says:

It is not easy to live alone without a husband. I left mine and took my three children with me to stay with a woman I knew. After a few days the walls of the factory were plastered with sheets of paper announcing that I was a slut who had run away to live with another man. Nobody would talk to me. I would sit alone in a corner and cry. My husband came to call me many times but I did not go. But after two years I went back. My friend's house was getting overcrowded and there was no place. Also my eldest daughter had reached puberty. Everyone said unless I went back nobody would marry my daughter.

But the women who come back get totally disillusioned. Most return on the husbands' terms. Life becomes a mere existence, often for the sake of the children. Family and friends rejoice because the couple is reunited or because the woman has learnt to adjust. In our survey we found that the beatings continued. But the women had learnt to accept the violence as something inevitable, a fact to live with and die with. But years later the women begin to think of leaving the house once again, this time when they feel that the lives of their children were being threatened. When the women see the bodies and psyches of their innocent children getting scarred due to the violence in the family they began their search for alternatives all over again. Thus we noticed that women leave their home either during the first five years of marriage and again after a lapse of 10–15 years when the children are grown up.

Despite societal conditioning women no longer said marriage is the ultimate goal of a woman and choose not to remain beaten. They had no hesitation to break the 'sacred knot of marriage'. But it is only when they realized that there is no way out, that they were trapped within the marriage because of a) lack of education, b) economic dependency, c) lack of support structures, d) the difficulties in obtaining divorce/job/house, e) the burden of child care, that they became passive, resigned and negative in their approach. They had numbed themselves. The beatings and the negative response of society to their needs had succeeded in making the women helpless, passive and negative.

The Cycle Theory of Violence

The women we interviewed spoke of their experiences as follows:

I know when a big fight is coming. It's preceded by small fights over nothing. I get really tense then. I try to stay out of his way and try to do the right things. But despite that, the fights, the small beatings occur. I know, I just know that a big beating is going to come—if not today, then tomorrow. I know because this has been the pattern for the past 15 years. And often rather than live under the tension, I think it is best to let him beat me now. At least the tension will cease after the beating and it will be calm and peaceful.'

Most women had similar stories to recall. The husbands were very considerate after a beating. After sometime the tension begins to mount, small fights leading to a big bang and then the calm loving husband.

These experiences support Walker's (1979) three-phase theory of battering, 1) a tension building period followed by 2) acute battering and 3) then the calm-loving respite. The women who have gone through many such cycles know the pattern well. These women—the ones who are put out of their houses, hospitalized or seek the aid of institutions are the ones who are further victimized. The woman leaves the house when the man is in phase 2. The social workers and counsellors find it very difficult to accept the women's version of the battering. When they meet, the husband has moved into phase 3. The loving, affectionate and contrite man they meet is quite a different person from the aggressive, dominant brute the woman had portrayed earlier. Every case history, like a worn out old record, carries the same old remarks, 'Husband seems loving and kind. He loves his wife and children' and 'She was rude to her husband. She needs counselling'. 'Which man will tolerate such behavior?'

There is yet one more trend among the modern social workers and psychotherapists. They accept the fact that the man is at fault. But they attribute this fact to the man's mental condition. They tell the woman that he is a sick man and that he needs help. The woman is given the responsibility of nursing and doctoring him. The message implied is that only she can give the psychological and social help that he needs. If she leaves him, he will fall apart. She is his only hope as he refuses to seek help outside.

Thus the women are physically and psychologically abused by their husbands and then kept in their place by a society that is indifferent to their plight. They are blamed for getting beaten and then blamed for not ending their beatings. They are blamed for not seeking help, yet when they do so, they are advised to go home and stop their own inappropriate behavior. Not only are they held responsible for their own beatings, they must also assume responsibility for their husband's mental health. If only they were better persons, the litany goes on, they would find a way to prevent their own victimization.

The exact length of phase 3 cannot be determined. It is longer than phase 2, but much shorter than phase 1. In some cases it lasts only briefly. You cannot see when it ends. Before the woman realizes, the calm, loving behavior gives way to a few batterings and verbal abuse and the cycle begins once again. When the cycle is repeated many times, the woman's suppressed rage leads to loss of control, and some times women stab or lash back with lethal weapons causing serious injury. The men do not seem to benefit in any way by their violent behavior. While trying to possess the woman psychologically, and physically dominating them, in actual fact they lose the love and respect of the woman. They may gain their fear and obedience. But the wives resent the husbands because they do not possess this power. The resentment builds up into anger and the woman tries to retaliate in other ways—sexual deprivation or verbal assault—which further deteriorates the situation.

Why Wife Beating Occurs

Frustrations build up in a man's life at two levels—individual and societal.

Individual

Man's expectations of himself and his inability to face problems and failures lead to a sense of insecurity. If frustrations in a man's life leads to violence, why is it that the wife is the inevitable target of his violence? Frustrations build up in a woman's life as well, but why is it that this does not lead to spouse abuse? We have put forward some reasons:

a The unquestioned authority of the man in his home/marriage.

b The consequent subservient role of the wife.

c The wife's total dependency on her husband because of which she cannot either rebel or escape from the situation.

d The social sanctions which the husband has to discipline his wife.

e Male arrogance – a man's sheer confidence that he can make a woman forget and forgive the worst with a show of love and gifts.

f Of all adults, a wife is least likely to show resistance to her husband's beatings g If a man has witnessed wife beating in his childhood or has been physically abused as a child, he is likely to assume that physical violence is the acceptable way of resolving marital problems. Child abuse also leads to the belief that one who loves also has the right to beat.

Societal

The most fundamental factor which leads to wife beating is connected with the sexist structure of the society as well as the family. Although a man and woman enjoy equality under the Indian constitution, as long as the idea of a man as the head of the family remains rooted in our culture and in the eyes of the law, wife beating will be perpetuated in society.

While economically dependent and independent women are equally likely to be beaten, an economically dependent woman is more likely to stay on in a violent home. Lack of education and poor job opportunities for women are important factors due to which many middle class women remain married to men who constantly beat them. This, along with the burden of child care and the sexual stereotyping of parental responsibility force women to remain in violent homes. Under the circumstances, a man does not need to fear that if he beats his wife, she will leave him with the responsibility of looking after the children. So he can continue abusing his wife with relative impunity. He can be relatively confident that she will not leave him because, *a*) she is not economically independent, *b*) she has no place to go and *c*) she has the burden of bringing up the children because society feels that child care is exclusively a mother's job and women who leave the children behind become social outcastes.

Existing Alternatives

We contacted all homes in the city which give shelter for women in distress. The Shradhanand Mahilashram at Matunga said that they give shelter to all women in distress but added that they do not have any battered women in their home. When we asked the reason for this, their reply was that perhaps women do not know that the home is open to battered women. The Government Rescue Home at Deonar and Ashadan at Dongri, were homes basically for unmarried girls.

When we asked police officers during the various stages of our survey, they said that if a woman has nowhere to go they are sent to Bapnu Ghar. At one level, Bapnu Ghar offers the woman an alternative to getting beaten in her home daily. She can, at least, seek temporary shelter there. The whole emphasis of Bapnu Ghar seems to be on reuniting the family. They call the husband and wife for counselling and try to understand the viewpoint of both sides. When asking the husband why he beats his wife, there seems to be a tendency to assume that wife beating is justified in some cases. However, can we say that a man has the right to beat his wife for some valid reasons, e.g., if she does not do the housework well, or if she is negligent of home and children, or if she is engaged in a love affair? In cases of wife beating it is the woman who is always the victim—there is no question of faults, and any counselling should be carried out in a way which does not at any level imply that if she was at fault then the beating was justified. Any institution that deals with this problem should always be kind and sympathetic to the women and see the problem from their point of view. We see wife beating as a crime of sexual violence against women.

The two major problems at Bapnu Ghar are that women with jobs cannot come there because residents are not allowed to leave the premises daily, and secondly, the home does not accommodate children above the age of 6. Women are allowed to go out only once a week. Some of our respondents indicated that this lack of freedom was one reason why they left and went back to their husbands. They also complained of boredom since there was no activity they could get involved in. Another major drawback was that there is no follow-up of old cases and women who are discharged are back again and again. Many times the women were sent back on the husbands' terms with conditions like, for example, her mother or relatives should not visit her. This kind of condition makes the position of the woman weaker in her own home once she goes back.

Suggested Changes

Any institution which tries to deal with the problem of wife beating has to take a preventive rather than a curative approach. Unless we try to change the structure of the family, the help given to battered women will prove to be only superficial. This does not mean that we should ignore the desperate and immediate situation in which millions of women find themselves, and live their lives in constant fear of violence and death in their own homes. Their need is urgent. To expect lone women to fight individually against institutionalized family violence is both cruel and unrealistic, despite occasional successes. We desperately need more homes for battered women where the women can take refuge when their lives are threatened. But we need homes which will look at the problem of wife beating from a pro woman point of view, and which will help the women to rebuild their shattered lives and induce faith and confidence in themselves. Moreover these homes can serve an important educational and consciousness-raising function. The time spent in these homes can be utilized in teaching the women useful skills which can eventually make them self-sufficient. In cases where the women choose to go back to the husband, the home should lay down rules that the husband allow her to continue her job training and should not send the women back on their husbands' terms. In most cases the husband is most anxious to get the wife back once she leaves, and this is the only time you can lay down terms and conditions for the man. This can be very useful in maintaining contact with the women, so that when the beatings recur, prompt action can be taken in pressing charges against the husband.

Community action like having a morcha or a dharna outside a wife beater's house will go a long way in acting as a deterrent to marital violence. Men and society at large should recognize once and for all that women are no longer going to take the beatings lying down.

The women who decide to break away need free legal aid, a place to stay and a job. The homes for battered women should be linked up with organisations which help women with self employment. We need more committed lawyers who are sympathetic and understanding and would help to provide legal protection and relief to the women who are beaten. The Government should be made to realize the urgency of the problem and battered women should be allotted a certain percentage in government housing schemes. Hostels for women with children with common kitchens are urgently needed where battered women can start living an independent life but at the same time be close to other women who have faced affliction and derive strength, sustenance and support from each other.

We need to create an awareness in society so that the attitude of doctors, counsellors, institutions, social workers and the police is more sympathetic towards victims of marital violence. The attitude of the institutions and counsellors should be to make the partners in a marriage more complete human beings rather than to preserve the marriage at any cost.

At another level, we have social workers who say that only psychopaths and alcoholics beat their wives. Asking the woman to change her life style in order to prevent getting beaten indirectly implies a social sanction for wife beating. The counsellors and social workers also need to recognize the '3 Phase' cycle theory of wife beating, so that they will not be taken in by his behavior in phase 3 and blame the woman for getting beaten, as the husband, after having given went to his anger and frustration is kind and loving towards his wife.

Wherever the woman shows a desire for reconciliation, she should be given some advice as to the precautions she should take in case of an attack on her. Getting help from her neighbors, locking herself in a room, running away from the house, throwing objects or chilli powder at the husband, kicking him in the loins are some of the simple things most women can do when a husband turns violent. They may seem scandalous to a religious mind which is conditioned to accept the husband as 'lord and master', but unless women can stand up to the beatings and fight back, the power relationship within the family will not change.

Getting help from the neighbors and involving them will make the women less isolated and help to create a social awareness that there is no stigma to being a victim of marital violence, in fact it is the agressor that should be chastized. It will also challenge the assumption that no one has the right to interfere in his personal life.

Unless women organize we cannot fight male domination. So we need to organize and start a Mahila Atma Suraksha Sangh in every area to fight this aspect of women's oppression.

The Law and Wife Beating

There is no special law to cover wife beating. It is covered under the general law for assault. These are sections 319–326 of the Indian Penal Code (IPC). Sections 319 and 321 are non-cognizable offences, i.e., cases in which the police can take no action against the assaulter.

Sections 320/322 cover 'grievous hurt', which is defined as:

a) Emasculation
b) Permanent privation of the sight of eye
c) Permanent privation of the hearing of either ear
d) Privation of any member or joint
e) Destruction or permanent impairing of the power of any member or joint
f) Permanent disfiguration of the head or face
g) Fracture or dislocation of a bone or tooth
h) Any hurt which endangers life or which causes the sufferer to be during the space of twenty days in severe bodily pain, or unable to follow his ordinary pursuits.

Sections 324/326 cover those cases where the assaulter uses dangerous weapons or means.

Wife beating is the most under-reported crime in the country. Going through the crime register of 1979 of two police stations in Bombay city we could find only one out of a total of 56 cases of assault at one police station, and one out of 42 at the other. Of the two cases in one case the wife was not staying with the husband. Both were registered under Section 324 of the IPC.

The first point to be noted is that these laws are ineffective for protection of a woman. A woman who fears that a severe beating is imminent can find little protection from the police under the general law of assault. If there is a grievous hurt involved, the police take little immediate action. Very few of the wife beating cases actually reach the police station and the police take action on only a few of these. The usual form of action is to call the offender, the husband, to the police station and to give him advice or counselling. Sometimes the man may be kept in the station to sober him down. The police officers themselves say of this treatment that the poorer men listen to us; the middle class men openly tell us that we have no right to interfere in their private family lives. At least for the working class cases the police seem to feel that this treatment is effective. However, as one woman recounts the situation is actually different:

> The children ran to call the police because they were really scared for me. The police came only four hours later after all the beatings were over. I might have been dead.

The police response to the problem of wife beating is obviously hopelessly inadequate. And it is essential to make changes in these practices to make them more beneficial to women. In view of these problems, we maintain that it is essential to argue for the following changes in the law/police set up as it currently exists:

1) There should be a *woman* police officer who meets a beaten woman when she comes to the police station for assistance.
2) In the absence of a woman police officer, the woman should be taken to the nearest women's home.
3) In every case the police should have the power to take preventive action, i.e., when the women comes to the police because she fears an assault she must be given the option of staying at a home for women.
4) A woman should never be interviewed in the presence of her husband.
5) Since the practice of talking to the man without a stern action leads to a situation where a woman is beaten further, every action of the police must be followed by stern punishment.
6) Since the situation of assault of a husband on a wife is quite specific, in that the wife is economically dependent on the husband, in that the assault occurs in the house in which both reside, it is essential that the police operate under different laws than those which cover general assault. A law such as Domestic Violence Act should cover the points made above and several others.
7) The police should be educated on the nature and problem of wife beating so that they are better equipped to handle the problem.

Under all the marriage laws except the Christian Marriage Act, it is possible for a battered wife to get divorce. For the purpose of this paper it is not necessary to cover the Divorce Act in detail. Therefore, we will only put forward certain suggestions:

1) If a victim of wife beating goes to court for a divorce she should be given free legal aid.
2) Though divorce is available on the grounds of 'cruelty', this term is left undefined. We feel that it is necessary to concretely define the term and this should include any threat of violence to the woman.
3) If a woman has been married under a religious ceremony she should have the right on the basis of a signed statement to have the laws of the Special Marriage Act applied to her marriage, since as yet we do not have a uniform civil code.

Although this study was done in 1980, its findings are confirmed by our day-to-day experience in dealing with the problem of wife beating even today.

BRIDE-BURNING: THE PSYCHO-SOCIAL DYNAMICS OF DOWRY DEATHS

Rehana Ghadially and Pramod Kumar

Introduction

Many people think that the only way for a woman to be happy is to be married and to have children. But a woman is not always happy in marriage. In fact, in quite a few cases it is a passage to misery and violence. Marriage may define a woman's existence but it can also blow her out of it.

At the time of marriage, it is customary in India for the bride's parents to give gifts, viz, dowry to their daughter, the groom and his family. The nature and origin of this custom and the general economics involved have been sufficiently documented (Srinivas, 1984; Sambrani and Sambrani, 1983; Rajaraman, 1983; and Nair, 1978). In contemporary times however, dowry is no longer a gift but rather a demand for cash and/or goods made by the groom and his family on the bride's parents. Increasingly, it has become difficult to meet these demands and many a young woman has died for not fulfilling the expectations of the groom's family.

In a study of unnatural deaths of young married women in Delhi for the year April 1981 to March 1982, Khan and Ray (1984) found that according to the official record of 179 cases of unnatural deaths, 12 per cent were dowry related. Of these two-thirds were cases of suicide and the rest homicide. On the basis of interviews with parents-in-law and husbands of the young women, 16 per cent of the unnatural deaths were estimated to be dowry related. Of these, three out of five cases were suicide and the others homicide. To take the example of another state, it was announced by the Minister of State for Home Affairs in the Maharashtra legislative assembly in early July 1986 that dowry deaths in Maharashtra have increased from 120 in 1984 to 211 in 1985—an increase of 64 per cent in one year (*Sunday Observer*, 13 July 1986).

Dowry death is one of the most frequently publicized crimes in the mass media. In order to get a better view of the dynamics involved in dowry deaths, *Manushi* was reviewed from January 1979 to December 1985. The rationale for reviewing a feminist magazine was to provide a women's perspective on this social evil. In all, 36 cases were located. These were described in full length articles, short articles or in the form of reports sent from different parts of the country by parents of dowry victims, friends, neighbors and women activists. Letters exchanged between daughters and parents and autobiographical writings were also reviewed.

Demographic Information

The analysis showed that 69 per cent of the cases were from Delhi, 8 per cent each from Punjab and U.P. and 3 per cent each from Kerala, Karnataka, Rajasthan, Maharashtra and Madhya Pradesh. While dowry deaths have been labelled as a typically north Indian phenomena, the over-representation of cases from the north is also partly due to the location of *Manushi* in Delhi.

In 47 per cent of the cases where the age of the women was reported, it ranged from 18 years to 28 years with a mean age of 22.7 years. Nine of the women were employed. Their occupations included typist, stenographer, personal secretary, school teacher, college lecturer and doctor. Where length of marriage was reported it ranged from 11 days to 10 years with a mean length of marriage equal to 2.33 years. Eleven per cent of these women were pregnant, 36 per cent had children and no information was stated in the remaining cases.

Majority of these women were married to professionals and in the remaining cases the husbands were businessmen. The professional group included scientific officers, college lecturers, medical doctors, bank officers and a communication assistant. The businessmen included those in whole-sale hosiery business, motor spare parts and export business.

Dowry Demand and Violence

Dowry demands are made both before marriage and at the time of marriage, but in most of these cases they were made after marriage. Where demands were made after marriage it was perceived either as an exercise of the rightful prerogative of the groom and his family, or to express discontent at what was given at the time of marriage or in social comparison with neighbors, at a later date, the dowry was perceived as inadequate.

The most common item of dowry demanded was hard cash (58 per cent). Cash was demanded not only for its own sake but usually to expand business, cover marriage expenses or to buy expensive articles. This was followed by household furniture (28 per cent). Color television, sewing machine, dunlop sofa, bed, radio and cupboard were the most commonly demanded items of furniture. Jewellery ranked a close third (25 per cent) followed by vehicle, clothes and household linen. Other dowry demands took the form of demanding a nice wedding, finding a job for the groom, bringing a certain number of people to the wedding, share in the bride's father's house, holding the marriage ceremony and feast in a particular town or a five star hotel.

When these demands were not met, it precipitated serious consequences for the young bride. Domestic violence was reported in 78 per cent of the cases. In 31 per cent of the cases, the violence took a milder form such as shoving, kicking, quarrelling, taunting, harrassment, blackmailing and mental torture. The daughter-in-law was not permitted to speak to the neighbors, to attend social functions or to step out of the house. In almost half the cases (47 per cent) violence was of the severe kind including beatings with belts, iron rods, starving, chaining and threats of murder.

In a majority of cases (67 per cent) the parents were aware of the violence their daughters were being subjected to. In more than half these cases the daughter-in-law had been either thrown out of her husband's home or had returned to her natal home on her own. With the exception of one who filed a case for divorce on grounds of cruelty, in each case she returned to her in-laws home after working out some semblance of a compromise. Domestic violence accelerated upon her return to her husband's home and reached a climax resulting in either suicide or murder.

While the husband and the in-laws have been the favorite targets of vituperation especially among women activists, the role parents play in compounding their daughter's problem must be accepted as part of the pressures acting on the young woman. It was observed in many cases that she had been persuaded by her own parents to bear everything quietly, not discuss her misery with others and encouraged to go back to a violent home. The increase in violence followed by a compromise, paradoxical as it may sound, has also been observed in case of young married Chinese women. Wolf (1975) by way of explanation stated that by the time she returns, her husband's family has been humiliated by the negotiations, by the group of curious neighbors and the mother-in-law has heard her treatment of the son's wife openly discussed by her women friends. The family resents this adverse publicity and the continuing attention the slightest row in the family brings. They are unlikely to feel charitable towards the woman who has caused them so much trouble.

It is pertinent to note here that in most cases neither the woman nor her family reported the violence to the police or took legal action against the demand for dowry which is a punishable offence. Why do victims and their families fail to report dowry demands and violence that precedes death? It is possible that there is insufficient awareness of the Dowry Prohibition Act and its subsequent amendments. Moreover, the Act itself deters families from reporting because it makes the givers of dowry offenders too. While there is no systematic information available as to why families fail to report dowry demands, it is worth the while to examine data available on lack of reporting in other kinds of crimes such as rape and robbery.

It is estimated that in U.S.A. between one half and two thirds of all crimes are not reported to the police (Kidd and Chayet, 1984). While examining the psychology of criminal victimization researchers have concluded that three factors are responsible for non-reporting. First, victimization produces fear, particularly about one's own safety and security. The woman fears that reporting may aggravate domestic violence or result in the breakdown of an institution she considers sacred. Secondly, crime victims commonly come to see themselves as helpless, vulnerable and impotent. Thirdly, the victim may come to believe that even others are ineffective in changing life's events. This projected helplessness does have some basis in reality as will be noticed when discussing the role of police and the courts in dowry deaths. When the victim does not report because of her belief that nothing can be done, it has serious negative consequences for the community.

Since victims cannot reduce their fear by reporting the crime to the authorities, they may seek to reduce it by talking about their fears to family members, friends and colleagues. Such in-community reporting results in what Lavrakas (1981) calls a 'victim set', i.e., persons acquainted with the victims are also apt to perceive less confidence in the authorities. According to Berg and Johnson (1979), following victimization, a person simply avoids contact with any persons or organizations that might further victimize him/her. For example, the victim and her family may feel and rightly so that the police and the judicial system may exact further cost in terms of time, money, energy and peace of mind in an already costly situation.

The end result is that these factors combine to produce self-blaming tendencies (Kidd and Plotkin, 1986). This tendency is seen in two suicide notes written by one woman to her husband and sister-in-law respectively:

From the moment of my coming to your house, your family has had difficulties which means that my coming was not a good thing . . .

With my coming into the family, his business came to a halt, I am so unlucky that wherever I go something goes wrong. (*Manushi*, No. 1, January 1979, pp. 13–14).

By blaming themselves for the occurrence, victims regain a sense of control and feel less need to report to the authorities. Unlike other crimes, however, not reporting led to the death of the victim.

Of the thirty six cases, thirty resulted in death of the woman. Of the remaining six cases, four resulted in an unsuccessful attempt at murder/ suicide, in one case there was no such attempt and the last resulted in a broken engagement. In so far as the nature of death is concerned majority (60 per cent) of the women died of burns. Hanging was the second most common form of death (13 per cent). This was followed by poisoning (7 per cent). Combination of strangulation and poisoning, shooting and death under mysterious circumstances constituted (1 per cent) each.

Interestingly enough, after the death of the victim many families willingly reported the crime to the authorities. This is because in most of these instances women's groups made the decision to call or acted as intermediaries in seeking assistance. Similar findings have been reported by Burgers and Holmstrom (1974) in case of reporting to the police of rape victims. Rape victims were more likely to report the crime to the police provided they had some social support.

Groom and Bride

For a crime to occur, two key elements are usually present. First, the perpetrator must be sufficiently motivated to commit the crime and secondly the victim must be sufficiently vulnerable (Greenberg and Ruback, 1984). The most common motives attributed to the groom and his family have been greed, rampant consumerism, materialism and the need for instant upward mobility (Oldenburg, 1984). Little or no information on the personality dynamics of the grooms is reported in the 36 cases. However, some inferences are possible. With the exception of a few, violence was present in the majority of the cases. It is possible that dowry seekers are nothing more than wife and daughter-in-law batterers and refusal or inability to bring dowry is simply an additional cause among many others for wife-beating. The psychological characteristics of wife batterers have been documented by Gondolf (1985). Some comparisons between wife-batterers and dowry-seekers are made here. Like most wife-batterers, dowry seekers also come from all walks of life, want their wives to return when they walk out of the house. They are not alcohol or drug abusers and respond to rigidly defined gender roles. Wife-batterers have low self-esteem, are over concerned about family's status and well-being and try to control not only themselves but others. When their demands are not met dowry-seekers also feel that the family's status and their sense of power and control are challenged. Sons-in-law in India not only enjoy special status and power in the family but they also act in ways that help them maintain it. And finally a wife-batterer's image is seriously threatened when there is a change or anticipation of extra responsibility and assertiveness on the part of the wife. It may be recalled that 11 per cent of the women were pregnant at the time of death and 25 per cent were economically independent. This may threaten the wife batterer's sense of security and self-image.

The vulnerability of the woman is highlighted in descriptions given about her by her parents and neighbors. She is 'passive', 'homely', 'dutiful', 'patient', 'quiet', 'sensible', 'nice', 'one who never emerged from the confines of the home' and 'one who took seriously the religious injunctions given at the time of marriage' according to which a wife should be dutiful and patient. The qualities expected of young brides is well captured in the words of the neighbors of the victims who stated:

> 'Teach your daughters patience. Girls must learn to bear everything patiently.'

> 'What is the use of such education when parents don't teach their daughters how to behave in their husband's house? Cursed be such education.'

> 'Nowadays girls can't put up with the smallest thing, they get into a temper.' (*Manushi*, No. 3, July-August 1979, pp. 16–17).

She is described by her parents-in-law and neighbors as 'mad', 'prone to violence', 'immoral', 'fashionable flirt' and 'adulterous'. In a puritanical society like India, character assassination on the part of the in-laws is a powerful technique in attempts at face-saving. However, discussion about a young bride's personality may be altogether a redundant exercise. At one temple ceremony at which he was present Lannoy (1971) noticed that,

> the bride was ignored while the heads of the two families sat in ceremonial attire with their accountants and their bulky ledgers to discuss the financial transactions associated with the marriage. Heaps of bank notes were piled in front of them on the marble floor at the feet of the diety. In such circumstances a bride would feel her prestige and status in economic terms, but have little sense of being regarded as a woman with a personality of her own (p. 106).

Nature of Social Support

Social support is emerging as the single most important factor in mitigating the impact of highly stressful situations (Brownwell and Shumaker, 1984). Who does the distraught family of a dowry victim turn to for help? Women's groups and organizations form a single most important source of help to the victim's family. Fifty seven per cent of the families received support from this source. Neighbors and residents (48 per cent) are almost as important in extending some form of help to the woman's family. Formal support systems such as women's organizations are often able to provide more expert information than informal providers such as neighbors (Shumaker, 1983). Friends and colleagues have extended support to 9 per cent of the families. Community elders, relatives, social work organizations, college students and human rights groups (4 per cent) play a small role in giving support.

A little over a decade ago the victim's existing social network had been woefully inadequate in dealing with the police and the judicial system. The emergence of more formal social support systems have made it possible for the bereaved families to take action beyond beating their chests in help-lessness. The assistance has been emotional, informational and tangible in nature. It has taken the form of public demonstrations, protest marches, slogan raising, giving media coverage, distributing pamphlets, holding exhibitions, enacting plays, assisting parents in filing cases in court, pres-surizing the police, pressurizing authorities to amend existing laws and following up cases with police and lawyers.

Perhaps the single most important function this kind of social support has served is to create public awareness of the crime. The knowledge that such resources are available, if needed, facilitates our adaptation to socially trying situations. Besides, there is evidence (Tyler, 1984) to indicate that information gathered from social networks such as friends and neighbors play a more important role than, say, mass media in estimating personal risk of victimization and the appropriate kind of action to undertake in order to avoid victimization.

The social support however has been overwhelmingly crisis intervention rather than crisis prevention in nature. Effective crisis prevention measures have yet to be evolved to deal with the crime of dowry demands and domestic violence. Bystanders have played a potentially crucial role in preventing street crimes like rape, robbery, etc. Shotland and Goodstein (1984) argue that this is because bystanders can serve as an extension of the 'eyes and ears' of the police. They are important sources of information, are potential witnesses and may influence the victim's decision to report the crime. In light of this the woman's immediate neighbors, her family and local residents are important bystanders and could minimize such victimization. The question is why haven't they done so? Again looking at the literature it is clear that bystanders don't intervene if they perceive the situation as not serious enough. The neighbors may dismiss her screams as simply a family quarrel. They may not intervene if they believe the victim provoked the incident. In cases of domestic violence there is enough misconception that it occurs because she must have pro-voked it (Rohrbaugh, 1981). Lastly, bystanders feel that the cost of inter-vention may be too high, neighbors may not act for fear of loosing the goodwill of another neighbor, her family may not act for fear that they may not find grooms for their remaining daughters.

The Role of Police and Courts

What role has the police played in dowry related problems and dowry deaths? In almost half the cases where some police involvement was mentioned, the police refused to take any action. When the police was informed that a young woman's life was in danger they refused to intervene in 'family affairs'. Police apathy manifested itself in several ways. The police appeared unconcerned, hesitated or refused to register a case. The police registered a case only after intense pressure from either the family of the deceased and/or members of women's organizations. If a case was registered the police refused to take any action after registration. Police indifference is primarily a function of the light view they and society take of dowry deaths. This seriously deters a woman and her family to report violence in the home. This light view is well exemplified in the speech of a district police commissioner at a college: 'This is not a case, rather it is an incident, it is a tragedy. I have five thousand incidents like these, it is very ordinary matter.' (*Manushi* 12, 1982, pp. 46–47). Take the example of another policeman who stated to the brother of the deceased woman: 'Go back to Punjab. Why are you wasting time and money here? Nothing ever gets done in such cases ' (*Manushi* 3, 1979, p. 21). The attitude of the police in dowry death cases is similar to the one observed in cases of wife-battering (Rohrbaugh, 1981).

Where a case was registered, 22 per cent were registered as cases of suicide or accused in-laws of abetment to suicide. In 8 per cent of the cases, murder or attempted murder was registered by the police. An equal number of cases (12 per cent) resulted in arrests, transfer of cases to the dowry prohibition cell and suicide changed to murder under intense pressure from the woman's family and/or women's organizations. The police have also been accused of being partial, of intimidating residents of the husband's neighborhood not to agitate, accepting bribes, tempering with evidence and exerting pressure on witnesses. In light of this it comes as no surprise that more dowry deaths are dismissed as cases of suicide rather than murder and all official figures will represent a gross under-estimation of the true extent of this crime.

Despite a large number of dowry deaths every year, very few reach the trial stage. When the journal issues between 1983 and 1985 were examined, the trial and judgements passed by the various courts in only 10 cases were reported.

Not surprisingly, only in three out of ten cases the accused were convicted by the Sessions Court and were sentenced to life imprisonment. In remaining seven cases the culprits were acquitted for several reasons. In four cases appeal was filed in High Court and one in the Supreme Court. In the lone High Court judgement reported, the culprits were acquitted. The Supreme Court case was yet to be decided. In two cases, bail was granted by High Court and in one, bail was reportedly refused by the Sessions Court.

The reasons for acquittal were several. The judges

   a) doubted the veracity of woman's dying declaration (4 cases)
   b) found fault in the investigating agency, i.e., the police (6 cases)
   c) found the evidence to be inadequate (7 cases)
   d) refused to accept the medical report of the doctor (4 cases)
   e) misinterpreted facts (4 cases).

The judges have doubted the veracity of the dying declaration on grounds that it was a wife's attempt to falsely implicate an innocent husband, that she was not medically fit to give a dying declaration (though doctor certified fitness) and finally why did she wait for the police before giving the dying declaration. In cases of rape, it has been the history of Western law that the words of a woman are not to be trusted (*Newsweek*, 1984). The same seems to hold true for dowry cases in India.

The judges' fundamentally sexist assumptions are manifested in many of their pronouncements. In one case the judge interpreted marks of strangulation on the neck to the gold chain the woman might be wearing. Also, the judge accepts the argument that women in unhappy marriages are prone to suicide. Another judge argued that since the husband was dark and the wife was fair and beautiful, he would feel fortunate to have such a wife and would not normally kill her. In two cases, the judges have refused to recognize harassment as abetment to suicide.

Faulty investigation and insufficient evidence constituted two other reasons for acquittal. The judges noted that the investigating turned hostile, the police did not take possession of incriminating evidence, they permitted accused persons to acquire vital information from police diary and often the police were corrupt. In a majority of the cases, there was no direct evidence by a witness, the witness was labelled as hostile and unreliable and the accused had attempted to destroy the evidence. Given the judges' male point of view and the incompetence and apathy of the police it will be uncommonly difficult to sustain a charge of dowry murder in court.

Dowry and the Law

The Dowry Prohibition Act of 1961 marks the first attempt by the Government of India to recognize dowry as a social evil and to curb its practice. The act was modified with the Dowry Prohibition (Amendment) Act of 1984, which has again been modified with Dowry Prohibition (Amendment) Bill 1986. Women's organizations have played a key role in this process of change.

The 1961 Act defines dowry and makes the practise of dowry, both giving and taking, a punishable offence. Any agreement on dowry is void. If it is given at all, it will be the woman's property. With increased awareness of dowry deaths and consequent public controversy, women's organizations made a thorough analysis of the implications of 1961 Dowry Act and criticized it for being theoretical and lacking in clarity.

The Dowry Prohibition (Amendment) Act of 1984 brought nominal changes and failed to meet the expectations of feminist groups. Nevertheless, it evoked a sense of hope. Changes were made in definition of dowry, and provisions for getting the dowry back.

In defining dowry, the phrase 'in consideration of marriage' was replaced by 'in connection with marriage' which widens the definition but does not adequately cover all situations. It may be difficult to prove that demands made a couple of years after marriage were 'in connection with marriage'. The distinction between dowry and voluntary gifts still remains unclear, and no ceiling was set on the value of gifts. The amendment provides that the gift should be of 'customary nature' and not of 'excessive value' with regard to the financial status of the giver. What is customary and what is excessive are difficult to ascertain. As Vanita (1984) puts it, this whole section will legalize any amount of dowry and provide scope for individual biases in interpretation, and arbitrary and contradictory decisions.

Regarding getting the dowry back, the provision has been made more stringent, by reducing the period of transfer of dowry to the woman or her heir within three months (earlier it was one year) and increasing the punishment in the event of failure to transfer with minimum six months and maximum two years imprisonment (earlier it was six months). The amount of fine remains unchanged up to Rs. 10,000/-. The amendment also empowers the judge to order return of dowry and if the husband or his family fail to do so, a fine equal to the value of the property may be imposed. This has been a boon for women who have been driven out of their matrimonial homes. Supreme Court's judgement in Pratibha Rani vs Suraj Kumar case upholding *stridhan* as wife's exclusive property, was a major breakthrough (Kumar, 1985). It was widely appreciated by women's groups as having strengthened the law. However, it still has loopholes, as it is difficult to identify dowry items. There is a need for legal registration of gifts to be made compulsory, so that women may not be cheated of their dowry.

Feminist organizations have resented government's failure to accept changes in other aspects of the law, e.g., one year limit for filing suit, considering both givers and takers of dowry as equally guilty. However, the 1984 Amendment makes it a cognizable offence and empowers welfare institutions to file complaint of offence. Overall, a feeling of positive outlook is visible.

Recently, the Dowry Prohibition (Amendment) Bill 1986 was introduced in the Rajya Sabha. It attempts to tighten the provisions of the Act, and includes dowry deaths in the list of offences in the Indian Penal Code. The Bill provides that if a woman dies within seven years of her marriage due to causes other than natural, her property would be transferred to her children and if she has no children to her parents. The burden of proving that no dowry demand was made will be on those who took or abetted in the taking of the dowry, the aggrieved person will not be subjected to prosecution.

This amendment bill has made the offence non-bailable and raised the minimum punishment to five years and fine upto Rs. 15,000. Provisions for appointment of dowry prohibition officers and their advisory board with two women members have been made. The feminist women's reaction to the amendment are awaited.

Concluding Remarks

The problem of dowry demand is not merely one of a family demanding cash and goods beyond the capacity and desire of another family to give but rather a question of the inter-relatedness of psychological, social and economic factors. As one reads the shocking stories of individual women and families, one notices that there is very little and often no awareness among them of the roots of the problem or any motivation to curb the practice and bring about a much needed social change. This can be attributed to an internalization of prevailing patriarchal values which view women as inferior and having only themselves to blame for their predicament. It seldom sees them as victims of a particular form of oppression or of socially prevalent sex biases.

The burden of tradition, a prevailing ideology of male superiority, an insensitive police force, an archaic judicial system and a society that condones violence creates a chamber of horrors where even angels would fear to tread.

SEX DETERMINATION AND SEX PRESELECTION TESTS: ABUSE OF ADVANCED TECHNOLOGIES

Vibhuti Patel

Various techniques of sex determination and sex preselection have been discovered during the last fifteen years (Kotala, 1983). Techniques such as sonography, fetoscopy, needling, chorion biopsy and the most popular one, amniocentesis, are increasingly becoming household names in India (Ravindra, 1986b). Though Bombay and Delhi are the major centers for sex determination and sex preselection tests, technique of amniocentesis is used even in the clinics of small towns and cities of Gujarat, Maharashtra, Uttar Pradesh, Bihar, Madhya Pradesh, Punjab, Tamilnadu and Rajasthan. Justification for these techniques is aptly put by a team of doctors of Harkisandas Nurrotumdas Hospital (pioneers in this trade) in these words: '. . . in developing countries like India, as the parents are encouraged to limit their family to two offsprings, they will have a right to *quality* in these two as far as can be assured. Amniocentesis provides help in this direction' (Panthaki, Bangkar, Kulkarni and Patil, 1979). Here the word 'quality' raises a lot of issues that we will examine in this paper. First, let us understand the technical details of this technique called amniocentesis.

Amniocentesis, a scientific technique that was supposed to be used mainly to detect genetic deformities, has become very popular in India for detection of the sex of a foetus. For this 15–20 ml. of amniotic fluid is taken from the womb by pricking the foetus membrane with the help of a special kind of needle. After separating foetus cell from the amniotic fluid, a chromosomal analysis is conducted on it. This test helps in detecting several genetic disorders like mongolism, defects of neuotube in the foetus, retarded muscular growth, 'Rh' incompatibility, haemophilia and other types of abnormalities. This test is to be conducted on women above 40 years because there are higher chances of mongoloid children produced by such women. In some cases, a sex determination test is required to identify sex-specific deformities such as haemophilia, retarded muscular growth which mainly affect males.

Limitations of Amniocentesis

This test can give 95–97 per cent accurate results. Thus it is not totally reliable. In Harkisandas Hospital and Pearl Center, Bombay, where this test is conducted on thousands of women, it was noted that the test had affected the foetus adversely in one per cent of the total number of cases. Thus, the test may lead to spontaneous abortions or premature delivery, dislocation of hips, respiratory complications and needle puncture marks on the baby (Chhachhi and Satyamala, 1983).

The test is conducted after completion of 16 weeks of pregnancy and within a week the findings are available. In our country, the facility of amniocentesis is available only in the cities and towns, hence, patients from villages and small towns get the results by post; that takes one more week. By the time they decide to abort the foetus, it is over 18 weeks of pregnancy. Abortion at such a late stage is quite harmful for the mother.

Popularity of the Test

The amniocentesis test became popular in the last five years though earlier it was conducted in the government hospitals on an experimental basis. Now, this test is conducted in private clinics, private hospitals, and government hospitals mainly for sex determination and thereafter extermination of female foetus through abortion. This perverse use of modern technology is encouraged and boosted by money-minded private practitioners who are out to make a woman, 'a male-child-producing machine'. Based on their survey of six hospitals and clinics in Bombay, a research team at the Women's Aid Center, Bombay estimated that 10 women per day underwent the test in 1982. This survey also revealed the hypocrisy of one 'non-violent', 'vegetarian', 'anti-abortion' management of the city's most reputed hospital. This hospital conducts antenatal sex determination test. Their handout declares the test as 'human and beneficial'. The hospital has out-patient facilities and there is such a great rush for the test that one has to book one month in advance. As the management does not support abortion, they recommend women to various other hospitals and clinics and ask them to bring back the female foetuses to them after abortion for further research (Abraham and Shukla, 1983).

In other countries, amniocentesis is very expensive and is under strict governmental control. In our country the cost of getting this test done is between Rs. 200 and Rs. 500. Hence, even the working class can easily use this facility. A survey of several slums in Bombay showed that many women had undergone the test and after knowing that the sex of foetus was female, had undergone abortion in the eighteenth or nineteenth week of pregnancy. Their argument was it is better to spend Rs. 200 or even

Rs. 800 now, than give birth to a female baby and spend thousands of rupees for her marriage when she grows up.

The popularity of this test has attracted young workers of Larsen and Toubro, a multinational engineering industry too. As a result, medical bills showing the amount spent on the test were submitted by the workers for their reimbursement by the company. The Welfare Department was astonished to find that these workers were treating sex determination test very casually. They organised a two day seminar in which doctors, social workers, representatives of women's organizations as well as the Family Planning Association were invited. One doctor with a flourishing business of sex determination test stated in the seminar that,

. . . from Cape Comorin to Kashmir people ring him up at all hours of the day to find out about the test. So much so that his six year old son has learnt how to ask the relevant questions on the phone like "Is the pregnancy 16 weeks old?" etc. (Abraham, 1984).

Three sociologists conducted micro research in Bijnor district of Uttar Pradesh. Intensive field work over a period of one year in two villages drawn from eleven randomly selected villages in two community development blocks adjacent to Bijnor town and an interview survey of 301 women who had recently delivered convinced them of the fact that clinical services offering amniocentesis to inform women of the sex of their foetuses have appeared in north India in the past ten years. They fit into the cultural pattern in which girls are devalued. As per the 1981 census, the sex ratio of U.P. and Bijnor district were 886 and 863 respectively. They also found out that female infanticide that was practised in Bijnor district till 1900 was limited to Rajputs and Jats who considered birth of a daughter as a loss of prestige. However, abuse of amniocentesis for female foeticide was prevalent among all communities (Jeffery, Jeffery and Andrew, 1984).

In Delhi, the All India Institute of Medical Sciences started conducting sample survey of amniocentesis in 1974 to find out foetal abnormalities. They were flooded with requests for abortion. As soon as the parents were told that the foetus was a girl, they started making arrangements for abortion (Chhachhi and Satyamala, 1983).

A sociological research in Punjab selected in its sample 50 per cent men and 50 per cent women as respondents for their questionnaire on opinions of men and women regarding sex determination tests. Among men the respondents, were either businessmen or white collar employees of the income group of Rs. 1000 to Rs. 3500 per month, while women respondents were mainly housewives. All of them knew about the test and found it useful (Singh and Jain, 1983). Why not? Punjab was the first to start commercial use of this test way back in 1979. It was the advertisement in newspapers regarding New Bhandari ante-natal sex determination clinic in Amritsar that activized the press and the women groups to denounce it equivocally.

Controversy around Amniocentesis

Three years back a controversy around amniocentesis started as a result of several investigative reports published in popular magazines like *India Today, Eve's Weekly, Sunday* and other regional language journals. What shocked everyone, from academics to activists, was that between 1978 and 1983, around 78,000 female foetuses were aborted after sex determination tests in our country (*The Times of India*, June 1982).

Sycophants of population control advocate this test because they think the government can achieve, Net Reproduction Rate of One (NRRI), i.e., replacement of a mother by only one daughter, with the help of sex determination test. According to them, if there are less number of women, there will be less growth of runaway population. The advocates of population control policy want to cash on socio-cultural values that treat birth of a daughter in the family as a great calamity and perpetuate modern method of femicide to achieve NRRI by 1990 asper the claims of 7th Five Year Plan of the Government of India.

The same government which refuses to ban amniocentesis exposed itself by not providing facility to pregnant women after the Bhopal gas tragedy inspite of repeated requests of women's groups and inspite of numerous reported cases of birth of deformed babies.

The government and private medical practitioners involved in this lucrative trade, justify the sex determination test as a measure of population control. Women have always been at the receiving end of all family planning policies. Harmful effects of pregnancy test, contraceptive pills, anti-pregnancy injections, camps for mass sterilisation of women with its unhygenic atmosphere are always overlooked by the enthusiasts of family planning policy. Ninety nine per cent of population control research is conducted on women without any consideration to the harmful effects of research to the women concerned. Advocates of population control will continue cashing on socio-cultural values that treat the birth of a daughter as a great calamity and perpetuate modern methods of massacre of female foetuses on a massive scale.

India has a legacy of killing the female child by putting opium on the mother's nipple or by putting the afterbirth over the child's face or by ill treating daughters (Clark, 1983). A recent survey by a leading magazine revealed that in Tamilnadu, among the Kallar community mothers who give birth to baby girls are forced to kill the babies by feeding them with milk from poisonous oleander berries (Venkatramani, 1986). It is quite possible that researchers could even today find cases of female infanticide in parts of western Gujarat, Rajasthan, U.P., Bihar, Punjab and Madhya Pradesh. Female members of the family get inferior treatment as far as food, medication and education is concerned (Kynch and Sen, 1983). When they grow up there is further harassment for dowry. No wonder many social scientists ask if is it not desirable that she dies rather than be illtreated? In Kumar's (1983b) words: 'Is it really better to be born and left to die than to be killed as foetus? Does the birth of lakhs or even millions of unwanted girls improve the status of women?' But the worst thing about amniocentesis is, it is practised by all, irrespective of their class, caste, religion, educational or cultural background, while female infanticide was limited only among certain castes (Jeffery and Jeffery, 1983).

What can be the long term implications if such a trend continues? Will it not aggravate the already disturbed sex-ratio? There has been continuous declining in female/male sex-ratio between 1901 and 1971. Between 1971 and 1981 there is a slight increase, but it still continues to be adverse for women. For the year 1981, the women per 1000 men stands at 933.

Here too, some economists and doctors have their reply ready, i.e., law of demand and supply. If supply of women reduces, their demand as well as status will enhance (Seth, 1984). Scarcity of women will increase their value (Bardhan, 1982). According to this logic, women won't be easily replaceable commodities. But here the economists forget the socio-cultural milieu in which women have to live. The society that treats women as mere sex-objects will not treat women in a more humane way if they are scarce in supply, on the contrary, there will be increased incidences of rape, abduction and forced polyandry. In Madhya Pradesh, Haryana, Rajasthan and Punjab among certain communities, the sex-ratio is extremely adverse for women. There a wife is shared by a set of brothers and some times even by patrilateral parallel cousins (Dube, 1983b).

To think that it is better to kill female foetus than give birth to unwanted female child, is very fatalistic. By this logic it is better to kill the poor people or third world masses rather than let them suffer poverty and deprivation.

Another argument is that in cases where women have one or more daughters, they should be allowed to have amniocentesis done so that they can plan a balanced family by having a son. Instead of going on producing female children in the hope of getting a male child, it is better for the family's and country's welfare that they abort the female foetus and have small and balanced family with daughters and sons. This concept of balanced family also has a sexist bias. Would couples with one or more sons undergo amniocentesis to get rid of male foetus and to have a daughter for balancing their family? Never. What is the cost of having a balanced family? How many abortions during 16 to 18 weeks can a woman bear without jeopardizing her health?

Time and again it is stated that women themselves enthusiastically go for the test out of their free will. It is a question of women's own choice. But are these choices made in social vacuum? These women are socially conditioned to accept that unless they produce one or more male children there is no social worth attached to them (Rapp, 1986). They can be harassed, taunted, even deserted by their husbands and in-laws if they fail to do so. Thus their 'choices' depend on the fear of society. It is true that feminists all over the world have always demanded the right of women to control their own bodies/fertility and choose whether or not to have a child or children and have facility for free, legal and safer abortions. While understanding these issues in the Third World context, we must see it in the background of the role of imperialism and racism that aims at the control of the colored population. Thus, it is all too easy for a population control advocate to heartily endorse women's rights at the same time diverting attention from the real causes of the population problem. Lack of food, economic security, clean drinking water and safe clinical facilities have led to a situation where a woman has to have 6.2 children to have at least one surviving male child.

These are the roots of the population problem, not merely desire to have a male child (Chhachhi and Satyamala, 1983). There are some who ask 'If family planning is a desirable thing, why not sex planning?' But we must not forget that this planning is envisaged within the matrix of patriarchal society. Sex choice can be another way of oppressing women. Under the guise of choice, we may indeed exacerbate our own oppression (Holmes and Betty, 1984).

Popularity of sex preselection tests can be more dangerous than that of sex determination tests because the former does not involve ethical issues related to abortion. So even anti-abortionists can use this method. Dr. Ronald Erikson, who has his chain of clinics conducting sex preselection tests in 46 countries of Europe, America, Asia, Latin America, announces in his handout: out of 263 couples who approached him, 248 selected boys and 15 selected girls. This shows that male preference is not limited to a Third World country like India, but that it is universal. In Erikson's method, no abortion or apparent violence is involved, still it can lead to violent social disaster if one thinks of its consequences in a long term. Through social consequences of sex selection as well as sex determination tests, the reality shatters the myth of neutrality of science and technology. Hence the necessity of linking science and technology with socio-economic and cultural reality. Class, race and sex biases of the ruling elites have crossed all boundaries of human dignity. After 39 years of revolution and socialist reconstruction, sex determination tests for female extermination have gained ground after government's adoption of a one-child family policy. Chinese couples willy-nilly accept a system of one-child-family but the child has to be a male. This shows how adaptive the system of patriarchy and male supremacy is. It can establish and strengthen its roots in all kinds of social structures, precapitalist, capitalist and even socialist by making savage use of science. This ethos of patriarchy has to be challenged consistently (Patel, 1984).

Action against Sex Determination and Sex Preselection Tests

In 1982, when national dailies first carried advertizements of Bhandari's sex determination clinics, women's groups organized protest actions against it. Sensitive journalists, women's organizations such as Saheli (Delhi), Women's Center (Bombay), Sabala (Calcutta) issued a statement against the tests. Research organizations such as Research Unit on Women's Studies, Center for Women's Development and voluntary health organisations also took stand against the tests. Medico Friends Circle and People's Science Movement also joined the campaign. None of them blamed the masses for propagation of the tests. They questioned the highly educated, enlightened scientists, technocrats, doctors and, of course, the state who help in propagating such a situation (Ravindra, 1986a).

The debate on sex determination tests have generated lot of controversy in the academic circles and among researchers too (Balasubramanyam, 1982; Dube, 1983a, Dube, 1983b). Most of the women's groups feel that amniocentesis, C.V.B., sonography should be allowed under strict governmental control and only for detecting genetic abnormalities (Singh, 1986). They are also aware of the fact that in that case unscrupulous doctors will illegally conduct the test. To avoid this, women's organizations and other socially conscious groups will have to act as watch dogs.

To consistently campaign against the notorious activities of money-minded doctors and antipathy of the government towards increasing female foeticide, a Forum against Sex Determination and Sex Preselection Techniques has been formed in Bombay. Lawyers, doctors, women activists, researchers and scientists are actively discussing the issue at the social level. Through their talks on public forum, media-coverage, poster campaign, exhibition, film, publications, they are trying to convey the social implications of the test. Because they know that mere reforms in legal or medical fields will not themselves do away with this ever growing phenomenon of female foeticide (Shukla and Kulkarni, 1986). To enhance social literacy of public, they have organised pickets in front of hospitals conducting such tests, pasted thousands of posters condemning the tests. They have demanded that:

1) Mass media should refuse to publish advertizements for sex determination tests, 2) The government must publicize the fact that a woman is not responsible for the birth of a girl.

A woman gives only chromosomes whereas a man may give an X or Y chromosome which is responsible for the sex of the baby. If a man's Y chromosome unites with woman's X chromosome, then a boy is born and if man's X chromosome unites with woman's X chromosome, a girl is born. Hence, woman should not be blamed for the birth of a girl child.

The forum has recommended that sex determination tests violate Article 14 and Article 15 of the Constitution of India that guarantees that there will be no discrimination against women. The advocate of the forum has expressed the need to introduce certain changes in the M.T.P. Act which would legally lay down the conditions under which amniocentesis can be carried out (Singh, 1986).

Public awareness and a consciousness-raising campaign can only bring positive results by changing societal values/attitudes towards women. The campaign should evolve newer forms to highlight the social issues and its various aspects. Some of the effective forms for campaign will be the parent-daughter yatra, march of school-going girls with flowers, sit-in (*dharana*) by prominent parents having only daughters (Lata and Harpal, 1986).

Conclusion

More research on the prevalence of sex determination tests needs to be done. So far we have micro studies on the subject only from some parts of Maharashtra, Uttar Pradesh and Punjab. Women's studies departments in colleges and universities and sociologists must give special attention to this problem as they can help in the process of change by working at policy levels and also by imparting knowledge to younger generation through the educational system.

FEMALE INFANTICIDE IN CONTEMPORARY INDIA: A CASE-STUDY OF KALLARS OF TAMILNADU

S. Krishnaswamy

The history of human culture is replete with examples of systematic oppression of women. One form of oppression of women is the practice of female infanticide. An example of female infanticide, as part of an adaptive strategy, was found among the Tapirape tribe of the Amazon region, which had a social structure that prevented the tribe from splitting into smaller groups, even when the community became too large for the subsistence base. The rationale for the existence of the practice was inadequate food supply (Scrimshaw, 1978). Another factor which lent credence to this practice was the patriarchal nature of the tribal society.

Scholars like Malthus, McLennon, Carr-Sander, and Krzywick have propounded theories in order to understand the basic relationship between population increase, want of essential necessities, and the need for an artifice for restricting rapid multiplication of human mouths (Pakrasi, 1970). These theories have justified the existence of female infanticide at a time when human civilization was still primitive and employed crude techniques and had reasons to eliminate their female members. But none of them hold true in the modern context.

However, what intrigues social scientists is the evidence that the practice of female infanticide has not completely disappeared. This paper, confines itself to an analysis of the custom of female infanticide in India, in general and among the Kallars of Madurai district in Tamilnadu, in particular.

Female Infanticide in Nineteenth Century India

There is hardly any written evidence of female infanticide in India prior to the coming of the British. When the British came to India this practice was common almost throughout India: from Gujarat in the west to the eastern borders of Uttar Pradesh, from Punjab in the north to Madhya Pradesh in the south. Significantly, there were only three tribal groups among whom this practice was prevalent at the time: the Nagas of the northeastern region, the Khonds of Orissa and the Todas of the Nilgiri hills (Pakrasi, 1968). However, female infanticide was suspected among several communities belonging to middle or upper classes: the Rajputs who were distributed in almost all the provinces of northern India, the Sikhs and Muslim Pathans of Punjab (Cave-Brown as in Miller, 1981), Khatris of northwestern India, Kanbis of Gujarat, Jats, Gujars, Tagas, Ahars, Minas, and Ahirs all of whom were inhabitants of northwestern India (Pakrasi, 1968).

One of the several reasons advanced for the existence of this practice was the prevalence of hypergamous marriages, a custom which forbids the marriage of a woman with a person of lower social standing. This invariably led to the giving of large dowry to secure a bridegroom of high social status. In fact, there is an old Tamil proverb which says: even a king with five daughters is sure to become a pauper. The financial burden of marrying off a daughter, and the social stigma of having an unmarried daughter in the house forced people to kill infant girls at birth.

There are also certain superstitious beliefs which have lent credence to the prevalence of female infanticide. A common belief was that if you kill a female child, the next one is sure to be a male. Another belief was that female children bring ill-luck to the family.

A possible explanation for the practice among tribal groups was inefficient family planning. Female infanticide has the same effect as abortion—the major difference being that in this case the progeny is being selected according to sex (Davis and Blake, 1956). According to Pakrasi, the Nagas practiced infanticide only 'to avoid raids by their strongest neighbours in quest of wives' (1968, p. 46).

The large scale practice of female infanticide attracted the attention of the British rulers and forced them to act. A notable feature of all the measures was the introduction of an Act for Suppression of Female Infanticide (VII of 1870). The British also organized conferences on the evils of infanticide, established a record of dowry deaths, helped fathers to pay for the marriages of their daughters, fixed a norm for the amount of dowry to be paid (Miller, 1981). The measures taken by the British Government, thus, helped in the noticeable decline of this practice in most areas in India.

The Kallars of Tamilnadu

The primary objective of this paper is to analyze the custom of female infanticide as is practised in the last quarter of the twentieth century, almost two hundred years after it was first reported. In order to understand

and appreciate the roots of this practice among Kallars, it becomes necessary to trace the caste history of Kallars.

In terms of caste history one finds a similarity between the Kallars of Tamilnadu and the Rajputs of northern India. The traditional occupation of both the groups had been as warriors. During certain periods of history members of both Kallars and Rajputs were seen as rulers in certain small pockets. Whereas Rajputs continued their traditional occupation as warriors even during the British period, Kallars ceased to be so. Nevertheless, Kallars were a fierce and turbulent race, famous for their military prowess (Thurston, 1975). However today the Kallars are found in such diverse occupations as landless agricultural laborers, watchmen, small businessmen, illicit liquor distillation etc. It is difficult, however, to pinpoint as to when this change in Kallars' occupation came about.

Though the maximum concentration of Kallars is found in Usilampatti taluk of Madurai district, they form a significant proportion in the adjoining taluks as well. They form a minority group in other districts of Tamilnadu. It has been noted that the role of women in their economic pursuits is insignificant. The women's role is confined solely to bearing and rearing of children and looking after the household activities. As such, the level of education among Kallars is very low.

Nature of the Custom

It is common for members of this community to openly admit to infanticide as if they are narrating their cultural habits. During the first encounter the author had with a female respondent, she had the following statement to make:

> Since I do not want the first child to be a female baby I wanted it to be killed. But my husband feels that we should wait for the second child. If that also happens to be a female baby we will definitely kill the second one.

The trained dai (midwife) at the local maternity center has been a witness to the practice of female infanticide. Some of the deliveries she performed at the center which happened to be female babies were done away with. She narrated ways in which the members of the community accomplish this task of killing their own infant daughters. In one instance, the father stepped on the throat of his infant daughter a few hours after the female baby was born while the mother was still unconscious; a second method was to feed the female infant with the poisonous milk of a wild plant (*calotropis gigantea*) or the oleander berries known for their lethal poison, with little sugar—the result being instant death. It is also observed that every Kallar household has this plant grown in the courtyard for use at an appropriate time such as the birth of an unwanted female baby. The third method of killing a baby is stuffing few grains of coarse paddy into the mouth. The infant breathes the grain into the windpipe and chokes to death (Venkatramani, 1986). There is also a widespread belief among Kallars that if you kill a daughter, your next child will be a son.

More recent evidence of female infanticide among Kallars has brought out few more interesting facts and figures regarding this practice. A doctor at a government hospital in the capital of one taluk, Usilampatti, lamented that when a pregnant woman of this caste delivers a female baby she invariably absconds immediately after birth with the baby. She returns after a week but without the baby and reports a natural death. The statistics at this hospital are shocking—which is indicative of the magnitude of the practice. Of the 1200 total number of deliveries performed on an average per year to women belonging to the Kallar caste, nearly 600 are female babies. Out of this an estimated 570 babies vanish with their mothers no sooner than they can open their eyes to the world. Hospital sources estimate that nearly 80 per cent of these vanishing babies, i.e., more than 450, become victims of infanticide. Similar trend is observed in private nursing homes, primary health centres and maternity hospitals/ centers (Venkatramani, 1986). This figure is an underestimation since the number of institutional deliveries forms only a small proportion of the total deliveries by the women of this caste, since many of them do not have access to medical facilities.

Who carries out the 'execution' of unwanted female babies? It is normally carried out by the parents, either on their own accord or forced by the in-laws of the women. Since the preference for sons is so strong among Kallars, a woman who gives birth to only female children is looked down upon by the members of her husband's family. In order to avoid the wrath of the in-laws the mother is forced to do away with the baby immediately after she comes to know that her baby is a girl, and the death is attributed to natural causes.

In cases where women cannot bear sons, even divorce is reported to be common. Which mother would dare to put herself into this position? It is interesting to note that in the 1891 Census, it is mentioned that as a token of divorce 'a kallan gives his wife a piece of straw in the presence of his caste people'. In Tamil, as used by Kallars (unheard of among other caste groups), the expression 'to give a straw' means 'to divorce', and 'to take a straw' means to 'accept divorce' (Thurston, 1975). Even today, the question of divorce among Kallars is reported to be the least complicated social issue. A less dramatic instance is that the husband will not visit the hospital ᶜ he hears the news that his wife has given birth to a female baby. This is an obvious sign for the wife of his displeasure and the unspoken message is very clear.

According to an available estimate it has been shown that the number of infanticide deaths were approximately 6000 during the last decade alone (Venkatramani, 1986). However, this seems to be an underestimate since it is not based on any empirical evidence, and the vital records do not provide this information as these deaths are not registered with local administration. The village visited by the author where this custom is still prevalent is marked as a high infant mortality area which probably could mean that the death of female infants, might have been reported as normal deaths.

Sex Ratio

One could infer the existence of female infanticide from the disparity in sex ratios provided by the Census. In the absence of 1981 Census returns for the selected villages we use 1971 Census figures instead. Of the four villages visited by the authors, the infanticide village, i.e., Kovil Kurivithurai had the lowest sex ratio when compared to the non-infanticide villages as given in Table 1. There is reason to believe that this sex ratio might have declined further keeping in line with the general decline at various levels.

Table 1
SEX RATIO IN FEW SELECTED VILLAGES OF NILAKOTTAI TALUK OF MADURAI DISTRICT -- 1971 (*No. of Females per 1000 Males*)

Area/Villages	Sex Ratio
Nilakottai (Rural)	998
Villages	
1) Kovil Kuruvithurai	926
2) Mannadi Mangalam	1029
3) Karuppatti	1035
4) Irumbadi	1007

Note: Computed from 1971 Census figures

As of 1971, village of Kovil Kurivithurai, inhabited mainly by Kallars, had a sex ratio of 926 females per 1000 males which is much lower than the sex ratio of the Nilakottai taluk as a whole. The adjoining villages (Mannadi Mangalam, Karuppatti and Irumbadi) located within a radius of 3–5 km, which had significant proportion of other caste groups had in fact been very favorable to women in general. Particularly in Karuppatti, the sex ratio stood at 1035 females per 1000 males. The above analysis could be taken as a fair indication of the low status of women in general in the predominantly Kallar areas.

During the last decade, the official birth rate among the Kallars of Usilampatti was only 1 per cent. Males now constitute 52 per cent of the Kallar population whereas 10 years ago they accounted for only 48 per cent. And 70 per cent of Kallar children below the age of 10 years are now boys. Ten years ago that figure was 50 per cent (Venkatramani, 1986). One notices a decline in the sex ratio in almost all the taluks of Madurai district between 1971 and 1981 (Table 2). The taluks with lowest sex ratio being Kodaikanal and Usilampatti. The lowest sex-ratio (938) in Kodaikanal (a tourist resort) is understandable, because it is hilly and men of different castes flock there for earning a livelihood leaving their families behind. The next lowest sex ratio (960) was found in Usilampatti taluk—a predominantly Kallar area, and this reinforces our thesis of low status of women once again.

Table 2
SEX RATIO IN DIFFERENT TALUKS OF MADURAI DISTRICT
DURING 1971 AND 1981 (*Per 1000 Males*)

Taluks	1971			1981		
	Total	Rural	Urban	Total	Rural	Urban
Palani	995	1005	966	977	979	966
Vedasantur	1012	1012	–	1000	1001	970
Natham**	–	–	–	981	983	974
Dindigul	989	997	972	978	985	965
Kodaikanal	935	930	953	938	936	945
Uttamapalayam	990	990	990	972	975	967
Periyakulam	987	991	975	976	980	965
Nilakottai	997	998	984	985	986	979
Melur	1008	1012	972	1019	1025	973
Madurai (N)	1029	1031	1011	984	985	976
Madurai (S)	952	979	949	953	972	951
Usilampatti	976	973	1003	960	961	949
Tirumangalam	1018	1026	977	1004	1012	963

Note: Computed from population figures of 1971 and 1981 Censuses
**Natham was not a district in 1971

Economics of Female-Infanticide

The custom of infanticide among Kallars (about 2 lakh in Usilampatti taluk alone) seemed to be motivated by the relative economic backwardness of the community and the social importance of males. These motivational factors are almost comparable to 'pride and purse' which underlined this practice in north India in the nineteenth century. In no other community in modern India, the economic value of male children is as pronounced as among the Kallars. This is borne out of the fact that the existence of this custom has not been reported from any other part of modern India. There are many instances of neglect of female children in education, health, nutrition and clothes, across the Indian subcontinent but none measure upto this custom of outright murder. The economic import of a male child is intertwined with the cultural practices of this community. As was noted, one of the hereditary occupations of the Kallars had been dacoity. Their status in the economic front, particularly those who inhabit the villages, has not changed in a major way and majority of them work as landless agricultural laborers. Thus, they are a merciless race as regards the value of human life. Having a son means perpetuation of the race, with all its valor and adventure. They take pride in calling themselves members of the Kallan race. In an age of increased competition for survival with other groups, more male hands ensure more physical power to the community. One would therefore, like to have only sons and do away with the daughters, since the destruction of a female infant is viewed psychologically in the same light as abortion. In this context, it is not surprising to note that a mother is looked down upon for not being able to beget a son.

Another practice that lowers the economic value of the female child and probably is the single most important factor is dowry. The evil nature of dowry among Kallars is similar to that among the castes practising infanticide in the nineteenth century. The female child becomes a liability in more ways than one. This is also attributed as one of the reasons for its existence in the past, wherein marrying off one's daughter into a caste higher than one's own was a desired social custom which needed considerable amount of resources. However, the system of dowry among Kallars assumes a slightly different dimension in that even if the Kallar bridegroom is not of higher status, the marriage still involves a considerable amount of expenditure. Invariably, all those respondents who were reported to have committed this crime resort to infanticide because they do not want to see their daughter suffer throughout her life as they cannot afford to pay an exhorbitant dowry. Instead they would prefer to bear the sorrow of their infant daughter suffering initially for few hours after birth which, moreover, does not result in any wastage of investment. The psychological impact of this custom is very profound on the mother, but she has to accept it since her position in her family becomes precarious otherwise.

When a mother does attempt to save her infant daughter, it results either in divorce or being sent to her father's place to bring more resources in the form of gold or money sufficient to marry off their daughter. What is the magnitude of this expenditure? If a Kallar family wants to celebrate a daughter's marriage in a decent manner, the minimum cost will range from

Rs. 30,000 to Rs. 40,000 including all the cost and jewellery and other marriage expenses. According to a member of this community:

> Even if you want to marry your daughter to a poor agricultural worker who does not own even a square inch of agricultural land and who has to lead a hand to mouth existence, you have to give Rs. 2,000 cash to the bridegroom and make jewellery worth five sovereigns of gold (approximately 50 grams) for your daughter. If the potential bridegroom happens, by chance, to own some land, however meagre the holding, the automatic demand is Rs. 10,000 and 10 sovereigns of gold. As the socio-economic status of the bridegroom goes higher and higher the cost and the jewellery to be given increases correspondingly. It is not considered unusual if the girl's father spends a lakh of rupees and in addition gives a kilo of gold when the son-in-law has the high status of an engineer, lawyer, doctor or member of parliament (Venkatramani, 1986).

The agony of parents do not end with dowry during the marriage of their daughter. The expenditure from the girl's side appears to be a life long process. The girl's parents are expected to offer gifts or invite the in-laws for each and every festive occasion. If the father of the girl is deceased, her brother is expected to attend the ceremonies of his sister's family.

Thus, the economic overtones in the form of dowry and post-marriage expenditures rather than the desire to kill, is the real culprit. This has been reflected in the responses of mothers who become emotional and they do not appear ruthless but seem to be unfortunate and hopeless victims of desperately cruel circumstances

Religious Reasons

The phenomenon of female infanticide among Kallars is found to have religious overtones as well. This religious importance of sons is not peculiar to this caste group alone. But one could note that the emphasis on the religious superiority of sons is more among the Kallars than in any other non-Brahmanic caste groups of southern India. Hindu scriptures put premium on sons. According to Hindu ritual *pind daan*, performed after death, ensures one to reach *moksha* (heaven). However, these rites can be performed only by the dead person's son. Absence of a son means no place in heaven, and the soul wanders without any abode. During most of the ceremonies in the household it is the son who stands next to his father, or performs himself if the father is deceased. The importance of a son assumes greater significance at the time of father's death, since only the son can light the funeral pyre, and the role of daughter is non-existent.

The religious reasons of infanticide could be viewed from the nature of Kallan worship. Their presiding deity, Kallalagar, derives his name from the name of the caste itself, or it could be vice versa. Among many stories about Kallans, there is one of a group of Kallan males who set out on a robbing expedition of neighboring villages and prayed to Kallalagar with the promise of due share to the god if their operation is successful. This story amplifies the importance of males among Kallars. The annual celebration of Kallalagar in the month of *Chithirai* (coinciding with April in English calender), called *Chithirai Thirunaal* in the city of Madurai, is one of the biggest festivals and is marked with utmost gaiety—the same gaiety which attends the arrival of a male child in the family.

Law and Female Infanticide

According to the law the deaths of babies under suspicious circumstances should be reported to the village administrative officers and the panchayats or local bodies. But in all these cases, the households keep the information to themselves, although what is happening is common knowledge (Venkatramani, 1986). The execution of law is non-existent. In order for the law to punish the guilty a formal complaint has to be lodged. Who will come forward to complain about any particular family killing a female child? It is very common that some informants openly challenge the legality of the government and officials who in their opinion have no business to interfere in their personal affairs. A typical attitude runs thus: 'If I and my husband have the right to have a child, we also have the right to kill it if it happens to be a daughter, and we decide we cannot afford it: Outsiders and the government have no right to poke their noses into this' (Venkatramani, 1986). This attitude is the result of a desperate economic situation in which the members of this caste are finding themselves in.

It must be stressed, however, that the Infanticide Act of 1870, which the British used so effectively, still exists and is strong enough to suppress female infanticide. In order for the law to be effective British administrators also employed various coercive measures. However, there is no mention anywhere in the literature of female infanticide as to whether anybody has been convicted for this crime as per the Act. In the present context, there appears to be a certain amount of reluctance on the part of government officials to act even though they know what has been happening. With the government's own strong family planning policies this custom has been ignored for it serves the same goal at no cost to the government. But there arises a serious question on the value of human life itself which all the civilized cultures hold so dear.

Recommendations

The *first* recommendation refers to direct intervention on the part of the government. The community may have any number of justifications for the practice of female infanticide. But, examples of successful suppression of this custom in the past is very much evident. There are laws in the modern world which prohibit the killing of animals—surely the law can be enforced to prohibit the killing of female children. But who would report these deaths? Even this is not an entirely unsurmountable problem. The hospital authorities could make absconding difficult; they could identify and report the suspected cases and these could be followed up by the law enforcing authorities. Concerted public pressure would go a long way in changing the attitude of the Kallars. The government could take action by demarcating this area as *active infanticide area*, and invoke the Infanticide Act.

A far better way to stop this inhuman practice is, of course, to strike it at the roots. Tightening of the dowry laws would surely help in bringing down the incidence of female infanticide. It is pertinent to recall that the British in their efforts to curb female infanticide fixed the rates of dowry to be paid at the time of marriage. Thirdly, social upliftment of the Kallars, in general, and the Kallar women, in particular, is essential, both educationally and economically. If the Kallar women could be seen as contributing to the family income, perhaps their stature in society would not be so pathetic. In this regard the role of women's groups, social welfare agencies and human rights groups is crucial. The spillover effect of this would be increased use of birth control practices which would help Kallar women in preventing unwanted births and not to resort to outright murder. The media should play an important role in enhancing the stature of women: by outlining the contributions a female child could make to the family and to society at large, if they are given the right kind of educational opportunities.

RAPE IN INDIA: AN EMPIRICAL PICTURE

Sohaila Abdulali

There is ample evidence that rape in India is a unique phenomenon which goes beyond the variable of sexuality in many ways, e.g., the way in which it is used by landlords to quell tribal uprisings. In this paper the role of institutions such as the police and the military in perpetrating rape is explored. Statistics and accounts of incidents collected from newsclippings, pamphlets, official publications and talking with people are included. Rape within the middle and upper classes, incest and marital rape are discussed, as are their connections with other forms of rape. The reasons why these forms of rape receive almost no publicity, in contrast with the more 'political' acts of rape committed by police, landlords, etc. are analyzed.

General Statistics and their Validity

Every year about 4,000 cases of rape are registered in India (Ranjan, 1982). According to an article in *India Today*, every two hours a rape occurs somewhere in India (Kapoor, 1983). This means a total of 4,380 rapes per year. This figure is almost identical to the number of reported rapes a year. I reject this as being unrealistically low. To presume that actual rapes equal reported rapes is highly optimistic, given the sanctions imposed on victims and the enormous pressures on women to be silent about all forms of exploitation to which they are subjected. Nevertheless, a look at the statistics on registered rape is useful as it provides some insight into the incidence of this crime. The following table shows the registered cases of rape in some years during the 1970s, according to the Bureau of Police Research and Development in New Delhi.

There were 2,962 reported rapes in 1974, and 3,899 in 1978; this means an increase of approximately 32 per cent in those four years of reported rape alone. Since I do not have complete statistical data on the figures in other time periods, this may or may not be a meaningful trend.

Reported rapes tend to increase in areas where there is political unrest and violence. For instance, in the state of Punjab, where there have been violent clashes between the Sikhs and the central government recently, registered rapes rose from 1,223 in 1982 to 1,500 in 1983, a 23 per cent

REGISTERED CASES OF RAPE IN INDIA

Major States	1972	1975	1978
Uttar Pradesh	577	760	820
Madhya Pradesh	433	565	787
West Bengal	285	408	477
Bihar	240	304	345 (1977)
Maharashtra	238	283	360
All India Total	**2,562**	**3,283**	**3,899**
Percentage increase over 1972		28%	52%

Major Cities	1972	1975	1978
Bombay	29	56	58
Delhi	30	52	57
Calcutta	15	21	23
Total for 8 major cities	**110**	**145**	n.a.
Percentage increase over 1972		30%	

The states of Uttar Pradesh and Madhya Pradesh accounted for 41% of the registered cases in 1978 (Rao et al, n.d.).

increase ('India', *Asian Labour Monitor*, 1984). Rape became an issue in Assam during the election violence in that state in 1983. The connection between political violence and violent crimes against women will be explored later.

Which rapes do not show up in the figures which are available? If only one case of rape is registered in Bombay every 7 days ('Rape a Day', *The Daily*, 1982), what kind of rape is it likely to be and what kind is it not likely to be? Inter-caste and inter-class rapes are much more likely to be reported than those which occur within castes and classes. This generally means rapes committed by upper-caste men on lower-caste women. In all my research the only case of an upper-class woman declaring publicly that she had been raped by lower-class men which I know of is my own. Perhaps the reason for this is that in such cases the woman is more likely to be blamed for her 'provocative' behavior, as the rape cannot be glibly explained away in terms of class oppression. It is also probably not as common as other forms of rape. Rapes within class are not reported either, for much the same reason. Even when rapes within class, especially the lower classes, are reported, they are not included in the usual rape statistics. In the 11 December 1982 issue of the *Free Press Journal*, it was reported that rapes of Adivasi and Harijan women in Madhya Pradesh are on the rise, and the monthly figure has risen to 15 as compared to 5 or 6 in 1975. The report specifically states that it does not include rapes committed by Adivasi and Harijan men on Adivasi and Harijan women.

Until the anti-rape movement began in 1980, rape was only an issue with political parties and activist groups for whom it was a symbol of political and caste oppression. It was not in the interest of these groups to take up the cause of those women who are raped by men of their own or a lower class. These rapes could not fit into an analysis of class-based capitalist oppression, and thus no political purpose was served by examining them. Failing a feminist explanation of rape, the only way to explain these rapes in a male-dominated society was by putting the responsibility for being raped primarily on the victim. Given this attitude, and the concept of women's elusive *izzat*, it is no wonder that the majority of reported rapes are those which are committed by men in position of power on women who are affected by this power. Other reasons for the under-reporting of rape include the lack of trust between law enforcement agencies and the public and attitudes towards rape which result in high social costs for the victim.

Rape by the Police

The Indian police force has the reputation of being extremely corrupt and repressive. The police are seen as rapists and brutes by oppressed groups, as political scapegoats by the ruling classes, as instruments of repression (or hapless victims of the system) by opposition parties. Whether or not they are indeed corrupt, police rape gets more attention than any other form of rape.

The most infamous case of police rape, the Mathura case, sparked the development of the anti-rape movement in India. Mathura, a lower-caste girl who was between 14 and 16 years old at the time, was kept captive by two policemen, Ganpat and Tukaram. She was raped by Ganpat and Tukaram tried to rape her but was too drunk to complete the rape. The Sessions Court found Ganpat not guilty of rape and declared that Mathura had been a willing party to sexual intercourse. The High Court found Ganpat guilty and sentenced him to five years rigorous imprisonment. The Supreme Court reversed the High court's decision and set both Ganpat and Tukaram free ('Rape', *Manushi*, 1980). This is typical in its circumstances as well as its outcome—condemnation of the victim, freedom for the offenders.

The Rameeza Bee case is another widely publicized example of police brutality. Rameeza Bee, a married woman who lived with her husband in the city of Hyderabad, was returning home with her husband after seeing a film late one night when some policemen took her away to the police station (because, they said later, she had unveiled her face and indecently exposed herself, and this led them to suspect her of being a prostitute) and raped her all night. The next day they took her home, dragged out her husband and beat him to death. This incident sparked off riots in Hyderabad and throughout Andhra Pradesh. The police station was burnt and police retaliation led to the deaths of about 26 people (Stree Shakti Sangathana, 1980). The rapists were acquitted by the Sessions Court judge, but this decision has been appealed (Bill on Rape, *Sangharsh*, n.d.). Rameeza has become a heroine of sorts, she is now regarded as a famous prostitute. In this case an impartial commission indicted the policemen who had raped her but the state government let them go free. This is just one instance of the government covertly sanctioning rape by policeman. Police morale must be protected, even if it is at the cost of justice (Rao et al, n.d.). There are numerous such incidents—incidents where the police have raped women not necessarily as part of larger political cause, but rather for the simple reason that the women are seen as available and rape is not punished.

In Baghpat, three men and a woman were sitting in a car in the market when a plainclothes policeman came over and began to harass the woman. He was beaten up by her companions. A short while later, a policy party came to the spot, shot and killed all three men, took the woman to the police station and raped her. They explained it by saying the men were dangerous criminals and the police had merely been rescuing the woman (Fernandes, 1983; 'Don't Complain to the Police', *The Economist*, 1980). In Bhatinda, Sub-Inspector Bhagat Ram and Constable Milthu Singh were arrested for the alleged abduction and rape of a young woman (*Maitreyi*, 1982). In Bellary, a 16 year old girl who was returning home with a male companion was accosted by the police. The pair were separated, the boy was severely beaten and the girl was raped by six constables. The public was outraged and there were riots. The police opened fire and 7 people were killed (Chakravarti, 1983). In Barabanki, two police officials were accused of the rape and murder of a Harijan village woman. They had gone to find her husband but on finding him gone had raped, tortured and then hung her (Rao et al, n.d.). In Garhwal, a 12 year old girl was reportedly raped by a police constable while she was in his house to do domestic work (Rao et al, n.d.).

Once in a while a policeman gets suspended from duty or arrested and these are the cases which get the most attention. The majority of police rapists go unpunished.

In addition to random rapes, the police also use rape as a very effective weapon in the suppression of leftist movements and tribal uprisings. In these cases the police, local upper-caste landlords and the government are all embroiled in a complicated system by which they all support each other and benefit from the suppression of peasant movements. Rape is a powerful tactic because raping women is a way of demoralizing and defeating men, as it has been in patriarchal cultures for thousands of years.

The Siswa incident is a case in point. In the village of Siswa, Hira Upadhyaya, a relative of a minister, lost in the election to another villager. In order to punish the village for this, Virendranath Nath Rai, a police officer, took 20 officers and 40 other men to the village, looted it and raped at least 16 women of all castes. The case is still under investigation but if past experience is any indication the rapists will probably go unpunished and the villagers will continue to live in terror of further violence (Ranjan, 1982).

The Naxalite movement is a political movement which concerns itself with the rights of oppressed groups, the tribals being one such group. The police rape tribals and also rape Naxalite women prisoners. Men and women alike are tortured, but rape is a special form of torture used against women who are often shunned even by their own colleagues after being raped (Rao et al, n.d.).

The Santhal Parganas case is an example of how rape is used by the police to suppress peasant movements. The pattern is very familiar—the Santhals, a group of tribal people, attempted to reclaim their land by forcibly harvesting it. Mahajans (money lenders, land owners, some of it illegal) called in the CRPF (Central Reserve Police Force) who proceeded to burn, plunder and rape in a spree of vengeance. Many tribal societies have not adopted private property notions of female sexuality and for this reason tribal women who are raped are much more likely to be accepted by their families than any other. Nevertheless, rape is humiliating on its own terms and not just a way of demoralizing men. It is unfortunate that some of the activists working for tribal liberation tend to ignore the question of women's issues and to look at rape only in the context of the damage it does to the tribe, not to women in particular (Kumar and Sadgopal, 1980).

Police brutality and specifically police rape are explained in different ways, depending on the perspective of the explainer. Labor leader George Fernandes analyzes police brutality by looking at the roots of capitalist imperialism in India, and at the way in which the British used the police as repressors rather than protectors of the public. 'It is upper caste policemen who are responsible for the atrocities . . .' Policemen are unwittingly drawn into a repressive system and cannot act in any way except the way in which they do (Fernandes, 1983). This analysis is certainly a valuable one but it does not explain the random rapes which are not politically motivated or the rapes in which the women are not likely to report the incident to anyone. Similarly, Sheela Barse has written about the ways in which the job desensitizes and brutalizes policemen by rewarding them for cruelty and sanctioning illegal violence (Fernandes, 1983). It must be remembered that while the analysis of police rape as a political weapon encouraged by the state is useful and necessary, it is incomplete without acknowledging the fact that the men who become policemen and commit rape are from the same society as other rapists and thus have the same sexist values. Thus their motivation for raping women cannot be rooted exclusively in on-the-job training and political pressures.

Rapes of dalit and tribal women

'The Indian national pastime is raping tribals,' says Dr. Rauf Ali. Dalits are oppressed groups without any political clout. When rape of dalits is reported it is usually rape of dalit women by upper caste men. Dalits are not likely to report rape within their communities—they do not trust the legal system and they have their own judicial system. If upper class women are raped by dalit men, which is probably not very common because there is not much opportunity for contact, this is certainly not a commonly reported crime.

Dalit men as well as women are oppressed by society at large; rape is simply one of the tools of oppression. It is special because it is directed specifically at women. Dalit and tribal women are raped for a variety of reasons, not least of which is the fact that they are vulnerable women and raping them is not likely to result in any punishment. They are also raped as a way of demoralizing them in their struggle for an improved existence; the Santhal Parganas case is a prime example of this. The rape of dalits by landlords in Tamilnadu is another example (Report, *Manushi*, 1981). Here rape is part of the repression of tribal attempts to reclaim land which was originally theirs. Economic, political and purely opportunistic motives are often combined to motivate rape.

The story of the Cholanaika tribe has not been written about anywhere as far as I know. The only reason I know of it is because my cousin Dr. Rauf Ali was living and working in the area at that time and was witness to the incident. It is a tragic story and it illustrates how rape was one of the ways in which a tribe was destroyed. The Cholanaika tribe lived in Nilangu Valley in Kerala. They are a hunting gathering people and they were completely undiscovered by anyone from the outside world until 1974. Each family controlled a river valley basin and they were self-sufficient. A film producer found out about them and decided to use the naked Cholanaika women in a pornographic movie. He introduced alcohol, loincloths and sexual exploitation to the tribe. Next came the government to civilize them. It set up cooperatives where the tribals gathered cardamom from the forests and traded it for rice—they got one kilo of rice (worth about

Rs. 2.50, or 25¢) in exchange for one kilo of cardamom (worth about Rs. 100, or $10). In addition to this, accounts were fixed to make the tribals look like cheats and force them into debt. In 1978, the government-sponsored collective decided to collect cane from the forest so they hired 22 local goondas who indulged in an orgy of raping the Cholanaika women. Forty to 60 per cent of the tribe now has sexually transmitted diseases and the population has dropped dramatically as their dependence and exploitation grows. Accordng to Dr. Ali these peaceful people who lived in rock shelters in an area of 300–400 square kilometres will probably be wiped out in the next decade and a half in spite of the latest government scheme for their salvation, which proposes to resettle them and teach them agriculture.

Thus the rape of tribal women by outsiders must be looked at in the context of the general brutality to which all tribals are subjected. Again, police and landlords often help each other in this regard. In Kodurpaka village in Andhra Pradesh, a peasant movement has been growing against the exploitative activities of the landlords. The women gave their full support to the movement and even formed an organization 'to make our lives worth living, to protect ourselves from rape and insult'. The land-lord's goondas, seven of them, raped 50 year-old Rajavva, one of the leaders of this group. At first the police refused to even register the case. Finally the whole area was declared disturbed, many activists forced to run away and police camps were set up to protect the landlords in the area (Rao et al, n.d.)!

Rape by the government and the military

The indignity, violence and infringement of human rights that were perpetuated in the name of conducting 'a peaceful election' by the government with the help of the CRPF (Central Reserve Police Force) and other paramilitary forces drawn from all parts of the country, are beyond the imagination of any civilized person . . . during the last election period and even now, the CRP and our own Indian govern-ment killed people with bullets, raped women and plundered the be-longings of the indigenous people of Assam. What pains us most is the fact that the atrocities were perpetuated by the police force of a demo-cratic country on their own sisters and brothers like occupation forces. (This is a part of a letter dated 3 April 1983 to the People's Union of Civil Liberties from Pragjyotika Mahila Sangha, an Assamese women's organization.)

It has become increasingly common for the State to use rape as one of its accepted tools in suppressing people's movements. The atrocities committed in the recent Assamese elections are examples of this. Members of the government's CRPF, the most hated force ever deployed in any state (Fernandes, 1983), went into Assam and burned, raped and killed as they were ordered to do so. I spoke with Anjali Bagwe, a graduate student at the University of California in Davis who visited some of the ravaged parts of Assam in April 1983. She had horrifying photographs and stories of some of the victims of CRPF rape. Many of these women were villagers who had nothing to do with political events. Many of them, although obviously brutally raped and marked for life with savage toothmarks etc., steadfastly refused to acknowledge that they had been raped, or were surrounded by in-laws who fiercely denied that rape had occurred. Even in such extreme circumstances, women are afraid of being blamed and strenuously deny the truth. In the northeastern states of Nagaland and Mizoram, the Indian army is engaged in a similar systematic terrorizing campaign to suppress freedom struggles.

It is not only the many incidents of organized rape which make the government and its institutions a threat to women's freedom; it is also the complicity the government lends to many individual rape cases. For instance, in the Baghpat incident mentioned earlier, Prime Minister Indira Gandhi and her late son Sanjay Gandhi protected the delinquent police officer because of favors done during the recent elections. It took protests by some 30,000 people to finally even appoint an investigative commission to inquire into the incident (Fernandes, 1983). Government officials are feared by the public and there are many incidents to validate this fear. In June 1980, a censustaker reportedly made three attempts to rape Adivasi tribal women in Maharashtra. In July of that year a young woman was reportedly raped in her hut in Raipur by four forest officials while her father was in Delhi to try and save the hut which the officials declared was in a reserve area (Rao et al, n.d.). Thus rape is covertly and overtly, randomly and systematically used by the institutions of the State.

Rape Universal, not just Institutional

It is important to remember that the widespread use of sexual violence is not the exclusive prerogative of men in the government, the police and the military. Political activists focus on this kind of rape but it is not only government employees who rape or even commit the majority of rapes. Women are raped at work, on the streets, in the fields, in their homes by men who are their employers, their acquaintances, their neighbors, their relatives, their in-laws and their husbands. It is not only dalit women who are victims and not only landlords and police who are rapists. This fact is often ignored or suppressed but it is very important if rape is to be exhaustively studied. Caste-related rape is important in Indian society where casteism and sexism are both very strong. The rape of lower caste women is a socially sanctioned way to express sex and class domination. Even without casteism, sexism is present in all strata of society and so is rape.

Rape on the Job

The rape of working women is a national scandal which is at least as widespread as custodial rape, yet it does not receive nearly as much attention. Perhaps this is because the idea of women working is frowned upon by many people, perhaps because when it is a question of a woman's word against that of her employer or male co-worker, the likelihood that she will be believed and be punished is not very high. The cases of on-the-job sexual coercion which are written about, almost exclusively involve lower class women. Domestic servants are molested by employers or the relatives or friends of employers. Factory and mine workers are often forced to have sexual relations with their superintendents. It has been reported that women workers of the relief works at Pali district in Rajasthan were being sexually coerced by a superintendent engineer (*Maitreyi*, 1982). Often working women are in the only jobs available to them and cannot afford to object to any treatment they get, be it substandard wages or rape on the job.

Rape by Strangers

Neither the streets nor the public transport system are safe for women. Within the last year there have been at least 2 reported incidents of rape by autorickshaw drivers in Pune, Maharashtra ('Two Pune women allegedly raped', *Times of India*, 1983). In these cases the police were instrumental in saving the women from being badly injured and perhaps murdered. Armed bandits often rape as part of their destructive activities. This is what happened in Ghatatoli in Madhya Pradesh on 20 March 1983. A 20 men armed gang went from village to village committing rape, arson and murder (Mathur, 1983). There are no statistics on rape in those rural areas which are not much interfered with by the outside world. I spoke with some women from various villages and got responses ranging from 'there is no rape in my village because girls go indoors at a decent hour' to 'Yes, it happens but we try to pretend it doesn't.' I will not hazard a guess about the extent of rape in rural areas. Rape is uncommon in some tribes but child marriages are common in some parts of rural India and rape is often an inevitable part of these arrangements. Rape by strangers is common in urban areas; in large cities like Delhi and Bombay women learn the secrets of being streetwise early. Urban slums are hotbeds of rape.

Rape of Children

The rape of children is particularly horrifying and yet it is not an uncommon crime. Newspapers and magazines regularly print accounts of the rape of minor girls.

On the afternoon of 24 December 1980, a group of children went to pick fruits from a forest in Tamilnadu. Suganya, an 11 year old girl was caught by a man who raped her, stabbed her in 16 places and then ran away. She was unconscious for more than a week. No action was taken in spite of a mass rally a few weeks later (Fatima, 1981). A 4 year-old child, Mamta of West Patel Nagar, Delhi was raped in a public park by an unidentified man in September 1982 (*Maitreyi*, 1982). A 15 year-old spastic girl was raped by a police constable at the Santacruz Police Station in Bombay. She had been taken there after being lost during a field trip from the institution in which she lived (*Maitreyi*, 1982). The rape of children cannot be explained in terms of political repression. A 4 year-old is hardly likely to present a threat to any existing institutions. Rather, the rape of children of all classes is a particularly sick crime by which men get gratification through perpetrating violence upon children.

Incest

The subject of incest is even more taboo in India than it is in the West. Hardly any cases of incest ever get publicized, the few which do are very sensationalist, e.g., the case of Balkrishna Engle whose wife caught him in the act of raping their young daughter and killed him (Ranjan, 1982). In most cases the crime is unrecognized and the victims forced to take part in a conspiracy of silence. Incest is one of the implicit reasons offered in support of child marriages, it is crucial to get the girl married off before she is 'spoilt' by her own relatives (if she is 'spoilt' by her in-laws after being married that is her own lookout; her parents' responsibility to marry her off while she was a virgin has been fulfilled). While I can offer no formal documentation of incest I have a very strong sense that it is wide-spread. I have heard too many stories of things which happened to my best friend to ignore my growing conviction that the incidence of incest needs to be further explored.

Rape among the middle and upper classes is another taboo subject. Even among middle class women, the general attitude towards rape is that it is something which happens to lower class women, something the rest of society is protected from by virtue of caste or class. This attitude is unfortunate as it does not help create a feeling of sisterhood among women and it also serves as a very isolating factor for those women who are raped. They have no way of knowing how many others have been through similar experiences and their confusion, shame and fear keep them from saying anything.

Why do I assert with such confidence that I know middle and upper class women get raped although I have no proof besides my own experiences and talks with people? For one thing, it seems unrealistic to assume that in a society where middle class women are subject to many of the same forms of oppression as lower class women (choiceless marriages, female infanticide, bride burning, etc.) they are in some way magically invulnerable to rape. An upper class housewife in Bombay may not be a likely victim of police brutality but she is certainly vulnerable to sexual assault in her own home. Secondly, there are so many obstacles in the way of reporting the crime that if no one is likely to find out it is no wonder women don't report it. Police disbelief and resistance to registering rape cases, familial pressure, social stigma and the certainty that it is usually the victim who is punished for the crime—these are strong incentives to keep the crime a secret. Lastly, marital rape and even rape by in-laws are not considered real crimes; they are seen as the natural lot of women. Unless these realities change, rape of upper class women will continue to be an invisible crime.

Conclusion

The main point here was to try and create an understanding of the many dynamics involved in the use of rape in India—personal and societal sexism, political opportunism and casteist practices, to name a few. The conclusion is that rape is dependent to a large extent on power based exploitative relationships and attitudes towards women prevalent in Indian society.

IV

MEDIA

To convey a message one needs a medium. The mass media have been interested in conveying to the public a particular kind of message about women. One need only flip through the pages of popular magazines and newspapers, watch television programs and commercial films to get the content of them loud and clear. Women's major concern is domesticity: they are capable of limited and highly stereotypical behavior, women are for sexual exploitation and are the safe and easy targets of male violence and abuse.

The power of mass media to create, select and convey particular kinds of images about women cannot be underestimated. At the first National Women's Studies Conference held in Bombay in 1981 the feminist media group blamed the media for perpetuating middle-class stereotypes. Participants agreed that by confining women's problems to separate programs or separate pages of the newspaper, the media had isolated them from mainstream problems and thus assigned them a low social value. The group recommended that a clear-cut policy at the national level be framed to regulate the portrayal of women in the media. It also recommended that media training programs include a course on women and communication.

Talking of television particularly, which is rapidly becoming a pervasive and powerful medium, the Report of the Working Group on Software for Doordarshan published in 1985 entitled 'An Indian Personality for Television', states that portraying women as equals is a subject that has been given low priority. Indian television has imitated the same negative, limited and derogatory images of women as commercial films have. The committee specially pointed out the need for a consistent and coherent policy regarding the portrayal of woman on TV and the importance of promoting a positive ideology and portraying the new, varied and emerging roles and images of women. One need not forget that the women's movement owes much to the mass media for giving publicity to its activities and efforts. Yet, paradoxically enough it has failed through its programs and commercials to turn its eyes to the new woman.

The medium that is most watched and does most injustice to women is the commercial Hindi film. Shamita Das Dasgupta and Radha Sarma

Hegde in their paper 'The Eternal Receptacle: A Study of Mistreatment of Women in Hindi Films' speak of the sheer quantity and variety of violence directed toward women and a weak rebellion against this aggression is drowned in the morass of overwhelming traditional images. That this violence is not without its purpose is amply documented by the authors. With the decade of women came a new wave of films on women's issues. C.S. Lakshmi's paper 'Feminism and the Cinema of Realism' analyzes a crop of films with the woman being the pivotal character. In the guise of modernism and liberation, these characters emerge as only two steps away from the usual myths about women. Caution must be exercised before accepting films purporting to handle the newly emerging woman. Jyoti Punwani's article 'Portrayal of Women on Television' points out that a woman's image on television is no better. The women-centered programs while depicting women's awareness of life's possibilities other than the socially given one, are rarely shown to translate these into action. The paper raises some critical questions regarding the creation of diverse images on this important medium. Besides images, words and language convey the existence of sexist values in society. Narendra Nath Kalia's article 'Women and Sexism: Language of Indian School Textbooks' highlights the mechanisms by which sexist language oppresses women and the consequences it has for students who read these books.

THE ETERNAL RECEPTACLE: A STUDY OF MISTREATMENT OF WOMEN IN HINDI FILMS

Shamita Das Dasgupta and Radha Sarma Hegde

Movies are perhaps the most popular medium of mass communication in India. The Bombay film industry is quite definitely the largest in the world and is supported daily by fifteen million Indian viewers (*India News*, 1983). Approximately seven hundred full length feature films are produced in Bombay every year. With regional films included, the number rises over an astounding 800. How deeply these films affect their viewers has not yet been directly fathomed. However, studies conducted on the relationship between television viewing and aggressive behavior, provide us with at least a suggestion of its magnitude and its long term effects (Eron, 1980; Huesmann, Lagerspetz, and Eron, 1984).

For some time now, media portrayal of the sexes and their roles have received some scrutiny in the western world (Tuchman et al, 1978; Ruth, 1980). In India, interest in the subject is more recent and is surely the by-product of the newly awakening consciousness about women's status in society. The few systematic studies that have been conducted on the topic, unequivocally claim that the social roles portrayed in the films are strictly dichotomous as well as stereotypical. Very few films show any cross over between the sex role boundaries. The traditional roles of the subservient female and the dominant male are repeatedly reinforced on the Indian screen ('Images of Women in Indian Films,' 1981; Hegde and Dasgupta, 1984). The modal personality of the virtuous woman in Hindi films is resplendent with characteristics such as, chastity, patience and selflessness. She is considered to be a *Devi* (goddess) by society, because of her readiness to sacrifice for the significant others in her life (Hegde and Dasgupta, 1984). Society expects her to efface her desires, rights and even her life for others. Yet, the films do not reward her for fulfilling these expectations. The more she endures, the more she has to suffer.

The present study takes a critical look at women as the recipients of a varied array of mistreatments in Hindi movies. It will be argued here that these mistreatments comprise a mechanism that perpetuates the traditional relationship between the sexes. To fully understand the dynamics of this relationship, we must take a look at the model of power inherent in the masculine role structure.

Power, psychological as well as physical, is pivotal to the male role. The male reserves the right to physical strength which automatically and continually decreases the number of choices available for the woman. Backed by credible threats of physical violence, the man is an effective coercer and forces the woman to construct her world in his terms. The central components of the female existence are, therefore, defined and controlled by him and by a world order that is patriarchal. Thus, it is only natural that the male view will perceive the two worlds of male and female to be complementary sets, with the positive elements portioned out to him, while suffering and sacrifice become vital to her being. The conception of the woman as an eternal receptacle of suffering, therefore, justifies societal mistreatments of her, and serves as a mechanism that reconfirms the status quo.

Purpose of Study

The purpose of this paper is to analyze the instances of mistreatments of women in Hindi films and the functions they serve in confirming the prescribed role dichotomies. The generic female role, as depicted in these films, seems to be one of subservience, which constantly endures abuse. The thesis here is that these mistreatments are not haphazard, but serve some specific functions. The functions served by such treatment of women can be summarized as follows:

(a) It reconfirms the patriarchal world order and perpetuates the existing dichotomy of sex roles. The virtues of the ideal woman on screen: chastity, dependence, succorance, passivity (Hegde and Dasgupta, 1984) etc. ensures her secondary status in society and asserts the primacy of the male. The recurring mistreatments that women receive affirm these already established social positions.

(b) It legitimizes and justifies mistreatment of women in society. The recurring representations of mistreatments of women have self-perpetuating effects as supported by literature on pornography (Brownmiller, 1976; Dworkin, 1979). Acceptance of mistreatment of women on screen eases the acceptance of it in reality.

(c) It cumulatively conditions both the sexes to play out their parts of doling out and receiving pain and suffering unquestioningly. The familiar styles of mistreatments ascertain the adherence of the male and female to certain preset behavior patterns. The male turns aggressor with no qualms and the female merges easily into the persona of the long suffering helpless victim. Each internalizes these characteristics and learns to play their parts with ease.

(*d*) It progressively debilitates the woman's self-image. Continual mistreatments meted out to the woman to ensure her subservience corrodes her self-esteem.

The mistreatments represented in the films serve not just one of the above functions, but cumulatively generate the mosaic of expectations that surround the female role. This paper will analyze these mistreatments and also attempt to focus on the voices of dissent that seem to be slowly emerging.

Method

Sample: Thirty Hindi movies were randomly selected from the available video-cassettes in a mid-western city in USA. Though almost all Hindi movies made in India are converted to videos and exported to the US, it is recognized here that there may be a bias towards the liberal in the sample. The films that are targeted for the US market may have been selected with the educated and westernized immigrant community in mind. There may be other unsuspected biases built in the sample due to the idiosyncrasies of the video-shops, availability of films at the time, demand in the community, etc. The sample spans a decade, 1973–1983, and both authors analyzed the films together.

The purpose of the paper is not to trace individual characters in a film, but to assess the patterns of mistreatments that are doled out to women on screen. It is not a cinematographic critique in any sense, neither does its scope include establishment of causal relationships.

It is almost impossible to catalog and examine every instance of mistreatment that women are made to undergo in these films. An atmosphere of general neglect and covert emotional battering of women pervade the film story lines. Only films with obvious instances of humiliations and actual physical and verbal violations of women were retained for the analysis (Table 1).

Analysis

From the initial sample of thirty movies, 21 (70 per cent) were selected for further analysis. This subset of 21 films contain instances of overt mistreatments of women. Five categories of overt physical aggressions, and two of other mistreatments were used as units of analysis for this paper. These categories were not chosen *a priori*, but they emerged from the analysis of the films. Eve-teasing, physical battering, assault, rape,

Table 1
LIST OF FILMS VIEWED

Name of Film	Year Released	Director
1. Aakrosh	1980	G. Nihalani
*2. Agni Pariksha	1981	K. Mazumdar
3. Ahista Ahista	1981	I. Shroff
4. Arth	1983	M. Bhatt
*5. Bato Bato Mein	1979	B. Chatterjee
6. Bazaar	1982	S. Sarhadi
*7. Bemisaal	1979	H. Mukherjee
8. Chakra	1981	R. Dharmaraj
*9. Chupke Chupke	1975	H. Mukherjee
10. Dillagi	1979	B. Chatterjee
11. Do Aur Do Panch	1980	R. Kumar
12. Don	1980	C. Barot
13. Ek Hi Bhool	1981	T. Rama Rao
*14. Grihapravesh	1980	B. Bhattacharya
15. Jeewan Dhara	1982	T. Rama Rao
16. Kabhi Kabhi	1976	Y. Chopra
17. Lakshmi	1982	B.S. Thapa
18. Log Kya Kahenge	1979	B.R. Ishara
*19. Main Intequam Loonga	1982	T. Rama Rao
20. Manchali	1973	R. Nawathe
21. Mehendi Rang Layegi	1982	D.N. Rao
*22. Panchwin Manzil	1982	J. Sidana
23. Rocky	1981	S. Dutt
24. Shakti	1982	R. Sippy
*25. Silsila	1981	Y. Chopra
26. Sindoor Bane Jwala	1981	D.N. Rao
27. Shradhanjali	1981	A. Gangooly
*28. Yeh Nazdikiyaan	1982	V. Pandey
29. Yeh To Kamaal Ho Gaya	1976	T. Rama Rao
30. Zanjeer	1973	P. Mehra

* Not retained for analysis due to absence of depiction of humiliation and violation.

homicide, miscellaneous punishment by society, and chivalry are seven types of mistreatments that seem to recur systematically in this sample of movies.

Although in most societies chivalry is taken as a form of tribute to women and not an affront, it was selected as a category of mistreatment here, as it plays an important role in objectification of women. Gallant behavior denies a woman separate will and existence and psychologically converts her into a possession of her male protector (Korda, 1976). Since chivalry undermines a woman's ability and competence in protecting herself, this study treats it as an instance of mistreatment of women in a patriarchal world order. Eve-teasing, physical battering, assault, rape and homicide are examples of mistreatments in an ascending order of degrees of violence. Miscellaneous punishments is a catch-all category which groups together sanctions ranging from slander to social ostracism.

The categories of mistreatments will be defined and discussed further here. Cited films will be referred to by their numbers, as elaborated in Table 1.

Eve-teasing: Any unwelcome verbal attention of a sexual nature by a single male or a group of males, encountered by a single woman or a group of women, mainly in public places (Stevens, 1984).

Eve-teasing probably is the most common form of harassment endured by women in Hindi films. It is a form of mistreatment that is portrayed as having comical overtones, as the woman becomes the butt of general ridicule due to male sexual bantering. Young, attractive women alone, or groups of women moving together, both fall prey to this type of mistreatment. Interestingly, eve-teasing always takes place when the female is on her own and quite often without any visible male protector. For example, in *Ek Hi Bhool* (13), the heroine, a young divorcee, is harassed by male fellow passengers while travelling alone in a bus with her child. Of the twenty-one films retained for analysis, seven (33. 3 per cent) portray similar incidents.

Physical Battering: Actual striking or physical abuse of a woman by her husband or any other man.

Numerous examples of slapping, violent shoving, and beating are strewn about in the films. Often, such instances occur in situations of argument or quarrel, where a man expresses his anger through abusive physical contact. In *Jeewan Dhara* (15), the only male in the heroine's family not only physically dominates his wife, but extends this rough treatment to his mother and sisters. Approximately 47.6 per cent (10) of the films show scenes of battering.

Assault: Eight (38.1 per cent) of the films have instances of violent attempt at forcible rape. Assault is distinguished from the previous category by the perpetrator's overt sexual intentions.

Assault seems to be a mistreatment that cuts across social classes. Women who are in unusual situations, that is, living or working without a male protector by their sides, seem to be selectively victimized. In *Arth* (4), the heroine who is estranged from her husband, is assaulted while seeking a job. In *Chakra* (8), the heroine who is a slum dweller, is assaulted on her way back from the village market.

Rape: Only two (9.5 per cent) films show forcible sexual violations of women. In both instances sexual intercourse is established by the perpetrators with brutal violence.

For women, rape seems to bring in its wake social ostracism. It changes their lives to the point that it becomes impossible for rape victims to readapt to their former life-styles. In the movie *Rocky* (23), a young woman is raped in her own home. She attempts suicide, and later chooses to become a courtesan, a profession supposedly befitting her defined existence.

Homicide: Murder of a woman, usually by a man or a group of men.

The two examples of homicide in this subset are from the movie *Aakrosh* (1). Thus, 4.8 per cent of the films fall in this category. Both murders occur in a lower socio-economic section of society. The first murder is committed by some politically influential and socially well established men in a small town. The lower class heroine is gang raped and then murdered, as a way of getting rid of the evidence. Later, the husband is framed for the murder. The rape itself is premeditated and planned as a punishment for the woman's husband, who is insubordinate to the local gentry. In the same movie, the second murder takes place when the hero kills his sister, as he believes that bereft of all male protection his sister's life will not be worth living.

Miscellaneous Punishments by Society: Societal sanctions, in the forms of public humiliation, ostracism, slander, etc. seem to await women who dare to transgress from the traditional role prescriptions of chaste wife and devoted mother. Four (19.1 per cent) films carry examples of mistreatments of this category.

In *Lakshmi* (17) society doubts the heroine's chastity, and consequently, she is banished from her home. She is then reduced to leading the life of a courtesan. In *Ek Hi Bhool* (13), the colleagues of a divorced woman spread rumors that she is a person of uncertain morals. As a result, she suffers such public humiliations that she is forced to crawl back to her husband on his own terms.

Chivalry: Chivalry is defined here as male interferences designed to 'protect' women's chastity and good name. Since the male world view perceives competence as a characteristic excluded from women's behavioral repertoire, men take it upon themselves to protect women. This type of gallant behavior usually takes the forms of beating up eve-teasers and avenging other physical violations of women. The men in 13 (62 per cent) films indulge in chivalrous behavior to protect 'their' women's virtues. A typical example of such behavior is in *Do Aur Do Panch* (11), where the two leading female characters initiate a rescue operation. The boyfriends of the women secretly accomplish the task, which of course, the women naively believe to be their own doing.

Table 2
SUMMARY OF CATEGORIES OF MISTREATMENTS*

Category	Films
1. Eve-teasing	3, 10, 13, 16, 23, 24, 29
2. Physical battering	1, 4, 6, 8, 13, 15, 20, 21, 26, 27
3. Assault	1, 4, 8, 17, 23, 26, 27, 30
4. Rape	1, 23
5. Homicide	1
6. Miscellaneous punishments by society	3, 13, 17, 18, 21
7. Chivalry	1, 3, 10, 11, 12, 13, 17, 21, 23, 24, 27, 29, 30

* All movies are referred to by the numbers as itemized in Table 1.

Discussion

This paper has scrutinized mistreatments of women in Hindi films. It is argued here that mistreatments of women in films are not purposeless actions introduced to strengthen story lines, but together, they constitute a mechanism that reinforces the masculine mystique. The male role, which is defined as powerful, aggressive, strong, active and instrumental (Parsons and Bales, 1955) is endorsed by its establishment of dominance over women. Since patriarchy dictates the parameters of the female role, any slight transgression on her part is severely punished by its representatives. Moreover, as the female role entails the negation of male characteristics, aggressive actions and femininity are considered antithetical. This puts a woman in a bind, and renders her virtually ineffective and helpless in any situation that requires competence and physical strength. Thus, she becomes dependent on the male for protection, and is often compelled to accept brutality in the bargain. The victorious establishment of male dominance over women, to a large degree, legitimizes their mistreatment and maintains the status quo. Psychological and physical mistreatment of a woman forces her to cower into the meek and subservient role that society has charted out for her.

From the thirty movies of the initial sample, twenty-one were chosen for critical analysis. Though mistreatment was never the central concern of any movie, the films in the subset had more overt instances of it. Mistreatments seem to regularly occur when women actively step out of their traditional roles. They served the common function of returning straying women to their stereotypical and socially approved behavior patterns. In *Ek Hi Bhool* (13), the heroine, who divorces her husband and tries to lead an independent life, is slandered, harassed, humiliated and ostracized by society. To escape the relentless persecution, she offers herself back to her ex-husband and docilely accepts the role of a wife and mother.

The movies have a definite bias towards the upper classes. Except for two (1, 8), all movies feature women of higher socio-economic status who are quite educated and westernized in their ways. Lower class women in the films are shown to suffer more blatant indignities at the hands of men. Women in both the above-mentioned films fall victims to violent rape, assault and murder. They seem to have fewer champions in society and their lives are clearly more insecure than their higher-class counterparts.

In six (28.6 per cent) out of the twenty-one films viewed, there is a minimal articulation about the woman as a victim of injustice in the patriarchal world order. These films which obviously question the traditional female role, represent a cross section of social classes in India. *Arth* (4) criticizes the unquestioned acceptance of the sanctity of marriage and the role definitions that are attached to it. The heroines in *Arth* (4) and *Mehendi Rang Layegi* (21) both break out of their role assignments and actively seek positive qualities such as independence, competence and assertiveness; characteristics hitherto, exclusively reserved for males. Such non-traditional behavior indicates a tentative beginning of a new and emerging consciousness about women and their social status.

The media's perspective on mistreatment of women is a very crucial subject of enquiry by itself. The popularity of films in India makes one speculate on the magnitude of the social consequences of such media portrayals even more. The Hindi film industry, similar to other film industries, is fundamentally a profit-oriented business. The dictates of the patrons of Hindi cinema, to a large degree, limits the choices of the directors of the films. The Indian viewing public must, therefore, be partially blamed for the unquestioning acceptance of mistreatments of women that we repeatedly witness in movies.

This paper asserts that mistreatments recur on the Hindi screen as an established mechanism to monitor and perpetuate the patriarchal world order. The regularity of such depictions is an important issue to be scrutinized. Despite a few weak voices of protest here and there, women's image as a traditional receptacle still endures on Hindi screen. Mistreatments of women seem to be an accepted institution in India.

FEMINISM AND THE CINEMA
OF REALISM

C.S. Lakshmi

Vimochana, a social action group in Bangalore organized a symposium preceded by a six-day show of films from 4–10 November 1985 on the theme 'Films: Cashing In On the Women's Issues'. The reason for holding the symposium was, according to their written statement, to understand the process of exploitation of women's issues. The blatant use of women in popular cinema is easy enough to identify and protest about. But what about cinema that is not as garish as the popular cinema in which also women have figured as central characters? 'Do we not see here', the statement asks, 'a using and selling not merely of content (in terms of the issues being raised) but also the commercialization of certain cinematic forms when innovative and radical packaging is used to sell played out content? . . . Can the camera eye itself therefore be sexist? . . .' Vimochana felt that 'while it is important to question the validity of the so-called women's film it is equally important to identify the new process of mythification that is setting in . . .' It looked at the outset that the symposium was all set to raise very relevant and valid questions. It was a pity that there was a little bit of 'cashing in' on the inaugural day itself—the festival was inaugurated by Smita Patil. It is difficult to forget that Smita Patil did live off the commercial cinema and took up roles that make many feminists want to do the Sita act of going under the earth in rage.

Apart from the Smita Patil handicap, the organizers also faced the problem of choice of films. They could not show films they really wanted to because award-winning films alone are allowed to be shown in non-theatrical viewings organized by private groups. So the organizers had a symposium with a very important question to discuss but not enough films to represent the symposium. The film-show and the symposium had to operate separately. Not many understood that, not having bothered to read the printed brochure. Despite the fact that the symposium did not quite work out the way it was planned because of this confusion, one of the things it made very clear was that the time had come for the feminists to take a stand with no doubts on what is referred to as realistic cinema.

What follows is a revised and expanded version of a paper shared in the symposium.

In viewing films, the feminists have focused on the question of the male 'gaze' which, in a patriarchy, repressed women through its controlling power over female thoughts and desires. The 'gaze' can be explained as:

(a) Scopophilia or sexual pleasure in looking which is enhanced by the very way in which the film is viewed—in a dark room with moving images controlled by a projector making it seem like a dream.

(b) The gaze in dominant cinema is built upon notions of male-female differences created by a culture. The three 'looks' that derive from this 'gaze' are:

(i) Gaze within the film text—how men gaze at women (ii) The spectator's gaze that identifies with the male gaze and objectifies the women on the screen (iii) The camera's original gaze that goes into the very act of filming (Kaplan, 1983).

Keeping the male 'gaze' in view, the images of women on the screen can be discussed either sociologically or semiotically. The sociological discussion centers upon role-types (housewife, beloved, vamp, etc.). Semiology views the entire film as a signifying system in which the woman functions as a 'sign'. In other words, semiology applied to cinema, speaks of how the film communicates. Every sign has a denotative meaning which is direct and a connotative one which is a suggestive or an associated one linked with the existing values in a society. For example, a white saree. At the denotative level, it only means a white saree, but at a connotative second level it signifies widowhood, virginity or purity. Take, for example, the colour red—its second level of meaning would be revolution. Image of a woman smoking would directly signify a woman smoking. But at the connotative level it would signify, in our society, a bold woman, liberated and defiant with fantasies of sexual promiscuity being signified along with these. In the film *Trikon Ka Chautha Kon* a woman smokes, reads Sartre and talks constantly with her lips curled up. At the denotative level this signifies only someone who is given to smoking and reading Sartre with a predeliction to curl up her lips while talking. At the connotative level this signifies a bold, intellectual woman who does not function by the normal codes of the society. The connotations in these signs, arise from myths about women that exist in the society and myths that exist about certain concepts like in the case of the color red. While the images are actually presented as if they were only denotative, the connotative aspect gets masked.

Feminists have now begun to draw a lot from semiotic analysis of cinema. Explained in very simple terms, this only means that in cinema, the woman is presented at the second level of connotation, a myth; she is represented as what she represents for a man, not in terms of what she actually signifies. While looking at realistic cinema one has to remember this level of myths constantly. Not only to understand the images on the screen but also to probe why presenting women in a particular way is attempted.

Women becoming popular as a subject in films is not very surprising. This is happening not just in films and not just in the case of women. A young girl who was least interested in any issue related to women was seen vigorously applying to American universities. When told that getting admission in Humanities has become a problem she replied: 'I can always get it for Women's Studies'. And sure enough she did. Another student wanted to work on rural poverty because it was the in thing. These are cold, calculated moves. Film-makers also take decisions like this. One director when asked what his next venture was going to be said: 'Oh, dowry death, of course'. He didn't have any specific reason for working on it except that it was a hot subject. Such films are like good trips—poverty trip, rape trip, dowry death trip.

There are those who may take up the woman as a subject with genuine concern but because of the mode they have chosen for expression and because they operate within a given set of myths they come out with portrayals that are flat without any dimensions catching only the surface reality. They belong to the school of realistic cinema which believes that cinema portrays the reality as it is or as if it is. Their effort is to create the illusion that the camera does not lie and that it captures reality in its totality. They attempt to do this by resorting to location shootings, long takes and natural light.

After the Second World War when human suffering was out in the open for all to see, there were talks of 'redemption of physical reality' by which it was meant that cinema has the capacity to 'mirror' reality without intervention. Documentary film-makers using this style argued that they were not making aesthetic objects and made roughly-hewn films which they wanted to use as organizing tools. Fiction films which use this mode of film-making are not different in their intention except that the fiction film has a plot and a resolution. But, of late, it is this capacity to be organizing tools that has been questioned, for realistic films use codes that cannot change consciousness. Eileen Mcgarry points out that long before the film-makers arrive on the scene reality itself is coded 'first in the infrastructure of the social formation (human economic practice) and secondly by the super-structure of politics and ideology'. The film-maker, according to her, is 'not dealing with reality, but with that which has become the profilmic event: that which exists and happens before the camera' (Kaplan, 1983, p. 126)[1].

It is important to dwell at length on these aspects of the realistic cinema while speaking of the images of women on the screen. It is difficult to take out elements from the whole and look at them separately. They have to be seen as parts of a whole in order to be viewed in the correct perspective. To elaborate on the concept of 'capturing reality', the moment the camera is placed one has excluded reality that is outside the frame. And the moment the first cut is done on the editing table one has excluded reality that is outside one's perception. Hence the reality that is presented is actually a reality modified, pruned and altered to suit one's world-view. This myth of realistic cinema has to be understood not only to understand women as characters in realistic cinema but also to be sure what myths we have to destroy when we think in terms of alternate or counter-cinema. Realistic cinema is based on the twin-pillars of narration and the concept of identification. The audience is made to feel that it is viewing reality unfolding right in front of it. In this process of presenting reality, the realistic cinema keeps a keen eye for details like objects, for example, creating a British Raj with all the objects and artefacts that went to make the British Raj. It will also keep a correct check on the real facts like food, clothes, mannerisms, speech, etc. Criticism is normally quelled when the director says that a particular incident took place exactly the same way. In other words, the cinema of realism claims to tell the audience the truth and how can one question truth? Attempts to look at representations of women on the screen, must hence not be on the basis of whether the facts are true or not, but on the basis of how in the total cinematic process the images appear in spite of being rooted in 'truth'.

With this understanding of the cinema of realism let us look at a few films that have women as central characters. Let us take *Ghare-Baire* by Satyajit Ray first. A woman confined to the women's quarters of a traditional household steps out to have an extra-marital affair, feels burdened with guilt once the force is spent out and feels justly punished when she becomes a widow or imagines herself as a widow. That is the textual material of the film. The film begins with a shot of her talking about herself after the affair. The viewer is given to believe that her eye is going to be the camera eye. But no. When the film unfolds, she is not the narrator anymore. The camera is now representing the director in terms of

---

[1] There is also a joke normally ascribed to the Italian film maker Antonioni about 'capturing reality'. There were two film makers. One was an early riser and the other slept until noon. The first one got up and took his camera and went out and came back in five minutes. Asked why he had come back so soon he quipped: 'All the reality has already been captured' (Kaplan, 1983).

the 'knowledge' it is imparting. If the film had been from her point of view we would have known how she felt about her confinement; what was that magic moment when she stepped into the common quarters; how did the world seem? When she took that first step did she feel a tingle? A sensation up her spinal cord? We don't know. We see them walking down the corridor as if they were two puppets in slow animation; we don't get to know because the director is not concerned about these layers of emotions. He is stating a fact of her stepping out; capturing it in realism that is lyrical. Like the geography maps that give minute physical details we know how she looked, dressed, spoke or responded. But yet we don't know her. The surface details are perfect; perfect enough to cause emotional up-heaval and identification, and yet we know her through physical events in her life, not through her private, non-expressed, repressed self. Picasso said that art and nature work differently. The work of art is to capture the concepts nature keeps hidden. These hidden emotions never surface in cinema of this kind for it wants everything broken into physical, tangible facts that can be detailed. Films such as this are about real women. But as Christine Gledhill asks, 'are they really about women?' (Martin, 1979, p. 34).

At this point it would be worthwhile to look at the theme of extra-marital relationship that has become a common theme to portray the 'bold' woman. These films seem to generally assume that every woman is just a few orgasms behind liberation. When the customary clandestine orgasms take place, lo and behold, her chains fall off; the world seems a different place and she is carried away on the wings of liberation. When the purity obsession works, it is normally through the body of a woman. A woman whose physical purity is tarnished, becomes impure. The present 'bold' woman portrayals are only an extension of this body obsession. She was bound by her body alone and now she is set free through her body.

Aval Appadithan is another film that is constantly referred to as a woman's film. The woman's characterization is brought forth entirely verbally by herself. According to her, she has become 'this way' (as if it is some communicable disease she is suffering from) because of a wayward mother. And 'this way' is nothing sensational. She had one boy-friend with whom she slept and another who left her. In its filmic-text, the film constantly resorts to existing myths about women and relationships. That a wayward mother destroys her children; that a woman who speaks the 'truth' is always alone, men are scared of her; the woman who is different is confused, not sure of herself and is only seeking love from a man but does not know it herself. In the way it has processed this filmic-text, the film uses all the known myths of sound (songs, dialogues to explain and a background score to match 'moods'). The only plus point of the film is that it does not 'expose' the body of women in the way it is customary to do. In all other visuals it sticks to myths normally adhered to—like showing her alone on the bed; insecure in her work sphere, she is almost always moving about in her office and we never catch her still at any moment; the room where she works is arranged in such a way that it appears as if the tables block her movement and become obstacles; plus the men in the office look lecherous as if out to use her. The visuals constantly play upon the fact that she is pitted against the outside world. All this could have been avoided if only she had a 'proper' mother! The last shot of the film leaves her on the road—that is where a liberated woman ends up. This final visual detail reveals the entire content of the film.

Another film which every women's festival must have is *Ghatasraddha*. There is a widespread belief that this film is about the plight of a widow. Actually this film is about two rituals—*ghatasraddha* and the ritual of abortion. The camera stands for the director and the little boy in the film. As in most films about true to life women who are seen by others, this widow is also seen by two persons. There is a motherly longing in her because her eyes linger on the little boy. Is that why she indulges in sex? One does not know for the enigma of the film is not this. The enigma is about what happens to a widow when she crosses her barriers. That she has a physical relationship is the only truth the narrative is concerned about. If, like Chantal Akerman, the Belgian film maker, one has to think of hierarchy of images, the most obvious shots that come at the top are the abortion and the ritualistic one (Martin, 1979). The others—even the shocking tonsured one—come below that. The father excommunicates her through one ritual; the abortion attacks her physicality and the film itself by making these the most important visuals of the film, removes her mind as if it has been accomplished by a surgical feat of a quack similar to the quack who aborts the unformed foetus in the film. The beautiful woman as a widow is another aspect to be noted. It is this that the audience reacts to. The beautiful woman who desired and got destroyed. If the casting had been done differently—with a not-so-stunning a beauty as the widow, her desire would have been viewed in a totally different way by the audience. The entire film is built upon the myth of the beautiful woman who is imagined by a man and desired by a man.

The realistic cinema has also used biography and autobiography for its narration. *Phaniyamma* is a biographical film. It is about a widow with a strong mind. It has been directed by a woman. The film is built on nostalgia but the trouble with nostalgia is that it hides a longing for the state one is nostalgic about. While it is true that those who have suffered have an enduring power it should not lead one to believe that it is directly linked to that suffering only, or the opposite—that in order to have moral power one has to suffer. When we look at these women we have to ask these questions repeatedly even if it is not a part of the biography the woman herself has written. *Phaniyamma* creates identification with people we know. It also creates tears and an acknowledgement about the truth about her statements. All the shots directed on *Phaniyamma* are unsure where to touch her, which aspect to capture. We have images that cannot even be put in an hierarchical order for almost all of them lack any definite conception. We do not know how she looked in the long years of her youth or for that matter how she felt during this period. Her statements showing strength of character—like the one sympathizing with the action of a widow who gets involved with her own brother-in-law—come later in her life. The statements come as factual details only, for we do not know from which inner corner these are echoed. At the end of the film, we know all the physical facts about *Phaniyamma* and the events in her life and her unorthodox statements and we are left with only these details articulated verbally constantly with no single image to carry home; not one gesture—a turn of the head, a budding smile—just good make-up showing you wrinkles.

Another film acclaimed as a feminist film is *Subah*. If one has to go by dominant images, the camera lingers most on the lovemaking scenes. If one considers these images, one has to assume that her physicality means a lot to this woman. And yet, the director is supposed to be telling us that she is a woman who wants to fulfil herself by work. In the text there are a lot of researched facts about female reformatories which are shown as strained documentary exercises with a whole lot of myths bundled together about suffering women and powerful women. But what does the main character herself do? She comes back when she fails in her work sphere for another long session of lovemaking. She leaves again not because she wants to pursue her goal again but because her understanding husband has taken another woman. The heroine of this film, in the last shot is in the train looking out of the window. When the actress doing this role gave an interview she said that the director had not asked her to smile but she smiled a little in that shot. Why? Is it a triumphant smile? What is her triumph? That she got a good, sentimental, emotional excuse to leave home? The film is filled with myths. The woman has her motherhood taken away because her own daughter is taken away emotionally by her brother and sister-in-law; her space at home is undemarcated because of a dominant mother-in-law. She has no place at home which is why she seeks an identity outside. All these facts make the opposite true, that if all these were not so this woman would have had no reason to go out of the home. A happy household creates a fulfilled woman. It is a dissatisfied housewife who ventures out. The fact that a woman in a completely satisfying household can still feel unfulfilled in herself and seek something more, does not fit into the myth about the new woman who is essentially portrayed as frustrated, exploited, angry, revengeful and ruthless. Underlying all that need to be herself is almost always a disappointment connected with a man. In other words, all that she needs is a nice, understanding, warm man who would indulge her.

It is not enough to have counter-content if there isn't a counter language. Jutta Bruckner, the German filmmaker, argues that it is not really a new language as much as a new identity (Harbord, 1981). A new identity would certainly mean a new expression. There are a lot of opinions on what exactly this new language should be. Some have felt that viewing cinema with feminist spectacles has only confirmed the 'absence' of women both on screen and as audience. They have also said that there are some real pleasures in the progress of the narrative and are doubtful to what extent these pleasures can be broken and subverted (Montgomery, 1984). What it really means is that there is no one language that can be identified as a feminist language and defined and categorized. There will always be as many languages as there are women. While one is not asking for one universal feminist language one should be definite that the present myths of realism in cinema would be of no use in helping to find a language which will be a woman's own. This new language will not emerge until the changed values and attitudes towards women become part of the living consciousness of the director, male or female. Anything else would only produce a fake creation. It is difficult even as a writer, to sit down, open a pen and say: 'Here I am going to write a feminist story'. It has to become a natural part of the creator's life for it to seem noncontrived and simple. For in actuality, truth is very simple—as simple as the falling of an apple. Any creation with loud, overt attempts to portray women one has to hold suspect even if it is packaged as a 'woman's film'. Like the old Zen master who lay dying and his chief disciple, who knew everything, came to ask him if there was something still lacking in the disciple that the master was dissatisfied about. The master replied: 'Yes, you are still stinking of Zen.'

PORTRAYAL OF WOMEN ON TELEVISION

Jyoti Punwani

The sudden growth of television over the last two years has made it the most influential medium of mass communication in India. Television's influence lies in its reach, i.e., 7 million television sets in 1983 (T.V. Network Grows, *Manorama*, 1987) as well as in its projection of social values. This it does through its sponsored serials, most of them soap operas, i.e., dramatization of short or long narratives, episodic in structure, dealing with real life situations and characters.

Sponsored serials on television started in 1985 with *Hum Log*: India's first soap opera, which changed the character of television. Very soon, other sponsored serials started being aired, and today, television can be said to be dominated by soap operas. Viewer's identification with these serials is very high. Serial makers state that they get regular mail advising them on how the story should develop.

Hum Log, was inspired by a Mexican soap opera, in which the dramatized, fictional narrative helped propagate the government's message of family planning. The succeeding torrent of soap operas on Doordarshan have had nothing to do with official propaganda. They are varied in content, form and origin, ranging from little skits written specially for television to literary classics.

How are women portrayed in these programs? Do these programs reflect the myriad aspects of women's lives in contemporary Indian society? To answer these questions, it was thought necessary to study in detail 12 representative serials, telecast over the past two-and-a-half years. Data regarding reactions to these serials was also collected through informal interviewing with viewers and directors of serials.

What immediately stands out in these programs is both the presence of women in significant numbers, as well as their importance to the theme. Unlike present-day Hindi films where women are generally just decorative pieces, on television women play important roles. Recently, a trend has started wherein women play the central character in the serial. However, this does not mean that one can get to see in these programs, the complexities which form part of women's lives today. Certain generalizations can be made about the women portrayed on television.

1. An overwhelming majority of them are home-based, whether married or unmarried.
2. Working women are always shown to be so, through circumstances, not choice, that too, unhappy circumstances. Also rarely are they happy in their jobs.
3. Marriage is seen as a natural state for a woman, if single, the woman is working towards achieving that state; if widowed/divorced, she is rarely happy. She may be making a success of her life, but underlying that is her sadness at her single and lonely state.
4. In their relationships with men, the ideal women are supportive and dependent; those who are aggressive or independent minded, are not considered desirable role models.
5. Women who try to break out of their traditional place in society and family, do not meet with a happy end. At best, they have to compromise to some extent, but by far the commonest fate reserved for them is failure and humiliation.

Hum Log, the first Indian soap, was clearly a story with a moral. The story of a lower middle class Delhi-based, Hindu joint family headed by an upright patriarch, it upheld all the traditional social values. *Hum Log* illustrated certain characteristics that were to become the norms for the future serials:

1. With some token exceptions, women are conventional and stereo-typed. Each of the three main female characters is a distinct individual: the traditional, long-suffering wife and mother, the rebellious elder daughter and the ambitious and flighty younger daughter.
2. As the character of these women develop, they move towards a stereotyped personality and conservative values. This is seen in Badki who begins by defying societal values but eventually succumbs.
3. A terrible fate awaits the ambitious woman who deviates from the traditional path. The classic example is of Majhli, who had to be scarred by a series of horrifying experiences, ending up as a nervous wreck and with a complete lack of self-esteem, before she can be rehabilitated and made into a docile wife.
4. The type of husbands given to aggressive or independent women—always kind, soft-spoken, decent gentlemen—only served to highlight the unreasonableness of the women, e.g., Badki's doctor husband.

There is a dilemma posed by the portrayal of conventional women in serials. Should they be reflected as reactionary and retrograde, or recognized as realistic? To take the example of the long suffering mother in *Hum Log*, would it have been in keeping with her character, her age and her background, to be shown fighting with her insensitive husband? The idea, however, is not to totally reject the conventional women but to highlight the limitations within socially sanctioned roles.

The above two characterizations were also present in the two other major family sagas: *Khandan* and *Buniyaad*. These serials telecast between 1985 and 1987, revealed more clearly what one could expect from television's portrayal of women, and strengthened the belief that no matter how vast the variety of women portrayed, the message they conveyed did not fill one with hope.

Both *Khandan* and *Buniyaad* made their own contribution to strengthening traditional sexist beliefs about women. *Khandan* gave viewers the modern stereotype: affluent and ambitious career women for whom marriage and children were obstacles. The serial assumed that women could not reconcile career and marriage successfully. Both the ambitious career women portrayed had unsuccessful marriages, both were aggressive, even ruthless. In an interview to the *Sunday Observer*, the director of *Khandan* Shridhar Kshirsagar claimed that his serial presented a 'spectrum of women: the traditional Indian women in the mother; the young widow who seems always ebullient but is in fact, very unhappy; the traditional *bahu* who, being educated, can't play the role. The thesis being: if you want to keep the woman as a chattel, don't educate her.' He added, that 'for a woman, these three roles (that of wife, mother and professional) are very clearly defined personae . . . Most women have just acquiesced, they haven't really resolved these conflicts. For a man, however, he felt these roles were just three facets of the same personality.'

Despite the letters received from women viewers protesting that his portrayal of the two career women was chauvinistic, that he need not have shown such agonizing conflict between marriage and career, the director went on to take his belief to its logical extreme. The heroine Ketaki, a ruthless career executive, who was also the most popular character in the serial, played out a doomed scenario. An unsatisfactory marriage drove her to prove herself in a career, her ambition made her lose her unborn baby and the subsequent depression led her to suicide. All this while being married to a perfectly naive husband who very soon found a more caring replacement for her.

Buniyaad gave women some status but saw to it that they exercised it within their families. Its values were Arya Samaji, its women were correspondingly the ideal, reformed Hindu women: educated, if not learned, intelligent, principled and wise. All these positive qualities were, however, confined to the home. These women were the guiding spirits for their husbands, they instilled the right values in their children. All the role models in the serial showed flashes of independence till marriage tamed them completely, harnessing their capacities to their homes, turning them into guardians of the family honor.

Correspondingly, the negatively portrayed women in *Buniyaad* hated the security of marriage, thirsted, even after her children were born, for a career on stage, lost no opportunity to undermine her 'good' husband's authority, and worst of all, looked down on Indian values, and admired the modern West. She was the butt of universal contempt. In contrast, the male villain of the serial was a powerful evil man, cunning and undeterred till the end. The good men, of course, were all doers who rose by sheer hard work, talent and support of their women, to become powerful men in post-independence India. The dramatic shift in life, the tragedy, loneliness and guilt that awaits a woman who engages herself in pre-marital sex is brought out in the role of Veerawali. Her lover, no doubt depressed, continues to have a normal life—a wife, son and business as usual.

The second category of serials important to this subject are the women-centered ones. From *It's a Woman's World* and *Rajani* telecast in 1985, to the very recent *Kashmakash, Chehre*, and *Rahen Aur Bhi Hain*, telecast in 1987, these serials have taught women viewers two bitter lessons:

1. the mere fact of them being women-oriented serials does not make them free from sexist values;
2. even when women are portrayed as trying to break old values and myths, it becomes equally important how they do it and at what cost.

Thus *Rajani* which made everyone sit up with its portrayal of a fighter who is not afraid of the various manifestations of small-time urban corruption which citizens have to encounter at every level, soon became repititive and predictable. Its early potential which inspired many women to emulate the spirited heroine, did not last and viewers started finding Rajani unnecessarily abrasive and even started pitying her 'victims'. She became a caricature simply because the director, who declared in press interviews that he chose a woman to be the central character because women were more honest than men and didn't compromise as easily.

The other women-dominated serials were even worse; few of them broke any new ground. Most of them were adaptations of literary work, but their low production value as well as their sheer number, rebounded on the intention with which they had probably been made. Viewers saw weeping women on the screen night after night. This only strengthened the stereotype of helpless, weak and powerless women.

Even *Kashmakash*, which was based on short stories written by women failed to make any impact. A character like Kitty in *Karamchand*—a self-consciously exaggerated dumb secretary, became immensely popular. Despite the program's late night slot, many women sat up just to watch Kitty say 'Sir, you are a genius', and make the most absurd remark as her detective boss went around solving crimes and replying 'Shut up Kitty' (Punwani, 1986). The Kitty and Karamchand pair epitomized the unequal relationship between the sexes in all walks of life.

In both *Rathachakra* and *Poornima* the central characters were left to fend for themselves by selfish families. Both managed well for themselves despite a hostile environment, but while one emerged finally as a survivor, the other succumbed.

While Poornima emerged as a strong and admirable character, her eventual fate, viz., suicide, undoes her actions. Her story is in fact, the story of many working women in the country today—forced by economic circumstances to start earning a living, initially as a temporary measure, but slowly develop into pillars of their families, from whom everyone draws sustenance, but who are finally left alone. The serial exposed the real status of the obedient daughter in most lower middle class homes today: the first to make sacrifices for their family, and yet condemned when they try to pursue personal happiness. *Purnima* showed the tension of being a young, single working woman who needs a job at any cost. In a country where marriages are arranged by parents and the terms set by the groom, it showed how difficult it is for a woman to marry (on her own initiative) without the backing of a family. Purnima is not shown to wallow in self-pity instead, she grows hard and cynical.

Interestingly, both these serials as well as many of the other women-oriented ones drew criticism from television critics for what they described as negative and degrading depictions of women. Undoubtedly, most of them showed women being ill-treated by families and bound down by custom almost seeming to choose unhappiness when given a choice, but most often given no choice or control over their lives. Even the well-known Marathi writer Vijay Tendulkar's serial on the life of a divorcee: *Swayamsiddha* conveyed only pessimism. The heroine's constant long suffering, martyred expression, the difficulties real and imagined, she encounters all the time, made many viewers wonder whether it wasn't easier to suffer in a bad marriage rather than suffer after divorce.

What should be the best way to portray women in television? Should they be shown as overcoming or trying to overcome all obstacles? If not inspiring, should they at least be sympathetic characters with whom viewers can easily identify? What if such portrayals are rejected by viewers, as happened with *Basanti*, the story of a slum girl fending for herself in a rich man's world, which got low viewership ratings despite high production standard because viewers complained that she was too plain? Or should ordinary heroines be more effective, women who fought some battles and gave up many more?

What about the literature on which these serials were based? Surely one had to be faithful to them even if it required showing women as suffering more than overcoming suffering. Should the choice of literature be different, then? The work of women writers have been tried without much success, for they too have internationalized sexist values of society. The answer may be in a search for enlightened and emancipated women and men writers.

One serial *Chehre*, based on Bengali short stories about women showed, almost without exception, women submitting to circumstances, rather than trying to change them. But were all these women to be rejected? Weren't many of them being true to their nature and their environment? Could a teenager in a village elope with her boy-friend and leave her little siblings at the mercy of an alcoholic father? If she chose, reluctantly, to stay behind, was she being a coward or just obeying her nurturing, protective instincts which proved stronger than her desire to find personal happiness? If a wife refuses to escape with her fugitive husband in the dead of night to avoid the scandal it would bring on his family, was she being hopelessly traditional? Or doing what most women would do? Would it have had a better impact if she had been shown choosing personal happiness at the cost of social disgrace to her family? There is little doubt that women's lives are full of sacrifice, letting go, giving priority to others' needs: it is time they made self-fulfilment and personal happiness central to their lives.

In one serial, *Kala Jal*, a Muslim wife, adored by her husband was shown bringing home a second wife on her own initiative only because she hadn't been able to bear him children. Was she just being a masochist or just following the custom in her community? Many of the women are aware of alternatives that would give them dignity and integrity but they resolve their conflict in a manner that takes them back into the shelter of tradition.

By allowing viewers to think of the alternatives these women could have followed, do these serials give an insight into our traditional society which is constantly putting pressure on women? Or they strengthen the belief that women have no real choice, that it is best for them to succumb to tradition, that honor is more important for them than happiness? Do these serials promote a fear of breaking social mores? All these serials were literary adaptations, and in many cases the writers were alive. Perhaps if the serial had ended with a short discussion with the writers, many of these questions could have been explored satisfactorily.

If television has succeeded in depicting shades of Indian women rarely depicted on the big screen, it is because the producers come from the educated middle class, unlike the financiers who control the film industry. But more importantly, it is their knowledge that women form the larger part of their audience, so they have a stake in making their programs credible and popular among women. Moreover, the sponsors of their programs and the advertizers regard women as the largest consumers. These very producers have no qualms about showing advertizements on television which depict women as sex objects. As Tuchman (1983) has said, 'Radio, television, newspapers and magazines all seek to deliver as many consumers as possible to advertizers'.

It is not as though general guidelines do not exist on the depiction of women on television. The P.C. Joshi Committee (1985) had recommended ways in which women should be portrayed. It has said:

The government must at the earliest formulate clear-cut guidelines regarding positive portrayal of women on television. This portrayal must take note of women in all facets of their lives: as workers, and significant contributors to family survival and the national economy. Women must not be portrayed in stereotyped images that emphasize passive, submissive qualities and encourage them to play a subordinate secondary role in the family and the society. Both men and women should be portrayed in ways that encourage mutual respect and a spirit of give and take between the sexes.

In order to promote a positive ideology that is sensitive to women's needs and permeates the total programing and also to have a coordinated, consistent policy it would be necessary for all Doordarshan policy-makers, programming, and production staff to have regular orientation courses that sensitize them to women's issues.

At the time, the committee submitted its report, the only reference point it had were film-based programs and a few television plays, and discussion programs, including women's programs. But despite all this, have things changed? Are women being portrayed as workers and significant contributors to family survival and the national economy? Despite the number and variety of women being portrayed on television, the answer must be no. The picture of Indian women on television is of a housebound, tradition-bound, passive person. Given the fact that the majority of women workers are housewives, there is hardly a glimpse of everyday adjustments women have to make in the home; the burden of housework; their contributions as housewives and mothers—all this is to be taken for granted. There is no attempt at changing relationships and expectations even among the most protected of Indian women. There have been momentous social developments, which have influenced political events, like the Shahbano affair, yet such developments are not reflected on TV serials. Issues like this or the recent judgement which has made it compulsory for a married daughter to look after her old parents rarely form the basis of discussion programs either. As Tuchman (1983) has said: 'The very unrepresentation of women, including their stereotypic portrayal, may symbolically capture the position of women in American society—their real lack of power.'

The remedy does not lie in putting more women in decision making positions in Doordarshan or in handing over these programs to women's groups/women directors alone. The P.C. Joshi Committee (1985) recommended a system of regular monitoring of the portrayal of women on television. It stated:

There should be a weekly program of viewer's views in which the audience as also critics and commentators from newspapers, women's organizations etc. are called to analyze and evaluate the week's program. The evaluation must have a specific focus in the way in which women are portrayed (p. 146).

To do this Doordarshan needs to build up a commitment not only to women, but towards promoting a changing image of Indian society. Given the control of government and of commercial interests over the medium this seems rather unrealistic right now.

WOMEN AND SEXISM: LANGUAGE OF INDIAN SCHOOL TEXTBOOKS

Narendra Nath Kalia

Almost 20 years ago, India's official educators promised to deliver a curriculum that would recognize and nurture the fundamental equality between men and women (Education Commission, India, 1965, p. 4). The Indian government agreed to rewrite the textbooks of independent India to prepare its young for an era of equality by inspiring

> each sex to develop a proper respect toward the other because . . . it is unscientific to divide tasks and subjects on the basis of sex and to regard some of them as 'masculine' and others as 'feminine'. Similarly, the fact that the so-called psychological differences between the two sexes arises, not out of sex but out of social conditioning, will have to be widely publicized and people will have to be made to realise that stereotypes of 'masculine' and 'feminine' personalities do more harm than good (Education Commission, India, 1965, pp. 4–5).

However, our government's performance never neared its promise (Kalia, 1979, 1980). Indian school textbooks have continued to exude sexist bias despite the pompous proclamations of our official educators and their almost dictatorial control over the content of these textbooks. To determine the extent of sexism in Indian textbooks, I conducted a computer-aided content analysis of 21 English and 20 Hindi language-instruction textbooks, prescribed yearly for more than 13 lakh students in Haryana, Punjab, Rajasthan, Uttar Pradesh and Delhi. These 41 books included texts prepared or used by two national agencies: National Council of Educational Research and Training (NCERT) and Central Board of Secondary Education.

What I found was damnable. Not only were the majority of characters male, but in 75 per cent of the lesson plots men also emerged as dominant figures. There were 47 biographies of men, only seven biographies of women. Men routinely abused and violently beat women in many lessons. Over 100 female characters were victimized as a result of their sex roles. In most lessons, men ventured out to seek fame and fortune, while women stayed home to wash dishes and clothes. Males in Indian textbooks occupied high-prestige occupations. Both in and outside the home, they appeared the dominant decision-makers in the wide range of activities. Of the 465 occupations held by characters in the plots, women were completely excluded from 344. Most women were relegated to low-prestige, low-income positions (housewife, servant, prostitute). Their authority to make decisions was generally restricted to domestic matters. As if catering to a male readership alone, the authors and editors of Indian textbooks used nouns and pronouns that excluded females from generalizations about human society. In the following sections, I have attempted a prescriptive analysis of this last feature of Indian textbook writing—sexism in language.

Does Sexist Language Contribute to Sexism in Society?

In discussing the issue of sexism and language, partisans are often drawn to the metaphor of illness: symptoms and disease. One side of the argument maintains that where sexism is the disease, sexist language is its natural manifestation, as red spots are of measles. Just as a physician would not cure measles by bleaching out the red spots, we must not hope to cure sexism by blanching language of sexist constructions. Such an enterprise would, in fact, be a ridiculous waste of time. On the other hand, while sexism remains the disease, sexist language is the critical symptom that actually defines the disease and, like seizures in epilepsy, sexist language can itself be debilitating.

Since arguers for the first case do concede that some linguistic changes are justified when terms or the usages demean members of a group through innuendo and implication, thus causing psychological damage to the subject and reinforcing prejudice in the speaker, the question to ask is: how do we define sexist language? Vetterling-Braggin provides one answer:

> A word or sentence is sexist if . . . its use creates, constitutes, promotes, or exploits an unfair or irrelevant distinction between the sexes . . . and if its use contributes to, promotes, causes or results in the oppression of either sex (1981, pp. 3–4).

In a more inclusive sense, sexist language is a symbolic device that 'limits the activities of one sex, but not those same activities of the other' (Shute, 1981). Sexism in a society complements the existence of sexist language. Sexist terminology distinguishes between people purely on the basis of biology. It defines the 'masculine' or 'feminine' labels attached to role, status, idea, behavior, activity; and condemns those who in any way overstep the bounds of their sex role stereotypes. Sexism in language allows an ideology to legitimize the prescriptions and appraisals of every human endeavor solely on the basis of gender.

Language uses us as much as we use language. Thus sexist language spreads and reinforces sex role stereotypes. Our opinions on any given matter are generally shaped by the way in which the original facts were presented to us. Lakeoff explains:

> If we feel positively towards any given thing in the world, we are more likely to describe that thing by using words with positive connotations than we are by using words with negative connotations. For example, if I admire a person who is capable of independent thinking, I am more likely to describe that person as 'strong-minded' than I am to describe that person as 'pig-headed' (cited in Vetterling-Braggin, 1981, p. 56).

The same process applies when we receive sexist messages. If we speak the way we think and if our thinking determines our behavior, then sexist language has serious negative consequences for social interaction. By enabling us to speak/think of women in unfavorable terms, such language actually prompts us and those who hear us to believe that women are, in fact, bad or inferior. When you think negatively of a group, you are unlikely to treat them fairly. When such attitudes become group held convictions, they help to dig the moat between the oppressors and the oppressed.

Specifically, sexist language oppresses people through metaphoric identification (Ross, 1981), exclusion, labelling, and referential genderization (Beardsley, 1973). Metaphoric identification involves the deep structure of words and phrases—their etymologies, allusions, psychological undertones. Sexist language conveys prejudice through the everyday vocabulary used in social intercourse. Many gender-related words metaphorically insult or belittle women by identifying them as children, animals. or objects: girl (used in reference to a woman), 'baby', 'dish', 'chick', 'hot tomato', 'bitch', ('son of a bitch' for men), 'dog', 'sugar', etc.

Exclusion involves the creation of sex-based names, terms, and expressions to characterize essentially sex-neutral positions, occupations, etc. Through exclusionary devices, sexist language restrains one gender from pursuing activities similar to those allowed the other gender in the same society. Words such as 'chairman', 'foreman', 'fisherman', exclude women by calling to mind male actors; thus, implicitly eliminating qualified women from consideration in these positions and occupations.

Labelling assigns the arbitrary tags 'masculine' and 'feminine' to areas that have no relation to gender. In everyday life, activities such as washing dishes or playing quietly may be despised by boys simply because they carry the label 'feminine', the bane of 'masculinity'.

Referential genderization involves linguistic practices that encourage the use of one gender pronouns as universal generics appropriate for signifying both the sexes. The use of masculine pronouns as generics is the most blatant example of such incorrect locution. By legitimizing the ambiguity of the masculine pronoun (it may mean a man or it may mean a man or woman) referential genderization ignores the fact that for every 'he' in the language there is a reciprocal 'she'. In perpetuating such usage, patriarchal grammar also promotes the notion that women as individuals, and feminine pronouns as words, are inferior and limited in comparison with their male counterparts.

Male Centered Language

Sexist language—what I shall here call male-centered language, since there are few examples of female-centered language and none of them appear in the Indian textbooks—reflects more than linguistic preference. By redefining social reality, it mirrors and enhances a collective strategy for gender-based discrimination. Take, for example, the criteria of excellence in a patriarchy. In her discussion of the 'otherness' of women, Simone de Beauvoir (1970, p. 493) showed how men and male achievement have come to represent the standard, the ideal. In comparison, women are always the 'other'—somehow unintelligible and inferior. The language of Indian school textbooks promotes similar arrogance with an eagerness bordering on obloquy: the best of humanity is masculine. The ideal of 'man' is often used to measure a person's worth. A character aspires to 'meet death like a man' (T10, p. 31), implying that to be brave is to be a man, or vice versa. In another textbook story, knowledge is incarnated as a male. Most essays on greatness lean so heavily on the use of 'man' that the females are virtually excluded from the realm of higher achievement. When used to describe a woman, 'man' is usually intended as a supreme compliment, as in: 'Though a woman, she played a part any man might be proud of' (T9; p. 43); or this gem from Mahatma Gandhi, 'India is less manly under the British rule than she was ever before' (T4, p. 75).

How does this affect the readers? Couching all our broad statements about the human race in male-centered language has dangerous consequences: female readers might not identify with what the 'man' has done. When women are excluded from the 'man's' achievements, they are left as spectators. Subsuming females with the word 'men' confirms the patriarchal dictum that men are somehow the legitimate, real members.

Women are the exceptions, the outsiders. Just as a boy might feel that a book entitled *Women and Her World* isn't meant for him, girls may feel excluded from books with titles like *Man and His World*.

Nowhere is this more apparent than in the use of 'man' to mean all people. 'Mankind' in Indian textbooks denote humanity, 'womankind' does not. 'One step for womankind' does not include both females and male persons as 'one step for mankind' does. Our linguists at the Central Institute for English at Hyderabad do not regard 'mankind' as a mere vestigial ellipsis for 'humankind': they continue to assign to the word 'man' a special privilege in relation to humans, while denying it to the word 'woman'.

I concede that sexist language is a necessary evil in ancient literary works. I also concede that the responsibility for sexist language may sometimes lie less with the textbook authors than with the way grammar evolved in patriarchal societies. I am not suggesting that editors and textbook approvers should strike from their anthologies all literary works, however important, that contain male-centered language. Yet, today's writers and editors can no longer evade the responsibility for sexist usage in materials specifically produced for classroom consumption. An editor, adapting a work of literature for textbook lessons, need not slash its soul by falling prey to linguistic insensitivity. Witness this adaptation of Rabindra Nath Thakur's story 'Horse' in the NCERT's *Dear to All the Muses: An Anthology of Contemporary Prose* (Prescribed for class XII: semester three of the +2 course):

To the new animal He made, He gave neither horns nor claws; He gave it teeth that could chew but not bite. The energy He gave it was enough to make it useful on the battlefield, but He gave it no taste of its own for battles. The animal came to be known as the Horse (T2: 2).

The same passage in *New English Course Reader* (prescribed for class IX of Rajasthan Secondary Schools) reads:

The new creature was given neither horns nor claws, and his teeth were only meant for eating, not for biting. The care with which fire was used, made him necessary in war without making him warlike. This animal was the Horse (T1: 55).

How can one explain the masculinization of the horse in the Rajasthani version? Perhaps with these words by the editors of the *New English Course Reader*:

A great deal of license has been taken with the original works which have been adapted to fulfil the requirements of the structures and vocabulary prescribed for the Secondary School syllabus (T1: Preface).

Such liberty to assign gender-linked pronouns to animals is unnecessary and undesirable. With creativity and a little caution, we can create language free of past debris, and truly reflective of reality. Examples in the following portions of this paper will provide suggestions and models for such writing.

Man as a Generic Term

Why do we operate under the delusion that the word 'man' and its pro-nominalized attendants 'he', 'him', 'his' inevitably include women? English-speaking people derived this notion from the earliest Anglo-Saxon linguistic tradition in which 'man' meant person or human being. An entirely different word distinguished male human beings from female human beings. In the course of time, patriarchal writers eliminated the dichotomy by using the word 'man' to generalize about both sexes. By the eighteenth century, the generic use of 'man' has been established as common usage. However, it still bothered some writers enough to prompt parenthetical clarifications. Witness Edmund Burke, writing about the French Revolution: 'Such a deplorable havoc is made in the minds of men [both sexes] in France . . .' By the time Thomas Jefferson wrote 'all men are created equal' and 'governments are instituted among men, deriving their just powers from the consent of the governed', such clarifications had become so unnecessary that Jefferson probably never even suspected that his statement, in an era before women's vote, would apply only to males and not to all citizens of the young American republic (Miller and Swift, 1980, p. 10).

Using 'man' to mean people causes ambiguity and confusion. What is one to think, for instance, of this exchange between Yudhisthir and Yaksha in the 'Enchanted Pool': 'What rescues man in danger?' 'Courage is man's salvation in danger' . . . 'Who accompanies a man after death?' (T9, pp. 29–30). Such usage of 'man' to signify both genders is rare in spoken language. Hearing a speaker address an audience of males and females as 'men' would seem strange indeed. Who would say, 'All men in my family have always been dark-skinned' when they mean, 'Everyone in my family has always been dark-skinned'? Only an odd reporter would inform readers that 'Every man is dead!' when referring to the male and female victims of a fire.

It is incorrect to presume that 'man' is universally understood as a term denoting the image of a person. The use of masculine pronouns almost always brings to mind male human beings (Miller and Swift, 1976). Children have particular difficulty in discerning the images of both males and females in the word 'man'. Studies of children's perceptions in the classroom clearly indicate that students, whose reading assignments use the so-called generic, subliminally perceive male characters significantly more often than students who read similar assignments in which the word 'people' replaces 'man' (Nilsen et al, 1977). Another recent study found students from elementary through secondary school confused over the nature of the referent in common expressions such as 'The child is father of the man'. Even their teachers could not answer with certainty whether the terms in question were generic or specifically male-related (Pincus and Pincus, 1980).

The currently acceptable generic use of 'man' is also illogical because one cannot say the same kinds of things with 'woman' or 'she' as one can with 'man' or 'he'. The generic application of masculine nouns/pronouns is inherently faulty, as this famous syllogism attests:

All men are mortal. Socrates is a man.

If 'man' were really neutral, one would be able to substitute any name for Socrates, even to say Lata Mangeshkar is a man.

Tokenism will not do

In some textbooks, token attempts to include women result in even more confusion and greater insult.

The franchise widened continually until it became universal, until the elections were held on the principle of 'one man (or woman) one vote' . . . 'One man, one vote' is also called the principle of political equality. Implicitly, it gives equal weightage to every citizen whatever his (or her) sex, race, caste, religion or class. Men are divided in many different ways (T5: 79).

The above appears in *We and Our Government*, an NCERT social studies textbook that continually uses 'man' and male pronouns to mean both men and women. But when women are specifically included here, what are we to think of the numerous other times when they are not? When previously the 'citizen' always did 'his' duty or acted for the benefit of all the 'men' in the village, are we now to assume that 'his' denotes men and women? And then, what does a word like 'everyone' represent? In saying 'whatever his sex', the writer's generic usage is foolish—'his sex' being understood only one way—a problem similarly faced by writers trying to describe how difficult childbirth was for 'primitive man'.

The parenthetical use of 'women' or 'her' in the above quotation also insults women because it treats them as an afterthought. The overriding impression is that their inclusion is not really legitimate; it was merely added on when feminist screaming got too loud.

Sexist Classification of Occupation

Since most chapters in textbooks are not protected by poetic license and since modern language does not lack non-sexist synonyms, male-centered language is especially inexcusable in discussions about human labor. A glossary in *An English Course for Secondary Schools* describes the word artificial this way: 'made by the art of man; not real or natural' (T8: 38). In other words, man-made. Why not use more sensible terms like 'synthetic', 'hand-made', 'manufactured', 'fabricated', 'machine-made', 'hand-built', or 'constructed'? Besides being more fair to the women who actually produce much of what is brazenly called man-made, these words have the added advantage of being more specific. As shown below, sex-linked words can be easily converted to their generic equivalents:

man (verb)	operate, work, staff, serve on (at)
manhood	adulthood, maturity
manpower	work force, workers, staff, personnel, human resources
man-sized (job)	big, enormous, challenging
manpowered	muscle-powered, unmechanized
man-eating	meat-eating, carnivorous
man-hour	work hour
middleman	go-between, liaison, trader
right-hand man	assistant
manhole	utility hole, access hole
manhole cover	sewer cover, sewer lid

Sexist classification of occupations advances the fallacy of socially significant work as 'man's business' through the use of three linguistic devices:

— 'man' as a suffix in job titles
— diminutive endings ('-ess', '-ette' and '-trix') for females
— 'woman' as a modifier in job descriptions.

The first two linguistic devices are obverse sides of the same coin. They both evolved when the occupations they described were generally held by men. Lately, one common technique of creating job titles that acknowledge women's entry into previously male-only domains is to replace the suffix '-man' with '-woman'. This kind of suffix juggling simply highlights the hasty patchwork. We would never call a man who cleaned a building 'charwoman'; instead we would call him a 'charman' (uncommon), 'scrubber', 'custodian', or 'janitor', even though the last three are generic and could as easily be applied to a woman who cleans. I am not suggesting that the man who calls himself a 'watchman' must suddenly be forced to use another term; rather a woman in the same position could be called a 'guard', and this term should be used in the general job description applicable to both. The same goes for words like:

salesman, saleswoman: sales agent, sales associate, sales clerk, seller, salesperson, sales representative.
businessman, businesswoman: business executive
spokesman, spokeswoman: representative, agent, speaker
statesman, stateswoman: leader, diplomat
chairman, chairwoman: chair, chairperson, presider.

Obviously, with all these words the correct sex-neutral noun will often depend upon the capacity of the position. For precision, business executives can be described by their specific roles: manufacturer, retailer, importer, merchant, etc. If we want to suggest something about the person's character as well, there is always entrepreneur, speculator, capitalist. And, when referring to the business community as a group, business can replace businessmen.

If you find the substitution of fisher for fisherman a little strained, let me point out that the *Oxford English Dictionary* has used fisher to mean somebody who fishes since the ninth century, and this term frequently appears in the King James version of the Bible. By comparison, fisherman has a significantly shorter history. The English language provides a distinct tradition for sex-neutral terms. The 'crown' refers to the monarch, the 'bench' to judges. As shown below, sex-neutral titles carry no additional psychological baggage:

cameraman	camera operator
caveman	cave-dweller, primitive, early human
chambermaid	housekeeper
charwoman	office cleaner
deliveryman	delivery person, deliverer
draftsman	drafter
gateman	gatekeeper
lineman	line installer, line repairer
mailman	letter/mail carrier, postal worker
newsboy	newscarrier,

paperboy	paper carrier
newsman	newscaster, reporter, journalist
pressman	press operator
repairman	repairer, mechanic
signalman	signaller
stuntman	stunt performer
workman	worker, laborer

Although some writers mistakenly assume that '-or' or '-er' endings signal occupations held by men (witness actor, waiter), these endings are sex-neutral regardless of their referents. In English traced from Latin, the '-er' or '-or' suffix means 'do or, more specially, one who does'. Thus, a teacher is one who teaches; and actor is one who acts; a farmer is one who farms, and so forth. In distinguishing jobs done by women from those same jobs done by men, diminutive endings only belittle women, because the endings '-ess', and '-ette', and '-trix' connote smallness of size or the qualities of substitute or imitation (witness leatherette), they delegitimate the worth of the labor described. They imply that work done by a woman is neither as genuine nor serious as the same work by a man. No female writer of stature would ever accept the label authoress. Yet, India's textbooks continue to describe Sarojini Naidu as a poetess, Amelia Earhart as a aviatrix, and numerous other women by the titles seamstress, actress, songstress, etc.

Table 1

People get born the sons of kings, and they grow up to inherit power and riches and then they say to themselves, 'Now, what do I like best?' (T3: 78).
This comes from 'A Dialogue on Civilization', the introduction to *The Story of Civilization* by C.E.M. Joad. In one form or another, sections or adaptations from this book appear in numerous language-instruction textbooks.

WHAT TO DO: After reading through the lesson, ask students to reread this particular page. Then ask whether they think anything seems unusual about its language. Draw their attention to the usage of the word 'sons' to illustrate the reasons behind the use of male-centered language and the reasons such language should be avoided. Ask students about the grammatical impropriety here: What does 'people' mean? What does 'sons' mean? What is the logical parallel to people in this sentence? To 'sons'? How does the meaning change when you use the logically parallel terms? Who are children born to? Why do we read about the 'world of our fathers', 'the children of kings', and so on? What is the female equivalent of kings? What words carry the same meaning but include both sexes? Ask your students to recast the sentence in as many nonsexist ways as they can think of without sacrificing meaning. Their various answers will probably come down to: 'People are born the children of monarchs . . .'

Following the -er, -or rule of definition, both sexes can be termed actors, aviators/pilots, singers, dressmakers/tailors/ designers, executors, stewards, waiters, bartenders, majors, and governors. The last two words become especially ridiculous when converted by diminutives, since the work they describe is far removed from the tasks of a majorette or a governess, as we have come to understand those terms.

If so many Indian students and teachers were not trained to take textbook lessons seriously, I could label the ridiculous grammar exercises that follow most lessons just that, and could move on to something more important. But the damage inflicted in our grammar exercises is too serious to be dismissed as innocent folly. Here is what *A Textbook of English Prose* (prescribed for Class IX by Board of School Education, Haryana; 4,25,000 copies in print) asks students to do:

> Change the gender of the following words and use them in your own sentences: maid, princes, queen, elephant, tiger, priest, (T7, p. 92) poet, wife, she, man, girl, master (*Ibid.*, p. 112).

What is the male equivalent of maid? Butler? But a maid's job includes housecleaning—something no pursed-lipped butler in his coat tails would dream of touching. Charman? But that suggests dingier work than that normally done by a maid. And what in the world is one to say to denote the sex-change of an elephant? Elephantette, elephantess, elephantrix? Nor is mistress, which is more likely to mean lover unless preceded by head, thus signifying a school principal, a proper feminine equivalent for master. Of its many definitions, mistress has almost never meant an exceptional achiever. While we may say: 'Da Vinci was a master of many arts'. It would indeed be odd to read: 'Sirimavo Bandarnaike is a mistress at political manoeuvring'.

Perhaps the Haryanvi educators would like us to use mistress as the female equivalent of master in such forms as: 'She was a mistress pianist', or 'Prabha Dixit has mistressed the art of investigative reporting'.

Why Eliminate Sexist Language?

In the beginning of this paper, I had mentioned that when feminists argue that eliminating sexist language is an important precondition to destroying sexism in a society, their critics maintain that social change affects linguistic change, nor vice versa. However, this line of reasoning fails to

> . . . . distinguish between words qua words and words qua used by speakers of the language. Words qua words are powerless to effect any change in the world, but the use of words . . . . can have the same effect as . . . paying employees on the basis of sex rather than ability (Shute, 1981, pp. 25–26).

By disavowing sexist language, we make it possible to eliminate its societal extensions. To paraphrase Pascal's wager on the existence of God:

If sexist language is dangerous and we act as though it were not, we have all to lose. If it is not and we act as though it were, we don't lose anything. The risks lie in doing nothing, in remaining silent.

Table 2

1 Put the verb in brackets into the past perfect tense: The firemen went away when they . . . put out the fire. (T1, p. 125).
Change fireman to firefighters.

2 Policemen do not either build roads or run hospitals or manage steel plants or shoot satellites into orbit (T5, p. 21).
Change policemen to police or police officers.

3 In politics, the common man can no longer be treated as an outsider (T5, p. 19).
Change common man to common voter or average citizen.

4 Laymen usually, and quite rightly, associate the entire government with the Prime Minister (T5, p. 49).
Change laymen to citizens or people.

5 Even democracies realise the importance of propaganda, and that has led to the growing importance of public relations men (T6, p. 75).
Change public relations men to public relations personnel/agents, or simply use public relations.

6 Knowing that a storm was coming, the fishermen . . . (T1, p. 123). Change fishermen to fishers.

List of Textbooks
(Cited in the paper by numeral T)

T1 Marwah, M.K. and Mathur, A. eds, *New English Reader*, Raj Prakashan, Ajmer 1978 (Prescribed for Class IX, Rajasthan).

T2 Mohan, R., Tickoo, M.L., Pant, H. and Ram, S.K. eds, *Dear to All the Muses: A Anthology of Contemporary Prose*, National Council of Educational Research and Training, New Delhi, 1971, (1978) (Prescribed for class XII, Semester Three).

T3 Tickoo, M.L., D'Souza, J., Jayaseelan, K.A., Sasikumaran, V. and Gunashekar, F eds, (1977) *English Reader: A Textbook for the Core Course*, National Council of Educational Research and Training, New Delhi, 1980 (Prescribed for Class XI).

T4 Matta, R.N. ed., *Reading for Pleasure*, Panjab University Publications Bureau Chandigarh, 1978 (1977) (Prescribed for Class XI, Punjab).

T5 Kaviraj, S. *We and Our Government: A Textbook for Class IX and X*, Oxford an IBH Publishing Company, New Delhi, 1977.

T6 Deshpande, N.R., *Political System: A Textbook for Class XI*, National Council Educational Research and Training, New Delhi, 1977.

T7 Board of School Education, Haryana, *A Textbook of English Prose*, Board of School Education, Haryana, Chandigarh, 1975 (1972) (Prescribed for Classes IX and X Haryana).

T8   Central Institute of English and Foreign Languages, *An English Course for Secondary Schools*, Central Board of Secondary Education, New Delhi, 1979 (1978) (Prescribed for Class IX).

T9   Board of School Education, Haryana, *English Reader, Book IV*, Board of School Education, Haryana, Chandigarh, 1976 (1971) (Prescribed for high school classes, Haryana, 5,42,000 copies in print).

T10 Collocott, T.C. ed., *New Radiant Readers Book VIII*, Allied Publishers, New Delhi, 1974 (Standard VIII of English medium schools in UP and Maharashtra).

V

AWARENESS

Having discussed the persisting images of women in society, the social-ization of young women to fit into these images, the derogatory and secondary treatment meted out to them in real life and in the media, the final section addresses itself to what has been done and is being done to eradicate some of these problems. Awareness of injustice and discrimi-nation, awareness of unequal distribution of power between the sexes is but the first step in bringing about a much needed social change.

The last decade has seen *yatras*, street plays, protest marches, exhibi-tions, consciousness-raising sessions, training camps and opening of women's aid centres in several cities in the country. These have been crucial in raising public awareness. Another common medium of raising awareness by feminists is the extensive media coverage of women's prob-lems including the publication of the first feminist magazine, *Manushi*, in 1975. Some of these attempts have involved symptomatic treatment of the problems, a few others have examined more deeply the roots of women's oppression and have provided radical solutions and new life-style options for them.

The emergence of women's groups has been the single most important achievement of our time. It is worth mentioning that, contrary to the West, in India informal social networks and togetherness among women at all age levels has been in existence and approved of. Surprisingly, this solidarity has probably been never systematically used to examine the dependent and oppressive nature of women's lives. The new women's groups working at the grassroots level have mobilized and sensitized women to the quality, or rather the lack of it, in their lives and created in them a desire to challenge social and legal conventions. Their major function has been to bring many silent voices to articulation. However, no single umbrella group has emerged at the national level to incorporate these smaller groups and provide an overall momentum.

This section begins with Vibhuti Patel's article 'Emergence and Proli-feration of Autonomous Women's Groups in India (1974-1984)'. The paper highlights the essential difference between the new groups and those women's organizations that have traditionally existed in the country.

There is a need among these groups to look at women's issues in specific terms and also in the larger context to connect their concerns with those of other oppressed groups in society.

In his article 'Forming a Women's Group in Chandigarh: Experiences of a Male Activist', Pritam Singh shares his personal experiences of how one such autonomous women's group emerged on the campus of a North Indian city, sustained itself for a period and then gradually disintegrated. The article shows that the contribution of sympathic men to women's cause cannot be underestimated. The hesitation experienced by young college women in assuming leadership makes room for pessimism towards this cause.

Imparting information (awareness) at a more formal and systematic level the article 'Teaching Men about Women' by Rehana Ghadially describes the uphill task in educating men about women's problems. Prejudice and masculinist values are rampant among elite, intelligent young men who aspire to leadership in society.

Speaking of a truly radical feminist movement, Lawrence Babb in his paper 'Indigenous Feminism in a Modern Hindu Sect' refers to the awakening of feminist thought in a group of very traditional women. The family has been one of the most oppressive institutions for women. Dissatisfaction with married life and knowledge of double standards in society have driven some women to pursue a radically different life style. Renouncing sexuality is held as the key to true liberation.

EMERGENCE AND PROLIFERATION OF AUTONOMOUS WOMEN'S GROUPS IN INDIA: 1974–1984

Vibhuti Patel

Around the mid-seventies, India witnessed the emergence of women's groups and organizations which have taken up feminist issues from a totally new perspective. Their activities were not restricted to merely passing resolutions or sending delegations to various authorities. These groups engaged not only in militant activism to assert women's rights but also made serious attempts to articulate their thoughts on the roots of oppression of women. Moreover, they were not guided by any political leader or party. Young educated women took the initiative to form autonomous women's groups.

In India, the earliest efforts to enhance the status of women were made in the nineteenth century. Male social reformers, their wives and some British administrators worked for the abolition of sati, child-marriages, female infanticide, purdah, and other cruel customs affecting women's lives. They advocated women's education, widow remarriage and such other social reforms. Raja Ram Mohun Roy, Ishwar Chandra Vidyasagar, Mahatma Phule, Karsandas Mulji were some of the important social reformers who worked for the upliftment of women. Their contemporary, Pandita Ramabai, was a radical reformer of her time.

During the Nationalist Movement thousands of women actively participated under the leadership of Mahatma Gandhi. Unfortunately, after 1947, women again stopped taking interest in larger social issues.

With the establishment of autonomous women's groups, things started changing. Established women's organizations, and women's fronts of political parties were forced to sit up, and think of revitalizing themselves (Patel, 1982). These autonomous groups and organizations are run by women and for women, and not by political parties. This does not necessarily mean that members of these organizations are apolitical. However, these organizations are not women's fronts of specific political parties. They do not exclude male membership, though they insist that women should decide the course of the movement. To many members, it is also not independent of class struggle or the problems of the toiling masses. We strongly believe that the women's movement is inseperable from movements of the working class (Patel et al, 1982).

Characteristics of Autonomous Women's Movement

1) Women organize and lead the movement.
2) Fight against oppression, exploitation, injustice and discrimination against women is the first and foremost priority of the movement, any other considerations cannot subordinate women's rights.
3) It cannot be subordinated to the decisions and necessities of any political or social group/organization.

Western women's liberation movement, its literature and the issues raised by them influenced many women with higher education. It was primarily a revolt against women being treated as objects and not as individual human beings. The women's movement demanded that 'equality', and 'liberation' be perceived from a women's point of view. Initially women's liberation was a matter of jest. Anyone who talked of women's liberation was labelled 'anti-man'. Feminists were labelled ambitious, egocentric, individualistic or careerist. It was said that all these women were frustrated, humiliated and rejected by males because of their ugly looks and were unsuccessful in their lives and therefore they joined the bandwagon of women's liberation. In spite of this, during 1975, many small groups of women's liberationists started appearing. Many young women activists who were involved in various progressive, radical and leftist organizations also started raising their voice against sexual discrimination within these organizations. All these organizations which were sensitive to the problems of the poor, openly denounced casteism and communalism, talked of fighting against oppression and exploitation of the toilers were utterly insensitive to the oppression of women. Not only that, they were just perpetuating patriarchal values directly or indirectly, in political as well as personal spheres. This angered women activists who found it necessary to form independent and autonomous organizations of women.

Socio-economic Background of the New Awakening

The crisis of the mid and late 1960s radicalized the working class. Not only were there trade union and anti-price rise movements but other movements like anti-war movements, colonial liberation struggles, students movements and black movements which developed outside the sphere of the official communist and socialist parties. Women too had been very much a part of this process of struggle and self-expression (Manohar, 1984).

Many women participated actively in anti-price rise movements of

Madhya Pradesh, Gujarat and Maharashtra (1974); student's movements in Gujarat and Bihar (1974), struggles by tribals in Dhulia (Maharashtra), Bhojpur (Bihar), Chhattisgarh (Madhya Pradesh), Andhra Pradesh (1970 onwards), the Naxalbari movement in West Bengal, Punjab and Andhra Pradesh, and other struggles of the oppressed masses in other parts of the country (Patel, 1978). But in these cases, issues around which struggles were launched were price rise, unemployment, low wages, unequal distribution of land, etc. (Omvedt, 1977).

Since then many women activists have found it necessary to take up issues related to oppression of women like dowry, violence in the family, alcoholism, sexual discrimination of women at their work place (*Manifesto of the Progressive Women*, 1977–78). During the International Women's Year (1975), a conference of women activists was held in Pune. The same year, in Trivandrum, á national level seminar on women's problems was held at the initiative of the Communist Party of India (Marxist). Except for the representatives of CPI(M) and CPI, all women activists emphasized the necessity of autonomous women's organizations.

In the 1974 students movement in Bihar, many girls had taken part. After the agitation, some girls who faced problems in their personal lives as a result of their activities got sensitized to women's problems. In Patna, their first action was to protest against sexual objectification of women in an advertizement and to organize an anti-dowry campaign. Mahila Sangharsh Vahini (Patna) was very active in these campaigns. Progressive Organization of Women (Hyderabad) launched a massive campaign against eve-teasing and dowry during 1974–75. In Delhi, conscious women's groups started raising their voice against dowry-murders.

In 1971, an unprecedented struggle started among women in Dhulia. Some activists of Magova, members of a radical organization, mainly based in Bombay and Pune started working among tribals of Dhulia. Their crusade was against exploitation and oppression of tribal masses by rich peasants, moneylenders and corrupt government officials. Their organization Shramik Sangathna became very popular among the toiling tribal masses there. The tribal women were very active in Shramik Sangathna right from its inception. Tribal women who came out to campaign against economic exploitation realized the necessity of fighting against alcoholism, wife-beating, sexual harassment of tribal women by the rural rich.

Their campaign against alcoholism and its associated corollary wife-beating had a unique feature. Women activists, without waiting for the green signal from their male leaders, launched a furious battle against bootleggers and broke wine pots. Any man who consumed alcohol and beat up his wife was beaten up with brooms by groups of women and forced to pledge that he would not beat his wife in future. Any man who molested a woman was made to wear a garland of footwears and was given a donkey ride in the village. In Marathwada, too, such campaign took place between 1976 and 1978.

In Bombay and Pune, independent and autonomous women's groups like Stree Mukti Sangathana came into existence in the same period. Members of these groups were from middle class and enlightened by women's liberation movement abroad. These women were also active in other organizations working for poor and oppressed masses. This new awakening and radicalization of young women should be seen in the context of anti-corruption, anti-price rise and trade union, other general struggles of the period between 1971 and 1975.

Political Background of the Anti-Rape Movement

With the declaration of emergency in 1975, even women's groups and organizations engaged in protest movements had to slow down their activity as a result of heavy repression. Women's organizations with massive membership had to face repression and their activities were more or less stopped but in the context of International Women's Year, activities like holding seminars, writing articles, making resolutions, and forming committees to highlight women's problems got state patronage and it also became a reason for the development of a new consciousness and alertness on women's problem for the media, policy-makers, academicians and the general public.

After the withdrawal of the emergency the issue of civil liberties was hotly debated. Repression of political activists and political prisoners by the state was highlighted in the media. Police atrocities on the Harijans, the tribals and the poor made the democratic-minded intelligentsia furious. News of mass rape of poor, dalit and tribal women in Madhya Pradesh, Bihar, Rajasthan, Uttar Pradesh and Maharashtra appeared in the press. Awareness of democratic rights brought with it awareness of atrocities on women (People's Union for Democratic Rights, 1982).

Organizations like Mahila Daxata Samata Manch and Stree Sangharsh Samiti were formed in Delhi. In Bombay, Stree Mukti Sangathana, Socialist Women's Group, Feminist Network Collective came into existence (Singh et al, 1982). Purogami Sangathana (Pune), Stree Shakti Sangathana (Hyderabad), Pennurimai Iyyakum (Madras) are also autonomous women's organizations that came into existence in the post-emergency period. In Kanpur, Patna, Kolhapur, Madras, Aurangabad, Raipur and other smaller cities too autonomous women's groups started blooming. Pune Women's Liberationist started a bi-monthly magazine called *Baija* (i.e., rural women) in Marathi. In 1973, when Socialist Women's Group—an autonomous group of feminists—organized a workshop of women activists in Bombay, many thought-provoking papers were presented. After three days of rigorous debate, it was decided to form a coordination committee of women activists working in various parts of the country, to start a newsletter in English and Hindi called *Feminist Network* and *Stree Sangharsh* respectively, and to publish a women's magazine in Hindi and English called *Manushi*. Women's fronts of the left parties also got activized during this period (Chakravarti, 1981).

During 1978–79, six issues of *Feminist Network* were published. This newsletter got very good response and feedback from women's groups and organizations all over India ('Hundreds of Women', *Feminist Network*, 1979). In January 1979, when the first issue of *Manushi* came out, many feminists felt a need to support it because it was a big venture and to sustain a non-commercial feminist journal required resources. *Manushi* was treated as a mouthpiece by autonomous women's movement in the country and was seen as a product of the collective effort by feminists.

At this stage, differences of analytical framework started coming to the fore. Those who merely wanted to make some minor reforms in the existing social structure and remain contented with liberal statutory measures were known as bourgeois feminist. Those who found men alone (to be specific, power relations between men and women), responsible for miseries of women were known as radical feminist, and those who admit the role of patriarchy in subjugating women in our society but at the same time believe that in this system other oppressed and exploited masses like dalits, tribals, working class are allies of women's liberation movement and therefore believe in solidarity with these groups are known as socialist feminist. In the context of *Manushi*, sharp discussions took place on trends in feminist thought (Desai, 1982).

Nationwide Anti-Rape Movements in India

Police gang-rape of Laxmi, a beggar-woman in Punjab and on Remeezabee and Shakeelabee in Hyderabad, caused public fury and civil liberties organizations took up these cases. Democratic rights organizations and bold journalists brought to light cases of mass-rape in Pantnagar, Dalli, Rajhara, Goa, Singhbhum, Marathwada, Agra, Bhojpur, Karimnagar and in the northeastern states (Farroqui, 1978). It was against this background that the Mathura rape case sparked off the anti-rape movement throughout the country. At the end of 1979, when four professors of law of Delhi University wrote an open letter to the Supreme Court of India condemning it for its judgement on Mathura rape case, women's organizations all over the country came out in the streets demanding the reopening of the case and amendments in the rape law.

Mathura, a fourteen year-old girl, was called to the police station in Chandrapur late one night, where two police constables raped her. The Sessions Court at Nagpur, alleged Mathura to be of loose morals and declared the rapists innocent. The High Court convicted the rapists and imposed 7 years rigorous imprisonment. But the Supreme Court reversed the judgement and alleged that Mathura had willingly submitted to sexual intercourse with the policemen. From every corner of the country, women's groups protested against this judgement, and demanded a rehearing of Mathura case. In this movement, autonomous women's organizations took the initiative. All over the country many demonstrations and rallies were organized on 8 March 1980. The government was pressurized by debates in newspapers and magazines, through signature campaigns and slogans, through posters etc. Anti-rape organizations and women's organizations were set up in various cities. Political parties, which initially did not take this problem seriously started issuing statements and started calling for public meetings and rallies after March 1980.

At the time of Maya Tyagi rape case, all opposition parties started agitating about the deteriorating law and order situation. In the winter session of the parliament, government declared its intention to introduce a bill relating to rape and presented a draft. Women's organizations, political parties and conscious people started discussing different aspects of this bill. Never since independence, had people shown such consciousness against police repression.

The government was forced to reopen the Mathura rape case. Thus such a situation was created that political parties could not be indifferent to this current of autonomous women's organizations.

Two autonomous women's groups—Forum Against Rape (new, Forum Against Oppression of Women) in Bombay and Forum Against Rape in Nagpur had also taken up individual cases of women's oppression. The Bombay based organization did active work on questions like dowry, rape, wife beating, etc. (Forum Against Rape, 1980). In Kanpur, Patna, Ahmedabad, Baroda, Raipur, Pune, Calcutta, Delhi, Hyderabad (Stree Shakti Sangthana, 1980), Madras, Bangalore such groups came into existence (Lalitha, 1980). These organizations attracted lawyers, doctors, professors, students and working women in particular (Stree Atyachar Virodhi Parishad, 1981). This nationwide movement enhanced the awareness of women's problems. All political parties started strengthening their women's wings. There had been a stage when those with pro-women attitude were condemned as anti-men. But now a stage has reached when to discuss women's issues, and publish material on it, have become measures of progressiveness. This, of course, does not necessarily mean that the condition of women has improved in reality.

Achievements of the Autonomous Women's Movement

Autonomous women's organizations have made efforts to make feminism acceptable among masses through plays, skits, songs, posters, exhibitions, newsletters, magazines, etc. Presently, many feminist magazines are being published. For example, from Delhi, *Manushi* and a newsletter, *Saheli* are published in English as well as in Hindi; from Calcutta four Bengali journals are published: *Sachetana, Sabala, Ahalya* and *Maitreyi*; from Patna *Apni Azadi Ke Liye, Stree Sangarsh* and from Chhatisgarh *Awaz Aurat ki* in Hindi; from Bangalore *Sangharsh* in English and *Samata* in Telugu; from Gujarat *Narimukti, Anasuya*; from Bombay *Women's Centre*, a newsletter in English.

Autonomous women's movement has also given rise to special interest groups. In Delhi, Bombay, Pune and Kanpur many feminists who had been involved in the anti-dowry (Shukla, 1985) and anti-rape campaigns felt the necessity for a women's centre—a place where women who have problems could go to for support—emotional, legal and medical (D'Mello, 1982). These are not forums for agitation but many of their members are also actively involved in agitational organizations. In Bombay, Women's Center, in Pune, Stree Adhar Kendra (Stree Adhar Kendra, 1981), in Delhi, Saheli (Saheli, 1982) and in Kanpur, Sakhi Kendra are such centers that provide services to individual women.

Autonomous women's groups have also generated feminist cultural groups with new songs, skits, plays, audio-visuals, slide shows, dance, dramas, films, etc. More research is being carried out on subjects related to women. In the academic field, women's studies are taken more seriously (Bhasin and Malik, 1979).

As a result of the pressure created by the women's movement, amendments in the laws regarding rape, dowry, marriage had to be made. Muslim and Christian women have come out challenging their respective personal laws based on religion (Punwani, 1984).

Now many autonomous women's organizations are trying to become active on the problems of working women (Melkote and Tharu, 1980). Social customs, responsibilities of housework and patronizing attitude of male trade union leaders are responsible for indifference towards specific problems of working women in trade unions and elsewhere. That is why, autonomous women's organizations have started efforts to build separate wings within trade unions exclusively for women. In Bombay and Poona, Nari Sangharsh Samiti is such a feminist organization which struggles for the working women. These organizations have attracted industrial women workers, nurses, etc. In Dhulia, the tribal women of Shramik Sangathana have after years of arguments, ultimately formed Shramik Stree Mukti

Sangathana. In Madhya Pradesh, Chhatisgarh Mahila Jagruti Sangh and Mahila Mukti Morcha (Sen, 1984), in Ahmedabad, Self Employed Women's Association (SEWA) are also autonomous organizations of women (Bhatt, 1981). This shows that autonomous women's organizations are not limited to educated urban women only. In Maharashtra, women activists have also made attempts to organize maid servants in many towns and cities (Bhaiya, 1982). Issues of temple prostitutes and tobacco workers are also taken up by them (Report, *How*, 1982). State level coordination committee of women's organizations has been active since 1979 (Stree Mukti Andolan Sampark Samiti, 1979).

Women's Movement and the Working Class Movement

Like casteism and communalism, sexism is also one of the most effective weapons utilized by the ruling class to divide the masses and to maintain status quo. To combat sexism, women's movement must evolve strategies to ally with other protest movements, because women's movements cannot sustain itself in isolation from the wider political movement. A very small proportion of women are economically independent. State security to women is impossible because of economic backwardness of our country. Socio-cultural factors have subjugated women and caged her in the four walls of her home. All these factors link women's problems to the problems of class and caste, etc. So women have to find a terrain where her strength, solidarity, confidence are enhanced, and she is seen not only as an oppressed sex, but also as a political struggling, asserting human being. Thus autonomous women's groups and organizations are a must, but they have to concretely and actively link themselves to the wider political movement. To establish linkages between women's movement and broader socio-political movement is the major challenge faced by women's groups. They have to address themselves to questions like casteism, class issues, communalism and how these factors affect every woman's life. For that it is a must for the autonomous women's groups to work in collaboration with various types of mass organizations like democratic rights organizations, trade unions and issue-based united fronts concerning the masses.

FORMING A WOMEN'S GROUP IN CHANDIGARH: EXPERIENCES OF A MALE ACTIVIST

Pritam Singh

This is an attempt to describe and analyze the efforts made towards forming a women's group in Chandigarh. Chandigarh is a Union Territory and is the joint capital of Punjab and Haryana. It has, predominantly, an urban population, middle-class in character. In the entire north-west belt consisting of Punjab, Haryana, Himachal Pradesh and Jammu and Kashmir, Chandigarh is the only city which is somewhat metropolitan in character in terms of its culture and the ethnic composition of the population. There is a medical research institute (PGI) of high repute, a university which is one of the earliest in the country, a college each for education in engineering, arts and architecture and about a dozen other colleges. The faculty and the students come from all over India though the preponderant majority is of Punjabi background. A large number of students come from Middle Eastern and African countries. The cultural ethos of the city represent all the complexities and contradictions of a society in transition. Though there is a heavy pull of the traditional values and ethos, yet there is a yearning for new ideas and a new way of life. The new middle class which has been continuously growing as anywhere else in India, does not openly oppose new modes of thought and living just in order to appear to be modern. Even this pretense for modernity is conducive to creating a cultural context in which progressive ideas find acceptance, how so ever half-hearted it may be.

When a small group of persons made attempts to form a women's group in early 1981, the environment in which they were working was characterized by the following major aspects as far as the women's question was concerned:

1. The past decade or so had witnessed growing awareness almost all over the world, including India, about the women's question. Women's groups and organizations had sprung up almost everywhere.

2. There was no women's group in Chandigarh which reflected the above mentioned change. However, there existed two kinds of women's group/organizations in Chandigarh. One set consisted of various ladies clubs comprising women of upper middle class background. Though such clubs provided useful avenues for women to get together and share some of their mutual interests and concerns, they remained within the framework of the traditional place occupied by women in society. There was almost complete absence of any critical debate on the status and role of women in society. The other set of women's groups consisted of Istri Sabhas affiliated to the left parties. Such groups did display a certain degree of militancy sporadically on ideas like dowry, women's right in property, employment of women, etc. Their activities however remained within the framework of militant economism. Though coming of women into the open, through such activities, helped in radicalizing the consciousness of both the participants and the general public, it served only a limited purpose. It gave a jolt to the traditional images and self-image of women but it did not lead to sharpening of an alternative perspective for women's place in society.

3. Given the cultural climate of Chandigarh, there existed a positive responsiveness to any discussion about women's question and any efforts towards forming a women's group.

The efforts towards forming a women's group started in early 1981. The initiative was taken by three persons—one woman and two men. The author was one of these two men. A few words about these three persons may be useful in understanding the process of starting the group and its subsequent weaknesses. The woman—a Muslim with a left liberal political orientation was teaching psychology at the university. She was also a leading activist of the teachers' organization on the campus. The other male member—a Punjabi Hindu—was the owner of a bookshop specializing in selling progressive literature. The author had come back to Chandigarh in 1978 after spending some years in Delhi first, as a research scholar in Jawaharlal Nehru University, and later as a teacher in a Delhi University college. He, like his woman comrade, was also involved in the work of the teachers' organization on the campus.

There were a few things common to the three persons. All the three had a left-wing political orientation and had been exposed to the various currents in the feminist movement abroad and in India. All three had varying degrees of alienation from their traditional family backgrounds. None of them had any organic links with Chandigarh. Thus on one hand, they did not have the handicap of being constrained by the traditional family network, and on the other, they suffered from the disadvantage of not being sufficiently rooted in the 'civil society'. This commonness of their background brought them together to discuss the question of starting a group in the city which could go into the whole gamut of men-women relationship in society. After a round of few discussions, it was felt that a meeting of a larger group should be called. The first meeting of such a group was subsequently called. The group consisted primarily of students and teachers from the campus. Most of the persons who came for the meeting had no previous background of having been even involved in any women's group and were not very hopeful that a women's group would get any positive response. However, a small group of girl students were very enthusiastic and determined to start some activity. Another helpful factor in the situation was the emergence on the campus of an independent student group called Democratic Students Forum (DSF). This group with a broadly left-wing orientation, had in it a number of very bright students who had gained some degree of popularity among the students. Some of the DSF members took an active part in the plans to start a women's group. Apart from this, some other individuals who were showing keen interest in starting a women's group, who were well known on the campus as leading activists of the teacher's and the research scholar's organization. The efforts to start a women's group received further boost from the support extended by a number of progressive-minded foreign students from Zimbabwe, Mauritius, Iran and Palestine.

After the initial consensus that some work towards forming a women's group should be done, two idea groups seemed to crystallize. One placed emphasis on spontaneity, i.e., everyone must talk whatever one felt was more crucial to one's and other's life. The second idea group emphasized the need to develop a general perspective. It argued that mere talking might help in establishing ties of solidarity but would not lead to any concrete set of activities. There was fear that an attempt to develop a general perspective might lead to alienation from the very beginning of those individuals who might not like to subscribe to any specific point. The danger toward sectionization was highlighted by this viewpoint. The healthy aspect of this difference of opinion was that both the groups should appreciate each others' point-of-view.

Eventually, everyone agreed on this that the International Women's Day on 8 March should be celebrated and in order to create awareness about the importance of the day and build enthusiasm to participate in the celebrations, a series of discussions should be held. These discussion topics were decided by keeping in mind the day-to-day problems as well as the need to initiate debate on developing a general perspective. A week-long program of following discussions was decided:

1. Marriage, dowry, prostitution
2. Our bodies and ourselves (for women only)
3. Society: Men and women in different roles
4. Working women
5. Problems of university and college girls
6. Women's movement: Past, present and future.

Some guest speakers were also invited from outside, out of whom only Veena Mazumdar came for one discussion. A summary of all these discussions was later published in the form of a booklet *Women and Society: Problems and Prospects*. It was also decided that the group of persons working together would do so under the banner of Adhoc Committee to celebrate International Women's Day. The nomenclature of the committee was considered as an apt representation of its spontaneous, democratic, flexible and non-institutionalized character.

The discussions aroused interest not only among the participants but also among the general public and especially in the university. Since such an open discussion about women's question was a new development in the culture of the city, the local press—English, Hindi and Punjabi—gave it a significant coverage. Another development—again signifying a new turn in the culture and life of the city and especially the university—took place during this week. A group of resident women students associated with the Adhoc Committee raised the issue of modelling and beauty contests held in the hostels. The Adhoc Committee appreciated their move to protest against such contests. This group of students put up posters in their hostel against modelling and beauty contests. The common theme of their posters was to project the idea that such contests commercialize, vulgarize and degrade women. This action led to a sharp reaction from the hostel authorities and especially from the women students who had been organizing and participating in such contests. Press publicity of the protest against these contests further enraged the organizers/participants and a group of them publicly burnt a few copies of *Indian Express*. Some journalists of the *Indian Express*, sympathetic to the women's cause, had taken keen interest in covering activities of the Adhoc Committee. It may be useful to mention here that though in 1981, the organizers held a well-publicized modelling/beauty contest almost as a retaliation against the protest, the hostel authorities have stopped holding these contests since that time onwards.

The week long discussions, the protest against modelling/beauty contest, the reaction against this protest and the press publicity to all these events generated a great deal of interest and curiosity in the rally which was proposed to be held on 8 March. On 8 March, a colorful and enthusiastic march of women started from the university campus. Indian and foreign students, teachers, journalists, lawyers, administrators, house-wives and a few domestic maid-servants added to the multi-faceted composition of the marchers. It was headed by two girl students—One Indian and the other African—carrying the banner of International Women's Day. The procession in a joyous yet defiant mood marched forward with banners, colorful placards highlighting the importance of the International Women's Day. It generated interest from the spectators and passersby. Some took the leaflets, others joined the march. A number of housewives came out to watch this procession, some of them came forward, to make enquiries, others asked for the leaflet. By the time the rally ended in Rose Garden it had doubled in size. Speeches at the rally in English, Hindi and Punjabi reflected a rebellious and critical mood. Some of the girl participants who had earlier been hesitant to shout slogans were so enthused by this collective activity that they finally took the lead in shouting slogans for women's unity and collective struggles. The rally remained the talk of the town for a number of days. It was a historic event—it marked the entry of women's movement in the life and culture of the city. The sympathetic press coverage took the news to the towns and villages of north-west India.

This enthusiasm however, could not, be sustained. Students, who constituted the main active section of the group, soon got involved with their examinations. The summer vacation following this, further added to the inactivity. By the time the university reopened, the overall political atmosphere in Punjab started changing. A leading journalist and the owner of a newspapers chain, which was spreading Hindu communal ideas and who was also an important figure in the communal politics of Punjab was assassinated. This was followed by the arrest of a Sikh extremist leader and the death of a number of persons in the violence following the arrest of this leader. This was the beginning of a turn in Punjab's political climate that had a severe setback for all progressive streams of thought and activity. The women's group was also a casualty of this process. The continuation of the group was further hampered by the difficulties arising out of the personal crisis faced by almost all the activists who had got on together at critical stages in their respective lives.

By the time 8 March 1982 came, the Adhoc Committee had almost disintegrated. Even some of those who had shown keen interest just a year ago, started becoming apathetic. Some of us, however, decided to celebrate 8 March again with whatever depleted strength we had. Some critics of the move objected to this as a mere ritual. We argued that though more systematic work is necessary, the celebration of 8 March must be made a regular feature. Our position was that even rituals are not without meaning and significance. Repetition of certain events become the means of forming a mutual collective and raising consciousness. We argued that

8 March must become embedded in women's collective memory as the symbol of their mutual solidarity and struggle against their oppression. We formed a street theatre group to stage a play *Cheekh* (The cry) in Hindi, the script of which had been written by a progressive poet-cum-playwright Kumar Vikal. The play is an attempt to weave together the different forms/aspects of women's oppression like female infanticide, child widow-hood, commercial exploitation of the female body, dowry murders and rape. It ends with a call for solidarity between people from all sections, and all walks of life to revolutionize their lives.

On 8 March, we had the first public performance of the play on the university campus. One of us explained the importance of the day to the audience and appealed to the assembled audience to join the procession. About 40 of us, both men and women, went through different sectors of the city to reach at the central office-cum-shopping complex in Sector D. On the way, we had two more performances of the play. At the terminating point, a big audience of about 300 persons, had collected to watch the play. It was so well-received that requests started pouring from different sections for repeat performances of the play. After a gap of about two weeks, we again had two performances of the play. Later, the Jalandhar centre of Doordarshan offered to televize it but we could not reorganize the theatre group.

Celebrations in 1983 consisted of a street play, *Om Swaha*, by the students of a local girls' college, an exhibition of posters/paintings depicting various aspects of women's life, a talk by a radical Sanskrit scholar, a procession on 4 March and a rally on 8 March. A public meeting, somewhat official in nature, was addressed by the Chief Commissioner of Chandigarh. Almost all the women's groups, mentioned earlier, participated.

By 8 March 1984, the political situation in Punjab and Chandigarh had become so tense, that public rallies and processions were banned. A small group of us, however, did not want to go unnoticed. The fact that 8 March had become an important day for a section of the local population, became known to us when some people started enquiring about the likely program on this day. Meanwhile, a new group of students from a local girls college had prepared *Cheekh*, which had been staged earlier by a different group in 1982. Since nothing else could be done due to the disturbed conditions in the region, we had one performance of the play on the university campus. The significance of 8 March was explained to the audience. The conditions under which we had the performance of the play, can be gauged from the fact that there was a significant presence of both uniformed and plainclothes policemen during the performance.

For four years from 1981 to 1984, we have regularly celebrated 8 March in one way or the other. *Manushi* had been carrying a report of the celebration every year. Since March 1984, the people of Punjab and Chandigarh have passed through such traumatic conditions which would make all talk of women's question separately, seem a sectarian occupation. Though some of us have started making attempts to regroup, we are not clear as to how we shall proceed. Uncertainty characterizes every aspect of public life in Punjab and Chandigarh.

I would like to sum up the achievements and weaknesses of our efforts. The major achievement of the four years of this sporadic activity is that a large number of women students have been conscientized in varying degrees. Even those who were not associated with the Adhoc Committee, are aware of the issue. Many of these women students are now employed as teachers, researchers, civil servants and journalists. There has come to exist a cadre of young educated women who would assist any effort towards activizing women. Apart from this, as an ideological base, the general public, and a unit of the press is now more responsive to the various aspects of the women's question. It is partly as a result of these four years of work, how-so-ever sporadic it might have been, that now a research cell on women's studies has been set up in the university.

Our major weakness is that we have not been able to produce even a small group of women activists. Though there are a number of good intentioned women who would assist any activity involving women, there are few who can take the initiative, co-ordinate and give the leadership. The task has become more difficult especially after the women comrade who was one of the founders of the group, has left Chandigarh. In this connection, the author is constrained to mention his somewhat bitter experience. From the very beginning, I have had an ambivalent attitude towards taking a leading role in forming a women's group. On one hand, I had the apprehension that taking a leading role might act as a hindrance in the natural process of the emergence of woman leaders and, on the other, I had the feeling that with my political background, I might act as a catalyst in the formation of a radical women's group. It is not for me to judge my role. In the course of my activities, I was, however, faced almost everytime with taking the major burden of organizing the various activities. Though reluctant, everytime I took the task upon myself knowing that otherwise the whole venture might collapse. Though I would take the final decision only after discussing the issue with fellow activists, I am toying with the idea that withdrawing at this stage may be more conducive to the emergence of a group of natural women leaders.

TEACHING MEN ABOUT WOMEN

Rehana Ghadially

In this paper I would like to share with you my experiences of teaching a
course in the Psychology of Sex Roles (with special emphasis on the
woman's role) to a predominantly male audience for 2 successive years.
Before I begin, let me give you some background information.

The Setting

I teach at an engineering institution that attracts some of the brightest
students in the country. There are five such major engineering institutions.
On the basis of a joint entrance exam, 2,244 applicants were chosen from a
total of 57,796 who sat for the exam in 1986. The academic program
consists of eight semesters—two semesters per year. At the institution I
teach, all students have to take humanities and social sciences courses in at
least five of the eight semesters. In the first three semesters, Introduction
to Humanities, Perspectives in Social Sciences and Economics are taught
respectively to all students. In the last two semesters students opt for one
course of their choice either in sociology, psychology, economics, literature or philosophy. Psychology of Sex Roles was offered as one such
elective for the undergraduate students in the final semester of their
academic program.

   The course was offered in the Spring semester of the academic year
1984–85 when 30 male and 5 female students registered and again in
1985–86 when 25 male and 4 female students registered. The class met 3
times a week, fifty-five minutes per period for 14 weeks. Student knowledge was assessed by an objective exam and an assignment.

The Course

Why teach sex roles to male engineering students? Raising consciousness
about the women's movement here and abroad was one reason. In line
with the ethos of the humanities and social sciences department, I wished
to sensitize the students to a current social issue. I also hoped that exposure

to such a course may help young men to participate and support women in their struggle to shape a new identity. From experience, I have learnt that male engineers and engineering students are generally quite conservative and rigid in their ideas. I was therefore interested in knowing their reactions to such a course.

The goals of the course were to help students critically examine the roles played by men and women in society, the consequences of playing these roles and to provide opportunities to students to examine their potential as human beings. Secondary goals included a need to be open-minded, to understand and respect many different viewpoints and to support one's own ideas with facts and research evidence.

In brief, the following topics—some more extensively than others— were covered in class. Content of sex role stereotypes in terms of personality traits and division of labor, sex role socialization and consequences of such socialization. Issues like power, self esteem, achievement and performance evaluation of the two sexes were considered. Along the way students expressed interest in the topic of masculinity. Wife beating and rape were covered in class as expressions of an exaggerated masculinity. Some time was also devoted to portrayal of men and women in advertizing and textbooks, use of sexist language and sex labelling of jobs.

While the emphasis in the course was on psychology, an attempt was made to draw material from other relevant disciplines. A feminist perspective was maintained in class and in keeping with this perspective, women's personal feelings and experiences were considered as real and important. Power was shared in class by keeping the idea of a teacher as an expert at a minimum and encouraging student participation as much as possible.

Student Reactions: Negative

A variety of reactions and emotions were generated among the students. Here, I outline briefly those that occurred fairly frequently.

1. If women feel that they have got a raw deal in society then no one is to blame but themselves.

2. Some of the things that women were demanding were trivial and that women were being misled fighting for such petty things as for example the insistence on the use of the word chairperson instead of chairman. Closely aligned to this response was a feeling that women were complaining about everything.

3. Students found fault with women in order to justify male shortcomings. They said so what if husbands beat their wives, women nag

and drive their men crazy too. Students felt psychologically comfortable and smug whenever they could point out a shortcoming in women. They preferred to deny and ignore the frequency and intensity of the difference between the sexes for such maltreatment.

4. They displayed exceptional knack in pointing out that things in this man made world were not as bad as some feminists have made out to be. In the context of dowry, for example, it was mentioned that in certain communities in Kerala, wealth moves in the opposite direction (from a man's to a woman's family). Exceptions to the rule justified man's (mis)behavior toward women.

5. Blaming women remained their favorite defense strategy. This was manifested in a variety of ways, most commonly it was felt that only if women changed their behavior or if they just did this or the other, things would be alright. If there is gross misportrayal of women in the mass media then why are women eager to model for sexist advertizers? Why do women go in droves to see popular Hindi films? To top it all, men are men simply because that is how their mothers reared them. There was a constant refusal to admit that the other half is responsible and must contribute to social change.

6. Students expressed the feeling that much of the violence against women is really perpetrated by women. Women are more against women than men are against women. How do you explain this? This was dealt with in class in the context of socialization and internalization of patriarchal cultural values by women.

Below, I quote some remarks of the (male) students:

'You have made five divorces possible' (referring to the five women in class who presumably will fight for their rights and upset the marital harmony).
'No matter what you say, I will have an upper hand in my family.'
'You are an over-feminist.' (meaning man-hater)
'But haven't they (researchers) found some innate ability by which the two sexes respond differently to many things.'
'I don't like you.'

These negative responses served major defensive functions. They were simply attempts to cope with threatening, anxiety-arousing and sometimes shocking information. These responses enabled students to examine course content while absolving them of any responsibility in the existing state of affairs.

Student Reactions: Positive

As the semester drew to a close much of the hostility in classroom discussion diminished and some hopeful and constructive thinking emerged. Occasionally, students showed a willingness to critically examine and challenge the culture's definition of power and masculinity. There was curiosity about the kind of society we would live in if one could free oneself from sex stereotypes. Many felt they had learnt something about themselves, were more aware and could look at man-woman relationship from a different perspective. Others felt this course should be made compulsory for all students and such an exposure would benefit even high school students. A few students promised never to beat their wives. Some topics aroused enough interest to hold informal talk sessions in their hostels.

Before I share my personal reactions to the course, a few observations are worthy of mention. Violence against women was one topic that sparked the most anger and hostility. It was at this time that students started looking at issues in a personal way. They seemed to be saying they were not that kind of men. The problem was the men in the class wanted to hear something nice about themselves and very little of it was forthcoming. It was during this time that students expressed maximum criticism of my teaching. It was their way of getting back at me.

When research evidence was presented in class, students wanted to know the sex of the researchers. They felt women researchers could be biased. There was often doubt about what was said in class, for example, when dealing with the topic of rape, some students challenged me and asked how I could be sure that women do not enjoy rape. Perhaps the women are lying. Besides there is a physiological response so they must have enjoyed it.

Thirdly, and most importantly the women students rarely spoke in class. The men students were genuinely eager to know what they thought and how they felt about the issues discussed. My attempts to encourage them met with little success as they said I was already representing their point of view. This does not come as a surprise as Burr (1974) has noted that women will disclose themselves significantly more in an all female group than in a mixed sex group.

Overall Impact

As part of the institute policy students fill out anonymous course evaluation sheet during the last week of the semester. These are returned to the course instructor within 2–3 months of evaluation. The following student comments are representative of the overall impact of the course on them.

'It has made me re-examine my role as a male. It has helped me to become a better human being in my interactions with females.'

'It has made a tremendous difference to my outlook.'

'All in all, it was an interesting and a thought provoking course.'

'By challenging male-oriented values, the course made me think hard. It has shown me a different and better way to relate and has left me with no option but to follow that.'

'The course should be made compulsory for all students. So that every year, 250–300 individuals will have a better approach to women. Isn't it great, because they are likely to pass the tips to others.'

'This course has made me realize my worth in society as a woman. There are so many things that we know, we read in papers but never stop to think. That these can affect us. I suppose this course will help me realize my potential as an individual rather than as a woman. I also hope that it has made the boys from my class aware of what injustice is being done to their opposite sex unconsciously and consciously. In a way I think the course has made me more insecure, I was living a comfortable life without thinking of the problems. I have now become aware of them.'

Personal Reactions

Emotions generated, as a result of my commitment to the women's movement came through in class. I felt transparent at times. My need to maintain a personal relationship with the students characterized by a sharing of power created some alienation. They found not only the content of the course threatening but also its delivery, as in the current patriarchal set-up they are used to an impersonal, idea-based, objective approach to teaching. My attempts to maintain an interdisciplinary approach tottered at times. I had much to read in the areas of women and law, literature and history. I also had difficulty finding psychological literature in the Indian context.

There were moments in class when I felt anger and exasperation not just to the lack of openness of students to information contrary to their belief system and lack of trust in the evidence presented in class but by the thought that the struggle ahead of us in India is a long one.

Despite the stresses and problems, I was often buoyed by the discussion with students inside and outside the classroom, by the gradual self-examination and growth that was taking place. Satisfactory classroom attendance (students here consider class attendance as optional) plus a request for a reading list on the male role encouraged me. I was particularly touched when students appreciated the excerpts I read in class from Anias

Nin's paper 'In Favour of the Sensitive Man' where she tells young women not to mistake sensitivity in a man for weakness and misuse of power by men as strength.

At the end of the semester I came out with a feeling that it was one of the most useful and relevant courses I had taught. I was convinced that if we are ever to eliminate sex role stereotypes, men must be educated in the psychology of women too. Besides, while technical education was presumably turning them into potentially good engineers, it would be too costly not to recognize the need to make them more humane men and emancipated women. I look forward to teaching this course again next year.

INDIGENOUS FEMINISM
IN A MODERN HINDU SECT

Lawrence A. Babb

Is a feminism with origins outside the western tradition possible? I pose this question not as a hypothetical problem but as a puzzle arising from the beliefs and practices of a modern Hindu sect, the Brahma Kumari (Daughters of Brahma) movement.[1] This sect seems to be feminist in at least some ways. But the idiom of its feminism, if feminism it is, is very different indeed from anything with which the western women's movements are familiar. Let me be more specific. One of the goals of the sect, though certainly not its only goal, is the liberation of women, but the kind of liberty sought by the Brahma Kumaris cannot really be understood except in the context of Hindu religious culture. Even their complaints about the institutions they consider oppressive are deeply colored by the world outlook of the Hindu tradition.

My object here is to describe Brahma Kumari feminism in its cultural context. To me it is intrinsically interesting that the will to be free can be nourished in different ways by different cultures. I shall leave the question of whether the Brahma Kumaris possess a 'genuine' feminism finally to my readers. For those who believe that a true feminism must seek radical change of existing social institutions, the Brahma Kumaris beliefs will probably seem misguided or beside the point. I hope to suggest the possibility of another view, one that encourages us to see feminism as the product of a transcultural motive that can be expressed in richly varied ways in different cultural settings.

Author's Note: The fieldwork on which this paper is based took place in Delhi between July 1978 and May 1979 and was supported by an Indo-American Fellowship. The research was concerned with modern sectarian movements in Hinduism, of which the Brahma Kumaris are an outstanding example. I acknowledge with gratitude the assistance of many members of the movement. I would also like to thank colleagues at the Department of Sociology, Delhi School of Economics, for the hospitality and intellectual companionship so generously provided during my stay. I am indebted to Deborah Gewertz for critical comments on an earlier draft. Final responsibility for errors of fact or interpretation is mine.

[1] 'Daughters of Brahma' is the English rendering prefered by the sect. A female member is Brahma Kumari, a male member a Brahma Kumar.

Origins of the Movement

The Brahma Kumari movement was founded in the late 1930s in the region of Sind (now part of Pakistan). Its original social setting was the 'Sind Worki' (*sindhvarki*) merchant community of Hyderabad. Belonging to the Lohana trading caste, the Sind Workis emerged as an elite class of merchants during the second half of the nineteenth century. They began as hawkers of Sindhi handicrafts in European settlements, prospered greatly, and by the time the sect started to form they had been taken by their businesses to other parts of India and overseas, where many had made quite sizable fortunes (Thakur, 1959). Informants characterize the Sind Worki men of those days as being rather conservative culturally, but because of business opportunities outside Sind, many were also quite cosmopolitan.

But if the world was wide for Sind Worki men, for their wives and daughters matters were very different. The world of women was the household, within which most of them were secluded. Excursions beyond the home were customarily limited to family gatherings, ceremonials, and visits to religious institutions. The education of these women tended to be desultory, and in general their lives were circumscribed by the many restrictions of movement and contact with outsiders characteristic of the women of northern India's upper castes and classes.

There is some evidence suggesting that the women's world of household and family was a troubled one at the time the movement began. The commercial life of Sind Worki men exacerbated this discontent. Business activities abroad often kept these men away from home for years at a time, leaving many families headed by absentee fathers and husbands. The statistical incidence of this pattern cannot be determined from existing evidence since the society in question was dispersed by the migration to India at the time of the partition between India and Pakistan. However, the accounts of older Sindhi informants and the Brahma Kumaris own portrayal of the period suggest that the pattern was pronounced enough to have disrupted some families and also to have generated strong negative stereotypes of the lifestyles of Sind Worki men and of family life in the Sind Worki community more generally.

For example, at the time the movement began to form, popular belief held that absentee husbands formed extramarital unions while abroad.[2] Although a double standard of sexual morality was certainly nothing new in India, and although we have no way of knowing to what degree such allegations were true, it is reasonable to conjecture that these images of

---

[2] Informants presented such allegations to me as facts.

the lives of absent husbands could have been quite damaging to the morale
of their wives and daughters and also to the esteem in which women held
the patriarchal family. This would certainly be consistent with the importance the idea of the libertine husband was to assume in the Brahma
Kumari critique of the family.

Informants report another stereotype of the time, that of the sex-
starved wife languishing at home while her husband has his good times
abroad. This also may or may not have been the case, but from autobiographical accounts of the period it seems evident that some women in
this community were quite dissatisfied with their lives in traditional families.[3]
Women were expected to fulfill the usual obligations of wives and mothers
in traditional seclusion. However, the families within which they were
expected to do so were sometimes truncated because of the absence of key
male figures. Probably more important, rumour and local stereotype pro-
claimed that the men in these families were leading lives of sin when away
and out of sight. Indeed, according to the Brahma Kumaris these men
were habitually given to vices of all kinds even at home.

The matter of male corruption seems to have been much on the minds of
the women who composed the early core of the Brahma Kumari movement. What they stress in their depiction of the period when the movement
emerged is the moral hypocrisy inherent in the marriage relationship
(Jagdish, n.d.). Husbands, they say, were supposed to be 'deities' to their
wives (this is, in fact, a standard Hindu usage), but because men's actual
behavior was often brutish and ungodlike, such husbands were certainly
unworthy of worship by their partners. The extent to which men ever
really adhered to the rules of virtuous family life is another matter, but it is
apparent that by the 1930s they were perceived by some women not to be
playing by the rules, which called into question (for some) the legitimacy
of the game itself.

The Brahma Kumari movement was founded not by a woman but by a
prosperous Sindhi businessman named Lekhraj. His later notoriety does
not seem to have been foreshadowed by his life prior to the formation of
the sect; neither obscure nor well-known, he is said by older informants to
have been just another rich Sindhi merchant. It is probably significant,
however, that his trade was jewelry. A jeweler is a specialist in women's
ornaments, and we may surmise that Lekhraj therefore came into more
intimate contact with women who were non-kin than would have been

---

[3] These accounts are preserved in the official biography of the founder of the movement
(Jagdish, *Ek Adbhut Jivan-Kahani*, Mt. Abu: Prajapita Brahmakumari Ishvariya Vishva-
Vidyalaya, n.d.). My discussion of the history of the movement is based mainly on details
given in this book, supplemented by conversations with informants inside and outside the
movement.

normal for a man of his class and time. It is conceivable that this contact could have fostered a more than ordinary insight into women's situation.

Lekhraj became a prophet late in life. Although the hagiography of the movement represents him as a lifelong vegetarian and teetotaler and a man of strong if conventional piety, it was only when he was about sixty years old that he began to acquire prophetic insight, which became manifest for the first time in a series of startling visions (*sakshatkars*). In many of the visions he saw deities from the Hindu pantheon, but the most significant was one in which he witnessed the destruction of the world; he reported seeing monstrous weapons used in a cataclysmic war and millions of the souls of the dead flying upward 'as moths flutter in the direction of a light'. Jolted by these experiences, he began to wind up his business affairs. Meanwhile there were more visions. He saw a strange light emanating from a vast and benevolent power and a new world where stars descended to become princesses and princes. A mighty being, he said, was instructing him to 'make such a world as this' (Jagdish, n.d.).

Lekhraj's visions attracted the attention of others, and the nucleus of a following came into existence. His first disciples, drawn primarily from his own family, were soon joined by outsiders. These followers were mostly female, which is not surprising since women, particularly older women, often provide the principal constituencies of lesser saints and gurus (Roy, 1975b). From this standpoint Lekhraj was initially little more than just another minor religious visionary with a certain local renown. Soon his disciples began to have similar visions, and his apparent ability to induce such experiences in others became one of the main bases of his growing reputation. His followers called him 'Om Baba', and the group around him began to be known as the *om mandli* (*om*, a sacred syllable representing the absolute; *mandli*, circle or association). This was the core of what was to become the Brahma Kumari movement. In 1937, Lekhraj established a managing committee of several women followers, and in early 1938 he turned his entire fortune over to this group.

From the very start the sect met with savage hostility from the surrounding society. Irate relatives of movement members formed an 'anti *om mandli*' association, and the local press undertook a campaign against the sect. Families of members were threatened with caste excommunication, and many of Lekhraj's women followers were physically abused by their families. Street rowdies insulted and intimidated members, and in 1938 an angry mob set a movement building on fire.

The ostensible reason for all the uproar focused on one of Lekhraj's most important teachings, celibacy. Husbands returned from long stays abroad only to discover that their wives had made vows of chastity and wished to transform their homes into 'temples'. Husband and wife, these men were told, should live as Lakshmi (the goddess of prosperity) and Narayan (her husband, Vishnu, a major Hindu deity), and should love each other with pure spiritual love (*atmik sneh*)—that is, with asexual love. Husbands and their families frequently responded with beatings, wife expulsions, and lawsuits for the reinstatement of conjugal rights. They regarded Lekhraj with deep suspicion. Some accused him of sorcery, and many believed that he was a man of inexhaustible sexual appetite whose real motive was the seduction of his female followers. Similar suspicions linger around the movement today.[4]

In actuality, the issue was never simply the denial of sexual pleasures to men, which in itself, in the Hindu context, could hardly justify the ferocity of the backlash that greeted the movement. A more fundamental issue concerned the family and the position of women within the family. In the Hindu world for a married or as yet unmarried woman to renounce her sexuality is to express a radical and unacceptable autonomy. It means withholding her maternal power, which she denies in the first instance to her natal family, whose right it is to bestow that power on another family in marriage, and in the second instance to the conjugal family into whose service marriage consigns her.

Because the Brahma Kumari movement began in tumult, its initial consolidation occurred in a seclusion necessitated by the hostility of the surrounding society. Driven from Hyderabad, the sect members sequestered themselves in Karachi, where Lekhraj and his principal disciple, a remarkable woman known within the movement as Saraswati, presided as surrogate father and mother over a predominantly female following numbering about three hundred. After the partition of India and Pakistan, they moved in 1950 to India and their present headquarters in Rajasthan at Mount Abu.

Following the move, the Brahma Kumaris at first resumed their former seclusion. Gradually, however, a change occurred in the general outlook of the sect. Lekhraj had previously characterized the movement as a fiery sacrifice (*yagya*) in which members would, in radical separation from the

---

[4] It is also frequently alleged that the Brahma Kumaris engage in secret tantric rites. In response it should be noted that relations between male gurus and female followers are sexually suspect in many areas of India. Moreover, the past members of the movement engaged in ecstatic dances associated with their visions, something that could easily be misunderstood by already suspicious outsiders. This aspect of movement life has been curtailed in more recent times. In the course of my contact with the movement I encountered no evidence that would support allegations of sexual misconduct. In any case, I do not believe it either slanderous or evasive to note that tantric sexuality is the very opposite of libertine sexuality and therefore would be, at a certain level, consistent with the stated ideals of the movement.

world, purify themselves through austerities while assimilating the knowledge (*gyan*) revealed by his visions. But now the founder began to emphasize active proselytization. It is likely that this resulted from the concern
that he and his followers must have felt about the future membership of a
movement of celibates. In part, too, he was probably encouraged by the
fact that the movement no longer had to confront the entrenched pre-
judices of Sindhi society. In any case, he began to speak of the seclusion as
a period of necessary preparation for the real mission of the movement,
which involved awakening the *bhaktas* (devotees, here, non-members of
the movement) from their ignorance and spiritual slumber.

To some degree, Lekhraj had already gone public. He had published
pamphlets almost from the start, and he was an inveterate writer of letters
to important public figures (Gandhi, the king of England, and many
others) in which he interpreted the meaning of contemporary events in the
light of his revealed knowledge. He began to intensify all of these activities,
and some of the most gifted movement members began to visit major
Indian cities for the purpose of spreading the word. Permanent centers
were ultimately established in Delhi and other urban areas, and by the
time Lekhraj died in 1969, the outer persona of the movement had changed
fundamentally. What was previously a highly reclusive sect had become an
aggressively proselytizing movement.

These efforts have been very successful. The Brahma Kumaris claim a
membership of one hundred thousand, although the number of truly
commited adherents is certainly much smaller than this. They are highly
conspicuous and an established presence. The movement presents itself as
a 'divine university' (*ishvariya vishva-vidyalaya*) and offers classes in
doctrine and meditation at hundreds of local centers. Most of these centers
are in northern Indian cities, but they also exist in other areas of India, and
there are a few overseas. The movement is now engaged in an energetic
campaign to internationalize.

My own perspective on the movement was local. For several months I
received instruction and participated in a variety of activities at a movement center in New Delhi. The constituency of this center was drawn
mainly from middle and upper-middle-class government-service families.
Of the hundred or so women and men who seemed to be in the orbit of the
center at any given time, there was a core of perhaps two dozen who
attended center activities regularly. An extremely high rate of turnover
characterized the outer fringes of this membership. It is very common for
individuals attracted to the movement to lose interest on more intimate
acquaintance. Most outsiders with whom I discussed the sect seemed to
regard it with a mixture of contempt and mistrust.

Sexuality and the Human Condition

Brahma Kumari views concerning the condition of women are embedded in a complex theological system. To a considerable degree this theology draws on ideas of wide currency in the Hindu world, but in some respects it is highly innovative. It was originally formulated in the discourses Lekhraj gave to his followers during his lifetime, many of which were recorded and continue to be read at Brahma Kumari gatherings today. The words, of course, are Lekhraj's own, but the views they express were probably influenced by others. He was in intimate and daily contact with a mostly female group of followers, and the content of his teachings certainly suggests the influence of a feminine perspective.

In consonance with other South Asian religions, the Brahma Kumaris teach that the single most important feature of the human situation is confusion about personal identity. 'Who are you?' Lekhraj always asked his followers. This continues to be the first question posed to potential converts today. Most people, the Brahma Kumaris say, have no idea at all of who they really are. The purpose of Brahma Kumari teachings is to enable those who are lost, those who have forgotten who they are, to recover their true identities.

Who, then, are we? According to the Brahma Kumaris we are souls (atmas), and our confusion takes the form of false identification with the bodies we happen to inhabit. The world consists of two utterly dissimilar constituents, souls and material nature (prakriti). The world of our bodies and senses is the material world. Souls are immaterial, massless points of pure brightness and power that have a true home at the top of the universe in a place called the supreme abode (paramdham). While there, souls exist in the company of the supreme soul (paramatma), who is the source of the light Lekhraj saw in his visions and who is identified by the Brahma Kumaris with the deity Siva. All souls, however, periodically leave this place and descend into the material world to inhabit human (never animal) bodies. When they do so, they forget their true nature and origin and transmigrate from body to body, wandering through the world in total ignorance of who they really are. This is our predicament; we are lost souls, lost children of the supreme soul, and we must recover our true identity.

When souls descend into the material world, as all souls must, they become entrapped in a rigidly determined historical cycle. According to the Brahma Kumaris, the history of the world occurs in five thousand year cycles of moral and physical decline, each divided into four ages (yugas) of 1,250 years. Every cycle is believed to be an exact duplicate of the others, like a movie that is screened again and again. The world is perfect in the beginning and totally degraded by the end, at which point the cycle begins anew. Souls may enter a cycle at any point, but obviously it is most desirable to do so at or near its beginning when the world is closer to perfection. The Brahma Kumaris believe that by means of self-purification and the realization of their true identities as souls they will enter the next cycle (and thus all cycles) at or near the beginning when the earth is a paradise.

At the start of the cycle, when the world is totally pure, there is no pain or hardship of any kind, and the deserving few who exist in the world at this time are deities (Babb, 1982). Indeed, they are the very gods and goddesses of the Hindu pantheon imperfectly remembered through texts today—the stars that Lekhraj saw in his visions who descend to rule a perfect new world. As time passes, however, the virtue of these beings gradually degrades; meanwhile, new souls, slightly less worthy than those who came before, continue to arrive from above. After 2,500 years of relative plenty and happiness, the decline of the world becomes serious and brings about a momentous transition at the halfway point in the cycle.

The great transition has to do with sex and procreation. One of the most fundamental elements in the Brahma Kumari conception of the human predicament, and one that is basic to their highly distinctive understanding of women's situation, is their belief (itself not novel in the Hindu tradition) that sexual intercourse is entirely unknown in the first and blessed half of the cycle of universal history. In the Brahma Kumari view, sexual intercourse is inconsistent with the purity of the deities who inhabit the world in that era. Sexual intercourse is unnecessary for reproduction because the souls that enter the world during the first half of the cycle are in possession of a special yogic power (*yog bal*) by which they conceive children. As the general level of purity and virtue declines, however, this power wanes, and at the midpoint of the cycle it disappears altogether.

With the advent of sexual intercourse the world changes from heaven (*svarg*) to hell (*narak*), and misery becomes the lot of humankind. Sexual lust (*kam vikar*), according to the Brahma Kumaris, is the parent of all other vices and the prime cause of the present unhappy state of humanity. Sexual passion, more than anything else, entrenches and confirms us in our false identifications with the body. All forms of violence, avariciousness, and exploitation arise from this. With the onset of sexual reproduction, the world begins an ineluctable slide into depravity and ever-deepening slavery to the body and its urges.

The fall of the world is also the fall of womankind. During the first half of the world cycle men and women are entirely equal, but with the beginning of what the Brahma Kumaris call 'body consciousness' (*deh abhiman*) women become mere objects of lust and fall under the domination of men. This, however, is but a symptom of a more general affliction because, with the subjugation of women, men and women alike become bound to the body and to the misfortunes and pain of life in a world ruled by passion and desire. Thus the bondage of women is the bondage of all.

We are now at the very end of the *kaliyug*, the final era of universal depravity, and the world is soon to be destroyed. This, of course, is the destruction Lekhraj foresaw in his visions; when it happens all souls will return to the supreme abode to await the renewal of the cycle. Just prior to the close of the *kaliyug*, however, the supreme soul favors humanity with a remarkable act of grace. At this point, when human beings languish in the deepest alienation from their true nature as souls, the supreme soul makes available special knowledge (*gyan*) of the true human situation to those few of special worthiness who are prepared to listen. He does so by speaking through the mouth of a human medium, who is, of course, Dada Lekhraj, the founder of the Brahma Kumari movement. To those who receive and accept such knowledge, the *kaliyug*, the present age of evil, becomes *sangamyug*, the 'confluence age', so named because it represents a time of transition to the renewed world to come. Members of the Brahma Kumari movement enter this fifth era with the expectation that they will become fit to be reborn in the paradisiacal phase of the next world cycle. By preparing his followers Lekhraj, in effect, creates that new world, thereby fulfilling the instructions he received from the supreme soul in his visions.

Subjugation

But what does all this have to do with feminism? A great deal, and the key lies in the way the Brahma Kumari portrayal of the human predicament invokes a particular image of women's condition. In the Hindu world there is nothing remarkable about the doctrine that worldly passions and attachments are the principal causes of bondage, nor is there anything truly striking about the use of woman as a metaphor for the human situation, a concept with deep roots in the *bhakti* (Hindu devotional) tradition. What is unusual in the case of the Brahma Kumaris is the incorporation of a critical point of view into this metaphor. Pervading the Brahma Kumaris' concept of the world is an idea of human alienation that draws its strength from the image of women as victims of corrupt institutions. I certainly do not mean to imply that the Brahma Kumari movement can be described as a feminist critique of society, for this would violate the complexity of an intricate and multifaceted theological system, but I do want to suggest that a feminist motive is at the very least a discernible element in Brahma Kumari theology.

Though it is not to be found in any single place, a Brahma Kumari account of the situation of women in Indian society exists. Elements of it are scattered throughout Lekhraj's discourses and the literature of the movement, but when the pieces are put together, what emerges is a coherent assessment of where women stand, focusing on the role of women in marriage.

As I have already noted, one of the principal Brahma Kumari complaints about the family and marriage is that women are subordinated to husbands who are unworthy of veneration. The question of the different religious value accorded to each sex is fundamental to this accusation. Men are full of vices, yet women are required to treat their husbands as gurus and deities while they themselves are regarded as no more than the 'heel of the left foot' of man. As if this were not enough, to the degree that man has fallen, women is regarded as the temptress who pulls him down. According to a common observation, women is the 'door to hell' (*narak ka dvar*), the implication being that women are not so much the victims of world-binding sexual lust as they are its source. Put otherwise (although the Brahma Kumaris never formulated it quite this way), women are truly viewed not as moral subjects but rather as provocations for moral choices made by men.

All this, however, is but a surface manifestation of what these materials point to as the fundamental injustice, namely, that women are not conceived as soteriolcgical agents. If man has fallen, he at least has the option of renouncing the world; he can become a *sannyasi* (ascetic) and seek what he believes to be his salvation. But *sannyasis* are men, not women. In the world as presently constituted, woman is not the renouncer but that which is renounced—the 'door to hell'. Bondage is worldly entanglement: liberation is release from this. The implicit gravamen in the Brahma Kumari assessment of women's condition is that women are not just bound to the world but also imprisoned in a concept—the concept of women serving as bait for the trap. And, in fact, at a more general level of Hindu symbolism, woman is *maya*, the illusion that is the created world and that draws the self into fatal bondage.

Because the subordination of women began when sexual intercourse became a factor in human existence, sexual intercourse is at the root of women's inequality. In the world as it exists now, women must enter into sexual relations with men and live as sexual beings if they are to be married. This offers no real choice, since to be an unmarried woman is to have no real status in society at all. Without the option of *sannyas* (world renunciation) women are trapped in 'worldly marriage'. This means that women are not merely housebound; they are also bound absolutely to the world. But so are men; they are as bound by their passions as women are by evil conventions. And in the present age of degradation even the freedom of the *sannyasi*, in the Brahma Kumari view, is finally a false liberty. The *sannyasi*, indeed, is an abettor of present miseries, making orphans of his children and a widow of his wife.

Marriage, or at least a certain kind of marriage, thus becomes a paradigm for the human condition, with the sexual role of women its focus. And because reproduction requires sex in the present era, it is ultimately the reproductive role of woman that underlies her predicament. The Brahma Kumari version of this predicament, however, differs somewhat from the one portrayed by western feminism. Consistent with the more general Hindu mistrust of passion, the Brahma Kumaris have concentrated on sexuality itself, rather than on the exigencies of child-rearing and house-keeping, as the significant factor in women's subordination. More important, they have not viewed the reproductive role of woman as a biological given. Intercourse is necessary for procreation, but only at the present time. Women can be free, and some women inevitably will be. And since the bondage of woman is the bondage of all, the world can be made free through her liberation. But a free world will have to be a world without sex.

Liberation and Power

In the Hindu milieu there is a close connection between sexuality and power. Intercourse is regarded as debilitating; it rapidly drains energies that are slow to accumulate in the body. Conversely, sexual restraint is a method of concentrating and storing power. The powerlessness that especially women experience in the present era can be partially attri-buted to women's inefficacy within unjust social institutions, but this powerlessness has a more basic root in the sexuality that binds both women and men to the world. Through sexual renunciation the Brahma Kumaris seek the power to make themselves free in a world that they themselves, by means of their power, will make.

Given Hindu ideas about the relationship between power and sexuality, it is not surprising that Siva is the presiding deity of the universe as the Brahma Kumaris conceive it, for he is the divine archetype of the sexual renouncer. Siva is the ascetic of the gods, dwelling apart from society and, during one phase of his existence, gathering fiery energy within himself by means of chastity (O'Flaherty, 1973). When the other gods wish to rouse him from his trance of withdrawal to prevent him from absorbing all the energy of the universe, it is Kamdev, the god of lust, whom they send. Although Siva was also an extremely important deity among the Hindus of Sind (Thakur, 1959), the Brahma Kumaris version is somewhat reduced from the Puranic original. As portrayed in Puranic mythology, Siva's character swings wildly between extremes of eroticism and asceticism (O'Flaherty, 1973). But there is nothing erotic about Siva as the Brahma Kumaris picture him; he is a purely ascetic deity whose character fulfills the values of the movement. Known to the Brahma Kumaris as Shiv Baba, he is visually represented not by the more overtly phallic conventional *linga* but by a red, egg-shaped emblem said to be the likeness of the halo of reddish light surrounding his real presence in the supreme abode. At the center is a tiny white dot representing the point of light (*jyoti bindu*) that is the locus of his immense power, forever retained by absolute chastity.

This emphasis on the connection between power and sexuality underlies what, to western feminists, might seem a rather odd feature of the Brahma Kumaris position with regard to existing institutions. Although they consider marriage, and thus a woman's family, to be oppressive in the present age, they do not advocate the dissolution of either marriage or family. Neither institution vexes them as such. Indeed, they believe there will be marriage in the world to come. Rather, it is worldly marriage, marrige with intercourse, to which they most object. Instead of directing the energies of the movement toward achieving the kind of institutional reforms sought by western feminists, they seek purity (*pavitrata*) within the family. By purity they particularly mean chastity, which in their view is the virtue from which all other virtues arise.

There are basically two levels of membership in the movement. At its core are fully 'surrendered' women and men who have either left or never entered family life and reside in the movement's many centers. Currently most of them seem to be recruited from families with strong and lasting movement connections. Women occupy the leadership roles and are the teachers who promulgate the movement's doctrines to the general membership and potential converts. Most of the resident men, a minority in the centers with which I am familiar, maintain outside employment and function as indispensible mediators between the secluded sisters and the outside world. Surrounding this core is a much larger lay membership with varying degrees of commitment to the movement. Lay members may live with their worldly families. If the movement expresses no positive enthusiasm for family life, if recognizes the family and marriage as institutional realities and sees in them a field in which virtues can be perfected. Families often participate in the movement as units, and although commitment to the sect by individuals has sometimes proven to be quite disruptive to households, the movement claims that the quality of family life can be radically improved if members adhere to Brahma Kumari teachings.

Brahma Kumari families must be 'lotus-like', that is, they must be unsullied by the mire in which they grow. Every home, the Brahma

Kumaris say, should become an *ashram*, a hermitage. Even for the lay members the rules governing day-to-day behavior are strict. Diet, for example, a major concern: meat, alcohol, and all other impure, passion-including foods and substances must be avoided. The most important norm however, is celibacy, the *sine qua non* of the virtuous life as the Brahma Kumaris understand it. It is for this reason that most of the converts in the center I knew best seemed to be persons for whom sexuality was no longer an issue: widows, widowers, and, in the case of married couples those in their middle years or older who had already had children. In chastity, husband and wife can live as god and goddess, a relationship that anticipates the divine partnerships that will exist in the new world to come. And by means of chastity they can accumulate the power that makes true liberation possible.

This liberating power is closely associated with a form of spiritual exercise the Brahma Kumaris call *raja yoga*. *Raja yoga* is a technique of meditation designed to cultivate 'soul consciousness' (*dehi abhiman*). Its object is the direct experience of the self as a soul rather than as a body, that is, the direct experience of one's true identity. There is no need to describe the actual technique here; the important point is that many practitioners have experiences that they regard as valid indices of spiritual progress (Babb, 1981). For them, *raja yoga* represents both a confirmation and a guarantee; it confirms their attainment of power-producing purity, since only the truly pure can engage in the technique with full success, as it guarantees their soteriological destiny, since the pure can be confident of a place in the *satyug*, the first age of the universal cycle, to come. In short, this technique enables its practitioners to answer Lekhraj's question— 'Who are you?'—for themselves. It is a way of knowing that you are not who you seem to be: you are not a physical and social being, bound to the world and the institutions of the world, but a soul. Knowing this, one becomes a witness (*sakshi*) to the material self, released from the bondage of this world and fit to live in a world of the free.

The Concept of Childhood

In Hindu India, renunciation is the key to liberation, but the problem for women is that renunciation is not a value that applies very easily to them. While there is nothing in the idea of liberation through renunciation that necessarily excludes women, and while there are and have been female ascetics in the Hindu world, the fact remains that *sanyas*, conceived as a stage of life, is not for women but for men. In the classical four-*ashrama* scheme (the four stages of life), a man's wife is permitted to accompany him to the forest in the penultimate stage of *vanaprasth*, but he becomes a *sanyasi*, a full renouncer, alone. In this image of world renunciation, the wife just seems to dwindle away.

But if the culturally dominant model of renunciation appears to bar women, the Brahma Kumaris have exploited another possibility inherent in that construct as a way of developing a culturally legitimate conception of world renunciation for women. Their beliefs incorporate an inversion of the dominant model: if men can become free through renunciation at the end of their lives, women can achieve a similar condition by recovering life's beginning.

The concept of childhood is a powerful theme in Brahma Kumari teachings. Not only do they consider the heaven for which they strive the childhood of the world, but it is also clear that the manner of life they seek in this world-dawn is in many ways a childlike existence. There will be no hardship, no worry, and above all no sex. Equally important, however, is the fact that the Brahma Kumari movement as it exists in this world consists of women and men who, in an important symbolic sense, have become children, the daughters and sons of Brahma. Brahma is the Hindu deity responsible for the creation of the world. Dada Lekhraj is known as 'Brahma Baba' within the movement because by promulgating his doctrines he creates the new world to come. Members of the movement consider themselves to be Brahma's (that is, Lekhraj's) daughters and sons because they are reborn through the knowledge he enunciates, which in some sense separates them from the world and from their families. Though in the world, they say they are dead to it; then existence is a 'death in life' (*marjiva janam*). In the *sangamyug*, an intermediate age, they are *bich men*, 'in between', neither of this world nor yet of the next. As such they are children in Dada Lekhraj's family.

But why should the Brahma Kumaris wish to be children? The answer seems to lie in their use of women's situation as a metaphor for the human condition. Brahma Kumari cosmology portrays the world as a paradise in its childhood; only when the world grows up does trouble begin. The point is, a similar 'fall' describes the changes a woman experiences over the course of her life.

That women in northern India undergo a change of religious as well as social status at the time of marriage is a matter of great symbolic importance to the Brahma Kumaris. A *kanya*, or unmarried girl, is considered a kind of goddess.[5] In northern India, one of the main occasions for the worship of the goddess (in the generic sense) is a ceremonial period known

---

[5] It should be noted that this conception is very important in Sindhi culture. Thakur reports that 'virgin or unmarried daughter is addressed as goddess (*Niani* or *Devi*) and is considered equal to one hundred Brahmins . . . who are substituted in several rites by virgins. She is identified with sacred energy (*sakti*) as she symbolizes chastity which is potent with enormous powers . . . She is frequently fed by the neighbors on various festivals including the Shradh festivities . . . No fruit or vegetable of the season is eaten unless first offered to a virgin, whose feet are washed and homage paid whenever she is fed.' (p. 78)

as *navratra* (nine nights). The Brahma Kumaris put great emphasis on the fact that one of the ways the goddess is worshipped during this festival is by homage (*puja*) to unmarried girls, which is offered just as it would be to an icon of the goddess on an altar. But a woman cannot be worshipped in this way after marriage; then the husband, not the wife, is regarded as *pujya*, 'worthy of worship'. A wife, by contrast, is merely *pujari*, 'one who worships'.

The analogy is obvious: just as the world falls with the advent of worldly marriage, so too the divinity of women is lost when they marry. To regain divinity, the Brahma Kumaris must become children, that is, they must be reborn as virgin daughters in the house of a new father.

It may seem an odd thing for a group with an apparently feminist orientation, but there is hardly a more pervasive concept in Brahma Kumari teachings than that of fatherhood. The supreme soul is imaged as masculine and paternal; he is the supreme father (*parampita*) who loves his children (the souls of human beings) with fatherly devotion. The Brahma Kumaris characterize *raja yoga* as 'remembering father', and they say that the world to come is an inheritance from him, theirs by right as children who have proved themselves worthy of their claim. And of course Lekhraj, too, is a father: he was the agency of the supreme father in his role as divine medium and also the father of the movement itself, a role he continues to fill from his present location in the supreme abode.

This emphasis on fatherhood is deeply rooted in the life experiences of northern Indian women. At the time of marriage a woman leaves her father's home for an altogether new kind of existence. The Brahma Kumaris characterize this transition as a kind of rebirth. As a woman is reborn into a new family and a wholly new life, her dominant identity changes from that of daughter to daughter-in-law. This change provides one of the staples of Indian folklore and literature, both traditional and modern, because of the potential for anguished separation and tragedy it carries. A woman no longer enjoys the relative freedom that was hers as daughter and sister in her father's house. Her station as a daughter-in-law is low, at least initially; and according to the Brahma Kumaris, her role is largely one of onerous servitude.

In a sense we are all daughters-in-law, men and women alike. Subordination means living apart from one's father in worldly marriage; liberation therefore is to dwell with one's father as daughter of the house. Thus we must all seek our true father, for it is only in his house that we can find real freedom. It is also only from him that we can expect an inheritance. As Ursula Sharma has recently pointed out, the inheritance system of north-west India is strongly masculine; one effect of rules of exogamy in this region is to ensure the exclusion of women from the inheritance of land by exporting them as far from their natal families as possible (Sharma, 1980). Against the background of Sharma's analysis, which is probably valid for most areas of northern India, the Brahma Kumaris' emphasis on claiming an inheritance through the recovery of childhood is as poignant as it is intelligible.

The idea of attaining autonomy and freedom by reclaiming premarital virginity has a context in the symbolism of the Hindu pantheon. The image of the goddess in Hinduism is extremely complex, and since it has been explored in detail elsewhere I shall merely note a few relevant points here. Amid the immense variety of forms the goddess takes, it is possible to discern two opposing images. One portrays the goddess as the spouse of the major gods. In these forms (as Lakshmi, Sita, Parvati, and others) she is associated with such positive qualities as prosperity, nurturance, and fidelity, but she is not a truly autonomous figure since her identity is closely linked to that of her divine husband. When the goddess's marital connection is not stressed, however, another of her selves comes to the fore. Then she appears as a supremely powerful, weapon-carrying killer of demons; in at least some of these forms, such as Kali, she is portrayed as fearsome and even potentially dangerous.

The autonomous goddess is an obvious symbol for a concept of woman as powerful and free. Her inherent power is unmodulated by the restraints of marriage; she is a self-sufficient and self-directing force in the universe. Moreover, her status is not derived. Devotees worship her on her own account since they believe all other deities are subsumed in her. This independent goddess is the one virgin girls primarily represent in the rites of *navratra*. This is also the goddess the Brahma Kumaris wish to emulate— autonomous, free, with inner powers protected by chastity, and worthy of worship like the virgins of the festival.

To recover childhood—and with it the virtues of premarital virginity— the Brahma Kumaris must die to old social roles (though they may continue to act them out) so that they may return to their true father's house. In their view earthly families are but temporary historical concatenations of material persons and have nothing to do with our essential souls. Thus one must be reborn as a special kind of child in order to recover one's true identity in the eternal father's abode. Within this divine family (*ishvariya kutumb*) the Brahma Kumaris believe they can achieve liberation from the injustices of this world and the promise of a life of full freedom in the world to come.

I must stress that feminism is not the only concern of the Brahma Kumari movement. Although women's interests are a conspicuous element in their conception of the world and the human situation within it, they regard the tragedy of our present existence as a human problem, not specifically as a women's problem. Moreover, men have been involved in the movement from the beginning, and were in fact a majority among the daily attendees at the movement center in Delhi where most of my investigation took place (I was told this was an exceptional situation). All this said, however, it remains the case that at the very core of the Brahma Kumari view of the world is an outlook that is feminist in the sense that it is based on a critical analysis of the position of women in Hindu society and seeks their liberation in accord with the Brahma Kumaris' idea of freedom.

It is possible, of course, that the Brahma Kumaris are in error about the relevance of their message to the women of India or, for that matter, to anyone. Certainly the message seems to have very little general appeal. The sect has prospered, but despite vigorous proselytizing it remains quite small in comparison with the size of the society within which it is situated. On the other hand, this may be an indication that its message striking about the career of the Brahma Kumari movement than the immense uneasiness and distrust it has provoked in Indian society. It is conceivable that this discomfort reflects what men and women alike perceive as a powerful symbolic challenge to heterosexual relations in a highly patriarchal society, relations that may be more sensitive and fragile than is commonly supposed. Suspicion of sexual misconduct is generally the expressed justification for hostility toward the movement, but I suspect a more fundamental cause involves the unwelcome and threatening spectacle of women running their own affairs.

Leaving aside, however, the question of whether the Brahma Kumaris' assessment of women's situation is in any sense valid, and leaving aside also the question of whether the movement offers anything resembling a genuine solution to women's problems. I believe that this rather unusual sect deserves our serious attention. If nothing else, it offers a striking illustration of the richness of the Hindu tradition and also of the ways in which elements of a religious culture can be reordered to serve goals ostensibly quite remote from tradition.

It is difficult to determine the degree to which non-Indian influences might have played a role in the development of the Brahma Kumari movement. As noted earlier, cosmopolitan patterns of commerce led to disturbances in the lives of some Sind Worki families, which may have provided some impetus to the formation of the sect. There may have been more specific influences as well, but the passage of time and the dispersion of the Sindhi society of those days make them difficult to pinpoint. However, even if it could be shown that the Brahma Kumaris' faith in the possibility of freedom for women was in some way exogenously inspired, the fact would remain that their feminism is essentially indigenous— indigenous in the sense that their notion of the wrongs done to women, their concept of the power that liberates, and their image of liberation itself are all in one way or another derived from the Hindu tradition. That the Brahma Kumaris have reacted critically to the situation of women in Hindu society is perhaps not in itself surprising. What is notable is that they have formulated a coherent analysis of this situation utilizing elements from within their own tradition. The result is a feminism that is both radical in its implications and true to its own past.

The Contributors

Sohaila Abdulali has a Master's degree in Sociology from Brandeis University. Currently she is working on her second Master's degree in Journalism at Stanford University. She has been the Director of the Boston Area Rape Crisis Center for a few years.

Mary J. Allen is Professor and Chair of the Department of Psychology at California State College, Bakersfield. Her research interests include psychological tests and measurements, program evaluation and the psychology of sex roles.

Lawrence A. Babb is Professor of Anthropology at Amherst College. He is the author of *Redemptive Encounters: Three Modern Styles in the Hindu Tradition* (1987). He has contributed articles on Indian religions to several academic journals.

Suma Chitnis is Professor and Head of the Unit for Research in the Sociology of Education and Head of the Unit for Women's Studies at the Tata Institute of Social Sciences, Bombay. She was a Jawaharlal Nehru Fellow between 1983–85. She is a member of the Advisory Committee on Women's Studies at SNDT Women's University, Bombay and the Indian Council of Social Science Research.

Sukanya Das is currently working on her Ph.D. dissertation, 'Parental Sex Role Orientation, Socialization Practice and Sex Stereotypes of Children' at the Indian Institute of Technology, Bombay. Her research interests include child development and sex roles.

Shamita Das Dasgupta is a member of the faculty of the New School for Social Research. Her research interests include psychology of women with emphasis on gender identity, socialization and sex roles.

Flavia is the founder of the Women's Aid Center in Bombay and a member of the Forum Against Oppression of Women. She was recently awarded the Ashoka Fellowship for evolving technical training programs for women.

Rehana Ghadially is Associate Professor in Psychology at the Indian Institute of Technology, Bombay. She has been a visiting faculty at

Auburn University, USA, University Sains Malaysia, Malaysia and Wake Forest University, USA. She has published several articles on sex roles, career aspirations of women and women in engineering in the *Indian Journal of Social Work, Sociological Bulletin* and *Journal of Higher Education*. She is a member of the National Women's Studies Association and the American Association of Women in Psychology.

Radha Sarma Hegde is a doctoral candidate in Communications at the Ohio State University. Currently she is a lecturer at Rutgers University. Her primary area of interest is intercultural communication.

Sudhir Kakar is a Fellow at the Centre for the Study of Developing Societies, Delhi. Among the books authored by him are *Personality and Authority in Work* (1974), *Inner World: A Psycho-analytic Study of Childhood and Society in India* (1978), *Shamans, Mystics and Doctors* (1983), and *Tales of Love, Sex and Danger* (1986).

Narendra Nath Kalia is Professor of Sociology at the State University of New York, College at Buffalo. His articles have appeared in several international journals. His publications include *Sexism in Indian Education* (1979), a novel and a multi-volume anthology of Pakistani Urdu poetry.

Pramod Kumar is a Junior Research Assistant and a Ph.D. candidate at the Indian Institute of Technology, Bombay. He has submitted his dissertation, 'Political Behavior in Organizations: Some Determinants and Consequences'.

S. Krishnaswamy is Director of Research at the Spastic Society of India, His major research interests include rehabilitation and special education.

C.S. Lakshmi is the author of *Face Behind the Mask: Women in Tamil Literature* (1984). She is currently working on a book, *An Illustrated Social History of Women in Tamil Nadu*.

Ashis Nandy is a Fellow at the Centre for the Study of Developing Societies, Delhi. Among the books he has authored are *Edge of Psychology: Essay in Politics and Culture* (1980), *Alternative Sciences: Creativity and Authenticity in Two Indian Scientists* (1980), *Intimate Enemy: Loss and Recovery of Self under Colonialism* (1983).

Vibhuti Patel is a member of the Forum Against Oppression of Women, Women's Aid Center and Forum Against Sex Determination and Sex Preselection. She is currently working on a resource kit on 'Women's Organizations, Participation and Consciousness' for the Asia and Pacific Development Center.

Jyoti Punwani is a journalist with thirteen years experience. Currently she is Chief of Bureau with *The Sunday Observer*, Bombay.

V. Nandini Rao is Professor of Sociology at Jackson State University. She has published several articles in journals on marriage and family, aging, alchoholism.

V.V. Prakasa Rao is Chairperson and Professor of Sociology at Jackson State University. His research interests include marriage and family, aging and sociology of sports.

Manisha Roy is a faculty member at Radcliffe Graduate Seminar, Radcliffe College. She is also a training analyst at the C.G. Jung Institute of Boston. Her teaching and research interests include psychological aspects of human behavior and relationship between the individual and his/her culture.

Renuka R. Sethi is Professor in the Department of Special Programs and Chairperson of the inter-disciplinary major in Child Development at California State College, Bakersfield.

Pritam Singh is Reader in Economics at Panjab University, Chandigarh. He is active both in the students' and teachers' unions. His research interests include political economy of development, the agrarian question and women's studies.

Susan Wadley is Professor of Anthropology at Syracuse University. She has written numerous articles on religion in northern India. Her other interests include folk literature, and calendrical rituals of Hindu practitioners.

Bibliography

Abraham, A. 1984. 'Larsen and Toubro Seminar on Amniocentesis', *Bombay Women's Center Newsletter*, 1, 4, pp. 5–8.

Abraham, A. and Shukla, S. 1983. *Sex Determination Tests*, Bombay: Women's Center.

Altekar, A.S. 1962. *The Position of Women in Hindu Civilization*, Delhi: Motilal Banarsidas.

An Index to Indian Periodical Literature. 1985. Bombay: Center for Advanced Research and Studies on Women and SNDT Women's University Library, October–December.

Archer, C. 1984. 'Children's Attitude Towards Sex Role Division in Adult Occupational Roles', *Sex Roles*, 10, pp. 1–10.

Arlow, J.A. 1961. 'Ego Psychology and the Study of Mythology', *Journal of Psychoanalytic Association*, 9, p. 375.

Ashmore, R.D. and Delboca, F.K. 1979. 'Sex Stereotypes and Implicit Personality Theory: Towards a Cognitive-Social Psychological Conceptualization', *Sex Roles*, 5, pp. 219–48.

Asian Labour Monitor. 1984. 'India', 10 February, p. 4.

Babb, L.A. 1970. 'Marriage and Malevolence', *Ethnology*, 9, p. 140.

———. 1981. 'Glancing: Visual Interaction in Hinduism', *Journal of Anthropological Research*, 37, 4, pp. 387–401.

———. 1982. 'Amnesia and Rememberance in a Hindu Theory of History', *Asian Folklore Studies*, 41, 1, pp. 49–66.

Baig, T.A. 1976. *India's Woman Power*, New Delhi: S. Chand & Co.

Balasubrahmanyam, V. 1982. 'Medicine and the Male Utopia', *Economic and Political Weekly*, 23 October, p. 1725.

Bandura, A. and Walters, R. 1963. *Social Learning and Personality Development*. New York: Holt, Rinehart and Winston.

Bardhan, P. 1982. 'Little Girls and Death in India', *Economic and Political Weekly*, 4 September, pp. 1448–50.

Barron, F. 1965. 'The Psychology of Creativity'. *New Frontiers in Psychology*, Vol. 2, New York: Holt, Rinehart and Winston.

———. 1969. *Creative Person and Creative Process*, New York: Holt, Rinehart and Winston.

Barry, H., Bacon, M. and Child, I. 1957. 'A Cross-Cultural Survey of Some Sex Differences in Socialization', *Journal of Abnormal and Social Psychology*, 55, pp. 327–32.

Beardsley, E.L. 1973. 'Referential Generalization', *Philosophical Forum*, 5, 1 and 2, pp. 285–93.

Beauf, A. 1974. 'Doctor, Lawyer, Household Drudge', *Journal of Communication*, 24, pp. 142–45.

Beek, E.F. 1971. 'Mariyamman: The Vacillating Goddess', unpublished manuscript, Vancouver: University of British Columbia, p. 2.

Bem, S. 1974. 'The Measurement of Psychological Androgyny', *Journal of Consulting and Clinical Psychology*, 42, pp. 155–62.

Bem, S.L. 1975. 'Sex-Role Adaptability: One Consequence of Psychological Androgyny', *Journal of Personality and Social Psychology*, 31, pp. 634–43.

————. 1977. 'On the Utility and Alternative Procedures for Assessing Psychological Androgyny', *Journal of Consulting and Clinical Psychology*, 45, pp. 196–205.

————. 1981. 'Gender Schema Theory: A Cognitive Account of Sex Typing', *Psychological Review*, 88, pp. 354–64.

Bem, S.L., Martyna, W. and Watson, C. 1976. 'Sex Typing and Androgyny. Further Explorations of the Expressive Domain', *Journal of Personality and Social Psychology*, 34, pp. 1016–23.

Benedict, R. 1938. 'Continuities and Discontinuities in Cultural Conditioning', *Psychiatry*, pp. 161–67.

Berdyaev, N. 1954. *The Meaning of the Creative Act*, trans. D.A. Laurie, New York: Harper & Row. (Quoted in Barron, 1969).

Berg, W.E. and Johnson, R. 1979. 'Assessing the Impact of Victimization: Acquisition of the Victims Roles Among Elderly and Female Victims', in W. Parsonage ed., *Perspectives on Victimology*, Newbury Park, California: Sage Publications.

Berger, L.P. and Luckmann, T. 1967. *The Social Construction of Reality: A Treatise in the Sociology of Knowledge*, Garden City, New Jersey: Anchor Books.

Bernard, J. 1942. *American Family Behavior*, New York: Harper & Row.

Bettelheim, B. 1962. *Symbolic Wounds: Puberty Rites and the Envious Male*, New York: Collier.

Bhaiya, A. 1982. 'Molkarnis of Poona: A Report on the Life and Work of Women Domestic Workers', *How*. 5, 1, pp. 15–19.

Bhasin, K. and Malik, B. 1979. 'Don't Sell Our Bodies to Sell Your Products', *Manushi*, 3, July-August, p. 23.

Bhatt, E. 1981. 'SEWA Women Break Free from Parent Body', *Manushi*, 2, 2, pp. 13–15.

Block, J. 1983. 'Differential Premises Arising from Differential Socialization of the Sexes: Some Conjectures', *Child Development*, 54, pp. 1335–54.

Block, J., Block, J. and Morrison, A. 1981. 'Parental Agreement-Disagreement on Child Rearing Orientations and Gender Related Personality Correlates in Children', *Child Development*, 52, pp. 965–74.

Bronson, W.C. 1959. 'Dimension of Ego and Infantile Identification', *Journal of Personality*, 27, pp. 532–45.

Broverman, D.M., Broverman, I.K., Clarkson, F.E., Rosenkvantz, P.S. and Vogel, S.R. 1968. 'Sex Role Stereotypes and Self-concepts in College Students', *Journal of Consulting Psychology*, 32, pp. 287–95.

————. 1970. 'Sex Role Stereotypes and Clinical Judgements in Mental Health', *Journal of Consulting Psychology*, 34, pp. 1–7.

Brownmiller, S. 1975. *Against Our Will: Men, Women and Rape*, New York: Simon and Schuster.

Brownwell, A. and Shumaker, S.A. 1984. 'Social Support: An Introduction to a Complex Phenomena', *Journal of Social Issues*, 40, 4, pp. 1–9.

Buhler, G. 1964. *The Laws of Manu*, trans., in Muller, M. ed, *Sacred Books of the East*, XXV, Delhi: Motilal Banarsidas.

Burgess, A.W. and Holmstorm, L.L. 1974. 'Rape Trauma Syndrome', *American Journal of Psychiatry*, 131, pp. 981-86.

Burlew, A.K. 1982. 'The Experience of Black Females in Traditional and Non-Traditional Professions', *Psychology of Women Quarterly*, 6, pp. 312–26.

Burr, R. 1974. 'The Effects of Same Sex and Mixed Sex Growth Groups on Measures of Self-Actualization and Verbal Behaviour of Females', unpublished doctoral thesis, Knoxville: University of Tennessee.

Bussey, K. and Perry, D.G. 1982. 'Same Sex Imitation: The Avoidance of Cross Sex Models or the Acceptance of Same Sex Models?', *Sex Roles*, 8, pp. 773–84.

Carstairs, G.M. 1957. *The Twice Born*, Bloomington, Indiana: Indiana University Press.

———. 1975. 'Village Women of Rajasthan', in Devaki Jain ed., *Indian Women*, New Delhi: Government of India, pp. 229-36.

Census of India. 1971. General Economic Table, Series 1, Part II, B (2), Table B-1, Part B, New Delhi: Govt. of India.

———. 1981. Key Population Statistics Based on 5 per cent Sample Data, Series 1, Paper 2 of 1983, New Delhi: Govt. of India.

———. 1981. Primary Census Abstract, Series 1, India General Population, Part II, B (1), New Delhi: Govt. of India.

Chakravarti, M.N. 1983. 'Rape Most Foul', *The Illustrated Weekly of India*, 6 March, p. 30.

Chakravarti, R. 1981. 'Role of Women's Organizations'. Paper presented at National Conference on Women's Studies, Bombay, April.

Chhachhi, A. and Sathyamala. C. 1983. 'Sex Determination Tests: A Technology which will Eliminate Women', *Medico Friend Circle Bulletin*, 95, pp. 3–5.

Clark, A. 1983. 'Limitations on Female Life Chance in Rural Central Gujarat', *The Indian Economic and Social History Review*, 20, pp. 1–25.

Cormack, M. 1961. *The Hindu Woman*, Bombay: Asia Publishing House.

D'Mello, F. 1982. 'Our Fight Against Wife-Beating', *How*, 5, pp. 9–10, 19–22.

Danielou, A. 1964. *Hindu Polytheism*, New York: Pantheon Books, p. 21.

Das, R.M. 1962. *Women in Manu and His Seven Commentators*, Varanasi: Kanchana Publications.

Das, S. 1988. 'Parental Sex-Role Orientation, Socialization Practice and Sex Stereotypes of Children', unpublished doctoral thesis, Indian Institute of Technology, Bombay.

Dasgupta, K., ed. 1976. *Women on the Indian Scene: An Annotated Bibliography*, New Delhi: Abhinav Publications.

Davis, K. and Blake, J. 1956. 'Social Structure and Fertility: An Analytical Framework', *Economic Development and Cultural Change*, IV, pp. 211–35.

Deaux, K. 1976. *The Behavior of Women and Men*, Monterey, Calif.: Brooks/Cole.

De Beauvoir, S. 1970. *The Second Sex*, ed. and trans., M.H. Parshley, New York: A Knopf.

Deepti and Shobha, 1982. 'Women Lecturers Mobilize Against Dowry Death', *Manushi*, 12, pp. 46–47.

De Mause, L. 1974. *The Evolution of Childhood*, New York: Psychohistory Press.

Desai, N. 1982. *Emergence and Development of Women's Organizations (mimeo)*, Bombay: SNDT University, Research Unit on Women's Studies.

De Souza, A. 1975. *Women in Contemporary India*, New Delhi: Manohar Publications.

Deutsch, H. 1945. *The Psychology of Women*, Vol. 2, Chap. 11, New York: Grune and Stratton.

Devi, G. 1967. 'A Study of Sex Differences in Reaction to Frustration Situations', *Psychological Studies*, 12, pp. 17–27.

Devi, R. 1972. *Dance Dialects of India*, Delhi: Vikas.

Dhamija, J.N. 1972. 'The Rising Star', *The Illustrated Weekly of India*, 30 January.

Donaldson, P. and Nichols, D.J. 1978. 'The Changing Tempo of Fertility in Korea', *Population Studies*, 32, pp. 231–50.

Dube, L. 1978. 'Sex Roles in Contracting Family System'. Paper presented at the World Congress of Sociology, Uppsala, Sweden.

Dube, L. 1983a. 'Misadventures in Amniocentesis', *Economic and Political Weekly*, 19 February, pp. 279–80.

———. 1983b. 'Amniocentesis: The Debate Continues', *Economic and Political Weekly*, 11 June, pp. 1933–34.

Dube, S.C. 1963. 'Men's and Women's Roles in India: A Sociological Review', in Barbara Ward ed., *Women in the New Asia*, Paris: UNESCO, pp. 174–203.

Dubois, J.A. 1928. *Hindu Manners, Customs and Ceremonies*, Henry K. Beaucham trans., Oxford: Clarendon Press.

Duncan, B. and Duncan O.D. 1978. *Sex Typing and Social Roles: A Research Report*, New York: Academic Press.

Dworkin, A. 1979. *Pornography: Men Possessing Women*, New York: G.P. Putnam's Sons.

Education Commission, India. 1965. *Recommendations on Women's Education*, New Delhi.

Education of Women In India 1850–1967, A Bibliography, 1968. Bombay: SNDT Women's University.

Engels, F. 1942. *The Origin of the Family, Private Property, and the State*, New York: International Universities Press.

Erikson, E.H. 1964. 'Inner and Outer Space: Reflections on Womanhood', *Daedalus*, 93, pp. 582–606.

———. 1968. *Race and the Wider Identity: Youth and Crisis*, New York: Norton, pp. 295–320.

———. 1969. *Gandhi's Truth*, New York: Norton.

Eron, L.D. 1980. Prescription for Reduction of Aggression', *American Psychologist*, 35, pp. 244–52.

Farroqui, V. 1978. *Women: Special Victims of Police and Landlord Atrocities*, Bombay: National Federation of Indian Women.

Fatima, B. 1981. 'Tamilnadu Rally Against Rape', *Manushi*, 7, p. 33.

Feinman, S. 1981. 'Why is Cross-Sex Role Behaviour more Approved for Girls than for Boys? A Status Characteristic Approach', *Sex Roles*, 7, pp. 289–300.

Feminist Network. 1979. 'Hundreds of Women Celebrate International Women's Day', 6, 1.

Fernandes, G. 1983. 'Brutalizing the Police', *The Illustrated Weekly of India*, 27 March, pp. 8–9.

Forum Against Rape. 1980. Introduction to Forum Against Oppression of Women, Bombay.

————. n.d. 'The Crime of Rape: Some Facts', Bombay.

Franken, M. 1983. 'Sex Role Expectations on Children's Vocational Aspirations and Perceptions of Occupations', *Psychology of Women Quarterly*, 8, pp. 59–68.

Germaine, A. 1975. 'Status and Roles of Women as Factors in Fertility Behaviour: A Policy Analysis', *Studies in Family Planning*, 6, pp. 192–200.

Gettys, L. and Cann, A. 1981. 'Children's Perception of Occupational Sex Stereotypes', *Sex Roles*, 7, pp. 301–08.

Ghadially, R. and Kazi, K.A. 1979. Attitude Towards Sex-Roles, *The Indian Journal of Social Work*, XL, 1, April.

————. 1980. 'Sex-Role Attitudes, Marriage and Career Among College Men and Women', *Indian Journal of Social Work*, XL, 4, pp. 441–47.

Ghosh, B. 1958. *Vidyasagar O Bangali Samaj*, Calcutta: Bengal Publishers, Vols. 1–3.

Gondolf, E.W. 1985. 'Fighting for Control: A Clinical Assessment of Men Who Batter', *Social Casework: The Journal of Contemporary Social Work*, January, pp. 48–54.

Gordon, I. 1975. *Human Development: A Transactional Perspective*, New York: Wiley and Sons.

Gore, M.S. 1961. 'The Husband-Wife and Mother-Son Relationship', *Sociological Bulletin*, 11, pp. 91–102.

————. 1968. *Urbanization and Family Change*, Bombay: Popular Prakashan, Chapter 1.

Government of India. 1974. *Towards Equality: Report of the National Committee on the Status of Women in India*, New Delhi.

Greenberg, R.P. and Zeldow, P.R. 1977. 'Personality Characteristics of Men with Liberal Sex Role Attitudes, *Journal of Psychology*, 97, pp. 187–90.

Greenburg, M. and Ruback, B. 1984. 'Criminal Victimization', *Journal of Social Issues*, 40, 1, pp. 1–8.

Hans, W. 1984. 'Knowledge and Legitimation: The National and International Politics of Educational Research'. Paper presented at the Fifth World Congress of Comparative Education, Paris, July.

Harbord, P. 1981. 'Interview with Jutta Bruckner', *Screen Education*, 2, pp. 48–57.

Hart, G.L. III. 1973. 'Women and the Sacred in Ancient Tamilnadu'. *Journal of Asian Studies*, February, pp. 233–50.

Hartup, W.W. 1983. 'The Peer System', in P. Mussen and E. Hetherton, eds., *Handbook of Child Psychology*, Vol. 4, New York: Wiley and Sons.

Hegde, R.S. and Dasgupta, S.D. 1984. 'Convergence and Divergence from "Devi": The Model of Ideal Woman on the Indian Screen'. Paper presented at the Annual Meeting of the Western Speech and Communication Association, Seattle, February.

Henry, J. 1963. *Culture Against Man*, New York: Vintage.

Hetherington, E.M. 1967. 'The Effect of Family Variables on Sex Typing, on Parent-Child Similarity and on Imitation in Children', in J.P. Hill ed., *Minnesota Symposium on Child Psychology*, Vol. 1, Minneapolis: University of Minnesota Press.

Holmes, H.B. and Betty, B. 1984. 'Prenatal and Preconception Sex Choice Technologies: A Path to Femicide'. Paper presented at International Interdisciplinary Congress, 'Women's World', Gromingen.

Holter, H. 1970. *Sex Roles and Social Structure*, Oslo: Universitetsforlarger.

Hoyenga, K.B. and Hoyenga, K.T. 1979. *The Question of Sex Differences: Psychological, Cultural and Biological Issues*, Boston: Little Brown.

Huesmann, L.R., Lagerspetz, K. and Eron, L.D. 1984. 'Intervening Variables in the TV Violence-Aggression Relation: Evidence from Two Countries', *Developmental Psychology*, 20, pp. 746–75.

Hyde, I.S. and Rosenberg, B.G. 1980. *Half the Human Experience: The Psychology of Women*, Lexington, Mass: D.C. Heath.

Inden, R.B. and Nicholas, R.W.. 1970 'A Cultural Analysis of Bengal Kinship'. Paper presented at the Sixth Annual Conference on Bengal Studies, Oakland University, May.

India News. 1983. 'Indian Cinema', New York: Consulate General of India, 11 March, pp. 5–6.

Inkles, A. and Smith, D.H. 1974. *Becoming Modern: Individual Changes in Six Developing Countries*, London: Heinemann Educational Books.

IS International Bulletin. 1977–78. 'Manifesto of Progressive Organization of Women', Hyderabad, Winter, 6.

———. 1981. 'Images of Women in Indian Films', 18, pp. 14–15.

Jacobson, D. 1977a. 'Introduction', in D. Jacobson and S.S. Wadley eds., *Women in India*, New Delhi: Manohar Publications, pp. 1–16.

———. 1977b. 'The Women of North and Central India: Goddesses and Wives', in Jacobson and Wadley eds., *Women in India*, New Delhi: Manohar Publications, pp. 17–112.

Jagdish, n.d. *Ek Adbhut Jivan Kahani*, Mt. Abu: Prajapat Brahmakumari Ishwariya Vishvavidyalaya.

Jain, D. 1975. *Indian Women*, New Delhi: Government of India.

Jeffery, R. and Jeffery, P. 1983. 'Female Infanticide and Amniocentesis', *Economic and Political Weekly*, 16 April, pp. 654–56.

Jeffery, R., Jeffery, P. and Andrew, L. 1984. 'Female Infanticide and Amniocentesis', *Social Science Medicine*, 19, 11, pp. 1207–12.

Jones, C.A. 1980. 'Observations on the Current Status of Women in India', *International Journal of Women's Studies*, 3, pp. 1–18.

Joshi, P.C. 1985. 'Women the Neglected Half', in *An Indian Personality for Television: Report of the Working Group on Software for Doordarshan*, Vol. 1, New Delhi: Ministry of Information and Broadcasting, Government of India.

Kakar, S. 1974. 'Aggression in Indian Society: An Analysis of Folk Tales', *Indian Journal of Psychology*, 49, 2, p. 119–26.

———. 1978. 'Life Task and Life Cycle', *The Inner World*. New Delhi: Oxford University Press.

Kalia, N.N. 1979. *The Lies We Tell Our Children: Sexism in Indian Education*, New Delhi: Vikas.

———. 1980. 'Prejudice Against Women: An Update of Sexism in the Indian Textbooks for the 1980's', *India Today*, 16–31 August, pp. 86–87.

Kaplan, E.A. 1983. *Women and Film: Both Sides of the Camera*, New York: Methuen, Inc.

Kapoor, C. 1983. 'Raped: Delayed Action', *India Today*, 15 April, p. 27.

Kapur, P. 1970. *Marriage and the Working Woman in India*, Delhi: Vikas.

Karve, I. 1968. *Kinship Organization in India*, Bombay: Asia Publishing House.

———. 1975. 'Indian Women in 1975', *Indian Journal of Public Administration*, 12, pp. 120–32.

Kelly, J.A. and Coorell, L. 1976. 'Parent Behaviors Related to Masculine, Feminine and Androgynous Sex Role Orientations', *Journal of Consulting and Clinical Psychology*, 44, pp. 843–51.

Kestenberg, J.S. 1956. 'Vicissitudes of Female Sexuality', *Journal of the American Psychoanalytic Association*, 4, pp. 453–76.

Khan, M.S. and Ray, R. 1984. 'Dowry Death', *Indian Journal of Social Work*, XLV, pp. 303–07.

Kidd, R.F. and Chayet, E. 1984. 'Why Do Victims Fail to Report: The Psychology of Criminal Victimization', *Journal of Social Issues*, 40, 1, pp. 39–50.

Kidd, R.F. and Plotkin, L. n.d. 'Self-Blame and Coping with Stressful Life Events', unpublished manuscript.

King, L.A. and King, D.W. 1985. Sex Role Egalitarianism: Biographical and Personality Correlates', *Psychological Reports*, 57, pp. 787–92.

Kohlberg, L. 1966. 'A Cognitive Developmental Analysis of Children's Sex Role Concepts and Attitudes', in E. Macoby ed., *The Development of Sex Difference*, Stanford: Stanford University Press.

Komarovsky, M. 1946. 'Cultural Contradictions and Sex Roles', *American Journal of Sociology*, 52, pp. 184–89.

Korda, M. 1976. 'Sex at the Office', in D.S. David and R. Brannon eds., *The Forty-nine per cent Majority: The Male Sex Role*, Reading: Addison-Wesley Publishing Company.

Kotala, G. 1983. 'Beyond Amniocentesis: New Techniques in Foetal Testing', *Ms Magazine*, December.

Krishnamurthy, J. 1987. 'Relationship among Persuability, Modernity and Value Orientation', *Journal of Psychological Researchers*, 31, pp. 116–20.

Kubie, L. 1974. 'The Drive to Become both Sexes', *Psychoanalytic Quarterly*, 43.

Kuhn, D., Nash, S.C. and Brucken, L. 1978. 'Sex Role Concepts of Two and Three Year Olds', *Child Development*, 49, pp. 445–51.

Kumar, D. 1983a. 'Male Utopia or Nightmares?', *Economic and Political Weekly*, 15 January, pp. 61–64.

Kumar, D. 1983b. 'Amniocentesis Again', *Economic and Political Weekly*, 11 June, pp. 1075–76.

Kumar, R. and Sadgopal, S. 1980. 'Rape as a Form of State Reprisal in Peasant Movement' Paper presented at the National Conference on Perspectives for Women's Liberation Movement in India, Bombay, November.

Kumar, V. 1979. 'When Police Shelter Criminals', *Manushi*, 3, p. 21.

———. 1985. ' "Stridhan" is the Exclusive Property of the Wife', *Eve's Weekly*, pp. 52–8, 18 May.

Kynch, J. and Sen, A. 1983. 'Indian Women: Wellbeing and Survival', *Cambridge Journal of Economics*, 7, pp. 363–80.

Lakhanpal, S.K. 1962. *Indian Women: A Bibliography*, Saskatoon: University of Saskatchevan.

———. 1970. 'Indian Women', *Bulletin of Bibliography*, April-June, 27, pp. 38–41.

Lalitha, K. 1980. 'Rape: A Case Study of Rameeza Bee'. Paper presented at the National Conference on Perspective for Women's Liberation Movement in India, Bombay, November.

Langley, R. and Levy, R.C. 1977. *Wife Beating: The Silent Crisis*, New York: Pocket Books.

Lannoy, R. 1971. *The Speaking Tree: A Study of Indian Culture and Society*, London: Oxford University Press.

Lata, P.M. and Harpal. 1986. 'Campaign Against Sex Determination and Preselection Techniques'. Paper presented at the Workshop organized by Forum Against Sex-Determination and Sex Preselection Techniques, Bombay, March.

Lavrakas, P.J. 1981. 'On Household', in D. Lewis ed., *Reactions to Crime*. Newbury Park, California: Sage Publications.

Lemaku, J.P. 1983. 'Women in Male Dominated Professions: Distinguishing Personality and Background Characteristics'. *Psychology of Women Quarterly*, 8, pp. 144–65.

LeVine, R.A. 1970. 'Cross-Cultural Study in Child Psychology', in P. Mussen ed., *Carmichael's Manual of Child Psychology*, New York: Wiley and Sons.

Lewis, O. 1965. *Village Life in North India*, New York: Vintage Books.

Lukas, J.A. 1974. 'India is as Indira Does', *The New York Times Magazine*, 4 April.

Lytle, E. 1978. *Women in India: A Comprehensive Bibliography*, Monticello: Nance Bibliographies.

Mackinnon, D.W. 1970. 'The Personality Correlates of Creativity: A Study of American Architects', in P.E. Vernon, ed., *Creativity*, Harmondsworth: Penguin Books.

Macoby, E. and Jacklin, C. 1974. *The Psychology of Sex Differences*', Stanford: Stanford University Press.

Madan, T.N. 1975. 'The Hindu Woman at Home', in D. Jain ed., *Indian Women*, New Delhi: Government of India, pp. 67–86.

Maitreyi. 1982. August-September, pp. 1–18.

Majumdar, D.N. 1958. *Caste, Communication and an Indian Village*, Bombay: Asia Publishing House, pp. 252–76.

Majumdar, G. 1911. *Folk Tales of Bengal*, New Delhi: Sterling Publishers.

Maloney, P. Wilkof, J. and Dambrot, F. 1981. 'Androgyny Across Two Cultures', *Journal of Cross-Cultural Psychology*, 12, pp. 95–102.

Mandelbaum, D.G. 1949. 'The Family in India', in Ruth Anshen ed., *The Family*, New York: Harper & Row.

———. 1970. *Society in India*, 2 Vols., Berkeley: University of California Press.

Manohar, M. 1981. 'Limitations of Trade Union Organizations'. Paper presented at the National Conference on Women's Studies, Bombay, April.

Manushi. 1979. 'Letters Written at Death's Door', No. 1, pp. 13–14.

———. 1980. 'Rape: The Victim is Accused', No. 4, pp. 42–46.

———. 1981. 'Reports', No. 7, p. 25.

Marriott, M. and Inden, R.B. 1972. 'An Ethnosociology of South Asian Caste Systems'. Paper presented at the American Anthropological Association, Toronto.

Marshall, M. 1984. *The Cost of Loving: Women and the New Fear of Intimacy*, New York: G.P. Putnam's Sons.

Martin, A. 1979. 'Chantal Akerman Dossier', *Feminist Review*, 3, pp. 22–47.

Mathur, M. 1983. 'The Rape of Ghatatoli', *Blitz*, 2 April.

May, R. 1972. *Power and Innocence*, New York: W.W. Norton & Co.

Mead, M. 1935. *Sex and Temperament in Three Primitive Societies*, New York: Morrow.

Melkote, R. and Tharu, S. 1980. 'Patriarchal Relations in Working Women's Hostels: Implications for Women's Movement'. Paper presented at the National Conference on Perspectives for Women's Liberation Movement in India, Bombay, November.

Menninger, K. 1942. *Love Against Hate*, New York: Harcourt Brace Jovanovich.

Miller, B.D. 1976. 'A Population Puzzle: Does the Desire for Sons in India Increase People ... or Sons'. Paper presented at the New York State Conference on Asian Studies, Albany.

———. 1981. *The Endangered Sex: Neglect of Female Children in Rural North India*, Ithaca: Cornell University Press.

Miller, C. 1980. The Handbook of Nonsexist Writing for Writers, Editors and Speakers, New York: Lippincott and Crowell.

Miller, C. and Swift, K. 1976. *Words and Woman*, New York: Doubleday Publishing Co.

Minturn, L. and Hitchcock, J.T. 1963. 'The Rajputs of Khalapur, India', in B.B. Whiting ed., *Six Cultures*, New York: Wiley and Sons.

Minuchin, P. 1965. 'Sex Role Concepts and Sex Typing in Childhood as a Function of School and Home Environment', *Child Development*, 6, pp. 1033–48.

Mitra, I. 1969. *Karuna Sagar Vidyasagar*, Calcutta: Ananda Publishers.

Montgomery, S. 1984. 'Women's Women's Films', *Feminist Review*, 18, pp. 38–48.

Mukherjee, R. 1958. 'Women in Ancient India', in Tara Ali Baig ed., *Women in India*, Delhi: Government of India.

Mumford, I. 1961. *The City in History*, London: Secker and Warburg.

Murli Manohar, K., ed. 1984. *Women's Status and Development in India*, Warangal: Society for Women's Studies and Development.

Nair, P.T. 1978. *Marriage and Dowry in India*, Calcutta: Minerva Associates Publications.

Nanda, B.R. 1976. *Indian Women*, New Delhi: Vikas.

Nandy, A. 1975. 'Sati, or a Nineteenth Century Tale of Women, Violence, and Protest', in V.C. Joshi ed., *Rammohun Roy and the Process of Modernization in India*, New Delhi: Vikas.

Nandy, A. 1976. *Alternative Science*, New Delhi: Tata McGraw-Hill.

Narayan, D. 1964. 'Growing up in India', *Family Process*, 3, pp. 148–52.

Newcomb, T.M. 1956. 'The Prediction of Interpersonal Attraction', *American Psychologist*, 11, pp. 575–86.

Newsweek. 1985. 'Rape and the Law', 20 May, pp. 60–64.

Nilsen, A.T., et. al., eds. 1977. *Sexism and Language*, Urbana: National Council of Teachers of English, III.

Nyrop, R.F., Benderly, B.L., Cover, W.W., Cutter, M.J., and Parker, N.B. 1975. *Area Handbook for India*, Washington, D.C.: American University.

O'Flaherty, W. 1973. *Asceticism and Eroticism in the Mythology of Siva*, London: Oxford University Press.

O'Neil, J.N. 1981. 'Patterns of Gender Role Conflict and Strain', *Personnel and Guidance Journal*, 60, pp. 203–10.

Oldenburg, V. 1984. 'Women Against Women or Culture Against Women?'. Paper presented at the New York State Asian Conference, Suny-Cortland, October.

Omvedt, G. 1977. 'Women and the Rural Revolt in India', *Social Scientist*, 6, 61, pp. 3–18.

———. 1980. 'Socialist Feminist Organizations and the Women's Movement'. Paper presented at the National Conference on Perspectives for Women's Liberation Movement in India, Bombay, November.

Ortner, S.B. 1974. 'Is Female to Male as Nature is to Culture?' in M.Z. Rosaldo and L. Lamphere eds., *Women, Culture and Society*, Stanford: Stanford University Press.

Pakrasi, K. 1968. 'On Female Infanticide in India', *Bulletin of the Cultural Research Institute*, 7, 314, pp. 33–48.

———. 1970. 'The Genesis of Female Infanticide', *Humanist Review*, July-September, 7, pp. 255–81.

Pakrasi, K. and Sasmal, B. 1970. 'Effect of Infanticide on Sex-Ratio in an Indian Population', *Z. Morph, Anthrop*, May, 62, 2, pp. 214–30.

———. 1971. 'Infanticide and Variation of Sex-Ratio in a Caste Population in India', *Acta Medica Auxologica*, III, 3, pp. 217–28.

Panek, P., Rush, M. and Greenwalt, J. 1977. 'Current Sex Stereotypes of 25 Occupations', *Psychological Report*, 48, pp. 668–73.

Panthaki, M.H., Bangkar, D.D., Kulkarni, K.V. and Patil, K.P. 1979. 'Prenatal Sex Prediction by Amniocentesis: Our Experience of 600 Cases'. Paper presented at the First Asian Congress of Induced Abortion and Voluntary Sterilization, Bombay.

Papanek, H. 1971. 'Purdah in Pakistan: Seclusion and Modern Occupations of Women', *Journal of Marriage and Family*, 33, 3, pp. 517–30.

Parsons, T. and Bales, R.F. 1955. *Family Socialization and Interaction Process*, Glencoe, Illinois: Free Press.

Patel, V. 1978. 'Role of Women in Middle Class Upheaval of Gujarat', *Readings on Women's Movement in India*, Bombay: Socialist Women's Group.

———. 1982. 'Indian Women on Warpath', *Lokayan*, December, pp. 1–3.

———. 1984. 'Amniocentesis: Misuse of Modern Technology', *Socialist Health Review*, 1, 2, pp. 69–71.

Patel, V. Ghotoskar, S. and Prakash, P. 1980. 'The Anti-Rape Movement and the Issues Facing Autonomous Women's Organizations'. Paper presented at the National Conference on Perspectives for Women's Liberation Movement in India, Bombay.

Pearce, M. 1975. 'Bibliography: Women in India', *Hecate*, 1, January, pp. 90–95.

Pincus, A.R.H. and Pincus, R.E. 1980. 'Linguistic Sexism and Career Education', *Language Arts*, 57, pp. 70–76.

Pinkham, M. 1941. *Women in the Sacred Scriptures of Hinduism*, New York: Columbia University Press.

Pleck, J.H. 1981. *The Myth of Masculinity*, Cambridge, Mass.: MIT Press.

Prabhu, P. 1962. *Hindu Social Organization*, Bombay: Popular Book Depot.

Punwani, J. 1984. 'A Muslim Woman Challenges a Muslim Law', *The Sunday Observer*, 15 April.

———. 1985. 'Don't Shut Up, Kitty: A Profile of a New Entity, the T.V. Woman', *The Sunday Observer*, 3 November.

Rajaraman, I. 1983. 'Economics of Bride-Price and Dowry', *Economic and Political Weekly*, XVIII, 19 February, pp. 275–78.

Ranjan, G. 1982. 'Raping the Woman to Penalise the Husband', *Femina*, 23 October, p. 31.

Rao, A., Vaid, S. and Juneja, M., n.d., *Rape, Society and State*, New Delhi: Peoples Union for Civil Liberties and Democratic Rights.

Rao, V.V.P. and Rao, V.N. 1982. *Marriage, the Family and Women in India*, Columbia, Missouri: South Asian Books.

———. 1983a. 'Sex Role Attitudes: A Comparison of Sex-Race Groups'. Paper presented at the meeting of Southwestern Social Science Association, San Antonio, Texas.

———. 1983. 'Sex Role Attitudes of College Students in India', *Working Paper, No. 72*, Women in International Development, Michigan State University.

Rapp, R. 1986. 'The Ethics of Choice'. Background paper for National Workshop on Women, Health and Reproductive Rights, Bombay, December.

Ravindra, R.P. 1986a. 'The Scarcer Half: A Report on Amniocentesis and Other Sex Determination Techniques, Sex Preselection and New Reproductive Technologies', in *Counterfact*, Bombay: A Center for Education and Documentation Health Feature, January, No. 9, Whole Number.

———. 1986b. 'Refined Techniques of Femicide'. Paper presented at the workshop organized by the Forum Against Sex Determination and Sex Preselection Techniques, Bombay, March.

Repetti, R. 1984. 'Determinants of Children Sex Stereotyping: Parental Sex Role Traits and TV Viewing', *Personality and Social Psychology Bulletin*, 10, pp. 456–68.

Report, 1982. 'Devdasis Meet at Nipani: Victims of Exploitation from Temples to Brothels', *How*, 5, 1, pp. 23–25.

Report on Democratic Rights of Women: Inside the Family. 1982. New Delhi: Peoples Union for Democratic Rights.

Research Unit on Women's Studies, SNDT Women's University, *A Select Bibliography on Women in India*, Bombay: Allied Publishers, n.d.

Rohrbaugh, J.B. 1981. *Women: Psychology's Puzzle*, London: Abacus.

Roiphe, A. 1973. 'An American Family: Things are Keen but could be Keener', *New York Times Magazine*, 18 February.

Ross, A.D. 1961. *The Hindu Family in its Urban Setting*, Toronto: University of Toronto Press.

Ross, S. 1981. 'How Words Hurt: Attitudes, Metaphor and Oppression', in Wetterling-Braggin ed., *Sexist Language: A Modern Philosophical Analysis*. New Jersey: Totowa.

Rowland, R. 1977. 'The Bem Sex Role Inventory', *Australian Psychologist*, 12, pp. 83–88.

Roy, M. 1973. 'Bengali Women as Respect Objects: An Analysis of Male-Female Relationship in Contemporary Urban West Bengal'. Paper presented at the Ninth Annual Conference on Bengal Studies, New York.

———. 1975a. 'The Oedipus Complex and Bengali Family in India', in T.R. Williams ed., *Psychological Anthropology*, The Hague: Mouton.

———. 1975b. *Bengali Women*. Chicago: University of Chicago Press.

Roy, P.C., n.d., *Mahabharata*, trans., Vol. 3, Calcutta: Oriental Publishing Co.

Rudolph, L. and Rudolph, S. 1966. *The Modernity of Tradition*, Chicago: University of Chicago Press.

Runge, T.E., Frey, D., Gollwitzer, P.M., Helmreich, R.L. and Spence, J.T. 1981. 'Masculine (Instrumental) and Feminine (Expressive) Traits: A Comparison between Students in the United States and West Germany', *Journal of Cross-Cultural Psychology*, 12, pp. 142–62.

Ruth, S., 1980. *Issues in Feminism*, Boston: Houghton Mifflin Company.

Sahai, S.N. 1985. *Women in Changing Society: A Bibliographical Study*, New Delhi: Mittal Publications.

Saheli. 1982. 'Profile of a Women's Group', *How*, 5, 1, pp. 9–10.

Sakala, C. 1980. *Women of South Asia: A Guide to Resources*, New York: Kraus International Publications.

Salzman, L.. 1971. 'Feminine Psychology Revisited', *American Journal of Psychoanalysis*, 31, pp. 123–33.

Sambrani, B.R. and Sambrani, S. 1983. 'Economics of Bride Price and Dowry', *Economic and Political Weekly*, Vol. 1, XVIII, 9 April, pp. 601–03.

Sangharsh. n.d., 'Bill on Rape: Protection for Whom?', p. 8.

Scanzoni, J. 1975. *Sex Roles, Lifestyles and Childbearing*, New York: The Free Press.

———. 1976. 'Sex Role Change and Influences on Birth Intentions', *Journal of Marriage and the Family*, 38, pp. 43–58.

———. 1978. *Sex Roles, Women's Work, and Marital Conflict: A Study of Family Change*, Lexington, Mass.: Lexington Books.

Scrimshaw, S.C.M. 1978. 'Infant Mortality and Behavior in the Regulation of Family Size', *Population and Development Review*, 6, 3, pp. 386–87.

Seligman, M.E.P. 1972. 'Learned Helplessness', *Annual Review of Medicine*, 23, pp. 407–12.

Select Bibliography of Indian Women. 1982. Hyderabad: ICSSR Southern Regional Center, Osmania University.

Sen, I. 1984. 'Mahila Mukti Morcha-Dalli Rajhare: A Report From a Women's Organization'. Paper presented at the Second National Conference on Women's Studies, Trivandrum, April.

Sen Gupta, P. 1960. *Women Workers of India*, New Delhi: Asia Publishing House.

Serbin, L.A., O'Leary, K.D., Kent, R.N. and Tonick, I. 1973. 'A Comparison of Teacher Response to the Pre-academic and Problem Behavior of Boys and Girls'. *Child Development*, 44, pp. 796–804.

Seth, S. 1984. 'Place of Prenatal Sex Determination'. Paper presented at the Larsen and Toubro Seminar, Bombay, September.

Sexton, K.G. 1979. *Between Two Worlds: Young Women in Crisis*, New York: Morrow.

Sharma, U. 1980. *Women, Work, and Property in North-West India*, London: Tavistock.

Shastri, H.P. 1962. *Ramayana of Valmiki* (trans.), Vol. 1, Ayodhyakanda, London: Shantisadan.

Shepard, W. and Hess, D. 1975. 'Attitude in Four Age Groups Towards Sex Role Division in Adult Occupation and Activities', *Journal of Vocational Behaviour*, 6, pp. 27–39.

Shotland, L. and Goodstein, L. 1984. 'The Role of Bystanders in Crime Control', *Journal of Social Issues*, 40, 1, pp. 9–26.

Shukla, S. 1985. *Dowry in Bombay: Some Observations*, Bombay: Women's Center.

Shukla, S. and Kulkarni, S. 1986. 'Social Implications of Sex Determination Tests'. Paper presented at the workshop organized by Forum Against Sex Determination and Sex Preselection Techniques, Bombay.

Shumaker, S.A 1983. 'Coping with the Crisis of Childhood Cancer: The Importance of Social Support'. Address given at the Institute of the Ministry of Sick. The Johns Hopkins Medical Institute, Baltimore, Maryland.

Shute, S. 1981. 'Sexist Language and Sexism', in Vetterling-Braggin ed., *Sexist Language: A Modern Philosophical Analysis*. New Jersey: Totowa.

Siegel, C.L. 1973. 'Sex Differences in the Occupational Choices of Second Graders', *Journal of Vocational Behaviour*, 3, pp. 15–19.

Singer, M.B. 1972. *When a Great Tradition Modernizes: An Anthropological Approach to Indian Civilization*, New York: Praeger Publishers.

Singh, G. 1986. 'Amneocentesis and Legal Provisions Pertaining to it'. Paper presented at the workshop organized by Forum Against Sex Determination and Sex-Preselection Techniques, Bombay, March.

Singh, G. and Jain, S. 1983. *Opinions of Men and Women Regarding Amniocentesis*', Ludhiana: Punjab Agricultural University, College of Home Science.

Singh G., Patel, V., Ghotoskar, S., Savara, M. and Banaji, R. 1982. 'Declaration of Socialist Women's Group', *How*, pp. 5, 6–7, 17–19.

Slater, P.E. 1968. *The Glory of Hera*, Boston: Beacon Press.

Smoker, B. 1975. 'Women and the Patriarchal God', *The Secularist*, 33, pp. 67–68.

Spence, J. and Helmreich, R. 1978. *Masculinity and Femininity, Their Psychological Dimensions, Correlates and Antecedents*, Austin: University of Texas Press.

Spratt, P. 1966. *Hindu Culture and Personality*, Bombay: Manaklalas.

Srinivas, M.N. 1942. *Marriage and Family in Mysore*, Bombay: New Book Co.

———. 1977. 'The Changing Position of Indian Women', *Man*, 12, pp. 221–38.

———. 1984. *Some Reflections on Dowry*, New Delhi: Oxford University Press.

Srivastava, S.L. 1974. *Folk Culture and Oral Tradition*, New Delhi: Abhinav Publications, p. 28.

Status of Women in India: A Synopsis of the Report of the National Committee on the Status of Women. 1975. New Delhi: Indian Council of Social Science Research.

Stevens, W.K. 1984. 'Across India, The English Tongue Gets New Twist', *The New York Times*, 19 March.

Stree Adhar Kendra. 1984. *Manifesto and Report of Activities*, Pune.

Stree Atyachar Virodhi Parishad. 1981. *Akrosh*, Nagpur.

Stree Mukti Andolan Sampark Samiti. 1979. *Report of 8th March Discussion Session in Marathi*, Pune.

Stree Shakti Sangathana. 1980. 'Rape: Case Study of Rameeza Bee'. Paper presented at the National Conference on a Perspectives for Women's Liberation Movement in India, Bombay, November.

———. 1980. 'Report from Karimnagar', Paper presented at National Conference on Perspectives for Women's Liberation Movement in India, Bombay, November.

Sutton-Smith, B., Rosenberg, B.G. and Morgan, B. 1963. 'Development of Sex Difference in Play Choices During Preadolescence', *Child Development*, 24, pp. 119–26.

Tangri, S.S. 1972. 'Determinants of Occupational Role Innovation among College Women', *Journal of Social Issues*, 28, pp. 177–99.

Tarrier, N. and Gomes, L.F. 1981. 'Knowledge of Sex-Trait Stereotypes: Effects of Age, Sex, and Social Class of Brazilian Children', *Journal of Cross-Cultural Psychology*, 12, pp. 81–93.

Thakur, U.T. 1959. *Sindhi Culture*, Bombay: University of Bombay Press.

The Daily. 1982. 'Rape a Day', 31 December.

The Economist. 1980. 'Don't Complain to the Police', 19 July, p. 40.

The Sunday Observer. 1986. 'Rise in Dowry Deaths Due to Consumerism', 31 July.

The Times of India. 1983. 'Two Pune Women Allegedly Raped', 2 April.

Tomeh, A.K. 1978. 'Sex-Role Orientation: An Analysis of Structural Attitudinal Predictors', *Journal of Marriage and the Family*, 40, pp. 341–54.

———. 1981. 'Correlates of Sex Role Attitudes of a Korean Student Population', *Journal of Asian and African Studies*, 16, pp. 169–85.

Tuchman, G. 1983. 'Women's Depiction by the Mass Media', in L. Richardson and V. Taylor eds., *Feminist Frontiers: Rethinking Sex, Gender and Society*, London: Addison-Wesley Publishing Co.

Tuchman, G., Daniels, A.K. and Benet, J., eds. 1978. *Hearth and Home: Images of Women in the Mass Media*, New York: Oxford University Press.

T.V. Network Grows. 1987. *Manorama: Yearbook 1987*, Kottayam: Malayala Manorama Co. Ltd., pp. 602–04.

Tyler, R. 1984. 'Assessing the Risk of Crime Victimization: The Integration of personal victimization experience and socially transmitted information,' *Journal of Social Issues*, 40, 1, pp. 27–28.

Vaid, J., Miller, B. and Hyde, J. 1984. *South Asian Women at Home and Abroad: A Guide to Resources*, CWAS Monograph Series, Syracuse: Syracuse University Press.

Vanita, R. 1984. 'Nominal Changes', *Manushi*, 24, pp. 29–31.

Venkatramani, S.H. 1986. 'Born to Die: Female Infanticide', *India Today*, 15 June, pp. 26–33.

Verma, R. 1981. *Mother's Sex Role Attitudes, Independence Training and Need for Achievement in Children*, unpublished doctoral thesis, Bombay: Indian Institute of Technology.

Vetterling-Braggin, M., ed. 1981. *Sexist Language: A Modern Philosophical Analysis*, New Jersey: Totowa.

Wadley, Susan. 1975. *Shakti: Power in the Conceptual Structure of Karimpur Region*, Chicago: The University of Chicago Studies in Anthropology: Series in Social, Cultural and Linguistic Anthropology, no. 2.

———. 1976. 'Brothers, Husbands and Sometimes Sons: Kinsmen in North Indian Ritual', *Eastern Anthropologist*, 29, 2, pp. 149–70.

———. 1977. 'Women and the Hindu Tradition', *Signs*, 3, pp. 113–25.

———. n.d., 'Woman, Wife and Mother in Ramayana', Unpublished paper.

Walker, E.L. 1979. *The Battered Woman*, New York: Harper & Row.

Ward, C. and Sethi, R. 1983. 'Cross-Cultural Validation of Bem's Sex Role Inventory: Malaysian and South Indian Research'. Paper presented at Third Asian Regional Conference of International Association of Cross-Cultural Psychology, Bangi, Malaysia.

Werner, E.E. 1979. *Cross-Cultural Child Development: A View From the Planet Earth*, Monterey, California: Brooks Cole.

Whiting B., ed. 1966. *Mothers in Six Cultures*, New York: Wiley and Sons.

Whiting, B. and Edwards, C.P. 1973. 'A Cross-Cultural Analysis of Sex Differences in the Behaviour of Children Aged Three through Eleven', *Journal of Social Psychology*, 91, pp. 171–88.

Williams, J.E. and Best, D. 1982. *Measuring Sex Stereotypes: A Thirty Nation Study*, Newbury Park, California: Sage Publications.

Williams, J.E., Best, D.L., Tilquin, C., Keller, H., Voss, H., Bjerke, T. and Baarda, B. 1981. 'Traits Associated with Men and Women: Attribution by Young Children in France, Germany, Norway, Netherlands and Italy', *Journal of Cross-Cultural Psychology*, 12, pp. 327–46.

Williams, J.E., Daws, J.T., Best, D.L., Tilquin, C., Wesley, F., and Bjerke, T. 1979. 'Sex-Trait Stereotypes in France, Germany and Norway', *Journal of Cross-Cultural Psychology*, 10, pp. 133–56.

Williams, J.E., Gilles, H., Edwards, J.R., Best, D.L. and Daws, J.T. 1977. 'Sex-Trait Stereotypes in England, Ireland and United States', *British Journal of Social and Clinical Psychology*, 16, pp. 303–09.

Williamson, J. 1979. *New Feminist Scholarship: A Guide to Bibliographies*, New York: Feminist Press.

Wolf, M. 1975. 'Women and Suicide in China', in M. Wolf and R. Witke eds., *Women in Chinese Society*, Stanford: Stanford University Press.

Women and World Development: An Annotated Bibliography, 1976. Washington D.C.: Overseas Development Council, 1976.

Women's Organization. 1981. *Newsletter: Research Unit on Women's Studies*, 2, 1, pp. 1–2.

Young, K.R. and Sharma, A. 1974. *Image of Feminine, Mythic, Philosophic and Human, in the Buddhist, Hindu and Islamic Traditions: A Bibliography of Women in India*, New Jersey: New Horizon Press.

Young, R. A. 1984. 'Vocational Choice and Values in Adolescent Women', *Sex Roles*, 7/8, pp. 485–92.

Zilboorg, G. 1944. 'Masculine and Feminine: Some Biological and Cultural Aspects', *Psychiatry*, 7, pp. 257–96.

Zimmer, H. 1956. *Philosophies of India*, New York: Meridian.

Zinkin, T. 1958. *India Changes*, New York: Oxford University Press.

Author Index